ENGLISHNESS IDENTIFIED

ENGLISHNESS
IDENTIFIED

MANNERS AND CHARACTER
1650–1850

PAUL LANGFORD

Illustrated by Martin Rowson

OXFORD
UNIVERSITY PRESS

OXFORD
UNIVERSITY PRESS

Great Clarendon Street, Oxford OX2 6DP

Oxford University Press is a department of the University of Oxford.
It furthers the University's objective of excellence in research, scholarship,
and education by publishing worldwide in

Oxford New York

Athens Auckland Bangkok Bogotá Buenos Aires Cape Town
Chennai Dar es Salaam Delhi Florence Hong Kong Istanbul Karachi
Kolkata Kuala Lumpur Madrid Melbourne Mexico City Mumbai Nairobi
Paris São Paulo Shanghai Singapore Taipei Tokyo Toronto Warsaw

with associated companies in Berlin Ibadan

Oxford is a registered trade mark of Oxford University Press
in the UK and in certain other countries

Published in the United States
by Oxford University Press Inc., New York

First published 2000
First published in paperback 2001

British Library Cataloguing in Publication Data
Data available

Library of Congress Cataloging in Publication Data
Langford, Paul.
Englishness identified: manners and character, 1650–1850 / Paul Langford.
p. cm.
Includes bibliographical references and index.
1. National characteristics, English—History.   2. National
characteristics, English, in literature.   3. England—Social life
and customs—18th century.   4. England—Social life and
customs—17th century.   5. England—Social life and customs—19th
century.   6. English literature—History and criticism.   I. Title.
DA118.L33 2000   306'.0942—dc21   99-41373
ISBN 0-19-820681-X (hbk)
ISBN 0-19-924640-8

1 3 5 7 9 10 8 6 4 2

Typeset by Best-set Typesetter Ltd., Hong Kong
Printed in Great Britain
on acid-free paper by
T.J. International Ltd.
Padstow, Cornwall

For Hugh

Preface

THIS book is an attempt to contribute to two distinct enterprises. In the first place it aims to offer a range of new or little-known evidence on the subject of social behaviour and manners. Most of that evidence consists of observations by contemporaries, many of them foreigners or at any rate outsiders. The history of manners does not always reflect systematic study of this kind of material. To a marked and understandable degree it has relied much on the didactic literature of manners, on the manuals, protocols, and rule books which centuries of European civility, courtesy, and etiquette have generated. These are valuable sources but they carry their own dangers. Guides to the 'dos and don'ts' of human behaviour do not necessarily reveal a great deal about the way people actually behave. If they did it would not have been necessary to write them. It may be true that those of them that condemn certain practices as well as recommend others may incidentally be revealing of prevailing behaviour. Even so, their empirical value is to say the least questionable.

Secondly, I hope this may contribute to current debate about the history of identity though my own concern is primarily with the things identified rather than the politics of identification. I seek to show how certain traits came to be seen both in England and outside England as typical of the English, and how those traits were defined and redefined to suit changing priorities and preoccupations. The significance that England and the Britain of which it was part came to acquire beyond its own shores between the execution of Charles I in 1649 and the Great Exhibition of 1851 perhaps gives the resulting characterization a particular interest. To the extent that it remains, implicitly or explicitly, a perception and a self-perception today, it may also say something about the influence that shadowy legacies of this kind can exert. Above all it perhaps demonstrates how dependent such long-lasting stereotypes can be on highly contingent historical circumstances.

P. L.

January 1999

Contents

Note on Sources

MANY of the sources used in this book were published in languages other than English in the first instance, though some were translated into English either in the lifetime of their author or later. In referring to the latter I have generally employed the most accessible English version. In certain instances, however, these represent translations which are contentious or misleading. In these cases I have cited the original version, while noting any points of interest that may be raised by the existence of dubious translations. Quotations from non-English sources represent my own translations, unless otherwise indicated. Throughout I have tried to combine the requirements of scholarship with the desirability of accessibility. In some instances the result has been the citation of a number of versions, in different languages, of the same work.

Englishness

*E*NGLISHNESS is a term much employed by historians, under-standably, given the current interest in matters of identity. The entire span of English history is affected, from the time when the presence of the English, or rather the Angles, in the British Isles, first makes such a formulation seem appropriate, to the present. Strictly speaking, as applied to the greater part of that span, the word itself is an anachronism. 'Englishness' is a relatively modern invention. Dictionaries place it no earlier than 1805, its first occurrence apparently being attrib-utable to William Taylor of Norwich, the radical poetaster who is cred-ited with bringing German romanticism to the attention of a British audience. It is pleasantly ironic that he should also have been accused by contemporaries of 'employing words and forms of construction which are not sanctioned or not current in our language'. In this respect Taylor cheerfully admitted to his own un-Englishness, boasting to Southey that his taste was 'moulded on that of a foreign public'.[1] Perhaps it was his immersion in German that induced him to coin a word that has something of a Germanic feel about it. Many languages to this day lack a substantive capable of summarizing the essence of their nationality, but German, with its 'Deutschtum', is not one of them.

Discussions of Englishness tend to imply interest in the process of identification as much as the things or values identified. Some major scholarly reappraisals have resulted. The rediscovery of Anglo-Saxon ethnic self-consciousness, for example, has powered a revival of interest in the vigour, originality and endurance of Old English institutions.[2] Similarly, features of Victorian thinking have revealed the centrality of specifically English nationhood to the social, political, and imperial concerns of the nineteenth century.[3] Not only the traditional concerns of the historian have been affected. Swathes of the literary canon have been subjected to analysis in terms of patriotic or nationalistic preoccupations, with large claims being made for their continuing relevance today.[4]

In this book, my focus is somewhat different: it is the things identified rather than the process of identification. By Englishness I mean those distinctive aspects of national life that struck either outsiders or insiders or both as characteristic. I give outsiders higher priority than they would normally be accorded by historians of English nationalism or patriotism. I hope this may be considered no bad thing. There is, after all, the freshness of perspective that foreign views bring, as intermediaries between the historian and his subject. In Madame de Staël's words, 'foreigners constitute a contemporary posterity'.[5] There is also the likelihood that if their testimony is not objective, it is at least disengaged. And above all, they shine light where it would not occur to their English contemporaries to do so. Things that are taken for granted as part of the fabric of everyday life may to outsiders be sufficiently novel to merit scrutiny. Moreover, they can rarely resist the impulse to generalize from their limited experience.

Such speculations have often annoyed by their glibness. The Spanish Anglophile Blanco White, not altogether innocent of the offence himself, denounced 'especially those theorizing Frenchmen, who would confidently run up some philosophical reflections on the state of the nation on the basis of a fortnight's tour'.[6] These more discursive reflections are often little valued by historians, so little that they have sometimes been suppressed even in the most scholarly translations.[7] Yet they can be highly suggestive of the relationship between a society and its competitors. They have, too, featured in some indisputable classics including Voltaire's *Letters on England* of 1733, better known in its grander French dress of a year later, as *Letres Philosophiques*, and Emerson's *English Traits* of 1856.

Such sources suggest a radical reassessment of the importance of England and things English. Between the execution of Charles I in the middle of the seventeenth century and the Great Exhibition in the middle of the nineteenth century, the place of Britain and therefore England in the comity of nations changed markedly. In terms of population it rose from being a minor demographic appendage of mainland Europe to one of its most populous states. As an exporter of people it made British institutions and the English language prominent features of the extra-European world. In point of power politics the overall trend from the time of Marlborough and the War of Spanish Succession was incontestably upward. Even a sceptical Frenchman reckoned that the century of warfare between Blenheim and Waterloo had lifted Britain from sixth place to first in the league table of international powers.[8]

The focus of interest in this phenomenon was not solely grand strategy, nor was it the same throughout. In the early eighteenth century the appearance of a new form of constitutional monarchy, and its implications for the liberties of the subject, attracted attention. Foreigners came to England, it was said, in search of government, as they went to Italy in search of arts.[9] Later on it was the commercial and colonial character of Britain's pre-eminence that seemed most striking. Later still, by the early nineteenth century, industrialization, with all it implied not only for the wealth of the State but for the ordinary life of countless human beings, was fascinating observers. And, throughout but increasingly, there was awareness of the cultural progress of the new Leviathan, which, as Disraeli's father Isaac, himself a second generation immigrant, put it, did as much as arms and wealth to ensure that 'An island, once inconsiderable in Europe, now ranks among the first powers, arbitrates among other nations, and the very title of its inhabitants ensures respect.'[10] Few outsiders would have contested the claim and to those from remote cultures, the impression of power, wealth, and sophistication was almost stupefying. As a Persian envoy to the Court of the St James's put it in 1810, 'It seems God who created the Universe chooses special people on whom to shower special blessings.'[11]

In all these matters innovation was the leitmotif. This was somewhat paradoxical considering what attention the English paid to their past and their traditions. But this may have been rather misleading. The cult of 'Old Englishness' was itself a natural reaction to the speed of change that the new England experienced in the eighteenth and nineteenth centuries. In any case interest in the physical evidence of the English heritage among the English themselves was not always very marked before the late nineteenth century.[12] Moreover, the growing part that Americans played in construing Englishness for a wider world had the effect of emphasizing their own particular needs. These were understandably concerned with ancient roots and traditions. *Our Old Home*, as Hawthorne expressed it, was meant to exhibit stability rather than change, age rather than youth.[13] To many Americans the reality came as something of a surprise. Landing at Liverpool, Harriet Beecher Stowe had to wait for a trip into the Lancashire countryside to find at Speke Hall 'the first really old thing that we had seen since our arrival in England'.[14] Before her lifetime few foreigners had set foot in England with the intention of seeing 'really old things'. They came to view tomorrow in the making, not yesterday.

In this respect Britain's failures were taken to be as significant as its successes. The greatest of these, the loss of the thirteen American colonies, was itself a portentous modernity. That one of the newest colonial powers should be the first to suffer in this way merely confirmed the impression that whatever was going on in the British empire was more dynamic, more prophetic than what happened in other empires. The fact that Britain not only survived this setback, but entered upon a period of unprecedented economic growth enhanced the impression that the new prodigy among nations was unique.

This belief that whatever the truth about British prowess, was a truth about the future, gained an increasing hold in the late eighteenth century and was rarely disputed in the early nineteenth. It was not necessary to agree that the future was a desirable one. Romantic travellers, who relished the opportunity to view societies that preserved the past in aspic, could not resist visiting one in which the future could be glimpsed.[15] And for those who saw in British industrial progress only political ossification and social retardation, it was no less instructive. Here in effect was taking place a grand experiment in the history of civilization, 'the new world of the old world'.[16] Not to have inspected it personally was not to have travelled. As the great Montesquieu himself observed: 'I, too, have been a traveller, and have seen the country in the world which is most worthy of our curiosity—I mean England.'[17]

These were sentiments that would not have been contradicted in England itself, with its growing faith in progress in general and the progress of Britain in particular. The cult of 'improvement' was a more satisfying aspiration than 'enlightenment', to the extent that it emphasized moral and material progress rather than an intellectual state. Significantly, the 'Scottish school' was always more ambivalent about the future than its English contemporaries.[18] For others, it was easy to assume that Britain was destined to be the great improver of the human race. Was it not after all, as Sir Richard Phillips meaninglessly but revealingly boasted in 1828, 'the most improved country that ever existed in the world'.[19] And if some were more restrained they did not deny that here was a kind of laboratory where the future was being tried and tested. This was as Mark Pattison put it 'the illustrative country'.[20]

The psychological impact of this transformation was enhanced by Britain's seemingly peripheral position on the margins of Europe, and also by older assumptions about its inferiority in the annals of civilization, though by the middle of the nineteenth century, it was possible to forget England's relative insignificance at earlier times in its history. It was Ralph Waldo Emerson who remarked, 'The problem of the traveller landing at Liverpool is, Why England is England? What are the elements of that power which the English hold over other nations? If there be one test of national genius universally accepted, it is success; and if there be one successful country in the universe for the last millennium, that country is England.'[21]

In truth most of this success had been achieved in a small fraction of that millennium. It is hard to believe that in 1650 any outsider, even one with some claim to be an honorary Englishman, as Emerson had, would have written in such terms. Rather the English had featured as Europe's mavericks, their history one of violence, turbulence, and instability, of achievement perhaps, but achievement unpredictable, unsustained, and unconvincing. They constituted a standing reminder of the spasmodic vigour of a people still close to barbarism. Nobody, surely, in 1650 could have observed, as Talleyrand did in 1806, that 'if the English Constitution is destroyed, understand clearly that the civilization of the world will be shaken to its very foundations'.[22] The word itself would not have sprung to the lips of Talleyrand's grandfathers. Civilization had for them been where the European tradition located it, in the heartland of Latin Europe, or among the Gallic and Germanic peoples who had taken on the cultural and political responsibilities once associated with Rome. But by the 1820s, Édouard de Montulé could exclaim, glimpsing the white coast of England just out of Boulogne, 'there is the centre of civilization'.[23] And the rounded nature of what was envisaged would have seemed extraordinary before the nineteenth century. The verdict of Madame de Staël's son, the Baron de Staël-Holstein, in 1825, was comprehensive. 'Civilization is there farther advanced than in any country on the Continent, that knowledge is more widely diffused, the science of government better understood, and all the movements of the social machine more rapid and more ably combined.'[24]

    If there was any particular point at which this acceptance of at least the possibility of English pre-eminence was attained it was probably the third quarter of the eighteenth century, and more particularly the 1760s. Then, Lord Normanby remarked, looking back from the 1820s, we 'led the way in human civilization'.[25] Or as Giuseppe Baretti put it in 1770, the English 'stand of course quite at the head of mankind'.[26] The stupendous victories of the Seven Years War, obtained at the expense of Europe's most populous and powerful State, naturally impressed contemporaries. At home they bred a fierce pride in the worldwide impact of a tiny island's prowess. In the words of the novelist Charles Johnstone, 'whenever England is at war with any of her neighbours, the effects are felt to the extremities of the globe'.[27]

    Understandably, England's nearest Continental rivals were particularly struck by the transformation. In his influential posthumous tract of 1772, 'De l'Homme', the French philosopher Helvétius selected the English as a spectacular example of progress, by what had once been 'a nation of slaves, inhuman and superstitious, without arts and without industry'.[28] This was written at a time when France was undergoing one of those periodic waves of fashionable *anglomanie* that punctuated the history of Anglo-French relations. Anglomania took its adherents in France, and later in Germany, far beyond an interest in British politics into realms of manners and culture that raised deeper questions about what constituted Englishness.[29] And above all there was the growing penetration of English letters on the Continent, a development that had its origins earlier but which by the 1770s was having a marked effect. It has been observed that in 1700 no educated Continental European would have thought it necessary to speak or read English whereas by 1800 it would have been considered essential.[30] The foreigners who came to Britain and wrote about their experience were precisely those who already had a mental picture of their hosts, much of it formed from imaginative literature.

What foreigners identified was what they increasingly described as national character. It is an expression that readily offends the sensibility of a late twentieth-century reader. The title which Sir Ernest Barker gave to his Stevenson Lectures at Glasgow in 1925, *National Character and the Factors in its Formation*, would certainly not appeal to an academic audience three-quarters of a century later.[31] The very idea that nation states are rooted in ethnic or racial origin, and that their behaviour either at the collective or individual level, is determined by the resulting organic tendencies, is repugnant to the liberal conscience of the West. This is understandable, but it should not be permitted to blind us to the prominence that the concept of national character has played in the past, nor to the less forbidding associations that the term itself has sometimes possessed. Attributing peculiarities of thought and behaviour to particular groups of people must be as ancient as human society itself, and does not presuppose any one explanatory model, let alone those that underpin nineteenth- and twentieth-century ideas of race. In the case of Europe there exists a long tradition of national characterizations, informing every kind of discourse from the common currency of diplomats to the proverbial wisdom of peasant folklore. As it happened, that tradition came under scrutiny at the time that Britain itself was being so closely inspected. It is tempting to attribute this to the political climate created by the rise of modern nationalist movements in the turmoil associated with an age of revolution. But it owed as much to the Enlightenment's search for the defining terms of the modern state and its fascination with the science of manners. Moreover, when the term national character became fashionable in the late eighteenth century it did so in a context that took little note of innate, inherited forces.

The prevailing fashions in what we would classify as psychology, sociology, and anthropology, treated nations merely as convenient, and often loosely defined units for analysis, rather than self-defining organisms. Character expressed itself in what was called manners, a term of wider extent and more fruitful ambiguity than it is today. Manners were largely the product of social interactions, whether in the past or present. Explaining an individual's manners was a matter of describing his upbringing, education, and experience. Explaining a nation's manners meant investigating its physical environment, its economic progress, and its political framework. Such themes are central to some intellectual projects of the period, among them the conjectural history of the Scottish Enlightenment, and the institutional analysis of the Montesquieu school. And they are not very remote from the concerns of modern anthropology, which in the words of one of its most distinguished students, Clifford Geertz, 'is firm in the conviction that men unmodified by the customs of particular places do not in fact exist, have never existed, and most important, could not in the very nature of the case exist'.[32] The sentiment is virtually that of the eighteenth-century historian Robertson, whose wisdom was approvingly quoted by travellers. 'The dispositions and manners of men are formed by their situation, and arise from the state of society in which they live.'[33] It followed that national character was a transitory expression of territorial units. 'The formation of national character cannot then be a work of Nature, since nations themselves are not a work of her hands.'[34] Nations rose and fell as they were active or inactive but essentially all human beings were the same.[35] More than that, national character was itself vulnerable to change and in need of continual tending. When Edmund Burke, leading the impeachment of Warren Hastings for corruption in 1789, told the House of Lords: 'We call upon you for our national character', he was expressing a commonplace view that it was the changing product of changing times, its virtues only to be preserved by combating the vices of the day.[36]

There were soon, indeed, to be other voices, as a growing preoccupation with ancestry and inheritance brought a more rigid notion of what constituted nationality. It belonged with a profound reassessment of man's place in the world, with what has been called a 'shift from a sense of man as primarily a social being, governed by social laws and standing apart from nature, to a sense of man as primarily a biological being, embedded in nature and governed by biological laws'.[37] This preceded Darwinism and was as marked as anywhere in England, with its vogue for Gothicism, Saxonism, and, eventually, Teutonism. Even so it was a gradual process and slow to harden. It remained the case that in its formative period as a concept, national character was little more than an attempt to describe the differences between peoples organized by geopolitics.

National character was thought crucial to Britain's success because it seemed a fair assumption that its people rather than its rulers deserved the credit. There were other successful states in the eighteenth century, Sweden at its commencement, Prussia later, but their achievements were attributed to their rulers, notably Charles XII and Frederick II. Even enthusiasts for the Hanoverian regime did not claim that George I or George II or George III was responsible for the extraordinary feats of the State each reigned over. Self-congratulation on the capacity of ordinary people to rescue their governors from the corruption and incompetence that often marked their conduct, was a more or less fixed item in populist and patriotic rhetoric, as relevant in an age of reform and democratization as it had been under would-be despots and oligarchs.[38] The belief, as the Scotsman Samuel Smiles put it, that 'the Men of England are, after all, its greatest products' was tantamount to an article of national faith.[39]

For foreigners, this lent a special significance to their analyses. Whatever was peculiar to this small island people might well hold the key to the ultimate State secret, a capacity to exert an influence on the world at large out of all proportion to demographic size and physical resources. It followed that students of greatness might do better to scrutinize the everyday behaviour of the people than its laws or arsenals. Character and manners, as a French Anglophile expressed it in 1817, could explain why 'the English nation, in little more than a century, that is, since the happy revolution of 1688, has increased more in population, in knowledge, in grandeur and in political prosperity, than any nation, ancient or modern, has been able to do in many centuries'.[40]

Such concerns were of well-established interest by this time, especially for the 'philosophical traveller' who regarded 'as a chief object of his speculation, the manners of a nation'.[41] The author of the Grand Tourist's vade-mecum, Thomas Nugent, urged his readers to shun cabinets of curiosities and study local customs 'to remove the narrow prejudices of education, and to fill their minds with more generous and

manly conceptions'.[42] There were other fashions in travel literature, but
this was never submerged. 'A great passion for seeing the manners of all
ranks of people' became more or less obligatory in travel writers by the
early nineteenth century.[43]

The lowest ranks of all were not the least interesting, for as the classical scholar Thomas Twining remarked in Paris in 1786, they might reveal
more clearly than their more polished superiors, the peculiarities of
national character. Letting a Savoyard clean one's shoes on the Pont Neuf
was time well spent and incidentally constituted the 'great charm of travelling'.[44] Which class best represented the supposed national character
was, however, debatable, not least in England. Those who believed that
the best of society was to be found in its middle ranks, where the golden
mean reigned, naturally assumed that the nation's heart was located
there.[45] On the other hand, there was a view that education and profes-
sionalism had made the middle class the most artificial of all and that the
nobility and peasantry were the repositories of true Englishness.[46]

Wherever it was to be found, there was something about the English
that made national character seem a peculiarly appropriate tool of analysis. Partly this may have been because much of their self-perception
seemed to depend on characterization. The English novel, the single
most potent agent of English culture on the Continent, was par excellence about character and manners. As soon as landing at Dover Frenchmen were liable to transfer their impressions of them from their
remembered reading to the scenes they encountered, as did the Shake-
spearean translator, Amédée Pichot. 'I certainly observed characteristic
traits in the appearance of the innkeepers. The English novel writers who
are so fond of painting these characters, copy from a given model, which,
though it admits of but little scope for variety, is nevertheless true to
nature.'[47] Fanny Burney's novels were described by a German enthusiast
as a History of National Manners in themselves.[48] The Italian Agosto
Bozzi thought he had collected from Smollett and Fielding 'not only vast
stores of English words and colloquial expressions, but of English
manners and peculiarities, the knowledge of which converted me almost
into an Englishman at once'.[49] In a culture that deemed the stage
of exceptional significance, 'a kind of thermometer to judge the civilisation of a nation', the English comedy of manners was particularly
revealing.[50] In fact the whole genre seemed itself characteristically

English, what Georg Forster called 'die englischen und anglisirenden Sittengemälde'.[51]

The traveller with a preformed idea of Englishness derived from English writings became an influential interpreter at precisely the time when interest in national character was growing in the last decades of the eighteenth century. Significantly, Prévost, who had visited England at the same time as Voltaire, in the 1720s, before it was fashionable for Frenchmen to visit Britain for anything but business, had waged a campaign single-handedly to bring to the attention of a French public the best of English literature. He believed that the English had been misunderstood by his countrymen precisely because they had lacked such insights in the past. They judged on the basis of what was assumed about a violent history from the time of the Saxon invasions to the Civil War. The English 'are separated from the continent by a dangerous sea. Travellers rarely visit them, and they are too little known. They are judged in the light of historical prejudice, and, deceived by appearances, people paint an imaginary portrait of them which bears no resemblance to the reality.'[52] This was certainly to change. Within half a century, it was the sensibility of the English novel rather than the brutality of English history that informed Continental assumptions.

It was also noticeable that the language of British patriotism seemed to be drenched in self-characterization. The cult of John Bull, assiduously promoted from at least the 1790s, and with roots that went back much further, had no parallel elsewhere. The French Marianne and the American Brother Jonathan, developed later and less fully.[53] John Bull seemed a flesh and blood character who might walk off the pages of a novel or out of a vulgar cartoon into everyday life. Foreigners thought they beheld him wherever ordinary Englishmen were to be found, not least on the streets of London.[54]

Character as the obvious point of reference did not, in any case, depend on John Bull. It seemed to foreigners the natural way of describing a society that was fundamentally unlike other societies. Crossing frontiers elsewhere was a gentler transition by far than arriving at Dover, Harwich, or Liverpool. England was completely and suddenly foreign. 'I feel as if I have crossed into another part of the world,' wrote Nicolai Karamzin, landing at Dover in the summer of 1790.[55] A remote part of the world, a new world, even another planet, these were common ways of referring to the experience. Here, everything seemed different, and, moreover, different in a way that suggested extraordinary coherence, deriving from a wholly unfamiliar human make-up. The point was put forcefully by Adolphe Esquiros, who sought refuge in England after the dissolution of the Second Republic and found himself in a land that seemed overwhelmingly alien. 'What strikes me most in British civilisation and the English character, is the personality . . . You feel yourself carried away by a civilisation, gifted like certain planets with a peculiar movement of its own.'[56]

If there was then a 'personality' so powerfully felt, whose personality was it? The ambiguity of the phrase used by Esquiros—'British civilisation and English character'—is telling, and perceptive in that it suggests the desirability of distinguishing between the two. The great majority of foreigners used the terms 'British' and 'English' indiscriminately and confusingly, sometimes as synonyms, sometimes not, and in most cases unaware of the confusion in which they were colluding. It is difficult to blame them. Those who visited Britain almost invariably arrived by way of an English port, London, Dover, Brighton, or Harwich in the case of Continental Europeans, London, Liverpool, or Falmouth in the case of Americans. Hardly any came via Ireland, Scotland, or Wales. Before the 1780s it was uncommon to venture beyond England, or even to leave London more than a day's journey behind. Thereafter foreigners did begin to cross Offa's Dyke, and even Hadrian's Wall and the Irish Sea, their awareness of diverse nationalities stimulated by the Welsh picturesque, the romantic appeal of Sir Walter Scott's Scotland, and the religious and political controversies of Ireland. But the experience did not necessarily cure them of their habit of confusing Britain with England.

In Romance languages there was a reluctance to coin a precise translation for 'British', or at least to use it once coined. Germans could, if they chose, differentiate 'Britisch' and 'Englisch' more accurately, but in practice rarely did so. Even Americans, with no linguistic barrier to surmount, did not necessarily show more discrimination. The result was that in much the way that the English used (and use) Holland to signify what might more properly be described as the Netherlands, most foreigners used 'English' as the principal way of referring to the British people as a whole.

The ambiguity was shared by their hosts.[57] It is a paradox that a nation state with such a long history and seemingly so marked a sense of its own apartness, should be so confused on the subject of the nation or nations that make up 'Britain'. Moreover this terminological chaos was compounded at a time when Britain was hauling itself up the roll of nations. The unions of crowns and parliaments which occurred between 1603 and 1801 naturally generated a process of rhetorical state-building, much of it quite conscious.[58] From the standpoint of the modern nationalist this rhetoric is easily treated as English imperialism, the creation of a centralizing state employing the language and imagery of Britishness to emasculate competing political traditions and subvert native cultures.[59] It would be a crude view, however, that made of it nothing more than that. Much of the success of Britishness derived from the way in which it offered a layer of identity compatible with potentially conflicting loyalties. Numerous Scots took advantage of a formula which left them national self-respect while participating in the commercial and professional possibilities of an empire whose metropolis was London, not Edinburgh. So too, did many Irish, including some Catholics. And for the Welsh, the Ancient Britons, it was even easier to slip into thinking of English ways as British, the most formidable eighteenth-century example perhaps being Mrs Piozzi, who throughout a life of cosmopolitan experience stuck firmly to 'British manners' and who even entitled her book on the English language *British Synonymy*.[60]

The English themselves had some difficulty with Britishness. Despite official encouragement following the Union with Scotland in 1708 they showed a notable reluctance to describe themselves as South Britons. Annexing symbols of British identity was another matter, and had been since the first Anglo-Saxon kings had proclaimed themselves *bretwaldas*, monarchs of Britain. But accepting that being British might involve some lessening of what it was to be English, was far more controversial. In periods when the expansion of the English state stimulated a commitment to a wider British identity, including the eighteenth and early nineteenth centuries, it did little to erode a deeper stratum of commitment to the language of Englishness. Indeed Britishness as an expression had to wait until the late nineteenth century, if the dictionaries are to be believed. And to be un-British was unexpressed until later still. But un-English was a term in use from at least the late seventeenth century. Nor was it an arcane or arch usage. When Fenimore Cooper visited Britain in the 1830s he noted 'They have a custom here of saying that such and such an act is *un-English*.'[61]

Historians are now well aware of the need to think of the history of England in a broader context. The candid editor of a volume that began with 'English' in the title but ended with 'British' has confessed his difficulty in having to resort to a term 'formal, abstract and remote' compared with one that has 'all kinds of pleasant connotations'.[62] The rush to convert English into British history has certainly been impressive. But it does not follow that all things English must be considered solely in such a framework. In what follows I deliberately avoid using the adjective British to describe the manners and characteristics that were primarily English even though contemporaries of all nations sometimes did so. The reason for this is simple. It is difficult to discover any alleged British characteristic that does not in practice coincide with an alleged English characteristic. Nor is it easy to find any supposed characteristic of one of the so-called Celtic nations that was not specifically contrasted with an English characteristic. English character, so to speak, was the dynamic force, squeezing out Celtic claims to determine what made Britain British, just as the English had once squeezed the so-called Celts themselves into the northern and western corners of the British Isles. To follow much English usage by employing the word 'British' in this context is indeed precisely to patronize as the English have often been accused of doing. This does not, however, apply to other matters. In speaking of the State or of other institutions and practices in which all the constituent parts of Britain or even the British Isles shared, 'British' was and is a more accurate description, even if the English have sometimes been reluctant to resort to it.

National character is necessarily a construct, an artifice. Whoever defines or identifies it is at best selecting, sifting, suppressing, in the search for what is taken to be representative. In the twentieth century a presumption in favour of the nation state makes it easy at least to assume that there is a unit to characterize. In the eighteenth century there was no such presumption. The British monarchy as a political entity comprehended a motley collection of peoples, from Hanover on the Continent, through the varied communities of the British Isles, to an increasingly diverse body of colonial or semi-colonial dependencies. Yet paradoxically at its heart was a nation that was thought of as having a distinctive history and a pronounced unity, making the identification of an English character seemingly quite easy.

'There is a great uniformity in the manners and customs of the English', wrote Prévost.[63] It became a common observation thereafter. Where were the varied customs and costumes of the provinces of France, Spain, Switzerland, it was asked.[64] An English peasant dressed much as a townsman did. Dialects notwithstanding, linguistic diversity was insignificant to an Italian such as Baretti, who found that even the Cornish were comprehensible.[65] It was not merely that different regions displayed little distinctiveness but that all bowed before the influence of the capital. Louis Simond was struck that everybody above poverty seemed to have visited London. The country, as a place where one would not meet town people, hardly existed. It seemed to consist of a country house to London.[66] 'Londres est aussi dans toute l'Angleterre', wrote the Bonapartist Pillet.[67] Such reflections were not necessarily pleasing to natives. With the boorish behaviour of the capital's lower class in mind, the poet John Armstrong insisted that Londoners should not be called English at all.[68]

Visitors were unlikely to encounter the kind of uncontaminated Englishman Armstrong had in mind. The highways that carried them into the provinces also carried metropolitan sophistication alongside them. Few ventured off the post roads, but when they did they were more prone to notice the difference.[69] Moreover, the kind of people tourists met with were unlikely to be representative of genuine English provincialism, which may even have been enhanced by the regional impact of industrialization.[70] Even so, the uniformity of manners remained impressive when compared with Continental countries. Any Englishman landing at Calais, Helveotsluys, or Hamburg would soon discover that he had passed the threshold of a province rather than a country. For a foreigner crossing the Channel this was simply not the case. Dover could plausibly stand for all, wrote the duc de Lévis in 1814, or, as Victor Hennequin put it thirty years later, High Street Birmingham turned out to be much like High Street Portsmouth.[71]

Approaching the far borders of England it might have been expected that this would cease to be true as the customs of the natives shaded into those of their Celtic neighbours. Nothing of the kind, as J. G. Kohl discovered on Tyneside. Northumbrians 'protested zealously against the idea of their having any thing Scotch about them. They were genuine Englishmen, they said, and more genuine perhaps than those that dwelt further south; for in Northumberland it was that the Angles settled in the greatest numbers, and thence it was that they extended their influence over the rest of England.'[72] This perceived uniformity was not necessarily a matter of compliment. It might be England's materialism that smothered diversity. 'No Gascons and Normans, Sicilians and Piedmontese, Catalans and Galicians,' wrote Blanqui. 'There are everywhere only English, united only by the same spirit; it is interest, which by a happy illusion, they take for love of country.'[73]

English travellers returning from the Continent noted the same contrast. The charming diversity of European peasantries stopped at Calais. Or rather, it had to leapfrog over England, to the outer parts of the British Isles. In Ireland, wrote John Gamble, a few hours' ride revealed every progression of manners. 'In England a man may travel much and see little. Gloucester is Lincoln, and a man or maid of Kent, little different from a man or maid of Salop.'[74] The comte de Melfort also remarked that the absence of picturesque provincial dress in England, was 'in contradistinction with the other parts of the British jurisdictions'. This was all the more striking when it was recalled that it was, after all, a matter of manners. Ideas and allegiances in England itself could be diverse. The polity that matured after the Revolution of 1688 was famous for its tolerance and pluralism, which contrasted strangely with the seeming monotony of so much of English life. It was also Melfort who remarked, mystified, that this was a country of 'twenty-four religions and only one sauce'.[75]

Was this rather particular kind of uniformity a question of ethnicity then? Anglo-Saxonism in the sense of veneration of the lasting value of ancient institutions, the jury, witenagemot, the militia, and so on, was admittedly deeply entrenched. But it did not go unchallenged. The controversies which had raged in the seventeenth century on the subject of the Norman Yoke and the place of feudalism in English history had never been decisively resolved, and in the new historical writing of the mid-eighteenth century, much of it from Scottish and Irish pens, the emphasis tended to be on the common legacy of Continental feudalism rather than the unique inheritance from the Anglo-Saxons.[76] According to John Millar, the Saxons' love of liberty was merely a result of their unimproved rudeness. Their characteristic institutions were to be 'regarded as the remains of extreme simplicity and barbarism, rather than the effect of uncommon refinement or policy'.[77] The celebrated Ancient Constitution of the English survived such douches of cold water, but perhaps the steady drip of historical scepticism served to restrain any tendency to racial triumphalism.

It might have been expected that English travellers would take an interest in fitting their Anglo-Saxon ancestry into its Continental cousinage, as the early seventeenth-century James Howell had, when he discerned traces of English physiognomy, complexion, and gait in 'Plat Deutsch' Germany.[78] But the subject rarely featured in English commentaries on the Continent. It took unusual curiosity to pick up clues to Anglo-Saxon government in Frisia, or to find early centres of emigration by comparison of English and Westphalian place names.[79] Alternatively, it needed the possibility of royal patronage to stimulate such interest, as when George III's marriage to a princess of Mecklenburg suggested the happy thought that the new Queen had come from precisely the zone where the ancient Angli had once flourished.[80]

Only in the 1820s, when interest in all things German grew, were determined efforts made to connect English national character with that to be found on Germany's North Sea littoral. Reclaiming England's kin then acquired a certain appeal, for instance to Thomas Hodgskin, who in Land Hadeln found numerous resemblances to England. Here were Germans thought odd even by other Germans, and in their oddity strikingly like the English. 'What they call sincerity and plain dealing, their countrymen name vulgarity and rudeness; what they call independence, other people stigmatise as pride and contempt. They are certainly at present a distinct people from the rest of the Germans; they want all the softness and gentleness which distinguish them, but they are more energetic and more independent; they are less book read, but they have a more manly port and a greater vigour of mind. Every lover of British freedom must admire this last remains of the freedom of his German ancestors.'[81] English visitors to Saxony were also on the look-out for ethnic resemblances in the mid-nineteenth century, though their historical grounds for doing so might not be very secure. Saxons, wrote John Strang in 1831, 'possess more of the English agricultural character, than any other nation on the Continent. Indeed, their resemblance to our yeo-manry is so striking, as to leave no doubt of the descent of the two nations from one common stock.'[82]

Thereafter serious interest in Anglo-Saxon history and the rage for things German supplied a historically rooted ethnic identity that had been largely lacking beyond antiquarian circles in the eighteenth century. For the generation of Herbert Spencer, future Darwinians, the search for an 'Anglo-Saxon nature' in one's ancestors seemed natural.[83] It helped when visitors of Germanic origin repaid the compliment. Friedrich von Raumer, in Britain in 1835, noted the debt to Germany in 'all her most essential characteristics and her most important institutions'.[84] One of the most striking of such judgements came from Carl Gustav Carus, who accompanied the King of Saxony himself, on a visit to Britain in 1844. The Welsh and the Scots he found 'cannot in any respect be compared in mental energy and development with those who, properly speaking, belong to the new British race, and are constrained to yield to the genuine English . . . It is this little England, this England containing about 15,000,000 of its inhabitants, which has made itself the centre of a kingdom, greater than any in the civilised world.' He noted with pleasure the Englishman's strong frame, oval skull, fair skin, and light hair, and decided that above all it was he who had preserved the old German customs and the old German laws.[85]

C. F. Henningsen, son of a Swedish immigrant, also gloried in what he called the 'unbending nationality' of the Anglo-Saxon whose energy and enterprise brought him into 'every variety of the human race, but without ever receiving any impress either physical or moral from those with whom he mixes'.[86] Other foreigners, by no means all of them Germanic, contributed to the new historical awareness that underpinned ethnic Englishness. One of the most explicitly racist as well as influential of interpretations was Augustin Thierry's *History of the Conquest of England By the Normans*, translated into English by that champion of English letters, William Hazlitt.[87] Such inquiries gave a harder edge to the safely picturesque nature of the antiquarian pioneers who had begun to explore the history of the English *volk*, such as Francis Douce and Joseph Strutt.[88]

By mid-century it was possible to believe that the English were racially pure. In his famous appeal to the 'youths of England' Ruskin described them as 'undegenerate in race' and 'of the best northern blood'.[89] This had certainly not been the eighteenth-century view. The mixture of Germanic and Scandinavian tribes which had erupted into Britain between the fifth and eleventh centuries were then thought of as having created a mongrel people.[90] Moreover in a country that cheerfully dispatched its convicts to its colonies there was readiness to grant what Continental authorities often supposed, that the invaders were the worst not the best ambassadors for their people. As the antiquary Sir John Spelman put it, they were the 'prommiscuous Vent of all *Germany*, and for the most part the Refuse-Scumm of all the Maritime Parts thereof'. The successive invasions of those times he called 'five great Plagues or Scourges'.[91] French commentators agreed. France had suffered only one conquest since Roman times, and that, by the Franks, had left the essential character of Gaul in place. England, on the contrary, had been conquered every time it was invaded, 'profoundly effacing in England all the characteristics of national individuality'.[92]

Ironically, the strongest sense of English nationality may have existed in Britain's American colonies, where the process of continuous immigration threatened the status of an old English elite. The American Revolution enhanced this self-perception for those of John Adams's generation in New England. 'The People are purer English Blood, less mixed with Scotch, Irish, Dutch, French, Danish, Swedish etc. than any other; and descended from Englishmen too who left Europe, in purer Times than the present and less tainted with Corruption than those they left behind them.'[93] Perhaps it is significant, too, that so many mid-nineteenth-century American visitors to Britain wanted to identify in ethnic terms with their hosts.[94] When Elizabeth Bancroft, wife of a United States ambassador, boasted to the Marquess of Lansdowne of her 'pure Anglo-Saxon descent' and the novelist Harriet Beecher Stowe declared 'Our very life-blood is English life-blood', they were exhibiting a sense of ethnicity which was not always manifested in England itself.[95] There it was also complicated by aristocratic pride in descent from the Norman conquerors of Anglo-Saxon England. Only the Earls of Northampton, it was believed, 'laid no claim to the blood of conquerors, but on the contrary believed themselves to be of pre-Conquest Englishry'.[96] It does not appear that in this respect they were the envy of their peers.

In England there was a well-established view that mongrelism might be no bad thing. Indeed it was precisely the charge against the Celts, that as the remnants of the once proud race of Ancient Britons they were too racially pure for their own good. 'The anti-diluvian pedigree of a Welchman' was something to be mocked.[97] Outsiders might agree. The Quaker Jabez Maud Fisher, visiting Britain in the 1770s, noted that the Welsh were the 'only People of Great Britain who can boast a pure uncontaminated Blood' but doubted 'whether this have been any advantage to them. The English, by their mixture with other Nations, have got rid of many peculiaritys in their Sentiments and Tempers. A Sort of Liberality has pervaded that part of the kingdom which the Welch know nothing of.'[98] Racial mixing was thought to have many advantages, including the legendary beauty of English women.[99] The antiquarian Thomas Fielding argued that the genius of the English people derived precisely from its make-up. 'We are a mixed race, and our character partakes of the compound nature of our descent—its excellence consisting not in one predominant quality, but in the union of several.'[100] The logical view of the Welsh and Highland Scots was that they should submit to the same miscegenation that had made the English so successful, 'for they are savages, have been savages since the world began, and will be for ever savages while a separate people; that is, while themselves, and of unmixt blood'.[101]

The advantages of mixed ancestry were more prominent even in nineteenth-century praise of Anglo-Saxonism than is sometimes remembered. Carlyle himself, for late Victorians the author who made them think of themselves as 'blond and blue-eyed nordic, threatened and infiltrated by decadent Celts and Latins', asked where the English would have been but for the infusion of discipline represented by the Normans. 'A gluttonous race of Jute and Angles, capable of no grand combinations; lumbering about in potbellied equanimity; not dreaming of heroic toil and silence and endurance, such as leads to the high places of this Universe, and the golden mountain-tops where dwell the Spirits of the Dawn.'[102] Moreover, many were aware that the English mongrel had a leavening of Celtic ancestry to set alongside his Nordic and Teutonic descent. The authoress Elizabeth Rigby observed in 1843 that the union of 'Celtic and Saxon heads has produced the best of all compounds, an Englishman'.[103] It did not go unnoticed that Palmerston, 'the intensest

Englishman in English public life', and Wellington, 'the impersonation of the English character', were predominantly of Irish descent.[104] Champions of Wellington in particular were put to some difficulty, explaining that 'one may talk of England and Ireland as one nation, in a general way', or 'a man may be an Irishman by birth, and an Englishman by adoption'.[105] Foreigners certainly regarded him as the supreme Anglo-Saxon, as a remarkable tribute by Engels testified.[106]

The chemist Richard Chenevix, whose last, posthumous publication was an extended inquiry into national character, wrote, somewhat startlingly, that the English character had remained the same ever since 'Caesar made his first irruption', some centuries before the Romano-Britons had heard of the Saxon Shore.[107] Historians provided a version of the Anglo-Saxon conquest itself that emphasized coexistence with those invaded rather than the genocide that featured quite unapologetically in some later histories. As late as 1849, John Kemble refused to accept stories of 'total exterminations and miserable oppressions . . . We may safely appeal even to the personal appearance of the peasantry in many parts of England, as evidence how much Keltic blood was permitted to subsist and even to mingle with that of the ruling Germans.'[108] Uninhibited pride in the cleansing brutality of the first Englishmen came later.

In the meantime, devil's advocates had to ask whether a mongrel nation could indeed possess a character. The American William Austin identified ethnic schizophrenia in England. Owing to successive racial engraftments, 'one part of their character is at least two centuries behind the other'.[109] Nor could it be assumed that the process was at an end. The infusion of Huguenot blood following the French monarchy's revocation of the Edict of Nantes in 1685 had a visible impact on numerous aspects of British society. French Anglophiles took pleasure in this fortuitous Gallic contribution to a maturing Anglo-Saxon civilization. For some of them it was additionally pleasing to reflect that it resulted from the folly of their own, absolute government.[110] By no means all the immigration of the seventeenth and eighteenth centuries was from the Continent. The German Uffenbach, in the England of Queen Anne, was one of many visitors astonished by the proportion of blacks in London and still more amazed to see them clothed in European garments.[111]

Above all, in terms of ethnic miscegenation developments within the

British Isles were still more tangible. The political unification of the three
kingdoms was only part of a process that concentrated both capital and
much of the labour it employed in England. Perhaps it was no coincidence that the desire to reassert the Anglo-Saxonism of the English
people in the nineteenth century was expressed at a time when fewer than
ever of that people could be sure that their ancestry included no tinge of
Welsh, Scottish, or Irish blood.

Ethnicity apart, there was also a kind of received wisdom that the
English were by definition incapable of anything that could be described
as a character. It depended on endlessly recycled remarks by two celebrated authorities, the sceptical Scottish philosopher David Hume and
the whimsical English novelist Lawrence Sterne. Hume wrote in 1741 that
because of the 'great liberty and independency which every man enjoys'
the English 'of any people in the universe, have the least of a national
character'.[112] Sterne, in his *Sentimental Journey*, drew a famous analogy
between the French and the English as coins, the former worn by incessant sociability into indistinguishable blanks, the latter so little accustomed to contact with others, that they retained their individual markings
in high relief.[113] There was an obvious rejoinder to these claims, put by
Kant, when he remarked that the Englishman's pride in his own
individuality was itself characteristic of the English as a nation.[114] In any
case, theorizing apart, interest in identifying what made the Englishman
English did not let up.

Characterizing a nation is done by the nation itself as well as other
nations, and the resulting portraits, if not closely coinciding, do have to
sustain a certain congruence it they are to serve any purpose for those
resorting to them. It is true that some foreigners thought the English little
interested in what they had to say. As the baron d'Haussez, who went to
unusual lengths to bring his thoughts before both his countrymen and
his hosts, put it, although 'one of the most commonly vaunted pretensions of English society is that of thoroughly knowing the interests and
the people of other countries', they intensely disliked foreigners forming
opinions about England.[115] If so the English must have been unusually
masochistic, for they offered a flourishing market for foreign commentaries. Many were indeed penned with a view to an English readership,
and some appeared only or at first in English. Whether this body of literature should be thought of as simply an addition to the stock of national

entertainment, or whether it was absorbed into English perceptions of themselves is, of course, a question.

There is no simple answer. Some portrayals provoked very diverse reactions. Louis Simond's *Journal of a Tour and Residence in Great Britain, during the Years 1810 and 1811* was on the whole well reviewed and received. Yet the novelist Susan Ferrier thought it 'a compilation of old newspapers, travellers' guides, Joe Miller jests, impertinent gossip, and vulgar scurrility'.[116] It was always easy to pounce on the misunderstandings of foreign commentators, as the *Monthly Review* did when one German author confounded 'boar' and 'bore', or the *Edinburgh Review* did when another misinterpreted the advertisement 'Funerals performed here'. 'The blunders committed by foreigners in describing this country are proverbial.'[117] They made it easy for the complacent to dismiss the whole genre of travel literature as ill-informed and useless, as indeed did that large body of publications which represented fraudulent or fictitious travellers.[118]

Clearly hostile portrayals were unsurprisingly assailed. Of these the most notorious was a work by René-Martin Pillet, a Napoleonic general who spent an unpleasant time in England as a prisoner of war, and gave free rein to his animus in print.[119] He was denounced in the London press and punished in effigy on the London stage. In Paris the Duke of Wellington felt compelled to request the suppression of his book by the authorities.[120] Almost as objectionable was the radical Ledru-Rollin's *De la déadence de l'Angleterre* of 1850.[121] Interestingly, in both instances the root of the problem was the extent to which each relied on what were considered misleading stories from the English press.

It also mattered that the pen in each case was that of a Frenchman. French views received greater attention in England than others. Before the French Revolution, they tended to be friendly, after it they were more divided and remained so throughout the nineteenth century. Regardless of national bias, such publications were far more noticed by the nineteenth-century press in Britain than by its eighteenth-century predecessor, and the chances of controversy were accordingly higher. Not that only the French were involved. Anything unfavourable from an American was likely to be picked up by journals that specialized in anti-Americanism, notably the *Quarterly Review*. On the other hand, transatlantic praise was received warmly, none more so than Emerson's in

English Traits. 'The prophet-philosopher of the New World sits in his retirement at Concord, and passes judgment on our land and our people. The old oracular voice is heard. It is the same tone; the same English, abrupt, rugged, forcible,—the English of the risen Plato; and the subject of its utterances is—ourselves.'[122]

The commonest criticism of foreign perceptions was of over-reliance on long-standing stereotypes. Charles Dickens was one of those who believed that generations of such writing had resulted in a ludicrous mis-representation of what the English were like, not only as the grotesque figures to be seen on foreign stages or in the pages of foreign novels, but in impressions retailed by serious students of English life. He thought outsiders less sophisticated than English travellers despite some popular images of 'abroad' which linger in the 'minds of some of our bold peas-antry and milder cockneys'.[123] Considering the abundance and pointed-ness of English caricature of foreigners, the assertion is hard to credit.[124]

Other criticisms of foreign reporting of Britain might be considered to have more plausibility. Foreigners often obtained strange notions of their neighbours, from the many Englishmen they encountered in their own countries. The English, it was pointed out, did not travel like others, in search of their fortune, but for pleasure. By the third quarter of the eighteenth century they were easily the most numerous of tourists, far outranking the German nobility who had once made the Kavaliertour their speciality. It seemed reasonable to ask how representative they were of national life.[125]

Certain features of this invasion of the Continent were prominent in forming images of Englishness. One was the evident prosperity it sug-gested. The English were the big spenders of Europe. To travel *en milord* or even as 'Monsieur Bull' was to travel in the expectation of being overcharged, and foolish expenditure was considered a sure sign of Englishness. It was by definition the wealthy who travelled for the most part. The exceptions, commercial travellers and the debt-ridden Eng-lishmen who fled beyond the reach of their own law, to spend their lives at Boulogne or Calais, wistfully gazing on the misty outline of the South Coast, did little to shake the resulting image. The travelling Englishman often complained about being treated as a 'walking mint' but the as-sumption was too entrenched to be easily shaken.[126] What Scott called 'the Englishman's characteristic of More Money than wit' passed into the common stock of national stereotypes where travel was concerned.[127]

The undisciplined and often violent behaviour of the English, especially the young English, was hardly less commented on. 'Europe he saw, and Europe saw him too,' Pope had said of the youthful Grand Tourist.[128] For the staff of British embassies abroad, the activities of English visitors, 'each vying with the other who should be the wildest and most eccentric', as Louis Dutens, based at Turin in the 1760s, put it, were a major preoccupation.[129] Even Russians, not considered by contemporaries the most sober of judges, were impressed by the cohorts of wild English youth they found in the cities of western Europe.[130]

Shifts in the social character of English tourism did not necessarily improve matters. When the Grand Tour became less fashionable it was not because it had diminished but because it had ceased to be grand as increasing numbers of middle-class tourists appeared, and also because less time-consuming forms of travel were becoming feasible. The word 'trip' was being applied to a short journey to France or the Low Countries by the 1770s, permitting the 'low-bred rich' to cross the Channel merely to boast of having done so.[131] The end of the Napoleonic Wars brought a further surge of tourism as the inhabitants of middle England began to exploit the opportunities for travel in a period of growing prosperity at home and more or less reliable stability abroad. But the results did not improve the image of the English tourist. The materialism of those who journeyed from one expensive hotel to another, more concerned with the quality of a replica English breakfast than the scenic views, presented an obvious target.[132] It might have been supposed that the increasing presence of wives, daughters, and mothers among these invaders would have softened the customary image. Certainly it was a distinctive feature of English travel. In the eighteenth century even diplomats had not commonly brought their families with them, and for a French woman to venture into foreign parts was rare.[133] But women brought new problems, including the whole paraphernalia of English social life. The resulting sense of formality and rivalry did not generally impress their hosts.

Opinion in Britain seems to have been more embarrassed by the image of the philistine John Bull than that of the irresponsible milord of earlier times. The bad impression made by the 'would-be gentleman' travelling abroad was much debated.[134] The *Edinburgh Review* offered a less than wholehearted apology. 'We have not much to say in defence of our countrymen—but what may be said truly, ought not to be suppressed. That our travellers are now generally of a lower rank than formerly, and that not very many of them are fitted, either by their wealth or breeding, to uphold the character of the noble and honourable persons who once almost monopolized the advantages of foreign travel, is of course implied in the fact of their having become vastly more numerous,—without supposing any actual degeneracy in the nation itself.'[135] Perhaps the difference between the old and new was exaggerated. Looking back on the 1820s, Fanny Kemble remarked on 'the travelling English, to whom the downfall of Bonaparte had opened the gates of Europe, and who then began, as they have since continued, in ever-increasing numbers, to carry amazement and amusement from the shores of the Channel to those of the Mediterranean, by their wealth, insolence, ignorance, and cleanliness'.[136]

No doubt the impression conveyed by the English traveller, like that conveyed by the English novel, brought the foreigner to Dover with certain expectations, including the unpredictability, arrogance, and profligacy that feature in many accounts. However, if this was the worst that their hosts could allege, it is of little consequence, for the fact is that there was a large measure of agreement between outsiders and insiders about the peculiar traits that constituted English character. This is demonstrated most clearly by the testimony of those who sought to distance themselves from their own society by posing as impartial outsiders. The mid-eighteenth century bred a whole tradition of such self-assessment in the *Persian Letters* vein, though it tended to focus more on the fundamental verities of human life than national idiosyncrasies. There was, however, another tradition of what purported to be highly specific accounts of English life from foreign pens. Southey's *Letters from England: by Don Manuel Alvarez Espriella* of 1807 was perhaps the most distinguished example, but there were others, such as P. G. Patmore's *Letters on England. By Victoire, Count de Soligny* of 1823, elaborate performances that fooled at least some of their readers. Whether they were satirizing their own countrymen, or satirizing foreign commentators, or merely seeking more credibility for their own commentaries, the degree of coincidence between what they said and what authentic outsiders said was high.

In some ways this is unsurprising. Stereotypes resemble a kind of solera to which each new pen adds but a drop. Flavour may change over time, but only gradually, and generally by adapting rather than substituting. Stray accretions are lost in the mass and only a sustained input of novelty over a prolonged period alters the taste. And where flavours seem to clash, the result can be misleading, for what was at issue in these differences of opinion was not so much the perceived characteristics, but the value judgements that they provoked. The same qualities could be presented either as virtues or vices. One man's pride was another's haughtiness, one man's overbearing another's independence, one man's taciturnity another's discretion, and so on, as commentators themselves were aware when they sought to delineate 'those nice, and frequently, complex traits which mark national character'.[137] A composite picture of the English national character was in essence the same, though it might be placed in different lights and viewed from different angles.

The perceived characteristics are, of course, a result of yet another element, my own reading of these diverse contributions as a late twentieth-century reader. I have grouped them around six major supposed traits of Englishness, none fixed, but developing over the two hundred years with which I am concerned. My choice is inevitably somewhat arbitrary, not merely because it represents my subjective assessment, but because the terms themselves could easily be changed, and in matters of this kind the semantics are important. To take an example, candour was only one of a cluster of associated words often used of the English both by foreigners and by the English themselves. Honesty, simplicity, directness, sincerity, and more might be cited. In each case I have selected what seems to be the most common occurrence and also the most neutral. But, as I hope to demonstrate, it is in the ambiguities of these characterizations and in the evolving purposes they served, that some of the most interesting features of perception and self-perception are to be found.

CHAPTER ONE

ENERGY

INDUSTRY

INDUSTRY, said the novelist Bulwer Lytton, was '*the* distinguishing quality of our nation'.[1] When this remark was made, in the early 1830s, the evidence of Britain's industrial prowess was accumulating rapidly. It was tempting to attribute it to the superiority of the English workman and make it a cause for patriotic self-congratulation. There were, however, other explanations, and other perspectives on the human resources of the 'first industrial nation'.[2]

Much depended on the way in which industry was defined. It might, for instance, mean a high level of self-discipline and personal commitment, an unusual capacity for painstaking care. Or it might mean frenetic, even wayward exertion, a state of incessant activity. And it might mean mere drone-like drudgery, a submissive acceptance of demands that others would have found intolerable.

In Lytton's time many would have considered the last of these alternatives the most plausible. Some distinguished foreigners were among them, including Stendhal and Heine. Each thought he observed a people uniquely subjugated to the requirements of a manufacturing economy, turning men into little more than machines and sacrificing everything that was life-enhancing for mere material gain.[3] On such readings the English constituted an awesome aberration, a freak in the history of progress, from which others might learn the perils of precociousness. The revolutionary exile Ledru-Rollin worked out a systematic thesis on these lines, concluding that the materialism that characterized the English people would end by destroying them. Much of the evidence that he provided had to do with the misery endured by ordinary workers in the acknowledged workshop of the world, as originally described by Henry Mayhew for English readers.[4] It was for France, inspired by the ideal of social equality rather than the lure of individual gain, to show humanity another way.

Many of Ledru-Rollin's comrades in the London émigré community would have agreed that England exhibited the extreme case of a people inured to labour by industrialization, the true home of 'white slavery'.[5] But not all thought that this was an exclusively English disease. Other economies were beginning to catch up and it seemed likely that such forwardness had little to do with nationality, but, on the contrary, represented the triumph of impersonal forces over all kinds of local or national characteristics. Political economists depicted it as the inevitable result of the specialization of labour in a market-oriented society. Adam Smith had predicted something of the kind, when he spoke of manufacturing labourers becoming 'as stupid and ignorant as it is possible for a human creature to become' and Marx made it the centre-piece of a theory of alienation that has exerted a considerable hold over students of industrial culture ever since.[6]

This did not rule out the possibility that there was something about the English that had given them a head start, explaining their early adaptation to the industrial mentality. If so, there was a paradoxical process at work. In the pre-industrial era an aptitude for labour was precisely what other societies seemed to have in greater supply. At home this was considered a matter for pride rather than embarrassment, in that it was believed to reflect the relative degrees of liberty among

Europe's working classes. Freeborn Englishmen chose when, where, and
how they laboured. The right not to work was almost a definition of
liberty, forced labour its antithesis. In the plantations the principle on
which an entire system of human degradation depended was slavery
sanctioned by law.

Nearer home, in the poorhouse, or, as it was known to many, the work-
house, the whip of the taskmaster might seem more humiliating than the
idea of incarceration itself. When chain gangs came into being in the
1770s the spectacle of manacled convicts marching to and from work
horrified the public at large. Prison 'reform' reinforced this mentality.
The treadwheel, introduced in the 1820s, drove home the association of
punishment with work, albeit useless work. Successive generations of
penal reformers were sensitive to the charge that they were turning
prisons into 'mere manufactories' and sought to establish a national pedigree for the discipline of the penitentiary.[7] This was, after all, a culture
rich in images that associated leisure with liberty and toil with bondage,
expressing a preference for a state that could be described, unkindly but
not inaccurately, as idleness.

Foreign observers were aware of this propensity. The received wisdom
was that the English were the laggards of Europe rather than its pace-
setters. The sixteenth-century Venetian envoys whose reports form such
a rich commentary on life in Britain considered its inhabitants slothful
and self-indulgent.[8] The obvious, and not flattering, comparison was
with the indolent Spaniards.[9] This continued to be a common assumption not only in Italy, but also in France, Holland, and Germany. Even
when their commerce was expanding, during the seventeenth century,
the English seemed to be less vigorous than their rivals across the North
Sea. The superior industry of the Dutch enabled commentators such as
Samuel Sorbière, in the 1660s, to understand how easy it was for tradesmen of the Netherlands to undersell their English competitors. A lazy
temper was natural to this nation of spoiled and self-regarding
islanders.[10]

Long after Sorbière's time foreigners continued to seek supporting
evidence for the charge of laziness. Leisure might be considered the
corollary of enervating luxury rather than healthy commercialism.
England offered a multiplicity of distracting and expensive forms of
diversion, and its inhabitants seemed to take every opportunity to desert

the workplace. The English weekend provided particularly promising material. Parliament led the way when it came to regard Saturday sittings as emergency measures.[11] The desertion of the City by London's business classes from Saturday to Monday seemed to set a worrying example to employees. Not that workmen needed much encouragement. Friedrich Wendeborn, in the 1780s, considered them far too addicted to holidays, especially by comparison with the Dutch.[12] The custom of 'St Monday', the English workman's unauthorized day off, was much cited. Evidently the Protestant Reformation had not had quite the galvanic effects on the labour force that might have been expected. Britons scoffed at the numerous days of idleness marked by holy fasts and festivals in the Roman calendar. Yet the reality in England seemed not noticeably superior. Growing recognition of Bank Holidays, the red-letter days in eighteenth-century almanacs and diaries, augmented the effect of less official festivals. There was evidently no reason for smug self-satisfaction here. The Irish, despised by the English for their Catholicism and indolence alike, allegedly made Monday their favourite day for work.[13]

Such attempts to distinguish the working habits of the English from those of their neighbours have an obvious interest. Modern students of labour relations treat the 'irregularity of labour patterns before the coming of large-scale machine-powered industry' as characteristic of pre-industrial Europe. It was in England that they were revolutionized to suit the work-ethos of Puritanism and the economic requirements of capitalism.[14] Yet foreign commentators found the English more lax and lazy than other peoples. English working hours were considered short. This was not simply a matter of successful trade unionism; it was thought to derive from some specifically national trait. That the English were late risers was one of the first observations of new arrivals from the Continent. Most Londoners were apparently still abed long after their contemporaries in Paris, Berlin, or Rome would have been about their business. Germans were particularly dismayed by such sluggish domestic habits. The idea that respectable life might involve starting the day at 9 a.m. was shocking.[15]

Even outside 'bürgerlich' London it was possible to be surprised by the leisure enjoyed. Heinrich Meidinger observed in 1820 that in country villages the poorest labourers expected to be in their own home by 6 p.m., consuming the famous English 'tea'.[16] Beyond the rural south a

quite different story had to be told. By Meidinger's time foreign visitors
were aware that without a sojourn in the industrial midlands or north any
tour of the new Britain would be incomplete. There they found long
hours, hard labour, and a routine of stultifying severity. But the very ferocity of this regime suggested not the industrial adaptability of the English
workman's temperament so much as the need to release industry from
its shackles. In the factory, that living social laboratory, Engels himself did
not consider the work demanding; it was 'no work at all, but pure
boredom, of the most deadening and exhausting imaginable kind'.[17]
Moreover, the notorious reliance of the new manufactures on the energies of women and children did not say much for the reliability of labouring husbands and fathers. The un-Englishness of industrial work
remained a potent theme in the literature of the mid-nineteenth century,
with the emphasis on the compulsion required to make workers productive rather than their natural laboriousness. They were 'the hardest
worked, and hardest taxed, and hardest pinched class of people on the
face of the earth'.[18] Disraeli's 'two nations' caught the sense of a divided
society, leaving no room for a truly shared identity.[19]

   English manufacturers were all too ready to agree that the discipline
of the factory had to be exerted against the natural grain of the workforce
rather than with it. The routine assumption was that the ordinary
workman would toil to avert starvation but not to earn a surplus or
acquire a superior standard of living. Such testimony to what is now
called the 'leisure preference' was hardly impartial.[20] On the other hand,
supposedly more objective judgements could be brought in support.
Arthur Young's remark that 'everyone but an idiot knows that the lower
classes must be kept poor or they will never be industrious' expressed a
wisdom deemed conventional from at least the time of Sir William Petty
and Sir William Temple in the late seventeenth century. By the nineteenth century it was being sustained by a growing body of official evidence, some of it genuinely comparative. Englishmen came to be much
in demand on the Continent on account of their familiarity with
advanced machinery and techniques, yet their allegedly unworkmanlike
habits infuriated employers. An inquiry in the 1830s recorded bitter complaints from Austria, Frankfurt, Saxony, and, above all, from Zurich,
where a manufacturer employing Bavarians, French, Danes, Norwegians,
Poles, Hungarians, Prussians, Dutch, Scots, and English described the

last as 'the most disorderly, debauched, unruly, and least respectable and trustworthy of any nation whatsoever whom we have employed'.[21] In America too, the English had a bad reputation with employers. They were criticized particularly for their unadaptability and their legalistic attitude to their duties.[22] Contractualism was considered an English disease long before the heyday of the trade unions.

Perhaps no theme in the vast literature of national improvement was more hackneyed than this. Making the freeborn Englishman conscious of his responsibilities was a constant preoccupation of those concerned with the generation of national wealth. State, county, corporation, and parish strove to render the 'unproductive' poor industrious. A whole array of charities, eleemosynary, educational, medical, religious, and humanitarian made the improvement of the national stock of labour their explicit or implicit object. Unfortunately, law and reason alike seemed destined to fail in this ultimate mission. From the Reformation to the Reform Act and beyond, the pundits lamented the limitations of coercion. 'You can confine this son of freedom in a nasty gaol for a trifling debt; you can send him to Tyburn for a pitiful theft; and yet you cannot oblige him to make himself happy, by earning a comfortable livelihood in the way of honest industry.'[23]

When it came to systematic comparison with others, the English themselves generally turned to their immediate neighbours to restore their self-esteem. With the growing popularity of the Welsh and Scottish 'Tours', peasant life in the Celtic uplands could be scrutinized and found wanting in the 'great exertion' that patriotic Englishmen discerned in the best of their countrymen.[24] Ireland permitted a still richer range of contrasts, not least to Anglo-Irishmen intent on combining Protestant evangelism with economic improvement. Bishop Berkeley traced Irish sloth back to an ancestry of Scythian vagabondage and Spanish idleness, claiming that it was a byword even among plantation negroes. By contrast, the English were aboriginally industrious. He painted naive portraits of plebeian life in England: northern folk who after a day's work in the fields would form a 'jolly crew' to work at a loom in a neighbouring house, cottagers at Newport Pagnell who would sit in front of their homes late on a summer evening making bone-lace.[25] The demoralizing immiseration that was to shock nineteenth-century commentators who visited Lancashire and Buckinghamshire evidently held no horrors for Berkeley a hundred years earlier.

There were, in any case, more sceptical judges of the superiority of Anglo-Saxon energy. For all the supposed inadequacy of the Irish peasantry on its own soil, there was testimony to the industry of imported Irish labour. The political economist Nassau Senior concluded that 'The Irishman does not belong to the races that are by nature averse to toil. In England, or Scotland, or America, he can work hard.' He argued that Irish indolence was to be attributed entirely to the political and economic conditions which obtained across the Irish Sea.[26] On the other side of the Tweed there was still more unpalatable evidence for the patriotic Englishman. Whatever Scots could be criticized for, it was not their want of enterprise. To witness the vigour of Scottish miners and manufacturers at first hand was to conclude that their English rivals were no better than 'lounging' and 'slothful'.[27] Such findings provoked some lively historical debates. Gothic enthusiasts sought to portray the industrial revolution as an Anglo-Saxon phenomenon, and more especially the work of those purer Saxons of the Pennines who had remained uncontaminated by successive waves of conquest and immigration.[28] On the other hand, Celts could turn to Tacitus and find that 'industry and a daring spirit of commercial enterprise' had characterized the British nation long before the Anglo-Saxons had arrived.[29]

The crucial comparison was with England's ancient rivals, the French. For long the general assumption was that they enjoyed the advantage. Edmund Burke, a tireless defender of English virtues, made no attempt to deny French superiority in this respect. On the contrary, he told a French correspondent: 'In England we *cannot* work so hard as Frenchmen. Frequent relaxation is necessary to us. You are naturally more intense in your application.' But the moral that he drew was not to the French advantage. 'They who always labor can have no true judgment.'[30] A measure of indolence was the price of a higher civilization.

Such admissions did not signify that the English were necessarily bad workers. Hard labour was not synonymous with effective labour. As Hazlitt explained, the drone-like consistency of the French peasant might not be an asset in an Englishman. 'We can do nothing without a strong motive, and without violent exertion.'[31] A contrast was also drawn with the 'phlegmatic' Germanic peoples, who were thought of as less energetic, if more methodical and dependable. The novelist Ann Radcliffe made the point when she visited the Dutch Netherlands in 1794: 'We never observed one man working hard, according to the English notion of the term. Perseverance, carefulness, and readiness are theirs, beyond any rivalship; the vehemence, force, activity and impatience of an English sailor, or workman, are unknown to them. You will never see a Dutchman enduring the fatigue, or enjoying the rest, of a London porter.'[32] Significantly, when the English found themselves directly competing with the Dutch in South Africa, they prided themselves on their superior activity and enterprise. Even languid Hottentots, it was noted, might be inspired to imitate them, whereas Boers offered only mechanical drudgery instilled by brutality.[33]

The supposition that when the English did work, they put exceptional effort into their labours, opened up a promising line of argument. A nation that knew how to rest might well toil all the more strenuously when roused. Indeed, as the Jacobin Jacques de Cambry pointed out, it might be that lethargy and sleep were the true secret of English success, in that they conserved energies that could then be released suddenly and forcefully to remarkable effect.[34] Late rising went with more intense labour. Even the tedious English Sunday made sense in these terms. It was the sabbatical coma of a people addicted to exhausting activity.[35] Such reasoning fitted a long-standing perception of the English as a people of erratic but extraordinary energy. In short, what appeared unusual about them was not so much their industry as their activity, more especially their restlessness.[36] 'Ohne Hast, aber ohne Rast', was a maxim coined by Goethe, but it might better have come from an Englishman, and when Goethe's English admirers presented him with a birthday seal bearing it, he admitted his surprise that they should make so much of an inconsequential remark. It must, he decided, have something to do with the nation's way of doing things.[37] He was certainly not the only foreigner to reach such a conclusion. This was a nation marked by 'a too restless activity, which, like the balance of a watch, is never in repose'.[38]

LOCOMOTION

An obvious manifestation of restlessness was what the editor of travellers' tales, Charles White, called a 'craving for locomotion, which is, perhaps, a distinctive characteristic of the English nation'.[39] This fitful, unsettled state was entirely compatible with sporadic slothfulness, indeed might be seen as its corollary, a kind of natural antidote. English travellers had often recommended travel as, in the celebrated Celia Fiennes's words, 'a souveraign remedy to cure or preserve from these epidemick diseases of vapours, should I add Laziness'.[40] Sloth and mobility were the recto and verso of the English temperament.

Many others agreed. To the marquis de Bombelles it seemed that wherever he found himself there were coaches about to leave for some destination or other: 'one does not travel anywhere so much as in England, nowhere has one so many means of departing'.[41] Before the railway age, London's Elephant and Castle, where so many stages stopped, was the ideal place to view 'the perfect mania that the English have for moving about from one place to another'.[42] Such travel was not necessarily long-distance. The duc de Lévis thought the English practice of living in a suburb while working in town an example of the 'déplacement' of all classes. Daily journeys of this kind would not have been tolerated elsewhere.[43] It eventually took Americans to invent a word for it, 'commuting', but the thing itself was considered quint-essentially English from at least the mid-eighteenth century to the mid-nineteenth.

Implicit in such reflections was a belief that it was the desire for constant motion, not the necessity of getting anywhere, that motivated English travellers. They suffered from 'la maladie de change de place'.[44] This was true not only of tourists. All English people with even a modicum of leisure seemed to be on the move, 'jaunting about' as the expression went. In town and country, by land and sea, they were never content. As the baron d'Haussez put it, 'It is a matter of little moment to them whether they shall be happier at this place than at that; their great object is, not to be to-morrow where they are to-day.'[45]

Washington Irving remarked the peculiar resonance of the phrase 'to get on' in English, signifying a constant anxiety to be up and away, always anxious to complete a journey, never enjoying it for its own sake.[46] Travelling hopefully was a characteristically English activity long before Robert Louis Stevenson elevated it into a moral precept.[47] There were less complimentary ways of describing it. English Grand Tourists acquired a bad name with many of their hosts for their habit of covering enormous distances without taking more than a nominal interest in the places through which they passed. Diderot considered this a kind of English sickness, though in fact the tourist who provoked this diagnosis seems to have been a Scot.[48]

Exertion of this kind had a paradoxical flavour. The legendary obsession of the English with 'home comforts' did not serve to hold them in one place.[49] Nor was it only travel that was at issue. This was, as was often remarked, a society in which the great aim was to become rich enough to be idle. And yet nobody was more active than an idle Englishman. He was incapable of immobility, even in an urban setting, where a sedentary life might be thought unexceptionable. His penchant for walking in the street, riding on horseback, or parading in a carriage, all without any actual business in view, 'but simply to be absent from home', was something on which almost all commentators agreed.[50]

On foot and in busy streets there seemed to be something quite distinctive about the English, something which shaped their entire urban environment. It was noticed that the French excelled in creating interiors, the English exteriors. The streets of London were constructed and maintained for constant use, whereas those of many other capital cities were cluttered and filthy. In most European towns and cities paving was provided for horses, carts and carriages. In London the very term 'pavement' came to mean what was intended for those on foot. The results were admired by those used to less comfortable urban walkways. London's famed flagstones, increasingly prevalent from the time of the great paving commissions in the 1760s, were the envy even of Parisians. One lived best in Paris, but only in London could one 'promenade', it was said.[51] The most unrelenting Anglophobe whom the musician Michael Kelly encountered conceded that London was superior for two things, mock turtle and pavements.[52] Not that all the results were equally laudable. The Englishman's custom of wearing boots indoors, while testifying to his delight in outdoors activity, said nothing for his delicacy and refinement. Even in the assembly rooms of Tunbridge and Bath, Masters of Ceremony had to frame express prohibitions to protect the dance floor from their encroachment.

Londoners were often identified as pedestrians par excellence. The poet John Gay hailed them: 'O ye associate Walkers, O my Friends, Upon your State what Happiness depends.'[53] The apostrophe would hardly

walking

have occurred to a French poet. Taking pleasure in walking, as much in
town as country, came to seem an English idiosyncrasy. Foreigners
indeed confessed to amazement at the briskly moving masses to be seen
on metropolitan streets. Cockneys were proud of their reputation, providing satirists with a fruitful subject. Cornelius Webbe, in the 1830s,
enjoyed himself categorizing the more irritating pedestrians. There were
waddlers, crawlers, wallers, strutters, butters, bustlers, hustlers, saunter-
ers, plodders, swaggerers, loungers, room-walkers. There was also a vast
class of true and best walkers: 'these are a million, and the best ten-toed
travellers in Europe.'[54]

The English generally were known for their rapid walking.[55] It was
something they evidently took patriotic pride in, as standing evidence of
superior Anglo-Saxon industry. To observe a Welshman's gait was to
'mark the Welsh as a lazy set of people'.[56] There were military implications. Regimental marching *tempi* varied, but observant foreigners
noticed that they were all faster than the more measured pace of Continental armies. Civilians were no less fleet of foot. To see a man saunter-
ing was said to be rare indeed, especially in London, where the pace set
by the busiest and fastest tended to determine the flow of human traffic
on the streets. Nor was it only men who possessed this characteristic.
Abigail Adams found it hard to keep up with ladylike life as the first
American ambassadress in England in 1784. 'The London Ladies walk a
vast deal and very fast.'[57] Men were also impressed. Women on the streets
of the capital walked 'as though they were flying'.[58] The Russian who
made this remark considered the result sexually appealing. But the customary verdict was that a leisurely gait would have been more fetching,
and that English women walked without grace. At Calais, where it was
possible to compare English and French deportment in the mass thanks
to the numerous 'daughters of Albion' disembarking, they were judged
sadly inferior.[59]

It was not that French women were noticeably slow moving but rather
that when they walked they seemed to trip delicately along, without
a trace of awkwardness.[60] English women took long strides, suggesting
an innate preference for speed even when they were proceeding at
a relaxed pace. On the Parisian stage, Englishwomen were depicted with
'Brobdingnag strides and straddles'.[61] Extended to men and considered

as a natural trait, this clumsiness was fatal to national aspirations in point of politeness. The French, who had invented the concept of promenading, were scornful. They concluded that however hard the English sought to emulate them they merely succeeded in some form of running.[62] The staunchest Anglo-Saxon found it hard to deny French superiority. The best that Hazlitt could do was to claim that this was a characteristically Gallic trick. 'French grace is a dextrous, artificial substitute for the real thing, taught by walking along the dirty, slippery streets of Paris.'[63]

The historian Michelet was impressed by 'this terrible concentration of power, this desperate acceleration in a straight line, found everywhere in England'.[64] Velocity seemed to be an obsession, going by the quality of the highways and the machines used on them. The coaches were the fastest in Europe, too fast for men like the classical scholar Niebuhr, accustomed to the agreeably gentle motion of a German carriage.[65] Prussian visitors admitted their dismay that their own vaunted posting system could offer no contest with that provided by the less bureaucratic English State.[66] It was also said that the horses were fleeter-footed than anyone else's. One or two French visitors patriotically contested the point, but others preferred to criticize the English breeder for reducing a noble animal to 'nothing more than a *locomotive* machine, a sort of *roulette* wheel whose speed determines loss or gain'.[67] The Englishman was the horse's knacker, not his friend.[68]

Not only horses were so treated. Most of animal creation, when bred in England, was apparently expected to have speedier wings, hoofs, or paws. This was even true of foxes. When a shortage of quarry led to the importation of French foxes 'the hounds themselves despise them . . . and once they have once tasted a wild, healthy British fox, will no longer stick teeth into such carrion'.[69] Nor would it have occurred to every nation to race either pigeons or dogs. Racing was not restricted to creatures with feather or fur. The readiness with which both men and women would run against each other seemed odd to foreign observers. And those of the English who preferred not to race put money on those who did.

The ultimate eccentricity was the respect accorded professional pedestrians. Some foreigners found it difficult to believe that this did not arise from a kind of abnormality. The feats of a Regency athlete who made a small fortune by taking bets on his long-distance walking were put

down to the fact that as a baker by trade he must be a compulsive insom-
niac, incapable of remaining still.[70] Others merely considered such habits
an extreme example of the national restlessness. Sometimes they were
exhibited abroad, for instance by the much-admired 'Walking' John
Stewart, whose wandering exploits extended over three continents and
whose memorable stride was still fascinating onlookers during his last
years in Regency London. It was not always appreciated by those who
first encountered this phenomenon that it had very little to do with
'getting from A to B'. The English had no respect for those walking
merely as a means of self-transport. Germans accustomed to touring on
foot were dismayed by the contemptuous reception they got from
innkeepers and other natives. And the English 'green-bag' travellers,
forebears of the modern ramblers, who appeared when romantic and picturesque scenery came into fashion at the end of the eighteenth century,
did not fare much better.[71]

Few doubted the physical benefits of such activity. Exercise, especially
outdoor exercise, was thought peculiarly the prerogative of the
Englishman.[72] To the American Charles Bristed, who spent five years at
Cambridge, it came as a surprise to find students occupying two hours
a day at fencing, riding, or rowing and to observe the roads around the
town between the hours of two and four 'covered with men taking their
constitutionals . . . Our Columbia boys roll ten-pins and play billiards,
which is better than nothing, but very inferior to out-door amusements.'[73]

The national obsession with taking an 'airing' puzzled visitors. Why,
in a country where humidity was high, winds rough, skies grey, and rain
frequent, should the open air seem so appealing, wondered the marquis
de Custine.[74] The fact that it was as much a female as a male obsession
seemed telling, especially when the resulting recreations, such as archery,
outraged the Continental eye.[75] Schoolgirls exercised as regularly as
schoolboys, with due allowance for the requirements of maidenly
manners. Their mothers were as accustomed to walk and ride, both in
town and country, as their fathers. Much of the idiosyncrasy of London
fashion as viewed from the Continent derived from this difference of
lifestyle. The prevalence of a masculine riding-habit, often worn out
of the saddle and even in the home, was much noticed, as was the liking
of the English gentlewoman for hats.

No less characteristic was the famed English complexion, supposedly

the consequence of living so much out of doors. The merits of this
'natural' look were vigorously debated. A Parisian journalist in 1801
feared that an Anglophile vogue for rosy complexions, braving the
weather and so on, might threaten French ideals of beauty by encouraging colour on the cheeks and fullness in the bosom. On the other hand,
he sarcastically conceded that fashionable English 'nerves' would mark
an improvement upon outmoded French 'vapours'. 'Nerves' did not
require a pallid look and a suffering air, but high colour, animation, and
vivacity. 'The chastity of Joseph might have been conquered if Mme
Pharaoh had had the power of this resource.'[76]

More than taste in matters of costume and cosmetics was affected.
Englishwomen were celebrated for their modesty, yet their passion for
the open air often put it at risk. An instance recorded by male visitors
was their readiness to take an outside seat on top of lofty stagecoaches,
something that would have been unthinkable on the Continent. The
resulting exposure of underwear and undercarriage proved a voyeur's
treat. Friedrich von Raumer, Prussian academic and administrator, could
not conceal his delight. 'A connoisseur may perhaps think this to be the
most agreeable part of the mode of travelling.'[77] The recurrence of
the theme in satirical literature and art suggests that it was not only
foreigners who were charmed by this female hardiness.

All over Europe, there were numberless unfortunates, including the
greater part of the labouring population, who braved the elements in all
kinds of weather. But the notion of doing so as a matter of policy and
pleasure seemed strange. The extreme contrast was with Germany, the
more striking because Germans had in common with the English both
their ethnic roots and their Protestant Reformation. Yet, as British travellers often observed, not only did they avoid bodily exertion, but their
houses were close and airless, their beds hot and stuffy, their whole way
of life enervating.[78] Even Latin Europe, though less housebound, was not
more given to exercise for its own sake. Italians, at least of the lower class,
contrived to spend much of their time in the open air but without the
least delight in bodily activity. The fact that across the Atlantic, even
among English stock in the United States of America, visitors were
thought eccentric to insist on taking a daily walk, as Charles Dickens did,
made this peculiarity seem all the odder.[79]

PHYSICALITY

The physicality of English life was indeed a subject of intense interest to foreigners. Many traced it back to upbringing, and in doing so could cite corroborative evidence from British authorities. The robust character of an English childhood was acknowledged long before *Tom Brown's Schooldays*. At every level of school life violence was taken for granted. Much of it was dealt out by masters or senior pupils, as often as not, so it seemed, without regard to anything that could be described as justice. But the most junior pupil was expected to be able to defend himself, and indeed to take the offensive, sometimes in circumstances that nonplussed observers. Where else but in an English academy could one imagine the scenes that occurred at Eton and Westminster, when a famous bruiser could make a living by letting 'the scholars hit him as hard as they could, even on the face, for a shilling'.[80]

The cult of athleticism at the public school—a well-worn subject—is generally associated with the reforming headmasters of the late nineteenth century. Yet as a recognized part of schooling, though firmly within the domain of the boys themselves, it goes back much further. In fact if Marlborough and Harrow are guides it seems likely that public-school sportsmanship was more in the nature of an attempt to control and channel the disorderly activities of pupils than an experiment in enlightened gymnastics. The physical exercise of the Georgian and early Victorian public school was not confined to playing fields such as those at Eton but tended to range over the property of neighbouring landowners and the streets of nearby townships, bringing with it a variety of irritations such as the poaching of game and the stoning of pets.[81]

The preferences of pupils doubtless varied, but in the recollections of generations of public schoolboys before Arnold extra-curricular activities tended to take precedence. This was as true of schools in what might be considered an urban or metropolitan setting as of those with easy access to open countryside. For Lord William Lennox, as for many other Westminsters, 'the football in the cloisters, the cricket at Tothill Fields, the rowing and sailing on the river, the skating on the duckpond, the shooting near the Willow-walk' were the principal attractions.[82] Small wonder that outsiders like Alexander Herzen decided this must be a matter of an Englishman's instinct. 'Though he practises no school gymnastics of the German *Turnübungen* style, he gallops over hedges and ditches, drives all sorts of horses, rows in all sorts of boats and in a fight with fists can make anyone see stars of all the colours of the rainbow.'[83]

This process started before school-days. The calculated importance of play in English child-rearing seemed to have no parallel in Continental societies, until the rise of the kindergarten movement in the early nineteenth century. Significantly, although its origins were Swiss it was readily adopted in Britain in the 1850s, perhaps because its methods, if not its theory, were familiar. Certainly foreigners had long been struck by the encouragement of infantile play in English families. When the young Johanna Schopenhauer was exposed to it in Danzig, thanks to her parents' acquaintance with a British resident, it seemed thoroughly alien. '"Let the little victims play," was his kind answer, when my mother scolded me for playing rather too roughly with my sister Lotty, who was then just four years old. Neither my mother nor I understood these words; when I learned English I comprehended them.'[84]

When, eventually, she got to England herself, Johanna Schopenhauer was none the less shocked by the freedom extended to playful children, especially if it resulted in their running recklessly between the wheels of street wagons. No nation seemed to take more literally the saying that everyone had a guardian angel, she thought.[85] It was noticed that London parents taught very young children the name of the street they lived in, a custom which supposedly kept many infants out of the orphanage.[86] Elsewhere in Europe, as the Tuscan Luigi Angiolini reflected, the idea of permitting tiny children to play in busy streets was unthinkable. Here was a nation which believed in inuring the young to physical danger. Surely this must be the source of that intense energy associated with the English character.[87] Significantly, Angiolini traced back this mentality to the earliest experiences of a child. An English baby hardly had time to cry, let alone sleep. It had to be picked up and played with, sung to and spoken to as if it was capable of responding to adults. It was subject to incessant stimulation and encouraged to be mobile before it could usefully move. Once on its feet, it was permitted an astonishing degree of independence. Freedom started young for the freeborn Englishman.

There were different ways of looking at this freedom. Even admiring foreigners found English children wild and unruly, both in and out of the home. Tolerance of the 'rough schoolboy', as a future King of Poland, Stanislas Poniatowski, remarked, was carried much too far.[88] But to the English this seemed preferable to the mollycoddling that went on elsewhere. When abroad they missed 'that constant gush of child life which overflows our London in park, street, alley and square', as Mrs Craik, author of *John Halifax, Gentleman*, expressed it on visiting Paris.[89] Moreover, encountering French youth, pampered into precocious politeness, was a disagreeable experience. The Caribbean traveller George Pinckard, who saw French boys alongside English in British-governed Martinique in 1797, decided that the advantages in health and spirits were certainly not with the French. 'From the cradle they are taught *de se soigner, de se ménager!* and habit begets a mode of self-discipline which puts nature to the blush!'[90]

The English child was not only father to the man but sometimes difficult to distinguish from him. Genteel recreations in England seemed unique in this respect. Foreigners understood why the young might engage in physical exercise, especially if they lacked the commitment to intellectual pursuits that Continental educators sought to promote. But that, for instance, 50-year-old men should play cricket in public, was astonishing.[91] Decorum, for which the English were celebrated, evidently placed no limits on the devotion to physical exercise.

The aristocratic pugilism that flourished from the 1770s was without parallel elsewhere, not least because it suspended the laws of honour, permitting blue-blooded boxers to exchange blows with plebeian. So was the contemporary craze for coachmanship, which resulted in the foundation of genteel clubs, the Whip, the Four in Hand, the Driving Club. The spectacle of a belted earl at the reins of a mailcoach, hobnobbing with coachmen and postboys, gave travellers a strange idea of British nobility. Royalty itself did not disdain association with humble sportsmen. At the coronation of George IV eighteen prize-fighters were employed to guard the external avenues leading to Westminster Hall, permitting the champion bruiser, Richmond the Black, to appear in the unfamiliar livery of a royal page.[92] Incongruous spectacles of this kind were taken to be an established part of official etiquette in Britain. Nor was the Continent immune. When an English nobleman perished in a steeple chase at Rome, Pope Pius IX was prevented from banning the sport by the threat of an English boycott and supposedly yielded with the remark 'that he would not prevent the English gentlemen from breaking their necks in his dominions if they liked it'.[93]

English low life was famous, or rather infamous, for aggressive physicality. A taste for combat seemed the most basic urge. Perhaps no scene figures so much in foreign accounts of London life as the impromptu boxing matches that settled disagreements on the street. Their frequency and orderliness in travel literature defy belief, though they certainly testify to Continental interest in such exhibitions. Those who went further afield found that an equally vigorous tradition of wrestling, boxing, and cudgelling was part of the rhythm of rural life. Visitors such as the abbé Prévost were impressed by the fortitude these practices engendered in English youth but found 'something ferocious and barbaric' in them.[94]

Their hosts countered by citing the martial advantages of unarmed combat, 'a practice of the highest antiquity, even reaching up to the time of Homer, that it served to form a manly population, and breed them up to contempt of danger; that the man who could beat another with his fists would never scruple to meet him with a gun and bayonet; and hence the superiority of the English over the French at these weapons'.[95] Various instances were cited. The famous victory at Dettingen in 1743 was attributed to the strength of the Englishman's arm, nurtured by boxing.[96] At Waterloo the heroism of a noted boxer, Corporal Shaw of the Life Guards, who was believed to have slaughtered or disabled at least ten of his enemies before he fell, provided powerful evidence, according to Sir Walter Scott, of the military value of 'the noble art'.[97] When Wesley's disciples set about 'reforming' the physical recreations of the people in one of their most secure redoubts, the West Country, some concern was expressed about the consequences for the armed forces. Similar arguments had been employed against Puritan zealots nearly two centuries earlier.

Even field sports, the universal recreation of European nobilities, took on a different character in England. Fox-hunting looked eccentric to a Continental observer, especially from the last decades of the eighteenth century, when it acquired an elaborate, minutely regulated, etiquette all its own. Englishmen exhausted themselves pursuing tiny creatures to a death inflicted not by them but by their hounds. The main object seemed to be exercise rather than killing. Visiting sportsmen were physically shaken by the experience of participating in an English 'chase', as some of them admitted in print. The baron d'Haussez, who sampled the fox-hunt in its most celebrated locale, at Melton Mowbray, was appalled by the speed and peril at which it was conducted.[98] For their part the English found Continental notions of hunting morally repugnant. They mocked the Nimrods of European royalty, such as Carlos III of Spain, whose idea of the chase was little more than slaughter.[99] The first gener-ation of English princes born and brought up in England, the brothers of George III, entirely shared this distaste. The Duke of Gloucester, on tour in 1769, was unamused by the 'barbarous diversion' of boar hunting among his German cousins.[100] As for shooting, the English gentleman went out on his own and worried little about the size of his bag. When the battue did become common in Britain in the mid-nineteenth century, it was denounced as 'un-Englishman like'.[101] The truth was that it offered the unfortunate game a better chance of survival than did traditional shooting, but this subtlety was lost on defenders of 'fair play'.[102]

English weather was taken to be part of the explanation for the sport-ing inclinations of the nation. One of the most quoted sayings of that quotable king Charles II was his remark that it 'invited men abroad more days in the year and more hours in the day than any other country'. Yet Britons overseas startled the natives by organizing such activity in far from favourable climates. As Henry Matthews concluded at Naples in 1818, when he witnessed *Eton versus The World* at cricket, his country-men were quite unmatched in their capacity for taking their amusements around the world with them.[103]

Empire created whole new playing fields. Modern accounts of the rela-tionship between games and imperialism understandably concentrate on the late nineteenth century.[104] But the subject has a considerable prehis-tory. The first colonizers of America had been Puritan critics of the Book of Sports, with unfortunate results for their successors, as it was thought. In New England sport was primarily encouraged as a form of military training. Elsewhere it was slow to catch on at all, and when it did, in the nineteenth century, its professional ethos was thought highly un-English.[105] No such mistake was made in Australia, where convict cricket was considered an important contribution to that zest for activity that came to seem so strikingly Australian. Australians were of English, or at least British and Irish stock, but the most unpromising ethnic subjects for treatment also responded to this medicine. At Singapore it was claimed that the effect of English ways was to be seen even among Malays, supposedly the most slothful of Asian peoples with whom traders came in contact. Water sports on the European model had a remarkable effect 'in the case of the watermen, or sampan-boys, in whom it has worked a complete change, almost amounting to regeneration'.[106]

A common view in Continental Europe was that the physical exertion taken for granted by the English was not feasible without exceptional physical capacity. French analysts often attributed it to an extraordinary meat intake. When English railway engineers arrived in France to construct a line from Rouen to Paris, their 'energetic seriousness' was so impressive that their hosts undertook an analysis of the dietary contrast between France and England.[107] This had long been debated where military matters were concerned. Numerous historical instances could be cited of English beef defeating Spanish oranges and lemons or French *soupe maigre*.[108] Eighteenth-century statesmen regarded a carnivorous diet as something of the highest importance to the success of British arms, and the preservation of the British and Irish livestock trade figured much in parliamentary debates, especially in wartime. The analysis remained appealing in the early nineteenth century. Fears that the beef-eating Briton was likely to be relegated to history made it all the more necessary to resuscitate him. William Cobbett pointed out that New England people were noticeably taller and stronger than those of Old England, a difference which he attributed to their practice of feeding meat to babies. He also believed that it was the superior size of Americans, not superior courage, that accounted for their victory in the War of 1812.[109]

In any event, French visitors continued to be impressed by the bodily vigour of the English. 'I am certain,' remarked Taine, 'that the animal physique, the primitive man, such as Nature bequeathed to civilisation, is of a stronger and rougher species here.'[110] His contemporary, the historian Michelet, strove to find the explanation. Time and again, as he travelled about England, he was struck by the ruddiness of complexion that marked its inhabitants. Redness was everywhere, redness that might perhaps suggest the influence of alcohol but still more revealed a diet of animal flesh. 'Chair et sang' provided the English with their energy. The influence of climate Michelet considered highly paradoxical. Here was a people that swam between two seas, one surrounding its island home, the other suspended perpetually above it. This profound and perpetual humidity should logically have had the most enervating effect. Yet in the encouragement it gave to pastoral agriculture it made possible an unparalleled consumption of meat. The English were in essence raisers and consumers of cattle. Their history showed that even commerce flowed naturally from this source, for when they were not eating mutton and beef they were living off wool, first by selling it to Flanders, later by making it the foundation of their own industrial revolution. Pastoral farming had unleashed huge energy and creativity. Had not Shakespeare himself been a butcher by trade?[111] Enthusiasts for cattle-breeding colonies, especially in Australia, were heartened by Michelet's historical analysis.[112]

Red meat was the main but not the only dietary foundation of red-bloodedness. Part of the English temperament was taken to be a craving for sensation and excitement which might be heightened by stimulants of various kinds. This was the subject of a considerable debate in the mid-eighteenth century. Frederick II of Prussia was convinced that diet was more important than climate or quality of air in the development of national character.[113] It was noted that he was himself unhealthily addicted to spicy food, precisely the failing that was diagnosed in English eating habits. The Englishman's taste for spice exceeded what was to be found generally on the Continent and was not to be explained merely by his contact with the Orient Spices were consumed everywhere, but only in Britain to excess. Like the national habit of mixing spirits with wine, this suggested a characteristic desire for excitation.[114] A matching interest was observed in colour. Vegetables were lightly boiled to preserve their greenness, white bread was preferred to brown, port had to be a violent shade of red even if it meant adding artificial colouring.[115] The treasured whiteness of English veal, brought to perfection by the cattle-men of Essex, fascinated foreigners.[116] There was no contradiction here. Spice and colour suggested a preference for gastronomic and visual sensation. The culinary formula of Continental chefs, offering food that needed little of either but provided a repertoire of gently graded and refined tastes, was simply not English.

Pronounced tastes in food were themselves easily associated with temperamental restlessness. This was the essence of Englishness, a craving for variety. For some, it constituted a priceless asset, fuelling the energy of a nation of traders and manufacturers, and also breeding up men of action whose enterprise would astonish and even conquer the world. 'May we found no hope', asked William Beckford, 'on our natural impatience, and love of change? or on those fits of enthusiasm, to which we are sometimes wrought up by accidental causes? These qualities and affections seem as inherent in Englishmen, as frigidity, heaviness, and phlegm in the people of Holland; and as naturally dispose men to action, as the others do to rest.'[117] Beckford, author of the bizarre *Vathek*, builder of the disastrous tower at Fonthill, notorious homosexual and endlessly discussed eccentric, was not, perhaps, a reliable guide to patriotic preoccupations. There were other, less reassuring ways of looking at English dynamism.

MELANCHOLY

Restlessness, it might be pointed out, was not a very likeable form of vitality, particularly when the alternatives on offer elsewhere were examined. Discoverers of Celtic character, such as Richard Warner in Wales in 1797, described it as 'vivacious, cheerful, and intelligent', qualities not generally identified with the English.[118] The contrast with French vivacity was no less marked. The French, too, were considered a restless people, but theirs was the restlessness of levity and gaiety. About the English variety there was something altogether more solemn. The very notion of restlessness without levity, as the marquis de Caraccioli expressed it, was a puzzling phenomenon.[119]

The semantics were found intriguing. English had no word for 'ennui', annoyance being something different. Henri Meister was baffled. 'I am at a loss to assign a reason why the word *ennui*, which has a meaning strongly expressive and peculiar to itself, has not been honoured with naturalization, as well as many others from the same country. Is this disease of the mind entirely unknown in England? or is it because, in this fortunate island, people always find amusement, and never suffer from satiety, or inaptitude for enjoyment?'[120] Meister's contemporary, Brissot de Warville, found an explanation in English politics: a free people had no time to be bored.[121]

So far as the English themselves were concerned, there might be grounds here for patriotic self-congratulation. Georgiana, Lady Chatterton, a lifelong student of the contrasting manners of European nations, believed that her compatriots had a higher mission which precluded mere boredom. 'The French always *mean* to amuse themselves, and therefore when they do not succeed in accomplishing this great object of their lives, they are ennuyés. The English seldom intend to amuse themselves, and therefore they rarely suffer from ennui. Business, or occupation of some sort, is the object of an Englishman's life. He may be melancholy all the time, and disappointed at last, but he will not suffer from the lesser annoyance of ennui. This is probably the reason that a word of the same meaning is not found in our language.'[122]

Lady Chatterton's argument came dangerously close to an admission that if the English did not recognize the existence of ennui it was only because they suffered from a more serious disease of the mind. Presumably, the phrase 'un mauvais quart d'heure' did not translate well into English because fifteen minutes of tedium would seem trivial by English standards. Sir James Mackintosh's friend George Moore argued something on these lines: 'the feeling is so general, and so considered, that it is taken as a thing of course and unavoidable, and not calling for a particular name to designate it'.[123] Interestingly, when a more or less matching term was invented, or rather adapted, 'boredom', it suggested irritation at the intrusion of others rather than dislike of being thrown upon one's own resources. This differentiated the English not only from the French but also from the Germans. 'Langeweile' was true tedium, the tedium of a passive and phlegmatic people. George Eliot, astonished by Germanic tolerance of endless plays, endless books, endless coach journeys, put it on a par with the most deadening of English beers. 'German ennui must be something as superlative as Barclay's treble X, which, we suppose, implies an extremely unknown quantity of stupefaction.'[124] The affliction of her countrymen was something quite distinct from both ennui and Langeweile.

When did melancholy register with others as an English malady? Certainly by the late seventeenth century, when the English themselves were reaching a similar conclusion, and terms such as hypochondria, hysteria, spleen, biliousness, vapours, were establishing themselves as part of a novel language of nervous disorder.[125] From an early stage the suicide rate featured in discussions of this subject. A much-quoted French witticism was that whereas other nations, notably the Italians, were given to killing each other, only the English were prone to kill themselves.[126] By the time Stendhal's Julien Sorel described the 'demon of suicide' as the English 'national deity' he was voicing a commonplace of Continental wisdom.[127] Why, it was wondered, should this people relish life less than others, with cause to relish it more? Why did they lag 'behind other nations in the great science of happiness'?[128] Why did their animal spirits, to employ the modish late eighteenth-century term, give way to such self-destructive despair?[129]

There is no sure means of ascertaining whether suicide was in fact a markedly English disease, though it would be unsurprising if London, with its rapid population growth, its perpetual inflow of the uprooted and insecure, and its concentration of urban stress, did not in fact suffer a high incidence, as it certainly did in the nineteenth century, when usable statistics first became available.[130] In any event, it merged into a wider concern about the innate mental depression associated with the English temperament.

Enlightened scepticism brought much analysis to bear on this matter, often directed to English cases that seemed baffling partly because they did not look at all like the self-murder of the ancients, the philosophical resort of the Stoic. The Smith family suicide of 1732, which was recorded in Smollett's *History of England*, and thence found its way into numerous foreign works, attracted the interest of many, including Diderot.[131] It featured a pact between a bankrupt bookbinder and his wife, who killed their only child and themselves, having left instructions for the care of the family pets. Here, seemingly, was neither lunacy nor genuine desperation, but a rational decision announced in a letter 'altogether surprising for the calm resolution, the good humour, and the propriety with which it was written'.[132] This kind of suicide seemed peculiarly English in origin, suggesting either some ethnic taint, or a stage of evolution beyond that experienced elsewhere.

This was the explanation advanced by George Cheyne, whose celebrated tract of 1733, *The English Malady*; *or*, *A Treatise of Nervous*

Diseases, commanded an international readership. He argued that nervous disorders were associated with the progress of civilization itself, and not found in primitive cultures. Material excess and psychological anxiety belonged in western societies whose elites were pampered into obsessive introspection.[133] If this were so, then the English malady was merely one of civilization's discontents. Other nations could in due course expect to suffer the disease as well as benefit by the discovery of a remedy. Historians find in this analysis the mentality of a commercial and medicated society, in which all were encouraged to view health as a commodity, sacrificing peace of mind in pursuit of the mirage of guaranteed healing and endangering their body with addictive stimulants.[134] At the time Cheyne's theory attracted much interest. Even so, among foreigners there was some reluctance to accept it without reservation. It was not particularly cheering to conclude that British prosperity could only be achieved at the price of English mental instability. Morever, the evidence of anomie seemed to go beyond what could be ascribed to the pressures of modern life.

The Englishness of melancholy was a favourite subject for satire, frequently with variations on the theme of climate. Most foreigners, it was jocosely claimed, could not spend more than a few hours in England without suffering an uncharacteristic deterioration of spirits. The Frenchman lost his *joi de vivre*, the Italian his singing voice, and 'The German,—if a genuine specimen of the most-German German—of the Goethe and Werter water,—is depressed down below the suicidal point in the mental barometer, but has not energy enough left to lift a pistol to his head.' Only the Dutch, accustomed to the malignant humidity of a land barely reclaimed from the sea, found it bearable.[135] Suicide was thought to be commoner in the mist-laden autumn, among the 'November spirited English'.[136] When the English started colonizing the southern hemisphere, supporting evidence came to hand. In New South Wales April, Australia's seasonal equivalent of November, was the worst month for suicides.[137]

It was asserted that the English aggravated the effects of their foggy climate with artificial pollution from coal fires, especially in London. Henri Meister's elaborate analysis of the fatal effects of coal smoke on English fibres offered numerous examples of the mental traits that resulted, all of them connected with that incurable melancholy that was universally agreed to be the inheritance of Anglo-Saxons. 'You will never remove the firm opinion I retain,' he wrote, 'that the sensibility bestowed by nature on such minute fibres and delicate nerves, when acted upon by the caustic vapour of seacoal in the slightest degree, will not, in length of time, be destroyed, and the parts themselves become divested of their energy and power.'[138] Even the English admitted, when they ventured abroad, that the sight of a Continental city without smoke came as a pleasant surprise, promising a cleaner and more invigorating environment than their own.[139]

Alternative explanations featuring lifestyle were offered. The sheer fatigue that resulted from English mobility must take its toll. The suburban Londoner, when he returned home from a day of travel as well as toil, was 'incapable of wit or gaiety and disinclined for the pleasures of conversation, music or dancing'.[140] Nor was his diet without disadvantages, especially where alcohol was concerned. The English would be gayer and happier if wine duties were reduced.[141] It was recalled that after Agincourt Henry V had prohibited the drinking of wine without water, and promoted the consumption of home-produced ale. This was the last form of beverage that the English should have adopted. A glass of porter would have deadened the wits of an exuberant Gascon or a Périgourdin, let alone a temperamentally melancholy Englishman.[142] On the other hand, it could be countered that beer had no such effect on the Flemings and Brabançons.[143]

Tea was another possibility, not least because the English themselves worried so much about its toxic qualities. Yet it did not seem to produce similar symptoms in the Netherlands. Montesquieu believed that it was ruining the physique of Dutch women but did not notice any nervous debility.[144] A further instance of self-poisoning was the dreadful coffee for which Britain was already notorious in the eighteenth century and which distressed some of the most undaunted Anglophiles.[145] Even the meat diet so prided by the British could be brought into the analysis, on account of its heaviness and indigestibility. The Russian Karamzin placed it alongside some other favourite explanations to propose a trilogy of causes: perpetual fog, perpetual coal smoke, perpetual roast beef.[146]

There was also a still more compelling analysis. The ancient constitution that constituted the Englishman's birthright had its part in this as in almost everything else that belonged in English life. Here the com-

monest argument was that put by Wendeborn, who believed that the
inculcation of liberty from birth sacrificed reason to passion. Unrealistic-
ally high expectations led to despair; an inborn belief in the individual's
freedom of action translated despair into the ultimate sin. Self-
determination logically entailed the right of self-destruction. Wendeborn
cited the Quakers' immunity to suicide as evidence of their un-English
educational discipline and rigour, the exception that proved the rule.[147]

There were other ways of relating English liberty to English melancholy. A standard mid-eighteenth-century belief was that a free state
placed a heavy burden on the shoulders of its citizens. 'An English John
Trott, with his head full of Politics, shall knit his brow, and grumble, and
plod, unhappy and discontented amidst all his boasted Liberty and
Pudding.'[148] Henri Decremps worked this up into a theory, ingeniously
assembling a cluster of related phenomena. First, the insubordination
natural in a free society militated against the gaiety promoted by secure
and unquestioned government elsewhere. Secondly, the courts of law, by
providing the accused with too many safeguards, sustained a high level
of criminality in the community, making people excessively suspicious of
each other. On the Continent the subject trusted his sovereign to detect
and punish the guilty. Thirdly, a nation in which the governed were
encouraged to put their own preferences before those of government
naturally pursued its individual self-interest at the expense of collective
jollity. Finally, the incurable insolence of the English *canaille* forced their
superiors to observe the most exact etiquette; societies with clearly
marked but unresented social boundaries enjoyed, by contrast, an easy
familiarity between ranks.[149]

Decremps advanced his hypothesis in 1789, the last year of what was
soon to be characterized as the 'ancien régime'. If anything, the tumul-
tuous events that followed rendered his analysis all the more plausible,
to the extent that it increasingly seemed to apply to France as much as
England. The Italian Giacomo Beltrami, startled by 'a certain reserve,
seriousness and disquiet' which he found in France in 1822, concluded
that 'all those great and extraordinary revolutions, which have followed
so closely upon each other during the last thirty years, must have produced some changes in their character'.[150]

Ordinary Frenchmen came to seem graver when equipped with
'rights' formerly enjoyed only by their ancient enemies. The free citizen

of a constitutional monarchy or a republic gradually lost the cheerfulness
that he had displayed when 'shut out of the regions of manly thought by
a despotic government'. He learned what the Englishman had learned
much earlier, that 'the continual exercise of the mind on political topics
gives intenser habits of thinking and a more serious and earnest
demeanour'.[151] This was the judgement of an American, Washington
Irving, but one for which ample French and English support could be
found. The poet William Taylor thought as early as 1802, visiting France
after the Peace of Amiens, that 'The French character seems to me much
altered, and in an English direction.'[152] After the Napoleonic Wars, some
Englishmen even claimed to find the Restoration Frenchman less frivolous than themselves.[153] And Anglophobe Frenchmen, such as Balzac,
were quick to blame their neighbours' influence for putting an end to
French gaiety.[154]

By then voices were being heard in Britain in favour of reviving 'Merrie
England' and the tradition of a people once given to festivity and recreation. It did not seem insignificant that these voices also endorsed the
ancient constitution in Church and State and opposed the political
demands of radicals and reformers. Campaigns for national holidays, to
relieve industrial workers from the perpetual drudgery of labour, were
supported by aristocratic Tories for whom the liberal vision of progress
had little appeal.[155] The proposition that English gravity could be attributed 'chiefly to the gradual increase of the liberty of the subject, and the
growing freedom and activity of opinion', was argued both on historical
and ideological grounds.[156]

GRAVITY

It was not, however, necessary to accept these explanations, or indeed to
explain at all. The commonest line of argument was simply that there was
something incurably tragic implanted in the English temperament.
Various kinds of evidence were adduced, much of it literary, and much
of that deriving from a superficial reading of Shakespeare, in whose plays
'most of the characters go mad, or get blind, or die.'[157] *Paradise Lost*,
which acquired a Continental readership in the mid-eighteenth century,

also provided quotable matter. More generally, Gothicism, and a propensity for what Dryden quotably called a 'fairy way of writing', was seen as part of this tradition of gloom.[158] The graveyard school incurred censure. What other nation could have produced, let alone relished, a work such as Young's *Night Thoughts* or Hervey's *Meditations among the Tombs*, or Thomas Warton's *Pleasures of Melancholy*?

It was not only in verse that the English gave rein to their characteristic 'hyp'. Tourists regarded the stage as the most revealing of media when it came to national character. A visit to the London theatre permitted reflections not only on the drama enacted and the players who enacted it, but also on the audience that paid to see it enacted. The results tended to confirm preconceptions about the English temperament. Theatregoers were considered impassive and unresponsive by Continental standards. Parisians were particularly dismissive: 'What a disparity betwixt the melancholy silence which reigned here and the agitation of sympathetic feelings which appear in our theatres!'[159] It was considered appropriate that when English dramatists excelled, they did so in tragedy. In comedy they could not match their neighbours. Their actors themselves were far more impressive when they simulated madness and agony.[160] Generalizations of this kind figured frequently in comparisons between the two capitals of drama.

None of this meant that an English audience could not be entertained. What was at issue was the manner in which it was entertained and the matter that was found entertaining. There was no mistaking the satisfaction, even delight, that reigned at Drury Lane and Covent Garden when one of the great masters of English tragedy, Garrick, Kemble, or Kean, took the part of Hamlet, Lear, or Macbeth. Paradoxically, the emotional engagement of audiences on such occasions could appear more intense, or at least more vital, than the sober attention with which Parisian audiences heard the elaborate declamations of a classical French tragedy. Moreover, in English tragedy there was always a kind of grim humour that conveyed pleasure in the dark side of life. Home-bred gaiety betrayed a touch of misanthropy, and resembled sarcasm rather than pleasantry.[161] English critics did not deny it, but rather boasted of the strange mixture of frivolity and gravity that marked the national taste and character. 'As a nation we have for the style of the serious French drama an ingrained antipathy. There must be a deeper earnestness than plays can demand, in whatever serious thing Englishmen are to look at without exercise of that sense of the humorous which is part of their life; so natural a part that every man is in every grade of society regarded as a bore who wants it; and the very phrase with thousands even among our educated men for not finding a thing acceptable is "seeing no fun" in it.'[162]

As in art, so in life, or rather in death. It had long been noted that the jollity wanting in English jollification seemed bizarrely present in tragic circumstances. The Anglophile Alphonse Esquiros considered this evidence of Anglo-Saxon hardiness and hard-headedness. 'The intrepid Saxon race likes to mock at everything which inspires man with a feeling of fear. Illness, death, the hangman, the gibbet, the terrors of the natural and supernatural world, become to him a subject for buffoonery in conversation and on the stage. "The English laugh, as if in defiance, and ridicule everything," one of them said to me, "excepting money losses." '[163] Petrarch was quoted to the effect that in the carnival atmosphere of an English public execution, even the condemned went to the gallows laughing. The modern historian of the public scaffold is sceptical: 'for every one such act of defiance many more felons died in terror or stupefied by drink.'[164] But there is no denying the prominence of the theme in much contemporary literature, including that penned by foreign witnesses. The gallows *mise en scène* at Tyburn, or, after its transfer in 1783, at Newgate, became a more or less obligatory subject for a chapter in the travels of visitors. Most felt that they were in the presence of a macabre English rite, one that included striking elements of the comic.

Other features of death in the English manner were considered distinctive, even unique. One was the taste for hatchments. Some put the practice down to vanity, a form of self-advertisement for genteel and propertied people.[165] Others took it more seriously as a specialized form of mourning, permitting owners to dress their homes as they dressed themselves. Experienced travellers like Fanny Lewald found the combination moving. To wander the streets of London picking out the houses with hatchments and the women dressed from head to toe in jet black— 'wirklich trauriger als traurig'—was to appreciate how far English grieving had diverged from its Continental counterparts.[166] Perhaps this was indeed a nation of philosophers, reluctant to abandon the deceased and accustomed to reflect on immortality. Its national emblem should be a death's head rather than a lion.[167]

The commercialism that permitted funeral shops openly to display coffins for public inspection confirmed the impression that the English took as much pleasure in dying as living.[168] So did the attention paid to graveyards. At Birmingham, it struck foreigners as very strange that the cemetery of St Philip's should be the principal promenade of the locality for gentry and plebeians alike.[169] Here, at the very heart of the most startlingly industrial of townscapes springing up in Britain at the turn of the eighteenth and nineteenth centuries, amidst the ceaseless bustle and clamour of numberless workshops, was a burial ground which constituted the principal boast of local politeness.

To some this seemed rather impressive. A nation wont to stroll among its dead must surely acquire a patriotic sense of its own continuity and experience a notable impulse to godliness. On the other hand, the sight of children running about by day and prostitutes lolling on tombstones by night was less bracing.[170] This was not, as Adolphe Blanqui remarked, the churchyard of Gray's elegy.[171] Nor was Birmingham unusual. Tradition made the graveyard a common resort of the fashionable and unfashionable alike in numerous towns and cities, well into the nineteenth century, until the requirements of public health directed the stroller to more hygienic parks and promenades. And even then some of these took the form of new-style cemeteries, elaborately designed and landscaped. The tourist arriving at Liverpool in the 1830s was likely to be told that the 'Symmetry' as locals called it, was the town's foremost attraction.[172]

In the meantime, the graveyard, with its tombstones laid flat to facilitate walking, and its seemingly magnetic power of attraction for all classes, was a national phenomenon, 'an Englishman's Lounge'.[173] Scots were as perplexed as other newcomers by it.[174] Irish churchyards were also quite different, less open to the public and even to English eyes more dignified.[175] Crossing Offa's Dyke equally brought contrasts. When the Welsh tour became popular in the late eighteenth century, visitors were surprised at the floral decoration which they found on graves, as if mourning was out of place in the presence of death. The English churchyard, the resort of the living yet unrelieved in its emphasis on mortality, was truly English.

Some characteristic obsessions took on new meaning viewed in the context of a predisposition to the melancholy or solemn. When foreigners looked at insular recreation, they found further evidence of restlessness and gloom. Country life, to which the English seemed devoted, was itself a curiously death-like affair as witnessed by outsiders. The English thought of it as a retreat from the cares of the town. But retirement *à l'anglaise* had little of Watteau or even of Horace about it. At best it was a form of furious diversion, a succession of mirthless house parties, assize meetings, and fox-hunts. This was dissipation without gaiety, a natural consequence of the warped character of the English.[176] Alternatively it looked like mere ritual, a parade of genteel ostentation before a guaranteed audience of rustics, during a season when no better alternative offered in London. The crippling etiquette of a country-house party suggested anything but a retreat to ease and informality.[177] Here was yet another obeisance to the crushing power of convention.

Activities designed for amusement took on a painful air of solemnity. 'Their amusement is the most *triste* affair in the world.'[178] Dancing, at least, must surely find the English expending their energy in joyful fashion. Countless observers testified to the contrary. John Bull was a reluctant dancer, always readier to stand and stare, 'silent, grave, heavy'.[179] When he and his wife Jane did take to the floor, the results were disheartening. This was true even in fashionable circles. At Brighton in the 1820s, Pückler-Muskau found 'the numerous company raven black from head to foot, gloves inclusive; a melancholy style of dancing, without the least trace of vivacity or joyousness; so that the only feeling you have is that of compassion for the useless fatigue the poor people are enduring'.[180]

Such impressions went back at least half a century. On his visit to Britain in 1789 Jacques de Cambry attended only one dance, also at Brighton. Such stultifying absence of gaiety he resolved never to bear again, 'despite the beauty, whiteness and virtue of English women; and despite the pride, profundity and gravity of English men'.[181] At Bath the marquis de Bombelles felt much the same in 1784. The prospect of three hundred beautiful English women at a ball, was, he remarked, most promising for a foreigner. But the event was disappointing. The women sat in three rows, like the Fathers at the Council of Constance; when the

dancing commenced it followed a tedious regimen laid down by the MC
with pedantic regard for rank. The whole thing was a sad affair.[182] Even
the English satirized their dancers, 'moving about with that happy
absence of animal spirits, so characteristic of English recreations'.[183]
Uninhibited dancing was for the Irish or Scots, or 'a drunken Welchman
on the first of March'.[184]

Why were holiday pleasures taken so gravely in England? To Johanna
Schopenhauer, Cheltenham seemed as dull as English domestic life.[185]
Haussez made the same point about the seaside and painted a depressing picture of a resort, families pacing up and down without accosting
each other, ladies reading on balconies while husbands watched the sea
with telescopes: 'in the countenance of all and each is imprinted an air
of lassitude and weariness which no one seeks to dissemble'.[186] Even in
London, famous places of resort often seemed tame by Continental standards. Holbach was appalled by Vauxhall; he compared the silent women
parading there with Egyptians processing around the mausoleum of
Osiris.[187]

None of this seemed to have much to do with class. All ranks were
equally subdued about their enjoyments. The coffee house, a favourite
emblem of the new sociability of the enlightened eighteenth century
throughout Europe, took on an air of gravity in England. The Russian
Karamzin reported: 'I have dropped into a number of coffeehouses only
to find twenty or thirty men sitting around in deep silence, reading newspapers, and drinking port. You are lucky if, in the course of ten minutes,
you hear three words. And what are they? "Your health, gentlemen!"'[188]
Perhaps, given the numbers frequenting English coffee houses, this was
just as well, for noise in proportion would have been unbearable.[189] As
for taverns, where the ordinary Englishman must surely be found relax-
ing, where was his animation, his *joie de vivre*? When artisans talked of
their daily concerns, they did so without animation. 'The pot of beer
emptied itself pointlessly; there was no gaiety at the bottom of it.' In
France there would have been gales of laughter.[190]

What the English did to the Sabbath was seen as conclusive proof of
a stunted temperament. An English Sunday horrified Continental visitors, as a Continental Sunday delighted Englishmen freed from their
domestic shackles.[191] Certain sacred English rituals, notably the weekly

roast beef dinner, and election canvassing and treating, were permitted
to take place on Sunday, at any rate before Victorian 'reformers' got to
work on them. But for the most part the Sabbath seemed deadening in
its solemnity. It had neither trade nor amusement, other than the combination of the two offered by an impressive number of prostitutes.[192] The
sense of alienation experienced by outsiders in the presence of this
bizarre rite provided traveller writers with a stock subject for trite
reflections. It also taxed the forensic resources of redoubtable English
apologists. Dr Johnson refused to defend the Sabbath's 'severity and
gloom'.[193] Hazlitt and Gissing simply considered it ineradicably English.
'Not to be dancing a jig and on our knees in the same breath' was part of
'our politics and religion', 'a part of our character'.[194]

Denying the Englishness of extreme Sabbatarianism was rarely
attempted, though it was common to locate it in a wider Protestant tradition. Until the mid-eighteenth century there was a reluctance to admit
that any cultural consequences of Catholicism could be desirable. Thereafter English travellers felt compelled to concede that it was possible for
Catholics to be both joyful and devout Christians. This was true even
within the British Isles. The Irish peasantry, like the French, were
meticulous about their attendance at church but followed it by innocent
recreation and merriment.[195] Further reflection on Protestant practices
elsewhere suggested that religion might have very little to do with the
matter, as even patriotic Englishmen admitted. Lutherans saw no necessity to make the Lord's Day one of joylessness, even in Norway, where
English visitors went expecting Norwegians to behave like Nordic
Englishmen uncorrupted by the advance of civilization.[196]

A superficial reading of Scottish history might suggest that Sabbatarianism was British rather than English. But the enthusiasm with which
nineteenth-century Scots took it up could be misleading. Candid English
observers noted, as Joseph Farington did at Glasgow in 1801, that on a
Sunday the streets were filled with people enjoying themselves, in contrast to Manchester and other populous towns in England, which 'proves
that a great change must have taken place since the days of John Knox,
and is very opposite to the Idea of puritanical Gravity and Seclusion'.[197]
Rigid Sabbatarianism was not simply synonymous with Calvinism; it
came, like many other changes in manners, from south of Hadrian's
wall.[198] Nor, indeed, as many complained, did it necessarily promote a

state of grace. An English Sunday might be solemn, but it was not sinless. The very absence of the harmless amusements that were permitted in many other countries drove the uneducated to choose between dullness and drunkenness, with predictable results.

Reformers seemed more interested in increasing the dose than curing the disease, as middle-class Evangelicals laboured to reduce still further the opportunities for plebeian celebration, especially on Sundays. The range of charitable associations established explicitly or implicitly to reinforce Sabbatarianism fascinated foreigners and also yielded a rich vein of satirical ore to irreverent Englishmen. Theodore Hook's merciless account of the Hum-Fum Gamboogee Society and the 'excessively correct persons who compose this grave body' was perhaps the most devastating of many such assaults.[199]

Continental tourists equipped with the standard knowledge of English literature were aware that respectable opinion in Britain took a very different view of Sunday from its counterparts elsewhere. Samuel Richardson, especially, left no room for doubt on this score.[200] Even so they were puzzled by the desire of the British bourgeoisie in its Evangelical phase to make observance of the Sabbath still more rigid. Perhaps, it was suggested, one had to be born of its number to understand why museums and art galleries were closed to the people on Sundays while public houses were open. Evidence of less repressive attitudes in the past aroused interest among students of English life. When Samuel Pepys's diary was published in 1869, Prosper Mérimée remarked: 'One sees why the epithet of merry England might have been employed at that time, though it astonishes the foreigner today, especially on a Sunday.'[201]

It did not follow, however, that the middle class was exclusively to blame for suppressing merriment. Numerous commentators testified that it was hard to find a lower class more intrinsically doleful than the English. One might, for instance, hopefully scrutinize the Spanish, well-known for their gravity, yet the fact was that travellers found ordinary Spaniards 'much more merry and facetious than the same class in England'.[202] There were, admittedly, peasantries so degraded or immiserated as to present a pitiable appearance. But this was considered quite different from the mournfulness of the English plebeian, in point of material comfort surely a prince by comparison with others. George Eliot pleaded for an honest appraisal of rural life in high art on these grounds, arguing that British artists drew their images from a Continental tradition based on an alien reality. 'No one who has seen much of actual ploughmen thinks them jocund; no one who is well acquainted with the English peasantry can pronounce them merry. The slow gaze, in which no sense of beauty beams, no humour twinkles, the slow utterance, and the heavy slouching walk, remind one rather of that melancholy animal the camel, than of the sturdy countryman, with striped stockings, red waistcoat, and hat aside, who represents the traditional English peasant.'[203]

Anglomaniacs sometimes claimed that English enjoyment was simply of a different nature from that of other peoples. The abbé Coyer observed that the English were not so much melancholy as serious about their amusements.[204] Alphonse Esquiros argued that there was more of the comic, not least in the English dramatic tradition, than his French compatriots generally supposed. But the comedy was of a different kind. 'Their laughter differs uncommonly from ours. English gaiety is that of a grave people, who, for all that, are only the more jolly in their moments of fun; it is what they call humour, with its sudden and unexpected sallies, daring metaphors, and a foundation of biting eccentricity, which is most frequently concealed under a cold and staid air.'[205]

Whatever the gloss put upon it, melancholy mattered much in analysing English energy. It was potentially devastating in its tendency to nullify motivation and ambition, especially if it were considered evidence of a flaw in the Englishman's mental composition, one that resulted precisely from his proneness to self-indulgence and idleness. Sir William Temple noted that the commercial but also workaday Dutch were immune to the spleen, 'a Disease too refin'd for this Country and People, who are well, when they are not ill'.[206] Moreover, it was the restlessness that characterized English energy even at its best that seemed to go so naturally with intermittent depression. Of course, if it was merely the consequence of a highly competitive, commercial society, ' "eels in a jar," where each is trying to get his head above the other', it was perhaps bearable.[207] But if, as many thought, idleness and the spleen were intrinsically English traits, the implications were disturbing. No wonder the manufacturer Josiah Wedgwood admitted his ambition 'to make such *machines* of the Men as cannot err'.[208]

ORDER

Restless, intermittent energy and a pronounced if sometimes inspiring tendency to melancholy, required an unusual degree of discipline if they were to be transformed into a recipe for national success. The English evidently lacked both the phlegmatic drudgery of other northerners and the frenetic enthusiasm of southerners. But did they have an asset wanting in both, a certain capacity to proportion their exertions to their objectives, a measure of self-control and self-direction that might bridge the gap between erratic exertion and solid accomplishment? Increasingly there was a readiness both in Britain and beyond to accept that they did, and that this explained 'the mystery of this mighty energy'.[209] The pay-off might be in the workplace, but it was not only there that the evidence of such strength of character was to be found.

Continental assumptions about the freedom-loving, individualistic Englishmen were deep-rooted. But when the tide of foreign visitors swelled in the late eighteenth century they often noted a countervailing love of order. This appeared to be true of the lowest as well as highest levels of society. For a vast and potentially turbulent city, London looked oddly tranquil to many newcomers. Generally, the 'menu peuple' of England seemed superior to their Continental counterparts in this respect whether at work or play. English recreation might be of a peculiar kind but it did seem to have the advantage that it needed no regimenting. French visitors regularly commented on the absence of armed sentries in the streets, mounted police on the highways, uniformed guards at the theatre.[210] Parisians wondered that 'the city is not a hell upon earth from riot and confusion'.[211] Flora Tristan felt the same at Ascot. In France the silence of the mass and the orderliness of the traffic could not have been achieved without three companies of mounted gendarmes.[212]

German visitors were also impressed. The Saxon Heinrich von Watzdorf was amazed to see the crowds enjoying Vauxhall without any sign of a grenadier or a fixed bayonet.[213] Sophie von la Roche was intrigued by the demeanour of ordinary families at ordinary entertainments, strolling about with easy manner and unhurried motion. In Germany there would have been much more vulgarity, boisterousness, rudeness,

always liable to erupt into violence.[214] Her countryman Georg Lichtenberg agreed. Viewing the Lord Mayor's procession in 1770 at a time of
Wilkite unrest he remarked that a handful of German students would
have caused far more trouble than 10,000 such people.[215]

The contrast with Germany was revealing because it seemed to distinguish Anglo-Saxons from others of Germanic or Nordic origin. It was
assumed that in northern Europe mobs were 'ungovernable herds', liable
to go on the rampage at the slightest provocation. Populous cities such
as Hamburg and Amsterdam regularly found themselves having to compensate foreign sufferers for the resulting losses.[216] London seemed to
offer no obvious parallel. The Gordon Riots of 1780 were a notable
exception but they appear to have made little impact on foreign opinion.
Visitors went by their own impressions, their own sense of atmosphere.
Considering their often disparaging remarks about the barbarous
manners of the English lower class encountered individually, their belief
in its collective inoffensiveness is all the more remarkable.

Comparisons with southern Europeans were equally suggestive.
Grand Tourists found much order among Italians in the mass, for
example at the great carnivals in Rome and Naples. Samuel Sharp
thought that in London such fairs would have presented a scene of less
calm and composure. On the other hand, he applied the contrast only to
a mob in a good humour. Vengeance and violence were terrible things to
behold in Neapolitans when 'exasperated'.[217] Similar judgements were
made about Parisians, especially when they showed what they could do
during the Revolution. Paradoxically, the English were likely to be worse
behaved in frivolous mood at a fair than in an earnest one.[218]

From the civic standpoint, this made them the ideal populace. Sir
Walter Scott thought he noticed a crucial difference between an English
and a French mob in the presence of authority. 'The English populace
will huzza, swear, threaten, break windows, and throw stones at the Life
Guards engaged in dispersing them; but if a soldier should fall from his
horse, the rabble, after enjoying a laugh at his expense, would lend a hand
to lift him from his saddle again. A French mob would tear him limb from
limb, and parade the fragments in triumph upon their pikes.'[219] The
political implications were intriguing. Reflecting on the relative meekness
of an English mob in 1749 the novelist John Cleland thought it 'one of
the best Proofs of the peculiar Power of Liberty, to inspire gentle and

governable Sentiments'.[220] A century later, when liberty had ceased to be an English monopoly, this seemed a less likely explanation. Viewing Chartist riots in the Potteries in 1841, J. G. Kohl noted 'how greatly an English mob stands in awe of shedding blood, and how easily it allows itself to be dispersed by a few soldiers. Had a French mob, with plans and views similar to those of the populace at Burslem, found themselves opposed to soldiers, the issue would have been of a much more sanguinary character. Whence comes this? Nobody will dream of attributing cowardice to the English as a national characteristic.'[221]

In fact there were those who did so dream, and unsurprisingly they were French. Samuel Sorbière asserted in 1665 that English independence consisted merely in one or two shibboleths which might readily be conceded for the sake of managing an essentially manageable nation. 'The English may be easily brought to any thing, provided you fill their Bellies, let them have Freedom of Speech, and do not bear too hard upon their lazy Temper.'[222] A hundred and seventy years later another French observer, the baron d'Haussez, even impugned the courage of the English lower orders. 'Taken collectively, the populace of England is remarkable for its cowardice.'[223] What else could explain the quiescence of a people who quailed before a handful of police with nothing more to control them than a wooden truncheon?

Some attributed the seeming ease of the British nobility in maintaining its hegemony during an age of revolutions to the submissiveness, perhaps servility of the lower class.[224] Others went further still, seeking to discredit the evidence of English bravery even in the armed forces. The duc de Lévis, Montcalm's successor as commander of French forces in Quebec, observed that Crécy and Agincourt had been won by the French subjects of Henry V, Normans and Poitevins, rather than by an English force.[225] In the eighteenth century foreign troops, Dutch, Hanoverian, Hessian, still had to be called upon to defend the British State. Whatever the feats of a Marlborough or a Wolfe, neither Blenheim nor Quebec were to be laid to the credit of those they commanded. On the other hand, it could be countered that the only defeats suffered by the English themselves had been inflicted by an English Jacobite general at Almanza and a Saxon, if not Anglo-Saxon, in French service at Fontenoy.[226]

These debates raised a question of engrossing interest. When national character was under discussion, nothing seemed more important than its adaptability to the requirements of war. It was a cherished belief among the English that their courage was of a superior kind, expressed not in superficial audacity but in steady, unflinching endurance. Frenchmen less biased than Sorbière and Haussez were prepared to admit that Gallic courage might suffer by comparison. 'The Frenchman has ample impulsive courage, product of national impetuosity and vivacity; but, after the first passion, discouragement follows and spreads with a rapidity unequalled elsewhere. We lack that cool and reflective courage, that calm amidst danger, that patience which surmounts difficulties and stands proof against obstacles.'[227] The martial virtue of their neighbours was valiant stoutness, coolness in the face of fire.[228] Charles Dupin, who came to Britain specifically to assess its naval and military strength, thought this 'steadiness of disposition' the crucial advantage that its troops possessed over those of his own country.[229] It was the quality above all that made the English infantryman feared and renowned by other armies. Even Napoleon expected French troops to dread it and was not above taunting them on this account. On the other hand, English forces did not want to be thought wanting in verve. During the occupation of Flanders that followed Waterloo, an officer of the line called out a French officer for saying the English army possessed 'more phlegm than spirit'.[230]

Naval warfare, too, depended on steadiness, or, as Lord Shaftesbury described it, 'ironsteadfastness'.[231] Hazlitt called it the passive part of courage, ultimately more potent than the active part. It was peculiarly suited to war at sea where sturdiness in defence counted for more than élan in attack. 'The British tar feels conscious of his existence in suffering and anguish, and woos danger as a bride. There is something in this Saxon breed of men, like the courage and resolution of the mastiff, that only comes out on such occasions.'[232]

Robustness in battle was not to be confused with the brutish courage often attributed to the Russians and other nations rendered insensible to hardship by their poverty.[233] It represented a voluntary choice rather than unthinking stubbornness. Some thought this made it inferior to the unthinking, innate courage of Continental peoples. 'Courage goes with us everywhere, from birth; bravery is voluntary, limited, it knows how to avoid danger if that is desirable.'[234] On the other hand, it could be argued that conscious choice implied a deeper commitment. England did indeed expect, and the English sailor or soldier was moved not by hope of glory but by belief in duty. His dying thought was likely to be: 'what will they think of us in England?'[235] At bottom, so the theory ran, he was inspired not by an imaginative engagement with his sovereign or his faith, but by a Spartan self-discipline that went with free membership of a free society.[236] This was precisely what Latin troops were thought to lack. It was also found wanting in the Irish, who in other respects made valiant warriors.[237] As Wellington remarked of his Irish troops: 'I could train my soldiers to do anything, except be masters of themselves.'[238]

Interestingly, the older Continental view of English valour closely resembled this English view of the Irish. In the sixteenth century their reputation had been for warlikeness, vengefulness, and fierceness: they were 'impatient of injuries and revenge them fiercely'.[239] Then they had been the barbarians of western Europe, pirates at sea and marauders by land, driven at best by a primitive code of honour rather than leadership and training. By the eighteenth century they had evidently evolved the discipline to control and direct their native ferocity. The result, as displayed at Waterloo, was 'its self-willed, defensive doggedness . . . which enables it, after eight hours of strenuous defensive fighting that would bring any other army to its knees, to launch yet another formidable attack in which lack of élan is compensated by uniformity and steadiness.'[240]

A shift in the emblematic representation of indigenous bravery nicely reflected this process of redefinition. At least until the 1770s the fighting cock seemed as acceptable an emblem as the bulldog. The two went together. Hume remarked in 1741 that bulldogs, like game cocks, seemed to be courageous only in England.[241] Certainly as much pride was taken in the latter as the former.

> If by Chance the Breed of France,
> Mix among our feather'd Throng,
> Those we lot, for Spit or Pot,
> For to feel, the Prick of Steel,
> Makes 'em cow'r and turn Tail.[242]

Such boasts were taken seriously. The French Huguenot La Motraye, who knew England well, was convinced that English cocks were of superior courage.[243]

By the end of the century the bulldog featured much more frequently. It is not difficult to see why. The cock represented the old, increasingly discredited version of English bravery, savage, merciless, uncontrolled. The bulldog represented the new, implying solidity, tenacity, indomitability. Not that the bulldog lacked a hint of the fighting cock's arrogance. Interestingly, one of the early depictors of American national character, Charles Sealsfield, contrasted American courage—not 'the swaggering British bulldog courage, but always the constant, composed, decided, calm, unshaken and unshakable courage of the Americans'.[244] In fact this was precisely what the English prided themselves on. Sealsfield, despite his name, was an Austrian, which may have affected either his image of bulldogs or his view of the British.

In any event the bulldog superseded the cock in English lore. No doubt it profited by the not entirely coincidental identification with its master John Bull. It is also possible that growing concern about the cruelty of cock-fighting lessened the appeal of Chanticleer. On the other hand, bull-baiting was at least as controversial as cock-fighting. The French were eager to proclaim the cock as their own; they never laid claim to a canine character. They did strenuously object to the expression 'French dog', noting the English illogicality of abusing their neighbours as dogs while proclaiming themselves dog lovers. It was indeed a common assumption that if the dog was not man's best friend he was certainly the Englishman's best friend. A rich store of historical anecdotes provided quotable matter for foreign commentators: the Earl of Wiltshire's dog biting the Pope's extended toe and thereby inadvertently precipitating the English Reformation, James II in a storm urging his servants to save his 'dogs and Colonel Churchill', and so on.[245]

Distinguishing English self-mastery from its Continental rivals was a matter of understandable importance. Self-control was not submissiveness. It went with a strong sense of individualism, not to say self-seeking. Even the celebrated order to be observed among the English in their daily activities did not lessen their characteristic egotism. Anything that interfered with their treasured mobility was despised. It was noticed, for instance, that while Londoners were past masters at rapid and orderly movement, they would not stand still even if the result would have been more speedy progress. The 'queue' was a French phenomenon, unknown across the Channel before the late nineteenth century. The Russian revolutionary Alexander Herzen found this intriguing, remarking that even at London's theatres it was impossible to make those attending form a line.[246] He considered it highly characteristic. When the English conformed they were conforming to their own will, not to the will of others, least of all to the will of authority. Here was a country where the police concentrated on catching pickpockets rather than calming the chaos of a crowded pavement. Alphonse Esquiros made the same point in relation to the national sport of cricket, which he considered truly the expression of national character. It required a degree of self-control that was beyond the most adaptable of foreigners. 'This game marks, to some extent, the limit of practical naturalization.'[247]

In the national character of the English, observed Engels, 'the most determined energy exists side by side with the calmest deliberateness, so that in this respect as well the continental peoples lag infinitely behind'.[248] This combination released the full potential of the English nation, both in the science of war and the arts of peace. It constituted the true basis of that industry which seemed to have made a small and once insignificant people the leaders, perhaps even the masters, of the human race. Here was not only power, but directed, dependable, durable power. Solidity of temperament, 'bottom', phlegm (formerly deemed quite inappropriate), came to be increasingly associated with a people earlier thought of as being highly unreliable and idiosyncratic. It was widely accepted that an Englishman who had made up his mind to something was peculiarly difficult to distract from it.[249] The English themselves took pride in being slow to rouse, but slower still to flag. The obvious metaphor was that of the oak, which 'refuses to put out his leaves at summer's early solicitations, and scorns to drop them at winter's first rude shake'.[250] The same tendency distinguished the emotional attachments of a people 'whose national character it is to be slow and cautious in making friends, but violent in friendships once contracted'.[251] Loyalty was the true-blue Englishman's second name.

Above all there was a sturdiness of character that constituted a kind of ethnic virility, a superior masculinity which had to do with the race as a whole, not merely the male sex. 'If, in a word, there exists one fact as to national manners, it is incontestably this; that in England, the men are more men, and the women less women than every where else.'[252] It was a Frenchman who said this, but much the same judgement was made by Burke, who remarked that when he used the term 'manly', he meant a quality shared by both sexes. He called it 'proper firmness' and admitted that English lacked a readily translatable word for it, no doubt because the thing itself was taken for granted in England whereas else-where it was sufficiently uncommon to require defining—in French, for instance, by a distinctive usage of the word 'caractère'.[253] Manliness was a much favoured term in nineteenth-century Britain, one that under-standably fascinates historians of gender. Yet it was often employed in this fashion, to signify the national characteristic of rugged robustness founded on extraordinary vitality. It was not only 'muscular Christians' among Victorians who made this connection. Leslie Stephen described energy as 'both the prerequisite and the expression of the manly life'. He also, casting back to that long tradition of idiosyncratically English pedestrianism, remarked, not at all in jest, that he was 'much inclined to measure a man's moral excellence by his love of walking'.[254]

Controlled energy made for a considerable reassessment of the English temperament. By the end of the eighteenth century there was a readiness on the part of foreigners to concede that it had about it a com-posure not recognized by their ancestors. Perhaps it was even content-ment, a hypothesis that suggested how far perceptions had moved from that preoccupation with melancholy taken for granted earlier. English opinion, too, had moved a long way, for by the mid-nineteenth century it was commoner by far to attribute gloom and despondency to the Celtic nations. 'Melancholy and unprogressiveness', as Matthew Arnold sum-marized it, went together.[255] Some Continental visitors were prepared to assert that the English looked positively happy. They could not achieve gaiety—that remained a Gallic prerogative—but they did possess a certain calmness and serenity, a notable tranquillity of spirit.[256] This was an intensely subjective judgement. To others, including some of the English themselves, the cost seemed high. 'One does not see', wrote Sarah Austin, in Berlin in 1828, 'the strife and struggle, the carking care, the soul-consuming efforts to get and to spend that are the pride and curse of England. Alas! we English pay dearly for our boasted energy, industry, activity, and so forth. Life is a toil and a conflict.'[257]

However it was evaluated, English self-discipline made for a fresh per-spective on international comparisons. Restlessness was coming to seem more French. Henri Meister reported in the 1790s that the 'characteristic of the English is that of method and steadiness, with less restlessness and more seriousness than we appear to possess; and activity less lively than ours, but more sedate'.[258] Sedateness went well with the self-conscious conservatism of the English at this time, and better still with the growing perception abroad of the English as a people uniquely capable of harnessing ancient talents and institutions to new requirements.

Before 1789 England had been the country of revolutions; after 1789 it became the country that did not have revolutions. It seemed all the easier then to grant the English their instinctive orderliness as 'the outstanding characteristic of the race'.[259] Alternatively, it might have resulted from a happy mixing of Teutonic and Celtic bloods. Midlanders and northerners prided themselves on their stability, detecting even in the mid-nineteenth century more pronounced 'energy and unrest of character' on the south and east coasts where successive invaders had once driven out the British and still retained something of their primitive unpredictability.[260] The industrial vigour of Lancashire and Cornwall where Celt and Saxon continued to mingle and 'constitute the most industrious and enterprising population of these isles' provided further evidence.[261] French opinion had always attributed the superior commercial success of northern nations to this quality of patient perseverance.[262] Somehow the English had come to share the doughtiness without losing their peculiar vitality. The result was an unmatchable 'stable heavy vigour'.[263]

PRACTICALITY

Such vigour was not enough on its own. The intelligence that directed it had to be dedicated to an end if it was to achieve what Guizot found when he passed from Calais to Dover, 'activity entirely engaged in its object'.[264] This was a matter of mentality. 'Nations like individuals have their habits of thinking', as the German scholar Niebuhr put it.[265] Interest in the English mind was often traced back to the influence of Voltaire, whose *Lettres Philosophiques* of 1734 popularized the intellectual achievements of a nation that could boast of Bacon, Newton, and Locke, creating, in Leigh Hunt's words, 'a fashion for English thinking, manner and policy'.[266] But Voltaire was rowing with a tide that had been flowing from the time of La Fontaine, whose observation that England was a country 'where one thinks' was worked up into an epigram by Montesquieu. 'One should travel in Germany, sojourn in Italy, and *think* in England.'[267] It fitted well with the image of a nation casting off its reputation for barbarism. The Englishman's mental capacity came to seem in its own right a distinctive contribution to the evolution of civilization.[268] Anglomaniacs made the most of this. Not only the stage Englishman, but also the stage Englishwoman, had to fit the stereotype. 'You are an English girl, learn to think,' Favart had his Lord Brumpton remark to his daughter, helpfully advising her to read Locke, Clarke, Swift, Newton, and Bolingbroke.[269]

Travellers were eager to verify English brainpower for themselves. Some thought the language itself evidence of a preoccupation with intellectual exertion. The Russian Oloff Napea observed, 'So general is the predisposition for thinking, that all classes of society misapply the word, saying they do think when they do not. It is not unusual to hear a tolerably well-educated person use, *I think*, for *I suppose*, or *believe*, or *fancy*, or *apprehend*.'[270] Unfortunately, the substance could be disappointing. Napea's compatriot Karamzin decided that an Englishman's thoughtfulness was a false impression, deriving from a grave manner of conversing. 'He talks as though he were reading, never revealing the sudden impulses of the heart which like an electric shock shake our entire physical system. It is said that he is more profound than others. Is this not because his thick blood circulates more slowly, and this makes him look thoughtful even when he is not thinking at all?'[271] In a similar vein was the story in which 'A French lady who had married an Englishman remarkable for his dullness, used to apologise for his silence in company by incessantly repeating "*C'est toujours Locke, toujours Newton*," as if these were the subjects that occupied his thoughts.'[272]

Hostile observers could rarely resist sarcasm on the subject. 'I am writing about the English and the absurdities of a nation which considers itself the only philosophical nation on earth', remarked Le Blanc.[273] Perhaps this was sour grapes, as the Swiss Zimmermann argued. 'The French in their own estimation are the only thinking beings in the universe.'[274] Germans had less cause for bias. Indeed their dislike of patronizing Gallic superiority often made them susceptible to British influence. Many came expecting to be dazzled by what they found. Yet as often as not they were disappointed by the topmost layer of intellectual life. When

Niebuhr visited Britain in 1798, he found 'almost universal cultivation of the burgher class' but among scholars no real depth or originality.[275]

The way was open for an Englishman remote indeed from La Fontaine's reflective inquirer, one whose thoughts ran in predictable channels and who, confronted with a testing challenge, 'muddled through' rather than reached a solution based on original thought and analysis. By the mid-nineteenth century the liberal philosophers of Voltaire's recollection were considered the exception rather than the rule, as Prosper Mérimée remarked when he met the free trader Richard Cobden. 'Cobden is a man of an extremely interesting mind; quite the opposite of an Englishman in this respect, that you never hear him talk commonplaces, and that he has few prejudices.'[276]

Admirers and detractors often agreed on the basic characteristic that was involved, even if they rated it differently. Mrs Piozzi emphasized mental regularity, contrasting it with the Italian mind—'like his country, extensive, warm, and beautiful from the irregular diversification of his ideas'. The English mind was 'cultivated, rich, and regularly disposed; a steady character, a delicious landscape'.[277] But regularity could resemble deadening monotony. Custine likened England to a mere abstraction, a mathematical formula applied to the great problem of civilization.[278] Heine, in a judgement that struck a chord with George Eliot, thought that English thinking, feeling, reckoning, digesting, even praying, were all essentially mechanical. A blaspheming Frenchman would be more pleasing to God than a praying Englishman.[279] Nothing seemed more telling about the clockwork machinery of the English mind and temperament alike than the obsession with time and punctuality. 'Their whole history and character may be derived or inferred from this national peculiarity.'[280]

Increasingly, characterizations emphasized 'that truly English attribute, *good common sense*'.[281] 'Sterling' came into use in this context, expressing a reliable solidity deriving from knowledge of the 'Manual of Life'.[282] Goethe, who never saw England, deduced from his reading and acquaintance with Englishmen that practicality was the 'main secret of their ascendancy amongst the various races of the earth', to the delight of his English followers.[283] His countryman Friedrich von Gentz, who did visit England, found it a 'theatre of practical wisdom'.[284] Or as Taine put it, facts were what interested the English; ideas were of little concern to them.[285]

His hosts could agree. 'Many many years ago we began to be a steady and matter-of-fact sort of people', wrote Dickens in 1850.[286] Another novelist, George Meredith, considered this a matter of pride. The 'question "are we practical?" penetrates the bosom of an English audience, and will surely elicit a response if not plaudits. Practical or not, the good people affectingly wish to be thought practical. It has been asked by them: if we're not practical, what are we?'[287] Significantly, when French novelists sought to imitate English, 'matter-of-fact-ness' was a quality to which they paid particular attention.[288]

Theory was for other nations. Even when they sought to generalize, the English seemed incapable of abandoning their boasted empiricism. John Stuart Mill complained that the 'universal maxims' of classical political economy were 'merely English customs'.[289] As always, Englishness, not Britishness, was at stake. It was often remarked that Scots exhibited 'a strong tendency to abstract argument quite unknown in England'.[290] Even the doubters recognized the solid dependability of a people who shunned the abstract. 'What foreigner could divine the union of invincibility and speculative dullness in England?' asked the young Matthew Arnold in 1848.[291] A nation of Newtons and Lockes became a nation of Boultons and Watts. If they remained philosophers it was only in the sense that a truly empirical thinker was more concerned to identify goals than uncover fundamentals.[292] The advantage of reliance on custom rather than questioning of assumptions was that it released the boundless potential of Britain for economic growth, unhindered by the desire to keep revising its laws.[293]

Speculation about the origins of the English genius strengthened the underlying line of thought. It was common to trace the English reputation for solid thinking to a no less solid diet. But as the Irish exile James Rutledge pointed out, Newton had composed his most demanding works on a diet of bread, water, and sugar. Solid thinking was better considered a result of politics, not diet. It had to do with the effects of 1688. During earlier centuries of despotism, the English had enjoyed no such reputation.[294] Not only was this a matter of liberty, in itself naturally stimulating. It was above all part of a necessarily practical approach to public affairs. The Revolution had required the English as a nation to attend closely to their 'business'.

Politics belonged with the other part of this equation, commerce. Centuries of commercial activity bred a realistic outlook on life.[295] A clear head and methodical thought were essential to consistent success in the matter of making a profit. The English were, quite logically, 'a rational and trading people'.[296] Politics and commerce, closely integrated, and mutually supportive, were essentially the same kind of activity. In England someone described as a man of business might be either a politician or a tradesman. This was a national vocation. 'The Englishman triumphs in Parliament and the Exchange, the German in his study, the Frenchman in the theatre.'[297]

The alleged contrast with Celtic habits of mind was a recurrent feature of such analyses, often endorsed by Celts. It was an early nineteenth-century Irishman, the landscape painter George Barret, who observed that the English were a 'people accustomed to business and always looking to the facts' whereas his countrymen were 'less accustomed to be diligently employed, and abounding in imagination'.[298] Some wondered whether the English had an imagination at all. Madame de Staël argued that at best it was stirred only by external stimuli, whereas the Irish and Germans, according to her sharing the same stock of instincts, brought to it innate creativity.[299] From an English standpoint, sentiment and imagination were no substitutes for good sense. When the Irish and British Parliaments were unified in 1801, this became a standard item in unfavourable accounts of the difference between Irish and English oratory. In an Irish legislator feeling supplied the place of thought.[300]

An obsession with business could explain numerous features of Englishness, not least that sense of urgency with which English people comported themselves in daily life, to the extent of unintended rudeness towards less preoccupied tourists.[301] Even an idle or pleasure-seeking crowd displayed 'a prevalence of grave faces, and an air of business'.[302] The marquis de Custine remarked that the only difference between English and French frivolity was that in London pleasure was a business whereas in Paris it was merely a distraction.[303] Language itself seemed to reflect this preoccupation. Why was it, wondered Mrs Piozzi, that the French thought of having business on the carpet, whereas the English put it on the anvil?[304] This must surely be a down-to-earth and literal-minded nation.

Refocusing the English genius involved a reappraisal of the way men of intellect and ideas were treated in Britain. The Voltairean wisdom was that they enjoyed a status not permitted their comrades elsewhere. It depended on anecdotal evidence, such as the respect accorded Newton by grandees competing to carry the pall at his funeral, or the presence in English parlours of a portrait of Pope rather than a Prime Minister.[305] The memorials and monuments of Westminster Abbey, the prime tourist attraction of London throughout the period, also figured largely. A nation that buried its poets, painters, and scientists alongside its kings, ministers, and generals, must surely have an unusual regard for talent humbly born.

Successive French visitors to England confirmed Voltaire's impression, dutifully parading before Poets' Corner and ritually reflecting on the wisdom of a nation that paid such lasting respect to the power of the human mind. Diderot did not visit England and was no Anglomaniac but he did not dissent. 'In England, philosophers are honoured, respected, they rise to public offices, they are buried with the kings. Do we see that England is any worse for it?'[306] German Anglophiles were also impressed. Archenholz described the funeral of David Garrick in terms similar to Voltaire's account of Newton's and recalled that but for his own desire for a peaceful retirement Garrick would have become a Member of Parliament. 'When shall we see our German actors honoured in this manner?'[307]

By the late eighteenth century this tradition was beginning to falter, and thereafter it came under sustained attack. Stendhal remarked that 'Intelligence and genius lose twenty-five per cent of their value on landing in England.'[308] His contemporary Custine, brought up on admiring accounts of the influence of 'gens de lettres' in England, thought them misleading. The English had passed through an age of intellectual activity and descended into materialism.[309] These were hostile judgements, but others had earlier come to question the influence of genius on the national character of the English. Louis Dutens was struck by the want of any sense of intellectual *esprit de corps* in London. 'Men of letters do not form a body in London, as they do at Paris: it is not a profession. There is no one house which the *literati* frequent more than another: they do not know what is meant by a *bureau d'esprit*.'[310] Germans thought societies of learning less numerous than in their own country

and deplored the tendency of English corporations and clubs to prefer
a public dinner to a public debate.[311]

Exposure to the laments of English intellectuals intensified such
doubts. A swelling body of cultured opinion believed, rightly or wrongly,
that it was significantly undervalued by government. Repeated campaigns for better public recognition of arts, letters, and science, were to
be recurrent features of Victorian England. These were not necessarily
mollified by the much-publicized gestures of High Society hosts and
hostesses. 'Some nobles', it was remarked in the Press, 'have, however,
thought to compromise matters by having two kinds of entertainment—
one for Society proper, the other for ordinary Members of Parliament,
Volunteers, Artists, and Opera-Singers; but this is held to be an evasion
of the rule, and is but sullenly accepted.'[312]

Some blamed materialism. The Englishman, wrote the journalist
Cyrus Redding, was 'insensible of the value of intellectual ability, because
he judges of all things by the quantum of return in money.'[313] Social snobbery also was uncovered and deplored. Bulwer Lytton expressed a
growing conviction that aristocratic life was inimical to artistic creativity.[314] This was particularly a problem for women. The reputation of
being a Blue or Bluestocking, itself a mid-eighteenth-century expression
in origin, was a social and sexual handicap. To be thought 'clever' was to
be relegated to a distinct and inferior species of being, one unlikely to
reproduce itself by marriage.[315] For a gentleman to be a scholar was per-
missible, if not very desirable. But for a lady it was almost unthinkable.
This seemed to be an English phenomenon. Women who ventured
abroad found that their Continental sisters were far less inhibited,
even when the social systems in which they dwelled seemed in other
respects less liberal than the English.[316] Resorting to French to describe
what she felt on returning to England after a period on the Continent
in 1818, Lady Frances Shelley remarked: 'en Angleterre il ne faut pas
s'attendre a cultiver son esprit'. This was, she decided, the necessary
sacrifice of an Englishwoman.[317]

There were numerous expressions and proverbs that implied the
untrustworthiness of the mentally gifted. Bagehot used one of these—'too
sharp by half'—to build up, only semi-satirically, a case for English
dull-wittedness. 'What we opprobiously call stupidity, though not an en-
livening quality in common society, is Nature's favourite resource for

preserving steadiness of conduct and consistency of opinion. It enforces concentration; people who learn slowly, learn only what they must. The best security for people's doing their duty is, that they should not know anything else to do; the best security for fixedness of opinion is, that people should be incapable of comprehending what is to be said on the other side.'[318] These qualities, Bagehot argued, were eminently those needed in the management of everyday affairs, and more especially in the art of politics. The idea that precisely because of their pragmatism the English were well equipped for the art of government could readily be deduced from his assumption.

It was a rather novel idea. The conventional wisdom was that all the northern nations were intrinsically wanting in this talent, whereas those in the south, the descendants of Roman civilization, had inherited their capability. In England itself the freeborn Englishman tended to be thought of as better at obstructing government than imposing it. Historically, the results were not altogether impressive. The crises of the seventeenth century were indeed blamed by some for permanently imparting to the national character its characteristic sourness and gloom.[319] In French eyes the arrangements of the eighteenth century were not necessarily superior. A comment by the comte de Dubuat-Nançay in 1778 to the effect that 'The English constitution is only a bourgeois government spread out over a kingdom' was meant to be a withering dimissal of a polity which for efficiency and rationality could not be compared with Bourbon absolutism.[320] And looking back from the mid-nineteenth century, Victorian reformers could be equally dismissive. John Stuart Mill and George Grote contrasted what they called the 'inglorious nullity' of government before the 1830s with the 'individual energy' displayed by its subjects.[321]

There were, however, other more reassuring views. Many foreigners were coming to think that the voluntary, participatory, amateur nature of English government not only had much to commend it, but suggested a kind of political wisdom that might be instructive. At a time when the expansion of the British empire was demonstrating that such skills might be increasingly called for and also suggesting that they might be superior to older modes of imperial rule, the resulting reflections were highly pertinent.[322] One of the most significant was that the English art of governing had little to do with the power of the State as such. Its most

characteristic form was the unforced and undirected authority of a JP, *ie. bord*
an alderman, or even a hospital governor. Germans were particularly
impressed, for they recognized a form of devolution that provided a compromise between the stark absolutism of their own princes, and the
radical republicanism of revolutionaries. Moreover, its minimalism, the
assumption that no more power should be adopted than was essential to
achieve an institution's purpose, seemed highly attractive. Fanny Lewald
linked the organizing talent to be seen, for instance, in a girls' academy
such as Queen's College, Harley Street to the English genius for practical self-government, unaffected by theorizing.[323]

The resulting mentality was as important in affairs of state as in a
boarding school. Lord Normanby remarked that whereas in Paris political wisdom was a matter of theory, in London it almost resembled an
occult art, learned only by apprenticeship, its way 'too dark and too mean
to bear the light, if written or in print. Its precepts are oral. They are
caught and communicated in conversation, are handed from politic
father to politic son.'[324] The seeming irrationality of English government
was the result, as Eugène Buret concluded. 'England is the country of
details, of isolated facts; each parish has its administration, its usages, we
might say almost its laws.'[325] Again, cleverness had nothing to do with it.
In English politics it was axiomatic that not being brilliant was a recommendation in a young tyro who aimed at becoming a man of business.[326]
Even the evolution of a new-model civil servant in the mid-nineteenth
century did not remove the preference for all-round ability rather than
specialist knowledge.[327]

Underlying such assumptions was a profound belief in the
Englishman as doer rather than thinker, who, as a modern French historian has observed, 'always conceived himself as a man of action; in every
age he has been the man represented by Hobbes'.[328] The carefully
directed dynamism that resulted was easily associated with the controlled
force evident in the technological supremacy of the English. Observing
one of the last mail coaches on an English highway, Esquiros thought it
summarized 'the traits of the Anglo-Saxon character—energy, perseverance, order, and intrepidity' and wondered whether its passing did not
signify the beginnings of decline.[329] Yet a year or so later he was concluding that the railways provided still more telling evidence of the Englishman's vigour and perhaps even 'to some extent spurred his physical

and moral activity'.[330] The evocative power of Turner's *Rain, Steam and Speed*, and Ford Madox Brown's *Work*, suggests that the English themselves were at least as aware of the aesthetics of national energy.[331] Understandably, politicians saw its rhetorical potential. Disraeli proclaimed order, 'the most efficacious assistant of industry' as 'the prime characteristic of the English mind' since the Reformation.[332] More intriguing still is that historians of Victorian Britain have been disposed to treat this as a matter of reality, not merely of image. Indeed their doyen Asa Briggs remarks: 'In looking back at "the Victorian age" it is impossible not to be impressed by its energy . . . The age had the same qualities as the steam engine which was given its own gospel . . . One of the genuine achievements of the Victorians was to motivate people in such a way that these values came to be thought of as "inner directed".'[333] Whatever the truth of the matter, as the reconstruction of a character from somewhat unlikely materials, it represented a considerable triumph, and an international one at that.

CHAPTER TWO

CANDOUR

PLAINNESS

*B*RITAIN'S rise to international greatness, in the course of the
eighteenth century, coincided with a fashion, or rather succession
of fashions, in which nature and the cult of the natural featured
largely. It seemed reasonable to relate the virtues and vices of the English
to these concerns. At the height of French Anglomania between the 1730s
and the 1780s the Englishman was often presented as the most natural of
Europeans, even a kind of half-civilized savage, whose honesty, on the
one hand, and brutishness, on the other, reflected this close relationship
with nature. The War of American Independence somewhat interfered
with this process of identification. From the 1770s natural behaviour
came to be considered a more obvious characteristic of the New World
than the Old. The British themselves were capable of celebrating Americans as 'a new people of manners simple and untainted'.[1] Even so, many
of the associated traits continued to figure in representations of English

character, as Charles Dickens remarked of French Anglophiles. 'I never saw anything so strange. They seem to me to have got a fixed idea that there is no natural manner but the English manner (in itself so exceptional that it is a thing apart, in all countries); and that unless a Frenchman—represented as going to the guillotine for example—is as calm as Clapham, or as respectable as Richmond-hill, he cannot be right.'[2] Continental visitors travelling in the opposite direction often continued to feel that in crossing the North Sea or the English Channel, they were about to set foot 'in the land of the half-civilized'.[3]

Travellers are collectors of impressions and examples of this naturalness were eminently collectable. Some of them seem rather unlikely to a modern eye. An English taste for undercooked meat and vegetables dismayed foreigners gastronomically but impressed them as consistent with their character, though as Edmund Burke pointed out, this ignored the Englishman's proneness to cover his food with sauces such as soy and catchup unknown to the French.[4] Other instances marked the recurrent association with liberty. The dress worn by the English was assumed to bring them closer to nature, especially in the case of children, whose loose-fitting clothes contrasted with the precocious artifice and adulthood suggested by Continental custom. And always there was the presumption that given a choice between two ways of doing anything, the English would invariably opt for the less affected. One vice unknown, wrote the abbé Coyer, in 1779, was hypocrisy—all showed themselves as they were.[5] Above all did this display itself in point of manners. He and many other tourists expected their hosts to observe 'that English frankness and cordiality which I prefer to all the ceremonies of politeness'.[6]

Genteel visitors were intrigued by insular horsemanship, and its seeming rejection of the classical precision of Vienna and the elegant prowess of the French *haute école*. For English equestrians submission to the unnatural Continental regime was like turning oneself into a poker.[7] And among human performers, the ultimate difference between the mid-eighteenth century's stars in Paris and London, Le Kain and Garrick, was the former's pomposity by comparison with the latter's simplicity of manners.[8] The joint triumph of Garrick and Shakespeare confirmed the 'reign of nature' in the English drama.[9]

A horror of theatricality none the less remained an impediment to national pride in the stage. One of the advantages of musical oratorio was that it escaped censure on these grounds. Those who appreciated it were able to congratulate themselves on their patriotism. 'These music meetings are the most thoroughly national amusement we have. Polished, pure, and dignified, they owe nothing to the glare of tapers, the false spirits of the evening hour, the splendour of ornaments, or any theatric illusion.'[10] Musical taste generally in England was thought to display an obsession with simplicity which might be lacking in the richness of Continental traditions yet did credit to the national sensibility.[11] Some foreign virtuosi found it hard to adapt. Others exploited it to their profit. The highly successful castrato Tommaso Guarducci told Charles Burney that the English 'love only a few notes in gracing, but they must be good—that they have been of great use to him'.[12]

The underlying human quality was taken to be an amiable, attractive disposition. Unrefined nature in a self-styled age of reason was good nature, and good nature was something for which the English were often praised, not only by themselves. Sir James Mackintosh 'Extolled, in warm terms—which he thought, as a foreigner (a Scotsman), he might do without the imputation of partiality, for he did not mean to include his own countrymen in the praise—the characteristic *bon naturel*—the good temper and sound sense of the English people; qualities, in which he deliberately thought us without a rival in any other nation on the globe.'[13] One way of summarizing such qualities was simplicity. The semantics required some consideration. It was pointed out that in France the expressions 'bon homme' 'bonne femme' implied simplicity amounting to innocence, almost backwardness. These qualities would have been boasts in England.[14] The English had no word of their own to match 'naïveté' precisely because they did not need a pejorative term for describing innocence.[15] German 'Einfachheit' came closer but did not quite convey the implied benevolence of English simplicity.[16] 'Amiable frankness and sincerity' were taken to be implicit.[17]

'Oh how the honest simplicity of the English character affected me at entering England,' wrote the artist Benjamin Haydon, when he landed at Dover after a trip to France.[18] It was a commonplace sentiment for returning travellers, even those who had been abroad seeking a coat of Continental polish with which to overlay this native rawness. Others, such as the physician Martin Lister, who was somewhat overcome when he visited Paris in 1698, could only reflect that after all the Parisian was prone to 'build and dress mostly for Figure', revealing an assumption that civility had to with appearances not reality and that the object was to persuade by flattery not honesty. "'Tis certain the French are the most Polite Nation in the World, and can Praise and Court with a better Air than the rest of Mankind.'[19]

The potential conflict was indeed a favourite subject for debate. The English gentleman's claim to fame, at least from the time of Addison to that of Rousseau, was that he uniquely combined good nature with civilized manners. His pretension to politeness depended on the redemption that Anglo-Saxon sincerity could offer a tradition sadly contaminated by Latin dissimulation. It was precisely the English complaint that the politeness of the courtly foreigner was a form of insincerity. John Moore pictured the Englishman abroad being treated to Continental hospitality and musing to himself: 'There was nothing real in all the fuss those people made about us.'[20] On the other hand, the counter-claim that English sincerity was merely evidence that the English did not care for anyone else's feelings at all might cause a certain twinge of guilt.[21]

Anglophile *Spectator*-readers on the Continent were forever worrying at this bone. How much could Old English frankness be imported without dispersing the polite hypocrisies that made Parisian sociability so delightful?[22] The converse worries might arise in English minds. Any Grand Tourist ran the risk of returning as Arthur Murphy's Jack Broughton did. 'He has forgot the plainness and honesty of an Englishman.'[23] The horror of an enemy within, such as Lord Chesterfield, with his Gallic code of manners, was that 'he did much, for a time, to injure the true national character, and to introduce, instead of open manly sincerity, a hollow perfidious courtliness'.[24]

None the less the threat was thought to have been beaten off. In any international table of sincerity the English would have figured high in the eighteenth century. The extreme contrast was taken to be with Italians.[25] If they had achieved nothing else Machiavelli and the Medicis had made them a nation of dissemblers in the eyes of others. Even southern Europeans expected northerners to be more open, and the English the most open of all.[26] Not that everyone agreed. Some colonial Americans awarded themselves the palm in this respect.[27] And when the Celtic 'fringe' became known in the late eighteenth century, its inhabitants were sometimes thought superior to the English. Ferri di San

Costante thought the Welsh in particular more sincere.[28] But by and large the English reputation persisted until the end of the century and beyond.

The fact that the most aristocratic of the English were supposedly as uncontrived in their behaviour as their inferiors seemed telling, for it might have been assumed that they would be prone to artificiality. Elizabeth Bancroft was struck by the unostentatious wealth and splendour that she found in England. 'Their manners are perfectly simple and I entirely forget, except when their historic names fall upon my ear, that I am with the proud aristocracy of England.'[29] The Frenchman Charles Cottu waxed still more rhapsodic on this point. 'In England one meets charming young men of candour; whose traits seem to belong to the earliest centuries of the planet, and are transmitted from age to age in families which are untainted by the corruption of the times. The calm of their physiognomy, the purity of their heart, the modesty of their air, has something enchanting. Nothing equals the innocence of their ways, and even of their thoughts. I have known those among them who have retained this kind of virginity of the spirit in the midst of the seductions of wealth, the dissipations of travel, and all the illusions of the world.'[30]

Civility had always nodded in the direction of simplicity. It went with self-command, self-control—what courtesy writers called 'moderation of affections' and 'collectedness of mind'.[31] In the eighteenth century there were various literary models of such simplicity, from Smollett's highly secular Lismahago to Henry Brooke's deeply religious Fool of Quality. The effect was much the same, however; simplicity and plainness were inseparable from questions of morality, not least Christian morality.[32] Simplicity of manners in this respect crossed class boundaries. Sir Roger de Coverley's simplicity was very like that of his tenants and labourers. It still seemed valid a hundred and fifty years after his time. The *Cornhill Magazine* in 1869 described the common features of the manners of the gentleman and the manners of the labourer in these terms, and hailed 'this sturdy mixture of frankness when they speak, with a perfect willingness to hold their tongues when they have nothing to say'.[33] Nor was this a male preserve. The same characteristically English mixture was represented in 'that beautiful union of refinement and simplicity (the perfection of female grace) which is found amongst English women'.[34]

Pushing 'simplicity to affectation' was considered by Fenimore
Cooper a characteristic English vice in eloquence as in literature and
manners.[35] There was much in the history of the preceding century to
support the accusation. Plainness was a favourite Augustan value,
expressed not least in the search for linguistic purity. Renunciation of
figure, trope, and metaphor was a prominent feature of the drive for a
lucid language. This not only separated the polite and plain-speaking
Englishman from his barbaric predecessors, it also distanced him from
his Celtic cousins, especially the Irish and Welsh, both supposedly given
to the flowers of rhetoric. A standard explanation of the Irish 'bull' or
blunder was that it derived from the misuse of an orderly language by a
people given to metaphorical confusion.

The assumption was that ornament not only inhibited clarity but also
concealed deceit, as the expression 'speaking one's mind' implied. Other
languages had insincerity built into them. French, especially, was a language of compliments, suggesting the extent to which hypocrisy had
become part of the nation's style. One of the arguments for allowing
English diplomats to use their own tongue rather than French was that
the latter was culturally contaminating. Making ambassadors read the
best of French writers was a sure way to prevent them being good Englishmen, as William Johnstone Temple expressed it in 1779, though it was
to be another forty years before Foreign Secretaries took the plunge and
promoted the use of English for communications with foreign courts.[36]

Language was taken to be a clear indication of the English obsession
with plainness and directness. Unmasking cant, it was noted, the Englishman would say 'The English of this is . . .'.[37] 'Plain English' or even,
by the mid-nineteenth century, 'plain Saxon' was a kind of tautology.[38]
Many observed the contrast with French evasiveness even when the sentiment was similar. Why did 'one shoulder of mutton draw down another'
in English when 'l'appetit vient en mangeant' in French?[39] Even the
Frenchified milord might be relieved to exude a 'downright English
sweat' when returning to London.[40] Such directness was not necessarily
shared by English speakers who had cast off from England itself. It was
an American who complained that his countryman had lost the ability
to call a spade a spade, inventing a kind of grandiose language all their
own.[41] The only exception to English directness was the growing
prudishness that marked all reference to bodily and more particularly

sexual matters. Ironically, in a Parisian salon 'speaking English' became a synonym for coarse or even obscene conversation; this was in reality one form of freedom that polite society in London certainly did not exercise.[42]

Directness was not without its inconveniences. Englishmen themselves could see that it might constitute a kind of verbal violence. As Hazlitt remarked, 'There are two things that an Englishman understands, hard words, and hard blows. Nothing short of this (generally speaking) excites his attention or interests him in the least. His neighbours have the benefit of the one in war time, and his own countrymen of the other in time of peace.'[43] 'Good, honest hatred' was a quality that the English need feel no shame about.[44] Even among people of education, the conventions of public speechifying assumed tolerance of what would have been insulting elsewhere. To an American tourist the 'good-natured and agreeable' way in which after-dinner speakers exchanged abuse seemed remarkable.[45] Freedom of speech evidently had an influence on national manners. Englishmen could say what they thought without fear of the consequences. Elsewhere, words could be dangerous. In France, at any rate before the Revolution, 'a shrug of the shoulders, an elevated arm, a contracted brow, or a gathering up, as it were, of one's whole body, may be, and frequently is, as well understood as words; and yet for these bodily actions, a man cannot be conveyed to the Bastille.'[46]

Unfortunately, there were arenas in which English want of subtlety was a disadvantage. Combating the French superiority in politeness constituted a war of civility. To encounter a Frenchman with his battery of compliments was to go into battle without adequate munitions. In diplomatic affairs this might count. The supposed inferiority of British envoys was to be traced to it. The English had never been famous for their ambassadors, even when educated abroad, and in the service of other states, as James II's illegitimate son the Duke of Berwick had been. Berwick generated some famous anecdotes, including the story of his being sent home by Elizabeth Farnese on the grounds that he could take no step that did not lie directly in front of him.[47] The common assumption was that the representatives of Britain had too much of the national frankness to make good career diplomats, and tended to act, as George III's son the Duke of Cambridge expressed it, 'entirely according to their own private feelings'.[48]

To say, as Count Gallina said of Lord Normanby in 1851, that he had never seen so much 'conviction' in an ambassador was at best a back-handed compliment.[49] When the British did engage in deceitful diplomacy they ran into heavy criticism at home, as Canning did in respect of Erskine's mission to the United States in 1809, all the more so in that in this case the deceived were former countrymen. 'To practise on America those politics, that are fit only for France, is . . . assuming a dress, more-over, that does not befit an Englishman; it sits aukwardly on him; and god forbid it should ever do otherwise. Whenever the garb of solid truth,—of stern old English honesty, is thrown aside for the motley jacket of a harlequin trickster, the nation is loser, gain what she will.'[50] All could agree, however, that in dealing with more primitive peoples, simplicity might be a useful servant of the State. Natural open-heartedness would eventually win over the Indian tribes in North America, it was argued, to the extent of defeating insidious French subtlety.[51]

OPENNESS

Plainness was first and foremost self-expression. It implied the presenta-tion of self as nature had designed it and in the guise of simplicity it gave free rein to the spontaneous virtue of the English race. But in terms of the resulting social relations it also assumed accessibility and openness. The preservation of liberty was not just about the protection of the indi-vidual against the State; it was about the maintenance of customs and institutions that made his doings as transparent as social existence permitted.

The outstanding example in the eyes of foreigners was the legendary freedom of the British press. In lore as well as law this was the story of successive capitulations on the part of government to the demands of the public for a free flow of information. The lapsing of State censorship in the 1690s, the refusal of opposition journals to be intimidated by prose-cutions for seditious libel in the Walpole era, the assertion by the Wilkites of the right to published debates of Parliament, the furious struggle against government measures to control the press during the Revolu-tionary and Napoleonic wars, all were so many milestones on the road to a truly free press. But this empowerment of the 'fourth estate', an expression that dated from the 1820s, could be viewed in various lights. As a check on executive power it had evident advantages. Yet there were those who wondered who would act as a check on the press itself. Even Englishmen sometimes asked themselves how 'the newspaper press should have attained to its present omnipotence among such a people as the British, seeing that it is an anonymous and irresponsible institution'.[52]

Foreigners were more impressed by the way it used its power than the way it acquired it. They were invariably fascinated and sometimes disgusted by the freedoms taken. The obvious example was the exposure of politicians to the public gaze, particularly from the 1770s onwards, when parliamentary debates became the staple fare of most newspapers, and when a whole genre of biographical literature—'portraits', 'memoirs'—sprang up. As Lord Liverpool's biographer observed in 1827, the lives of public men had become 'a species of public property'. The result was like living in 'a glass bee-hive'.[53] The quantity of print devoted to the personal doings and characteristics of people in public life struck foreigners as quite without parallel. When Carl Gustav Carus accompanied the King of Saxony to England in 1844 he decided that this incessant 'prying and observation' explained a style of statesmanship that contrasted with other modes he knew. 'The [British] statesman', he wrote, 'is not suffered to intrench himself behind . . . documents, but must come forth personally.' He was particularly startled to find that a man of importance in public affairs could not even board a train without being accompanied by newspaper reporters, pen in hand. He thought 'all this spying and universal small talk of the newspapers' a national disgrace. 'Such a people as the English should be far above such littleness!'[54]

Perceptive observers realized that it was possible to make too much of such exposure. As Georg Lichtenberg noted, what would have been sedition in Germany was barely noticed in England. The threshold of what was tolerable had moved so far that not even those most vilified troubled to take such abuse seriously.[55] Mrs Piozzi thought Italians gained a misleading impression from English newspapers circulated abroad, forming judgements of characters which were not intended even by those who had composed them.[56] Similar observations were made by travellers in Germany.

That this suggested something more about the English than their political sophistication was confirmed by the realization that press coverage of this sort was not in fact restricted to statesmen. Indeed it was the intrusion of the journalist into the private life of 'Society' that most surprised many visitors.[57] Some of the resulting scandal-mongering was of the lowest kind. When it was relatively new, in the 1770s, serving 'private distresses up the next morning for the breakfast and entertainment of the public' was often designed to extract hush-money from the great and the not-so-good.[58] The resulting form of blackmail seemed entirely English.

But not all social news was scandal, and the English appetite for tittle-tattle puzzled foreigners. Why newspaper readers should want to know the names of those who had attended fashionable parties was something of a mystery. So remarked Harriet Beecher Stowe. 'It always has seemed to me that distinguished people here in England live a remarkably outdoor sort of life; and newspapers tell a vast deal about people's concern which it is not our custom to put into print in America. Such, for instance, as where the Hon. Mr. A. is staying now, and where he expected to go next; what her grace wore at the last ball, and when the royal children rode out, and what they had on; and whom Lord Such-a-one had to dinner; besides a large number of particulars which probably never happen.'[59] This triviality was thought distinctive. Even when French newspapers were not censored, they showed little interest in such material, as Amédée Pichot observed in 1825. 'How delighted our Parisian coquettes would be to find the less spacious columns of our journals imitate the gallantry of the London newspapers, and attach as much importance to ladies' dresses as they do to political debates and the price of the fund! But, alas! the very *Journal des Modes* does not indulge in the smallest personality of this kind. After this, who shall say that we pay too great an homage to the fair sex.'[60]

In effect, the principle of public scrutiny was being misused to intrude on private lives. The English legal system suggested to some observers something of the manner in which this could have occurred. It was an axiom of Anglo-Saxon justice that no man should be condemned behind closed doors. Defending one's name and honour in the face of one's country not only implied the individual's right to trial by jury but the right of the public to see that justice was done. English courts were very public places. Until the 1830s the highest in the land, at Westminster, were physically separated from the public only by portable screens. The merest passer-by could pause to view their deliberations. Assizes and quarter sessions were similarly part of a public process which celebrated a characteristic mixture of justice, administration, and sociability. Technically judges had the power to control admission to their own courts, but in practice they exercised it with restraint. That audiences were drawn more by vulgar fascination than a passion for justice was difficult to deny. The results could be rather shocking to those who assumed that some matters were too delicate to be aired before any kind of public let alone the sort likely to collect in the Old Bailey. Sexual offences were particularly problematic. Maurice Rubichon remarked that in England a woman alleging rape had to have her private parts so to speak paraded in court.[61] Elsewhere she would have been heard in the privacy of a magistrate's chamber.

Unsurprisingly, crime reporting was one of the main preoccupations of the nation's newspapers, often taking priority even over politics. Some assumed that this was indeed a matter of national character or at least inherited practice. William Howitt, in the 1840s, noticed that by contrast the German authorities took great care to keep criminality out of the newspapers. Police officers were trained to 'hush up' the crimes they investigated.[62] But if the infection was of English growth it was capable of spreading. Fenimore Cooper thought that in his own time 'the practice of repeating the proceedings of the courts of justice, in order to cater to a vicious appetite for amusement in the public' had begun to spread, first to America and then France.[63]

The paradox of press freedom was heightened by an awareness that its agents were licensed in a way that would have seemed offensive in the case of any other parties, private or public. Journalists were essentially spies, privileged only because their discoveries were for public consumption. Any other form of spying subverted an open society, implying secret lives secretly detected. Nothing shocked British tourists travelling in central Europe in the early nineteenth century more than the operations of Continental police forces in this respect.

When a State police force finally emerged in Britain, in the second quarter of the nineteenth century, it went out of its way to distinguish its methods and mentality from those of other such bodies. But its success owed much to the fact that the police were able to operate effectively on the boundary between public and private according to ancient custom. The objection was not to intrusion into the life of the individual so much as the manner in which it might be done. Secret investigations were the essence of un-Englishness. They were just as objectionable when the spy was privately employed, as controversy about the growing use of private detectives revealed. In a notorious divorce trial of 1840, the Morgan case, the defence barrister asked how English jurymen, accustomed to 'throw in the teeth of France their system of espionage' could take seriously the testimony of a spy. 'Were they to trust to the oath of one who thinks the occupation of a spy an honourable one—a spy, which every honest man shrinks from? He would be glad to know where the man could be found who would consent for any consideration to be pointed out in the street and have it said, "There goes the spy."'[64]

It would not have been an answer to such arguments that secrecy was an efficient way of doing things, for the underlying assumption was that it was necessarily immoral. Various usages reflected this assumption. The term 'indirect' was a synonym for corruption in the late seventeenth century and remained so well into the eighteenth. Candour implied not only frankness but honesty. The furore that arose when Speaker Norton told an MP in February 1770 that 'he now found he was to expect no candour from him' arose from the contemporary belief that the charge directly reflected on his victim's honour.[65] Anything that could not be publicly avowed was assumed to be discreditable. 'Publicity was honesty, secrecy was fraud.'[66]

Emerson traced this attitude back to the Saxon's innate horror of craft and deceit. He thought that the English made bad traitors because they could never keep a secret.[67] Such attitudes were held to be revealing in point of national character. 'In keeping a secret—the German forgets what he has heard; the Englishman conceals what he should divulge, and divulges what he should conceal; the Frenchman blabs every thing; the Italian nothing; the Spaniard is indifferent to all.'[68] Opportunities to compare different nationalities under test conditions were understandably rare. However, when one such occurred at the Congress of Vienna in 1815 it was the British delegation, composed mainly of clerks, that thwarted the efforts of the legendary Austrian police to secure state secrets.[69]

Attempts by the British government to employ the methods of other states were inevitably controversial. There was general agreement that Britain was unique in the freedom of movement it accorded. Its citizens did not need their ruler's permission to travel either at home or abroad nor were foreign visitors exposed to unwelcome scrutiny. There was one awkward exception, however. Britain's customs officers were considered the most officious of all, providing an unfavourable first impression of insular life that figured in countless travels. Their inquisitions were invariably time-consuming. Less than two hours was getting off lightly.[70] Beyond that there was their impoliteness, what Dickens called 'a surly boorish incivility about our men, alike disgusting to all persons who fall into their hands, and discreditable to the nation that keeps such ill-conditioned curs snarling about its gates'.[71]

Body searching was a particularly sensitive matter. No exception was made for sex. Baretti was shocked 'to see even ladies treated with an indecency that the roughest Barbarians would be ashamed to practise'.[72] In her novelette *The Ring* Lady Blessington tellingly contrasted the brutal behaviour of officers to women with the national pride in liberty.[73] Nor did rank make a difference. The Marquis of Pombal was so enraged by his treatment when he went to Britain as Portuguese ambassador that he later imposed punitive wine regulations at Oporto on British merchants.[74] Admittedly, opinions varied as to the ferocity of an English search. The Saxon Watzdorf found running a hand from the shoulder to the hem of one's clothes unobjectionable. 'This they call pocket-searching. In Germany it is better understood.'[75] The real defence, however, was that English customs officials were interested in property not persons, however roughly the latter might be treated in pursuit of the former.

The Alien Acts, which required foreigners to register with the authorities at the point of entry and at their destination, were introduced as a result of the Revolutionary War with France. They were the cause of recurrent controversy at home and considered a regrettable if necessary break with tradition, though few foreigners complained about them.[76] Americans were among those who did. Benjamin Silliman thought that 'strangers are not treated at the alien office with that mildness and lenity which becomes the character of the nation' but admitted that it had been 'instituted in consequence of the abuse of the almost unrestrained liberty which foreigners had, till then, enjoyed in England'.[77] On the other hand,

innkeepers, hoteliers, and landlords did not record the identity of their
guests, something that was de rigueur on the Continent and even, to the
surprise of English visitors, in the United States. Americans were rather
embarrassed by the fact, and reduced to pointing out that while regis-
tration was indeed the custom, it was not in fact a requirement of
government.[78]

Every country had to have a secret service, if only for purposes of
national security. But it was a long-standing anxiety in Britain that it was
likely to be directed against the opponents of government at home rather
than abroad. The use of the Crown's Civil List for purposes that had
more to do with electoral corruption than the defence of the realm was
a recurrent grievance. Successive reforms of the public finances removed
this particular cause for concern, but the sensitivity of security questions
remained intense. If nineteenth-century governments employed debatable methods, the result was uproar. When Mazzini's letters were opened
on the authority of Sir James Graham in 1844, Graham was accused of
introducing the 'spy system of foreign states'.[79] The *Times* thundered:
'The proceeding cannot be English, any more than masks, poisons,
sword-sticks, secret signs and associations, and other such dark ventures.
Public opinion is mighty and jealous, and does not brook to hear of
public ends pursued by other than public means. It considers that
treason against its public self.'[80]

Here was a rich and ancient rhetoric that made secrecy a vice in itself.
Every offence attended by secrecy became worse. 'Screening' ranked very
high among the crimes of statesmen, not least the first Prime Minister,
Sir Robert Walpole, whose reputation as 'Screenmaster-General' made
him the most vilified of all eighteenth-century Prime Ministers. Murder
'out of the blue' or 'in the dark' was the most horrid kind, as a secretly
plotted atrocity was the most detested. In the space of a few years, the
assassination of the Prime Minister Spencer Percival in 1812 and the discovery of the Cato Street Conspiracy in 1820, aroused fears of 'a new
epoch in the English character'.[81]

Secrecy was illegitimate even when it could be argued that it served a
public purpose. Opposition to the secret ballot in parliamentary elections derived much of its force from a feeling that it was 'inconsistent with
the straightforward character of an Englishman, who loves to indulge in
the manly and open avowal of his opinions'.[82] Resistance to the intro-

duction of the ballot was not broken down until 1872, notwithstanding the passage of major reforms of the franchise in 1832 and 1867. In the meantime the view that it would be 'unmanly, ineffective, and enervating' was commonplace.[83] It reflected a conviction that publicity was the best check on corruption and intimidation.

There was a paradoxical quality about public participation. In Continental states the public had to be addressed by governments precisely because it played little or no part in government. In England it was supposed that the public did not need addressing. Wendeborn was struck by the fact that statutes were never proclaimed in England; it was simply assumed that the people would know from its representatives what was done in its name, 'a kind of imputed knowledge' which looked odd at a time when parliamentary legislation was increasing rapidly in volume and complexity.[84] Enthusiasts for rational government went about reforming this tradition with caution. When Pitt and Speaker Abbott started the process in 1796, 'We agreed that the less was said to expose the deformed and shapeless condition of the present mode of giving publicity to our laws, the more discreet it would be.'[85]

The obsession with publicity was by no means confined to politics. Openness was the essence of proper behaviour. Balzac, who knew English vanity if he knew England itself very little, took pleasure in depicting a noblewoman of 'un-English openness'.[86] Certainly English gentility depended on a readiness to confront a stranger frankly. Suspicion attended anyone who 'seldom looks a Person in the Face, and is as little of a Gentleman as his Neighbour'.[87] Genteel architecture was meant to convey the same sense of confidence. It was a source of pride that the great town houses of the nobility were not shut away in dark courtyards, like the 'hotels' of Paris, but open to view in the squares of Georgian London. The famous exceptions, such as Burlington House and Devonshire House, were taken to be the work of cosmopolitan noblemen who had betrayed their Englishness.

Significantly, it required commercial interest to make a case for concealment. Industrial espionage was seen as a major threat to economic power, alarming Parliament and the Crown as well as manufacturers themselves. The secret of English industrial pre-eminence was the most irritating of English secrets to foreigners by the beginning of the nineteenth century, as numerous visitors complained. The fact that many came to Britain precisely to view the wonders of the new workshop of the world made this all the more frustrating. Testimony on the point varied, and some thought criticism exaggerated, but the resulting debates were not without awkwardness from a patriotic standpoint.[88] There remained a sense that there was something demeaning about the need for concealment even when the argument in favour of it was overwhelming. One possibility was to argue that the manufacturers who were reduced to such tactics were driven to it by mercenary motives that most of their compatriots would have scorned. One reason why Scots were taken to be less frank than Englishmen was their neediness, which supposedly bred a certain canny cautiousness in the imparting of information. Even some Scots conceded that the English were the franker people.[89] The claim was to a superior national civility, what the American painter J. S. Copley called 'a great deal of Manly politeness in the English. There is something so open and undisguized in them that I can truly say exceeds rather than falls short of my expectation.'[90]

Horror of concealment was demonstrated in nothing more than the reservations that attended its use for purposes of social mixing. The masque is central to the story of European sociability in the seventeenth and eighteenth centuries. Yet in England it is almost irrelevant, and certainly ambivalent. It flourished under George I and George II when a foreign court provided it with predictable approval. But by their self-consciously patriotic successor George III it was strongly discouraged. Though it enjoyed a brief revival at the end of the eighteenth century it never attained the acceptance that it did elsewhere and throughout the period was the subject of much criticism.

It was a common observation that masquerades were ill-suited to the national character. Samuel Richardson believed that 'They are diversions that fall not in with the genius of the English commonalty.'[91] Or as a journalist put it nearly a century later at a time when public masquerades at Vauxhall enjoyed a brief popularity in celebrating success in the Peninsular War, the 'rugged soil of Britain' was not ideal for an exotic import such as this.[92] Various evidence was offered in support of such contentions. One of the more interesting was the claim that the essentially theatrical spirit of masking was beyond the down-to-earth English temperament. 'The pleasures of a Masquerade, that is, its *peculiar* pleasures, must result from good histrionic powers being prevalent throughout the community.' But most of the debate revolved around the moral dangers of masquerading in England, given 'the delicate and retired system of female education and female habits'.[93]

The assumption was that masquerades permitted womanizing men exceptional opportunities for sexual dalliance. Evidence that survives of what went on, particularly when masquerades were fashionable under George I, suggests indeed that this was the object for many men and women.[94] Reforming magistrates who employed the Black Act to outlaw such assemblies in London considered them inseparable from numerous forms of 'vice now reigning in the City'.[95] On the other hand, even Richardson did not necessarily assume the worst. It was the frivolity and futility of masquerades that shocked him in his persona as self-appointed guardian of English womanhood. 'I was disgusted at the freedoms taken with me, tho' but the common freedoms of the place, by persons, who singled me from the throng, hurried me round the rooms, and engaged me in fifty idle conversations; and to whom, by the privilege of the place, I was obliged to be bold, pert, saucy, and to aim at repartee and smartness; the current wit of that witless place.'[96]

The indignity was not merely intellectual. A mask might conceal social inferiority and presumptuous manners. This did not seem to entail the dangers on the Continent that it did in Britain. Masques were well established at Versailles and Paris by the early eighteenth century and spread rapidly throughout the German courts thereafter. Particular delight was taken in the opportunity to play at plebeian life. 'Wirtschaft' masques had a prince as innkeeper, his courtiers as peasants.[97] The bogus humility and equality of these occasions evidently added an appealing frisson to high life. But long before revolution made the dangerous nature of such games obvious the English had perceived the potential threat for a relatively open society such as London's. Giving low people the chance to be Arcadian shepherds and shepherdesses looked like a risky experiment.[98] Only where the rank and blood of all could be taken for granted was it wise to engage in such games. And even then it might be necessary to resort to punishments that would have been impracticable in Britain. For Elizabeth Hervey, wife of the celebrated traveller the 'Prince-Bishop' of Derry, the story of a footman who took the opportunity of a masquerade at Rome to dance with a princess and had to be put to La Corda in consequence seemed all too instructive.[99]

The association with foreignness was also significant. The introduction of the masquerade in England was blamed either on a French ambassador to the court of Queen Anne, or on the celebrated impresario John James Heidegger, whose masquerades in the 1720s were seen as pandering to the tastes of an alien court.[100] The use of French as the common masquerade talk did not increase its respectability. And it seemed significant that when George III was for once compelled to forgo his personal veto on a royal masquerade, it was in deference to a visit from his brother-in-law, the King of Denmark.[101] Christian VII's subsequently notorious sado-masochism, not to say his incarceration of his wife for misconduct with his minister, did not suggest that the morality of a Continental court was a recommendation for such amusements.

Masques never altogether died out, but there always hung over them an ambiguity making attendance a nice matter for judgement and requiring careful calculation of the relative decorousness of the venue. Two rules could be applied. One was that the audience must be invited or at least predictably select. Even the Opera House was preferable to the Pantheon, for instance.[102] Secondly, there was the important discovery that exotic garb could make for an agreeable evening without resort to concealment of identity. It was left to the English to take the masque out of masquerade, as Horace Walpole remarked.[103] The modern fancy dress ball was the safely Anglicized and sanitized result.

SEPARATENESS

It could be argued in defence of English practice in such matters that openness implied genuine sociability whereas less open societies could only find it through an elaborate form of secrecy such as the masquerade. The snag with this argument was that confronted with English practice foreigners often found evidence of unsociability, of exclusiveness rather than inclusiveness, enclosure rather than accessibility.

They were puzzled by the practice of dividing even the most common tavern or alehouse into compartments, from the sixteenth century when the partitions were of wood, to the nineteenth when they were more likely to feature green baize curtains on brass rails.[104] The American Calvin

Colton described the resulting want of communality. 'A room divided into stalls some six feet deep from the walls and four broad, with a narrow board for a table as a fixture in each, with wooden benches for the length thereof, and partitions rising as high as one's head while sitting, and above these corresponding scarlet stuff-curtains run on a brass wire, supported at the extremities by small brass posts about an inch in diameter—the whole apparatus constituting a line of recesses entirely round the room, into which any one, two, or three, or four persons may retreat, and partake of a breakfast, dinner, tea, or supper, without any connexion with other persons in the apartment. . . . Nobody is supposed to know his neighbour in an adjoining stall, or to have anything to do with him.'[105]

So secluded were these cubicles that early nineteenth-century parents felt confident about leaving their children in them. Alphonse Esquiros characterized them as 'separation in union—the type of English life'.[106] Even in the early Victorian gin-palaces, which needed space for purposes of sexual display, concessions had to be made to this spirit, as Flora Tristan noted. 'Upstairs there is a spacious salon divided down the middle; in one half there is a row of tables separated one from the other by wooden screens, as in all English restaurants, with upholstered seats like sofas on each side of the tables. In the other half there is a dais where the prostitutes parade in all their finery, seeking to arouse the men with their glances and remarks.'[107]

The English themselves told stories ridiculing their use of such space. Thomas Mozley, of Oxford Movement fame, recalled that 'in the city and along the river, there were "shades," in which wearied men retired to dark, cavernous holes for half an hour, and drank wine from the wood. I remember Mayo, of Oriel, mentioning that a city friend had gone to the same "shades," and the same stall, at the same hour, for, I think, twenty-seven years. The whole of the time another man had come to the adjoining stall at the same time. At last, one hot summer's day, Mayo's friend resolved not to quit this world without knowing who his neighbour had been. Lifting his voice, he said, "Sir, you and I have sat here with a board between us now for twenty-seven years. May I venture to ask your name?" The only reply was, "Sir, you're a very impertinent fellow."'[108] Well into the twentieth century it has been claimed that the English insistence on eating and drinking in seclusion has rendered inconceivable an English version of café society.[109]

This tendency to compartmentalism was not restricted to tavern life. What distinguished an inn from a public house was its provision of private rooms for sitting, dining, sleeping, and sojourning. When, in the 1780s, the French word 'hotel' was adopted, it was to mark the extension of the notion to an establishment in which not merely men, but women and children, could respectably be accommodated without recourse to weekly or monthly boarding. 'The Englishman brings his home to his hotel,' it has been said. 'It is not a meeting-place, but, quite on the contrary, a place for personal privacy and seclusion.'[110]

Spaces that might have been thought in their nature open to all were not less liable to enclosure. In the verdant squares considered one of London's glories, the gardens themselves were fenced, locked, accessible only to inhabitants, and usually empty. 'England is the country of grills and palissades' concluded Victor Hennequin, in 1844.[111] The historian Michelet was more appalled still to find that in church the Englishman guarded himself and his family with locked pews. 'No pleasure, if not exclusive.'[112]

Even a moving space could be confined. From at least the late seventeenth century the English became expert in devising forms of transport that avoided contact with others. The post-chaise was the envy of Continental travellers for its combination of luxury and speed in seclusion. The stagecoach, for all its technical sophistication in Britain, had to remain a communal enterprise, though one that native reserve could render relatively uncommunal. When rail travel was invented, some thought was devoted to the problem. Harriet Beecher Stowe, used to open carriages in her country, was surprised by the snug compartments found on British railways. 'Every arrangement in travelling is designed to maintain that privacy and reserve which is the dearest and most sacred part of an Englishman's nature. Things are so arranged here that, if a man pleases, he can travel all through England with his family, and keep the circle an unbroken unit, having as little communication with anything outside of it as in his own house.'[113]

The ultimate form of separateness was the home itself, not least because wherever possible, English families lived vertically not horizontally, occupying all the floors of one narrow-fronted house. The arrangement seemed all the odder in that the Palladian fashion of the eighteenth century created townscapes which made vertical living at odds with its architectural aesthetics. The pattern so common in Continental and indeed Scottish towns was quite different. There families would occupy one floor. The very terms to describe such dwellings had to be imported: 'flats' from Scotland, 'apartments' from France.

One explanation was the importance attaching to status in England. It was unthinkable to share the same house with other classes. On the other hand, horizontal living could be socially stratified in the most literal sense, though the preferred stratum might vary from place to place. In northern Italy the first floor or *piano nobile* took precedence; in southern, the very top floor. In Spain it was the second floor. In Edinburgh genteel living took place on an upper floor. The resulting contrast with London generated the well-known story of a Scotsman who refused to change his habits when he moved there. 'He ken vary weel what gentility was, and when he had lived all his life in a sixth story, he was not come to London to live upon the ground.'[114]

In any event, it seemed more sensible to look beyond rank to a deeper instinct, a 'long-cherished principle of separation and retirement, lying at the very foundation of the national character'. This particularly interested Germans, who saw it as exemplifying 'an ancient German tendency'.[115] The Teutonic model had the advantage that it helped explain a crucial feature of the English home, its association with the domestic virtues of women. As the historian of the Anglo-Saxons, John Kemble, put it, the German house had been a holy thing and its mistress an object of reverence. 'Even in the depths of their forests the stern warriors had assigned to her a station which nothing but that deep feeling could have rendered possible: this was the sacred sex, believed to be in nearer communion with divinity than men.'[116] Here was one respect in which Anglo-Saxons seemed to have clung closer to their traditions than other Teutons, given that Germans often had housing that matched the pattern of other Continental peoples. Still more shocking was the way those other Anglo-Saxons, in the great cities of the American seaboard, had abandoned their domesticity. The resort of young American couples to apartments in hotels utterly vitiated the idea of an English home, as even some Americans admitted.[117] In England itself, it was one that continued to inspire all ranks. The industrial working class of the nineteenth century unhesitatingly opted for domestic seclusion and enclosure as it gained in prosperity and accordingly in control of its environment. It took the full weight of central State planning to dent this tradition in the twentieth century, and perhaps then only for a while.[118]

This was believed to be a matter of deep national instinct. Archenholz noted that the English 'prefer the most miserable cottage hired in their own name, to more convenient apartments in another house. The national character is discovered in this very circumstance.' To be a 'house-keeper' was essential to a self-respecting Englishman.[119] The fact that some of the lowest of all Englishmen, travelling showmen, sought to live in a mobile home, furnished down to a door with a suitably imposing knocker, provided further proof of this propensity.[120]

The uniformity of London houses startled many visitors, especially to the extent that it implied 'cellular' living. Ferri di San Costante sarcastically remarked that the English had driven the monks from their land only to create one vast convent of housing cells.[121] The English admitted their distinctiveness in this respect, some of them finding unusual arguments in favour of it. Wellington pointed out that it made revolutionary insurrection highly problematic. 'He did not think the mob would ever be able to pursue with success in this country the same plans as at Paris, *viz*: to get into the houses as soon as the troops charged them in the streets, and fire upon the latter from the windows. The different mode of tenanting the houses, each house generally belonging to a single family, would contribute to this.'[122]

Whatever the cause, the impression of separation was overwhelming, and reinforced by the sight of iron fences, brick walls, and dense hedges. The obsession with enclosure appeared distinctive. 'An Englishman does not seem to be sure that his house will not be claimed by some one else, unless he makes it unlike all others, and puts his name upon it; he cannot be certain that his little plot of land will not escape from under his feet, until he has hemmed it in by a high paling, or a thick impenetrable hedge.'[123] Americans were particularly struck by the English desire for invisibility. William Austin noted the high walls that rendered the Englishman's home his castle in a double sense, and Nathaniel Hawthorne was intrigued that villas had to be positioned out of sight of the road.[124]

Towns, it was observed, oddly permitted far more secrecy than the countryside. 'A country gentleman cannot quarrel with his wife or his eldest son without it being known in a week all over the county.' But urban living was paradoxically secretive. 'Any one so minded may make his house an impenetrable mystery.'[125] In other countries domestic life constantly spilled out into the street. But in London houses were constructed to shut families off from the outside. Not the least of the challenges that the coming of the railways offered concerned this. As Alphonse Esquiros asked, 'Will not a steam-view of London allow us to discover some new phases of English life?' Railroads took no account of traditional street layouts. To be whisked through Whitechapel was to gather countless images of a world invisible by other means, girls fastening their hair, women and children playing together, nurseries in full view.[126] This was not merely male voyeurism. Fanny Lewald made very similar observations. Hurtling along at first-floor level on an elevated line in London she caught glimpses of domestic life such as no foreigner could have gained by other means: a handsome girl with hair unpinned and children playing, a family reading the Bible together, and so on.[127]

The obsession with privacy worried some British travellers who saw alternative lifestyles abroad, even among peoples whose ethnic origins and cultural traditions were comparable. Crabb Robinson, in Germany during the Napoleonic Wars, was intrigued to find families continuing to dine or drink coffee with their doors open. In Hamburg a hall was still a hall, not, as in England, a narrow passage or a large parlour. His belief was that 'our proud love of retirement' was to blame.[128] In France, wrote Archibald Alison a little later, there was indeed no distinction between public and private. 'The first thing that strikes a stranger is, that a Frenchman has *no home*: He lives in the middle of the public.' Alison was especially startled to see his wife and children in a café or restaurant with him.[129]

For their part, foreigners found an English home the most testing of all challenges. Politeness presupposed a certain accessibility to other polite people. This stopped short at the door of the Englishman's castle. It was a frequent source of complaint by foreigners that it was out of the question to call on an Englishman at the dinner hour and expect dinner. Indeed to attempt to do so was a breach of manners. Elsewhere the reverse would have been the case. Not cordially to welcome a chance visitor would have been grossly discourteous. The point gained added force in England because the quality of the dinner table was known to be so high. In Italy it was often difficult to be asked to dine with one's host because dining itself was so rare. The most distinguished of all complainants on this score, Montesquieu, recognized at Genoa that this had to do with the relative poverty of the Italian nobility, not their inhospitality as such.[130] Other comments made about Italy also heightened the distinctive nature of English life. At Naples it was unusual to be invited to a noble home simply because the extended family and numerous dependants of a Neapolitan noble would have made it impossible to provide a polite traveller with a hospitable reception.[131] Men of rank in Britain could offer no such excuse.

The principle applied to all levels of society. Royalty itself was increasingly resistant to intrusion notwithstanding a powerful tradition that treated the court as a form of perpetual exhibition. The English court was relatively inaccessible. Versailles seemed to be swarming with low people who would never have been seen within the precincts of Buckingham House.[132] And at the opposite end of the scale, intrusion was no easier if the home-owner was of humble standing. Pückler-Muskau expected to be able to rush into a cottage for shelter from the rain, but 'In England, everything domestic is held so sacred and inviolable, that a man who enters a room without having cautiously announced himself and begged pardon, instantly excites alarm and displeasure.'[133] In foreign reflections on English life and character this obsessive domesticity featured increasingly largely, as indeed it did in English portrayals of themselves.

DOMESTICITY

The idealization of the home and the consequences for women are well-worn themes among historians of the eighteenth and nineteenth centuries. At the time, foreigners took a lively interest in these matters, though more with a view to assessing the peculiarities of the English mentality than describing the plight of middle-class women. Not that they were uninterested in what would today be called gender relations. Many came to England expecting to find a 'Paradise of Women' and left convinced that this was a considerable exaggeration or distortion of the truth. But there were aspects of family life that struck them as especially revealing of national character. These were the paradox that rendered the

English male a fervent believer in home life yet a hypocritical practitioner of its virtues, the strange combination of material affluence and moral self-satisfaction that ruled in it, and above all the unique sentimentality that was associated with it.

The extent to which the rituals of English life had become home-based, and often impregnated with a spiritual quality, was much noted. An English Christmas was domestic in character not merely by comparison with its Continental counterparts, but also when compared to such celebrations in the United States, where common traditions might have been expected to produce common practices.[134] What the actress Fanny Butler called 'a species of home religion' was neglected in the America that she knew in the mid-nineteenth century. 'In this country I have been mournfully struck with the absence of every thing like this home-clinging. Here are comparatively no observances of tides and times.'[135] On the other hand, festive days that supposed commonality beyond the home were neglected in England. The contrast between New Year's Day in Edinburgh and London was revealing. The Austrian diplomat Philipp von Neumann concluded: 'it proves how little the English feel it necessary to give proof of their good feeling to each other.'[136]

The sentimentality was inescapable to anyone of the merest acquaintance with the English language. The very word 'home', 'that sound of British harmony which vibrates in perfect unison with the best and truest notes of happiness', had an emotional power that was difficult to match elsewhere.[137] The English themselves claimed that no other language recognized it. George Russell, born in a family of legendary English patriotism, was brought up to believe that 'the unhappy, decadent, latin races have not even a word in their language by which to express it, poor things! Home is the secret of our honest, British, Protestant virtues. It is the only nursery of our Anglo-Saxon citizenship.'[138] Used adjectivally, home provided endless assurance of quality. Home-spun, home-bred, home-grown, home-made, home-cooked, all were terms of approval. A rich range of proverbs, some of them of quite mystifying triteness, such as 'Home is home be it never so homely', provided evidence that this was a genuinely popular impulse.[139]

English travellers abroad were confirmed in their attachment by their experience abroad, as Matthew Consett, a pioneering tourist in Lapland, reflected. 'There is something in the very word *Home* that fills us with inexpressible affection. And if, according to the old English Maxim, it be *ever so homely*, still our wants and our wishes center there.'[140] Above all, the metaphorical adaptability of the expression suggested something of its power. Home implied heart, even soul. To have a conviction 'at home' was to be totally committed to something. To strike home, for a swordsman, was to penetrate to the bowels or heart. Commercial exploitation of so rich a range of associations was inevitable. Yet some of it was oddly impressive. The proliferation of self-styled 'home libraries', providing an entire fireside literature at affordable prices might be attributed to the mercenary motives of publishers 'but it possesses a peculiar interest for the moralist'.[141]

Home itself was not a space but an organism that ceased to function if reduced to four walls. The most shocking of all indictments of the factory system was the damage it inflicted in this respect. In the reports on industrial life that found a significant body of foreign readers, the point was much laboured. For Lancashire labourers the home became 'a mere shelter, in which their meals are hastily swallowed, and which offers them repose for the night. It has no endearing recollections which bind it on their memories—no hold upon their imaginations.'[142]

The associations of home tended to multiply under the impact of Victorian sentimentality, acquiring a somewhat 'heimat-like' quality more suggestive of German attitudes. Romanticized memories of childhood, nostalgia for a rural past, and a popular culture that made the theme of 'Home Sweet Home' ever more emphatic yielded ever more sickly invocations. 'Who does not love to recall, and yet more to revisit, Home? The field in which we learned to bat; the pond on which, . . . we made our first uncertain slide; the hedge in which we found our first bird's nest', and so on.[143] The connection between home and country both in its narrow sense as countryside and its broader patriotic sense was not infrequently made. Bonstetten thought it a generically northern phenomenon, explained by climate. Home for a northerner resembled a snail's shell, so vital was it to his existence. To a southerner it had nothing like the same significance.[144]

Yet, despite the patriotic associations of domesticity, foreigners did not generally find it productive of strong government in Britain. De Tocqueville pointed out that 'stay-at-home tastes' worked in favour of localism in both legislation and government, and impeded the growth of the central administration.[145] Ludwig Wolff noted the reluctance of the English to make country and home truly synonymous by resorting to a term such as fatherland, newly coined by Lord Byron but not widely adopted. Something prevented the Englishman from putting the sentimental power of the home at the service of the State.[146] At bottom the home was a focus of emotional loyalty rather than a political weapon. Its public function was moral, as Samuel Smiles insisted. 'The Home is the crystal of society—the nucleus of national character; and from that source, be it pure or tainted, issue the habits, principles and maxim, which govern public as well as private life.'[147]

Faith in the human warmth that home life permitted was recognized as an English phenomenon from at least the mid-eighteenth century, dating perhaps from the vogue of that time for the English novel. Johanna Schopenhauer's husband, in a Danzig threatened by the machinations of the great powers, proposed travelling to England 'to observe more nearly the domestic family life in this land of liberty, as he called it; that if the expected change compelled us to leave, England might, perhaps, be the land of his choice'.[148]

Yet to those who witnessed the English family at close quarters, warmth did not seem its most prominent feature. Sons, especially, enjoyed a depressingly artificial relationship with their parents. 'The very word employed by a child in addressing his father, *sir*, seems to indicate forced respect, rather than affectionate confidence.'[149] Moreover, the English custom of sending sons away from home at the earliest opportunity had long been considered an English aberration. Yet there seemed to be more male attention to very young children than elsewhere, 'men performing the office of nurses and bearing children in their arms'.[150] Chastellux found the same attitude in America: fondness for infants, lack of interest in children.[151] It was the transition to recognizable individuality that marked the hiatus. The result was to some, such as the baron d'Haussez, extraordinarily alienating. The early separation of children and parent, brother and sister created a situation in which members of the same family would have to be introduced to each other as if they were strangers.[152]

International travellers were well placed to observe the independence of an English child. On the road and on shipboard it was common to find children travelling on their own, with a minimum of supervision.

And on home ground they seemed strangely detached. Not that children were oppressed. Most foreigners found them forward and indulged, their parents' governors rather than governed. But such spoiling was neither accompanied by affection nor rewarded by it. Why, it was asked, is there 'such a dread of any display of affection, that, to avoid this, it seems sometimes thought expedient to strangle affection itself'?[153] The answer, it seemed, lay in filial preoccupations with inheritance of wealth, which made any but a calculating relationship between parent and child impossible. This was perhaps why a grandparent's preference for grandchildren over children could only be an English invention. 'The very *thought*', wrote Pückler-Muskau, 'could never have arisen but in an English brain!'[154] Others, such as Mrs Piozzi, thought that the commercialization of British life was creating an unbearable tension between the requirements of business and the demands of the family. Commerce required each one to take a 'separate road'. On the Continent the family was still sufficiently important as an economic unit to sustain its emotional integrity.[155]

Whatever the cause, children were evidently a secondary consideration in point of family feelings. To the extent that it involved real affection it seemed to be about man and wife alone. The emotional power of the English home, observed Guizot, derived from the 'the closeness of the conjugal tie'. Here was a heightened but wholesome affection, the bonding of free men and free women in a land of liberty.[156] So emphatic was English propaganda on this point that foreigners naturally entertained high expectations of English marriage. The iron link of sexuality and domesticity was marked in the novels that were most popular among Continental readers. '"Domesticate yourself," was the advice given to a young woman by Samuel Richardson: "The lovers like to come *home* to a girl."'[157]

The contrast with other societies was also explicitly drawn by English writers. Characteristic was the scene fancied by Constantine Phipps in his account of an English bride having to adapt to a Neapolitan marriage. 'Had she not from her earliest years known and been accustomed to witness pure English domesticity in her parents' abode, she would perhaps have become reconciled to the fond, though inconstant attentions of an Italian husband, and to the undomestic comforts of an Italian *ménage*. Had she not remembered Euston Park—had she not known the uninterrupted union of "wedded love" in England—and had not all her airy castles, her ideal scenes been framed upon a model of English bliss, then might the Countess have resigned herself contentedly to the very *acme* of Neapolitan bliss, that she enjoyed—a palace—wealth—society—consideration—and an adoring husband, *when* it so happened that the Count partook of his beloved wife's society.'[158]

Real-life examples of the damaging effects of removal from the healthy atmosphere of an English home, were sometimes offered by British travellers. For the Anglo-Irish Mrs Trench a visit to Napoleonic France in 1804 confirmed her prejudices when she discovered that even the daughter of an English friend, after a short residence in Paris, had lost the bloom of domestic womanhood. 'I was surprised to see how much less well-looking her pretty daughter is at home than *au bal.* I am sure this is in the air of France; for in London a fine girl is prettier at home, at her ease, in her white dress and in her hair, than ever she is abroad; but this young lady had the lounge, the home-stoop, the loose dress, the big shawl, and the neglected hair, of a French beauty *chez elle.*'[159]

There were naturally alternative perspectives. The rights that women enjoyed before marriage were not at all those they enjoyed within marriage. What resulted was a life of sweet vegetation.[160] Other metaphors could be used. The comtesse de Boigne, who lived as a French émigrée many years in Britain, likened English women to the occupants of a nest rather than a home.[161] Flora Tristan was more brutal. 'English women lead the most arid, monotonous and unhappy existences imaginable . . . Nothing reveals the materialism of English society so well as the state of nullity to which men reduce their wives.'[162]

Determined Anglophiles tried to put the best complexion on this state of affairs. If women seemed so sweetly submissive, it must be because they actually enjoyed great power on their own ground. If this was the only country where women were removed from the presence of men after dinner, it must be because women chose to withdraw from the frivolity and indecency to which wine gave rise.[163] If women seemed to lack the consequence they enjoyed in France might it not be because they had all the leisure and most of the liberty a rational woman could desire? And above all, had they not succeeded in making their husbands slaves to the routines and requirements of a home life?

Representations of the home often made it complementary to the active political life that English men were expected to undertake. It was a place for reflection and rest, wrote the civil servant and poet Henry Taylor. 'Lively talents are too stimulating in a tired man's house, passion is too disturbing.'[164] His formidable contemporary the Duke of Wellington perhaps concurred. 'After all *home* you know is what we must look to at last.'[165] There was a resigned quality to his remark which captured something of the ritualistic inevitability that went with the idea of home for upper-class men. It has indeed been argued that it was precisely the unexciting homeliness of the English gentleman that has made him resistant to Continental ideals of *sprezzatura*, and thereby significantly modified the application of ideals of civility in England.[166]

How true was it that an English husband was an ardent devotee of home life? Legend showed him as delighting in it, by contrast with his neighbours. 'French people have no idea of domestic and rational evenings at home; they would be devoured by *ennui*, were they obliged to endure them.'[167] For the Englishman sexual engagement was inseparable from ideas of home. As Madame de Staël sardonically observed, domestic life was so entrenched in the English character that even adulterers paid tribute to it. A 'kept' woman was a kind of second-rate housewife, set up in a home of her own and visited by her lover when he was excused duty in his first home. There was nothing Bohemian about sexual intrigue in the English manner; indeed it was more moral than marriage in Italy.[168] Those who had to satisfy English prejudices while moving in cosmopolitan circles, for instance Nelson in his relationship with Lady Hamilton, encountered considerable difficulties in consequence.[169]

Scenes of domestic bliss featured husband and wife dining alone. This was a sacred rite at the heart of English life. English travellers who found it wanting in respectable families on the Continent were shocked. Some foreigners concurred. Marc-Auguste Pictet took intense pleasure in 'those charming breakfasts en famille scarcely known outside Great Britain'.[170] Others were less impressed. It could hardly escape notice that the primary purpose of the gentleman's club looked very like escape from the company of women. Certainly that was its effect when Anglomania created a vogue for such clubs in Paris in the 1780s, according to Melchior Grimm, who throve on the salon companionship of fashionable women.[171] As London's clubland expanded in the early nineteenth century it seemed not unreasonable to suppose that the sheer tedium of home must be the obvious reason for its growth.[172]

One oddity of Regency and early Victorian clubs was that with increasingly large and elaborate establishments, they came more and more to resemble a great aristocratic household. When Adolphe Esquiros suggested that it would be easy to take them for noble houses, he was told by an English acquaintance that in effect 'each of these princely residences was occupied, as he said, by a collective Lord'. And when he actually ventured into one of these formidable institutions, he decided that club was in fact a kind of 'home, a domestic sanctuary'.[173]

Esquiros would have had considerable support among his hosts for this standpoint. When Lady Morgan inspected clubland in 1833, she was startled: 'I had a peep at club life,—the Travellers. It is the perfection of domestic life! Every comfort at once suggested and supplied; good reasons for not marrying! Women must get up to this point, or they will only be considered as burthens. Some of the young husbands of the handsomest wives live at their clubs.'[174] Thackeray ironically suggested that it was precisely for married men without a profession that the club should be maintained. 'The continual presence of these in a house cannot be thought, even by the most uxorious of wives, desirable.'[175] Some strange arguments had to be adopted by those defending clubs. It was claimed that they actually reinforced family life by providing an innocuous form of diversion far superior to the vice which had characterized earlier departures from domesticity. 'Clubs are a preparation and not a substitution for domestic life. Compared with the previous system of living, they induce habits of economy, temperance, refinement, regularity, and good order.'[176]

Not less interesting than the ambivalence of the human relationships that centred on the home, were its physical organization and material characteristics. A home, it has been said, has two essentials, a wife and a fire.[177] In contemporary accounts the latter featured as much as the former. Housing might exist without a fireside, a home could not. Domestic heating gave rise to much discussion. Why did the English insist on an open hearth, when an oven would have been so much more efficient? Why did they subject their constitutions to the toxic strain of burning 'fossils'.[178] Was it a puerile delight in wanting to see the flames burning, as Georg Wilhelm Alberti mused, or was the fire in some deeper sense itself a form of company, as Wendeborn speculated.[179]

It is easy to understand how foreigners got the impression they did. An English comedy was not complete without a fireplace and a crackling coal-fire. Moreover, the English themselves seemed to suppose that the fire was either an aid to sociability or even an alternative to it. Viewing Dutch stoves, the pseudonymous English traveller Joseph Marshall reflected on 'the cheerful society of an English fire'.[180] And an English noblewoman visiting Vienna could write 'what is to me hateful, is the want of fires. My mouth waters at the thoughts of a blazing fire.'[181] The fireside defined the communal life of the family, exclusive as well as inclusive. Hence the axiom of English domestic life that a female servant must have her own fire. Sharing the family hearth was a threat to the sexual integrity of the home, 'downright bigamy'.[182]

The coal-fire was often cited to explain features of English life. Moritz thought that the English habit of staring into it accounted for the number of spectacles to be seen.[183] Harriet Beecher Stowe wondered if it explained the longevity of English beauty, especially freshness of complexion and fullness of figure, by comparison with the fading charms of American women. 'Is it the conservative power of sea fogs and coal smoke? Have not our close-heated stove-rooms something to do with it?' She called 'bright coal fires, in grates of polished steel' 'the lares and penates of Old England'.[184]

The fireside came to dictate the very nature of human interaction and intercourse. It had its own laws of precedence, with pride of place accorded host and hostess and strict rules for the disposition of visitors. In its effect on furnishings it had considerable ramifications. As Louis Simond noted, it was the English who changed the arrangement of furniture in a domestic setting, scattering chairs around the middle of rooms and fireplaces. 'Such is the modern fashion of placing furniture, carried to an extreme, as fashions are always, that the apartment of a fashionable house look like an upholsterer's or cabinet-maker's shop.'[185] Many visitors found the resulting lack of symmetry distasteful. The obvious explanation was that the mobility of English furniture could be explained by the need to stay close to a fire. Little nests of tables, portable tables, light chairs, might never have evolved but for the bad heating technology employed by the English.[186]

Demonstrating that there were more efficient ways of heating a home made little difference. English travellers found Continental stoves depressing. If stirring a fire was the particular delight of an Englishman, how could a furnace serve? Such attitudes were challenged by various improvers, the most influential being Count Rumford, a soldier of fortune whose accomplishments included the invention of a stove that combined heating with cooking and threatened to revolutionize the English household to the despair of traditionalists. 'Rumfort, by his *philosophical* chimneys, is likely to destroy the comforts of our fire-sides. When will reformers and sciolists meet with that contempt which they deserve!'[187] Even the most salutary reforms were controversial where fires were concerned. Moving the smoky fires that traditionally dominated the middle of ancient halls to a side wall where they could be provided with a flue as well as a chimney was considered by the Tory Dr Johnson as one of the many Whig innovations that occurred after the Revolution of 1688.[188]

Wherever it might be placed the fireside was what made a social setting 'comfortable'. The idea of comfort was a subject of endless debate both at home and abroad. Part of its patriotic power derived from the claim, generally accepted by their neighbours, that the material well-being of the English was far above anything to be found elsewhere. This belief went back centuries and drew much of its plausibility from the evident prosperity of the peasantry compared with its Continental counterparts. The visible poverty that accompanied industrial and agrarian change from about the 1780s to the 1840s somewhat shook this confidence, though only to the extent of moving the emphasis on to the prosperity of the middle and upper classes. By this time English tourism was rapidly increasing and giving rise to comparisons which made even the most advanced of neighbouring nations seem at least fifty years behind Britain in 'the real conveniences and comforts of life'.[189]

There was no obvious synonym for comfort in other languages, as contemporaries noted.[190] It had to be exported into German and re-exported into French in the course of the eighteenth century. Its colloquial currency signified its power, as approving English-speakers noted on the Continent, when they found that 'the terms comfort and comfortable ... are now pretty common in the social parlance'.[191] Even so it was necessary to see it oneself to understand what the word 'comfort' meant.

Partly it was about a certain robust durability. An English book, for example, possessed characteristic solidity and quality.[192] But there was also a close association with the idea of the home, to the extent that the expression 'home comforts' was considered something of a tautology. Above all, foreigners commented on the quantity and quality of English furnishings. By comparison, other peoples did not seem very interested in the furnishing and decorating of their houses, as the English agreed. 'Properly speaking,' wrote Byron, 'the word comfort could not be applied to anything I ever saw out of England.'[193] The conclusive proof arguably lay in Ireland, where some at least of the landed class had access to the same material goods as their cousins in England. Yet an Irish country house, however cheerful, could not attain 'English exactness and finish', as a visiting American put it.[194]

There were doubters, including other Americans. Fenimore Cooper thought 'the far-famed comfort of England, within doors, owes its existence to the discomfort without'. The 'chilling dreariness of the weather' brought 'the warmth, coal-fires, carpets, and internal arrangements of the dwellings, into what may be truly termed a *high relief*'.[195] The baron d'Haussez was still more withering. '*Comfort* means a heavy, well-stuffed arm-chair in which the master of the house goes to sleep after dinner. You think I jest: no, verily! it is the exact truth. Independently of this chair, there is nothing which justifies the idea of general comfort which the word would seem to indicate. A dinner of boiled fish, and of plain vegetables destined to be mixed by way of sauce with all one eats—a piece of roast beef from the hardest and most tasteless part of the carcass; in place of napkins, a corner of the table-cloth; in lieu of dessert, nuts, cheese, and raisins; chairs with rush bottoms, sometimes covered with a cushion, which the least movement causes to fall to the ground; immense four-post beds, with feather bed, beneath which is a paillasse so arranged as to produce the effect of an ill-joined table—no clocks—and in each room coal-fire, whose dust and smoke soil everything—grooved window-shutters, windows with running Venetian blinds and sometimes ill-draped calico curtains of a dark pattern: these are some of the English comforts, of which the natives of Albion are so boastful.'[196]

The sanctity of the comfortable home was often used to explain the stultifying nature of English sociability. Diderot seized upon it as the key to understanding the difference between the French and other nations. Paris was one great house and Parisians, indeed all French people, one great family. Other cities were collections of houses.[197] No doubt this was why even fashionable French ideas of social organization broke down in London. As William Archer Shee put it, attempts to make salon society work failed because they were incompatible with the privacy of the fireside. The Englishman dined out by appointment and received formal company by appointment, but could not tolerate ease of access to his home. 'He expects to be in the enjoyment of his drawing-room, without fear of interruption from uninvited guests, who deprive him of his nap, disturb him in his perusal of the last new novel, and render the wearing of even a pair of embroidered slippers an indiscretion.'[198]

Arguably it was easier to take the home into society than to take society into the home. The English travelled, it was said, like snails, carrying their home along with them. Washington Irving drew a charming picture of an Englishman in Italy, eating in his own coach a meal prepared by his own servant, and consisting of beefsteak, 'ketchup, and soy, and Cayenne pepper, and Harvey sauce, and a bottle of port wine, from that warehouse the carriage, in which his master seemed desirous of carrying England about the world with him.'[199] And since home was ultimately an abstraction as much as a place it was transportable even by those who lacked such resources, as Fanny Lewald noted. 'In the Parks ordinary families are established as if at home—to "my house is my castle" should be added "wherever I am is my castle"—they sit or lie, reading a book as if they were unobservable at home—they look as if they had no interest in what others think.'[200]

Comfort was much discussed by English observers of Englishness. For Hazlitt it was the corollary of Englishmen's dislike of company. 'They are afraid of interruption and intrusion, and therefore they shut themselves up in in-door enjoyments and by their own firesides ... As they have not a fund of animal spirits and enjoyments in themselves, they cling to external objects for support, and derive solid satisfaction from the ideas of order, cleanliness, plenty, property, and domestic quiet.'[201] For Southey it was far more than creature comfort, as he observed apropos of a typically English invention, the pocket toasting fork. 'It is not for such superfluities that the English are to be envied; it is for their domestic habits.'[202] Foreigners agreed that comfort had implications beyond the material, some of them investing it with an almost mystical significance.[203]

For a nation of restless achievers home life served as an anchor. It sustained people subject to countless risks; actors and actresses, for instance, whose domestic life provided a haven of propriety away from the indecencies of the stage.[204] As a school of character it had a powerful influence on the moulding of men in public life. And for those of humbler ambition, it provided no less valuable training. Reformers drew heavily on this argument. 'There is nothing which so truly marks the character of a community, in a moral point of view, as domestic manners,—nothing which affords so correct a criterion by which a judgment may be formed of its happiness and comfort. Politically speaking, the common people may be a dead letter, whilst their homes exhibit private independence and social enjoyment. Politically speaking, a people may possess many immunities, many rights, may even exercise a very marked control over the actions of their rulers, whilst their homes exhibit social disorganization and moral worthlessness.'[205] Indeed the moral fibre bred in the home featured prominently in reform debates. As Bagehot noted of Bright's advocacy of the household franchise, 'He holds that family life is a sort of guarantee for English sobriety—a notion very dear to the British middle class, but not perhaps very adequately sustained by the testing of experience.'[206]

Matters of national policy could be affected by implications for the home. Debates about emigration touched on sensitive ground here. To send the seedcorn of England's youth abroad was to deny it an English root and incidentally to admit that home had failed it. Choosing between commercial survival abroad and degrading poverty at home was a dilemma explored in much eighteenth-century popular verse.[207] When the pressures to emigrate and the opportunities for emigration reached new levels in the early nineteenth century, it required emphasis on planting new homes and new roots of true English stock to deal with this difficulty.

Even then, something of a balancing act was required. Could colonial society ever quite match the English model? Enthusiasts did their best to assure prospective immigrants that home comforts in the fullest sense were not wanting. Travelling in New South Wales Daniel Tyerman was delighted by life in Sydney: it gave 'the English idea of comfort to the stranger who has long been absent from the only land (perhaps) in which genuine comfort can be found as the pervading *genius loci*, of houses, villages, towns, and great cities—for comfort in England is not merely a fireside companion on a winter evening, but "*a presence*" in which we feel ourselves every day and every where.'[208] In an expanding empire, home building itself became a major preoccupation. Those in no position to settle permanently, such as men in colonial service, received extra marks if they talked of their families, even if in some instances it was an oppressive family that had driven them to the colonies to earn a living.[209]

Home as a quintessentially English concept was a rising stock at the turn of the eighteenth and nineteenth centuries. It was 'that blessed, blessed, essentially English luxury. The Swiss have their mountains, the French their Paris, the English their Home. Happy English!'[210] In truth, domesticity and its attendant values were influential throughout the western world in the early nineteenth century.[211] Yet the very concept remained alien to foreigners, at any rate according to a patriotic Briton like the novelist Marianne Baillie. 'We are coming home, *Home!* that talismanic word, which thrills the heart of every child of Britain, and whose full import can never be comprehended by any foreigner to the soil.'[212]

It could be described in less idolatrous terms. The sagacious Emerson offered a sober judgement of the significance of the home in English life in the 1850s. On the one hand, it was a source of enormous vitality. 'Domesticity is the taproot which enables the nation to branch wide and high. The motive and end of their trade and empire is to guard the independence and privacy of their homes.' At the same time, it promoted a certain narrow patriotism and lack of principle as its concomitants. 'Their political conduct is not decided by general views, but by internal intrigues and personal and family interest. They cannot readily see beyond England.' Even worse were the moral consequences: the English displayed 'truth in private life, untruth in public'. [213] For all its recognition of the vigour derived from domesticity, of 'home-power', this was a serious indictment, threatening that moral aura in which the English had encased their home. It also directly challenged the national reputation for sincerity.

HONESTY

Unhesitating rebuttals of such criticisms were common in the early nineteenth century and no doubt all the commoner as the confidence in
national redemption grew under the impact of the Evangelical Revival.
Victorian high-mindedness could be traced in some instances to a
genuine belief in ethnic morality, often in rather unlikely quarters. John
Stuart Mill was one of those who believed the English a superior nation
in terms of conscience and thereby burdened with a higher duty to take
a moral lead.[214]

At bottom the claim to candour was indeed one to truthfulness. Lying
was thought to be innately un-English, at any rate by the English. When
Bishop Heber decided that American sailors had become less addicted
to lying than formerly he remarked: 'their character seems to have recov-
ered its natural English tone'.[215] If some English people did lie, the easy
explanation was that they were half-castes who had inherited the tendency from the ancient Britons, a different race altogether, and one well
known to Romans for its mendacity.[216] Among the public figures who
most seemed to represent the English spirit the most valued were those
who were most transparently sincere, whatever their other deficiencies.
Spokesmen for the nation were men such as Samuel Whitbread, 'an
epitome of the national character . . . the simple manners, sometimes
abrupt, but always kind,—the sturdy honesty, sometimes rough, but
always consistent,—the shrewd penetration, ever active, but ever
candid,—the boldness of spirit, sometimes violent but always steady;—
which altogether have ever been considered as the infallible marks of a
genuine Englishman.' Whitbread was notoriously plain of garb.[217] And
after him there was John Bright, who had 'an evident sincerity and bluff
bona fides about him, which goes straight to the hearts of Englishmen.'[218]
Every generation had such men, not leaders indeed, for unvarying
honesty and leadership were not expected to go hand in hand, but
beacons that kept the nation true to its traditions and rulers within the
bounds of what it would tolerate.

What, other than a divine gift or genetic inheritance, imbued the
English with such honesty? The obvious answer was an ancient tradition that made personal dishonesty especially liable to censure. Moritz
noted that in England lying was considered a far more serious accusa-

tion than it was in Germany.[219] This seemed to be because so much in English life depended on truthfulness judged by nothing but the reliability of the teller. It did not go without notice that English justice relied on a system of public prosecuting, testifying, and judging.[220] This was an oath-based law, little changed since the times of those Anglo-Saxon invaders who had introduced it. The idea that it was sufficient to make a man swear on the Bible to accept his word was a highly original and English one, as Henri Christophe, the King of Hayti, remarked to William Wilberforce.[221]

Eighteenth-century radicals had high regard for Anglo-Saxon practices that depended on individual pledges of integrity and did their best to reinforce them. William Beckford, as Lord Mayor of London, even proposed a Mansion House oath for guests attending the Lord Mayor's banquet to 'swear to act in public life purely according to dictates of conscience'. It took the intervention of a former Prime Minister, the Marquess of Rockingham, to dissuade him.[222]

There were other points of view, some of them shared by Englishmen. It might be true that as a tool of public policy, in the lawcourt, in politics, and in commerce, testaments of truth had a significance unmatched in Continental societies. On the other hand, a common criticism was that the extraordinary frequency of oaths in England resulted in trivializing them. Oath-taking seemed to have made the English casual about some of their vows. As William Hazlitt remarked, 'The English (it must be owned) are rather a foul-mouthed nation.'[223] From the standpoint of outsiders this was a considerable understatement. Why, it was asked, could an Englishman not get through a sentence without swearing? Common English greetings seemed to consist of nothing but oaths. Foreign audiences were provided with suitably colourful specimens of an encounter in daily life.

'Damn ye I am glad to see you!'
'Dam ye, you dog! how do you do?'
'You son of a whore, where have you been?'[224]

Such cursing was not solely a plebeian custom. Gentlemen were as prone to profanity as their inferiors. It was embarrassing for the English to find that Mr Godam was a standard French characterization of an Englishman. 'Pauvre Jean Bull, pauvre Godem.'[225] Even the Duke of

Wellington was so described.[226] Anglophile foreigners did their best to imitate such models, increasingly outdated, with incongruous results. Shortly after the Napoleonic Wars, Grantley Berkeley met Frenchmen using phrases such as 'Damn my eyes' and, at dinner, 'Damn my eyes, sud you have some of dis.'[227] The young Henry Fox found similar obsolescence in Naples in 1825. 'Many of the Neapolitan men I have seen, such as Prince Petralla, Juliano, Letitia and others, have an anglomanie about their horses, carriages and dress, and mean to be very idiomatic in talking the language by the frequent use of "*damme, dammed*" and "*God dam*".'[228] By this time, in Britain itself, there had occurred a considerable revulsion against genteel cursing, which made traditionalists stand out as increasingly eccentric, as the poet-civil servant Henry Taylor remarked. 'That the surviving majority of the gentlemen brought up in the last century should have contrived to get rid of such habits in the first half of this, is more surprising than that some of them, like Lord Melbourne and the Duke of Wellington, should have failed to do so.'[229]

Oaths were not the whole of the story. Some insisted that the English genuinely did possess high standards of personal morality and that evidence to the contrary merely indicated heightened sensitivity in such matters. When State scandals were at issue this convenient argument was much employed. The uproar occasioned by the Duke of York's alleged sale of army offices in 1809 led Lord Muncaster to reflect that 'the people of England were always affected by whatever appeared to be immoral. Even vicious people in this Country, respected moral conduct.'[230] It was admitted that this propensity might involve the sacrifice of more agreeable qualities. As the artist Joseph Farington put it in 1802: 'if there is less of what is called the *Amiable*, it is amply made up by a quality of a much higher kind, which is *integrity*. That is a word which the English may apply to their Character by the consent of the whole world more universally than any other Nation that exists in it.'[231]

Integrity helped explain the worldly success of the British, the outstanding example being the superior business morality of English merchants, tradesmen, and shopkeepers. This was not merely a matter of self-congratulation. The good faith of the English businessman was widely attested. Alessandro Verri, who spent time in both London and Paris, thought the merchants of the former infinitely more to be trusted.[232] Contemporary commercial practices had much to do with this. The tendency in Britain was for formally sealed documents to give way to verbal or informal contracts for many purposes.[233] The courts, for all their conservatism, adapted readily to this trend. If the Englishman's word was his bond, it was partly because bonds themselves were becoming such inconvenient devices in the hurry and rapidity of commercial transactions. Connections were also made with the English dislike of wasting time. If customers were to be attracted in the mass, it was essential to avoid unnecessary haggling. Bargaining, as many foreigners noted with surprise, was uncommon. A child could shop as confidently as the most street-wise market shopper.[234]

This trait possessed particular interest because it was not considered an inevitable concomitant of commercial vitality. The traditional prejudices of courts, nobles, and churches took it for granted that people preoccupied with the making of money could not be expected to maintain high standards of probity. A great chain of authority from Aristotle downwards could be cited to endorse this supposition. Nor did the Reformation break it, even in Protestant countries. There were successful commercial cultures which were considered grasping, mercenary, and corrupt even by other Protestants. Dutch and Scottish Calvinists were often so described. English stock in an un-English environment also fell under this heading. New Englanders had an unenviable reputation for sharp commercial practice, not least with French commentators.[235] This rapidly extended itself to all American merchants, and after American independence to all 'Yankees', especially of the lower sort. No doubt it was particularly convenient that the British should see their former compatriots and present rivals as below contempt, especially when they came under the scrutiny of naval parties searching for contraband. 'To lie like an American captain' became something of a proverb during the Napoleonic Wars.[236]

Even those well-disposed to America were shocked by its cynicism in this respect. The republican and dissenter Thomas Russell, in Philadelphia in 1795, reported: 'Here a man may break his word with impunity, and may without disgrace flagrantly violate those established customs, the infringement of which would in England irretrievably ruin his character. He may have been two or three times a bankrupt and be known to have defrauded his creditors, and if he thereby reacquires considerable wealth, he will nevertheless be received in the first company. In short, as wealth is the darling object of their attention, so a person with that needs no other letter of recommendation.'[237]

The lack of shame that attended bankruptcy in America was reinforced by a species of national vanity invented there, according to Charles Dickens, who called it 'the national love of "doing" a man in any bargain or matter of business.' Dickens's interest in the introduction of an international copyright law hardly made him an impartial authority on this point, but it certainly lent acerbity to his analysis. 'The raven hasn't more joy in eating a stolen piece of meat, than the American in reading the English book which he gets for nothing.'[238] The countervailing emphasis in England on consistency of reputation was often noted by visitors. As Prosper Mérimée observed. 'The English have the custom of showing the greatest trust in everyone possessing a character, that is to say recommended by a gentleman; but they do not give a character lightly: whoever obtains one is careful not to lose it, for he cannot regain it.'[239]

It was not only trade that made possible national comparisons of this kind. The most prevalent of all social pastimes, gaming, also did so. Italians appeared at the bottom of the resulting league table. Tourists found it shocking that in Italy it was necessary to use leather or ivory tokens for gambling because even high society could not be trusted to handle cash.[240] Belief in fair play was assumed to be one of the prime characteristics of an English aristocracy that made it acceptable and even appealing to its inferiors. A cheating lord was a class traitor as a result.[241] All ranks were supposed to share this horror of foul play, though one or two foreigners professed to have seen evidence of trickery in London for all the Englishman's vaunted sense of honour.[242] The usual verdict was that a high standard of honesty obtained even where the circumstances seemed unpromising. The vulgarity of a race-meeting hardly suggested respectability and integrity, yet as Count Kielmansegge reported in 1757, 'An Englishman, who would have no compunction about taking in his neighbours in other things, will never be found a defaulter in this respect; such bets are much too sacred for him not to act with the utmost sincerity in their settlement, as his credit depends upon this.'[243]

Some feared that economic progress threatened this presumed integrity. As with most English virtues, there was a certain 'Old Englishness' about it that made successive generations aware of a deterioration in standards while none the less sure that they remained superior to those of other nationalities. Such anxieties became sharper as the economy expanded and paper money multiplied in the late eighteenth century. The singer Michael Kelly claimed that in Italy, where he spent a portion of his youth, the honour of an Englishman had been proverbial, to the extent that 'if two Italians were making a bargain, it was clinched by one saying, "I pledge myself to do so and so on the honour of an Englishman."' By the time he wrote his memoirs, in the 1820s, he thought this was far from being the case.[244]

Later, by the time of the Great Exhibition, it was possible for a German visitor to be dismayed by the cynicism of shopkeepers, though even he noted the exception of those 'who after a period of years sell their business with its customers, a usage which has existed for more than a hundred years among the English bourgeoisie'.[245] The English themselves could always blame the conveniently reprehensible influence of Americans. Fanny Kemble believed that 'their speculating mania and rage for rapid money-making has infected our slow and sure and steady-going mercantile community. The plodding thrift and scrupulous integrity and long-winded patient industry of our business men of the last century are out of fashion in these "giddy-paced" times, and England is forgetting that those who make haste to be rich can hardly avoid much temptation and some sin.'[246]

On the whole it is surprising how rarely the English reputation for honest dealing was challenged. That is not to say that related accusations were not made. One concerned the matter of consistency. In English self-appraisals consistency, steadiness, solidity figured very largely. But on the Continent there was a tradition of scepticism on this point. Fickleness and inconstancy were synonymous with Englishness. Numerous examples of bad faith were dredged from Tudor times, much of it associated with the prevarications of Elizabeth I in her dealings with Spain.[247] The sufferings of the Stuarts at the hands of their people also figured prominently. A standard text was Bossuet's funeral sermon on Henrietta Maria, which dwelled on the faithlessness of the English over two centuries of shifting belief. Bossuet was careful not to blame racial origins, if only because, as he put it, they were ultimately descended from Gauls, and successive injections of Mercian, Danish, and Saxon blood could not have so corrupted the good sense implanted in them by their predecessors. Instead he blamed the spirit of disputation which had rendered them easy victims of the wickedness of successive Protestant governments.[248]

The successive revolutions of the seventeenth century merely reinforced such claims. To hear of yet another coup d'état was to remind oneself that this after all was a nation of king-makers and king-killers. As Marie de Rabutin-Chantal remarked in 1688 on learning that the Prince of Orange had been elected king eight days after reports directly to the contrary, 'mais ce sont les Anglois'.[249] But it was Reformation rather than Revolution that did the most damage. Fickleness in religion remained a recurrent Catholic charge against the English. The English dissenting tradition could be portrayed as cynical time-serving rather than principled toleration. English sects changed their divinity, like the Japanese, whenever misfortune shook their flimsy faith.[250] It was a Jansenist joke that the Jesuits had been driven from England not because they were hated, but because 'rivalry in deceit would have been too strong and too dangerous for its inhabitants'.[251]

Such mockery was all the more effective in that it coincided with an English self-assessment that remained current until the mid-eighteenth century. 'The fickle and inconstant temper of the English nation' was often admitted in a spirit of tempered pride, in that it went with libertarian instincts. Freedom and unpredictability were two sides of the same coin.[252] Thereafter, it dropped out of patriotic discourse. By this time Britons were engaged in recurrent warfare for commerce, empire, and status, and there were dangers to conceding fickleness as a national characteristic. It was after all uncomfortably close to admitting disloyalty to friends, unreliability in battles, and irresoluteness in defence.

Foreigners did not necessarily share this shift of perception. On the contrary, they built on the older view. The Prussians exploited it when they accused Britain of abandoning Frederick II during the Seven Years War. The French resorted to it whenever the propaganda requirements of war and diplomacy made it useful. Eventually, they coined the term that has remained common currency ever since, 'perfidious Albion'. Such challenges to the place of principle and integrity in the make-up of the English from time to time stirred uneasy feelings in England itself. Were they, after all, a nation of deceivers, and was their self-conscious high-mindedness merely hypocrisy, the tribute that vice paid to virtue?

HUMBUG

Hypocrisy, or as it colloquially became known at the end of the eighteenth century, humbug, was in fact increasingly an English concern. The word itself had a certain fascination for foreigners, though it sometimes gave rise to confusion. Madame de Staël caused amusement in London when she called it 'hugbum'.[253] There were in any case other ways of describing it. 'Gammon', from backgammon, gained currency from the 1820s. But the polite term was cant, the use of which had somewhat lapsed in the course of the eighteenth century but revived thereafter. Cant was often traced back to the Puritan moralizing of the seventeenth century. It seemed easy to relate its recurrence a hundred and fifty years later to the new Puritanism of the Evangelicals. But there was a common assumption that it represented an entrenched English characteristic, even if the vigour with which it flourished depended somewhat on circumstance. Continental commentators were scathing on this subject. Typical was the judgement of the German V. A. Huber, who set out to investigate English universities and found them riddled with what he called 'this mixture of hypocrisy and self-deception, of not seeing and not choosing to see; [it] is a part of that principle, with which English life is so thoroughly imbued, a characteristic of its own, for which the English language alone has supplied the appropriate term, CANT. It is a characteristic feature, we say, of the national physiognomy, which, in spite of all that is excellent and admirable about it, one cannot but see.'[254] This was not an exclusively foreign perception. As Byron put it, cant was an English obsession stronger even than cunt.[255]

The charitably inclined assumed that this arose from a commendable horror of hyprocrisy. Washington Irving spoke of the 'national antipathy' to anything that savoured of it, and his countryman Emerson called terror of humbug the ruling passion of Englishmen.[256] A less generous judgement might have been that humbug was more characteristic than terror of it and that Englishmen had good reason to fear something which had become all too typically English. It was the celebrated London hostess Lady Jersey who remarked in December 1839 'The fact is though I never say so that We are essentially a hypocritical nation. We are not only so but We like hypocrites and hypocrisy.'[257] As Lady St Julians in Disraeli's

Coningsby and *Sybil* she was given numerous opportunities to display her cynicism in print.

It seemed no coincidence that fictitious hypocrites exercised a hold on the national imagination. Perhaps the most famous of all these was the villain of *Nicholas Nickleby*, Pecksniff. Dickens's friend and biographer Forster went out of his way to defend his friend's creation. 'The confession is not encouraging to national pride, but this character is so far English, that though our countrymen as a rule are by no means Pecksniffs, the ruling weakness is to countenance and encourage the race. When people call the character exaggerated, and protest that the lines are too broad to deceive any one, they only refuse, naturally enough, to sanction in a book what half their lives is passed in tolerating if not in worshipping.' On the other hand, Forster took comfort from the fact that if France had no Pecksniffs it was because Frenchmen had ceased even to pretend to virtue, and quoted Taine in support. 'No principles being left to parade, the only chance for the French modern Tartuffe is to confess and exaggerate weaknesses. We seem to have something of an advantage here. We require at least that the respectable homage of vice to virtue should not be omitted.'[258] This defence, that only a nation of exceptional integrity could be so concerned by those who preached it without practising it, savoured of desperation but was often resorted to.

It was true enough, no doubt, that attempts to promote higher standards also promoted greater hypocrisy. A classic case was that of Sabbatarianism, a favourite cause of puritans throughout the ages. It seemed peculiar to visitors that London's day of devotion and abstention should be associated with promenading in Hyde Park for the upper class, gorging beef and pudding at Sunday lunch for the middle class, and drunkenness in suburban taverns for the lower class. It also struck them as extraordinary that Sunday newspapers were the most licentious of all. Yet it was quite logical that this should be so. Publishing newspapers on Sunday had long been discouraged, by opinion if not by law. When publishers plucked up courage to break this embargo in the 1770s, they larded their news-sheets with, as a French observer put it, 'truly English and frigid reflections' on various vices.[259] Before long this became an excuse for mere parading of salacious stories. The result was that the Sunday reader more than the weekday reader could be guaranteed a prurient pleasure, and 'Fathers of families, who would have thought their daughters' minds poisoned if they had casually at a theatre listened to a coarse expression of Shakespeare, systematically submitted to their inspection a paper teeming with the grossest allusions and the most flimsily-veiled *double entendres*.[260] At the height of the Evangelical Revival, between the 1790s and 1820s, the vulgar Sunday newspaper established itself as part of English life, despite attempts to legislate it out of existence.[261] Nor did it go unnoticed that when it suited even devout Sabbatarians to depart from their devoutness, they did so. In the Peninsular War Napoleon's troops hoped that fighting on Sunday would give them an advantage against English Protestants. Unfortunately, the English 'gloriously broke the Sabbath'.[262]

The semantics with which moral lapses could be shrouded, especially where class was concerned, also seemed indefensible. 'An adulterous intercourse in low life is an unfortunate partiality in high life.'[263] Clarissa's defiler Lovelace could only have been an Englishman, it was said, an observation which provoked the retort that the marquis de Sade could only have been a Frenchman.[264] Law, like language, was granted a morally cleansing function that struck outsiders as implausible. Amédée Pichot was amused by the miraculous effect of a wedding, which could make the most notorious slut a respectable woman. 'Such an occurrence is looked upon here as a sort of civil baptism, which washes away the original stain. Why should this sacrament have more virtue in England than in France? When a woman of equivocal character gets married here, her husband is said to make an *honest woman* of her: this phrase, you know, occurs in the Vicar of Wakefield.'[265]

Such defences of cant as were attempted emphasized the peculiar features of English society. Lord Normanby pointed out that in a country whose social conglomerations were often voluntary and sometimes ephemeral, rivalry naturally expressed itself in a heightened form of boasting. 'Go successively into an hundred different societies, and you will find established an hundred species of cant, each laughing at the idol of the other.'[266] Hazlitt thought hypocrisy very rare. Cant was something different, a desire to be thought better than we are. 'Cant is the voluntary overcharging or prolongation of a real sentiment.'[267]

Above all, there was the horror of social failure, which dictated conformity to all kinds of conventions and opinions. A commercial code of values made impressing or alternatively disappointing other people a matter of social importance. When every rank aspired beyond its station the result could not but be unnatural and hypocritical behaviour. Mrs Piozzi noted the striking contrast in this respect between Britons touring Italy and the society that acted host to them. 'No man in this country pretends either to tenderness or to indifference, when he feels no diposition to be indifferent or tender; and so removed are they from all affectation of sensibility or of refinement, that when a conceited Englishman starts back in pretended rapture from a Raphael he has perhaps little taste for, it is difficult to persuade these sincerer people that his transports are possibly put on, only to deceive some of his countrymen who stand by, and who, if he took no notice of so fine a picture, would laugh, and say he had been throwing his time away, without making even the common and necessary improvements expected from every gentleman who travels through Italy; yet surely it is a choice delight to live where the everlasting scourge held over London and Bath, of *what* will they think? and *what* will they say? has no existence.'[268]

The charge of hypocrisy went deeper than such petty snobberies and insecurities. It brought into question one of the most treasured of English values, consistency and dependability of character. Emerson thought this the true point of the ineradicable national anxiety about humbug. 'In the same proportion, they value honesty, stoutness, and adherence to your own. They like a man committed to his objects. They hate the French, as frivolous; they hate the Irish, as aimless; they hate the German, as professors.' An Englishman would even curb his own prejudices confronted by an opponent who stuck resolutely to his. An example was the mob's liking for the reactionary Eldon, on the grounds that he was no trimmer. 'Loyalty is the English sub-religion.'[269] The value that England attached to tradition and its status as a standard-bearer of stability in a world of reform and revolution reinforced this notion. 'Immutability seems to attach itself to everything that this nation does' observed a French tourist in 1821.[270]

The stout-hearted loyalty of an Englishman was a patriotic article of faith. Only a few heretics questioned it. It embarrassed some military experts who were aware that English troops had a propensity to desert, though not, fortunately, under fire. Wellington put this down precisely to fickleness and love of comfort: 'they liked being dry and under cover. And then, that extraordinary caprice which always pervades the English Character!'[271]

Empire as well as war made some wonder about English stoutness. In the American Revolution it was English stock that had rebelled. Some of this could be put down to the Puritan origins of American society. The betrayers of Charles I were unlikely to breed good subjects of George III. This link between Puritan hypocrisy and political treachery was a favourite theme of opponents of American independence. The belief of many, including George III, that Americans were devious and hypocritical, stemmed from the assumption that they retained the morals and manners of the Puritan forebears.[272] The War of 1812 reinforced this impression, particularly when it found Americans claiming English sailors as their nationals and using them against their own country. They must be 'the most perfidious Boasting Cowardly Men in the Universe'.[273] On the other hand, some of those who compared different strains of Anglo-Saxon stock thought that of the mother country less impressive than some of its colonists. Trollope was struck by the superior loyalty of Australians. English people, he thought, had a vague belief in English government and institutions, but no such deep-seated fidelity to their country.[274]

Politics provided the richest of all fields of inquiry. Charges of hypocrisy ironically gained credence from the very circumstances that made the English seem less unstable and unpredictable. The Revolution of 1688 eventually brought constitutional stability in its wake. This should have put paid to accusations of fickleness. That it did not could be put down to what seemed rather the institutionalization of fickleness. The English had not lost their waywardness, they had merely ensured that their rulers must follow them without endangering the fabric of national life. Whatever the public desired must be implemented, or at least publicly accepted, even if the implementation was likely to be unsatisfactory.

The effect was strikingly new in the eighteenth century, though later familiar in democratic politics. In all kinds of situations British governments were not only behaving badly, something that could be expected from any government, but defending their conduct in terms that condemned their own subjects. Not only did the nature of a parliamentary system expose English rulers to the charge of inconsistency, it made the inconsistency national rather than personal. For Frederick II to accuse his English allies of treachery would seem to be effrontery of the highest order. But the difference was that his changes of front could be seen as those of an absolute prince, whereas those of his ally were those of an entire nation. When Frederick betrayed his allies, nobody blamed the German character. When Queen Anne, or George III, did so, there were many indeed who blamed the English nation. Foreign monarchs came close to sympathizing with their opposite numbers in Britain on this account. There was a French view, for instance, that George II was a civilized and honourable statesman. If only he had the powers in England that he had in Hanover, dealing with the British would have been a simple matter. Popular politics imposed a barbarism which only absolute rule could control.[275]

Explaining the unpredictability of an English mob was a perennial problem that could be traced back centuries. But that a Parliament of gentlemen generated hypocrisy in those who had to answer to it was unsettling. Ironically, accomplished deceivers were rewarded for their sleight of hand with the respect of their audience, whereas less practised charlatans were condemned not for their ineptitude but their hypocrisy. Part of Castlereagh's unpopularity derived from the fact that he felt compelled to hold two quite different languages, one to Parliament and another to the Continental powers, without successfully deceiving either. His rival George Canning was less maladroit in this respect. Canning's Private Secretary Lord Edward Bentinck claimed after his death that there was documentary evidence of letters written specifically 'to throw dust in the eyes of the Parliament'. Not only did this mislead MPs, it caused considerable confusion among foreign statesmen, including the legendary Metternich, a man not easily confused.[276]

The famed accountability of the English, especially of English politicians, had evidently created a fatal gap between public and private morality. The comtesse de Boigne was startled when the Prime Minister, Lord Liverpool, objected to her bribing a little dog with meat to lure it back when it escaped beneath the dinner table, for fear of 'spoiling its morals'. 'No one can conceive, except by actual experience, how far in English opinion the private life of an individual can be separated from his life as a statesman. The one will refuse indignantly to countenance any step which can in the smallest degree hurt the most delicate feelings, while the other will unhesitatingly pursue the most Machiavellian policy and disturb the peace of nations, if any chance of profit for old England may result. The hand with which Lord Liverpool checked mine when I would betray the little dog was bold enough to sign the treaty to the cession of Parga, at the risk of the resulting tragedy.'[277]

The Countess was in good English, or perhaps Scottish company. Carlyle spent his life waging war on cant, the acceptance of moral, political, and religious doctrines which had submerged the natural sincerity of the English character, sacrificing duty to right and responsibility to liberty. His heroes were Frederick II and Cromwell, because both warred with a hypocrisy in others which had no part in their own make-up. Gladstone, whose moralizing necessarily belonged in the dishonesty of parliamentary politics, was another matter.[278]

These concerns are inseparable from consensual politics. But there exists a long tradition of analysis that ultimately blames national character for the unpredictable and contradictory actions forced on England's leaders by its whimsical people. Media managers who might have been accused of exacerbating this process, blamed those they were accused of manipulating. It was an English journalist, Cyrus Redding, who observed that 'The English people are remarkable in their public conduct for moving by fits and starts. They will race after every game that accident presents upon all occasions, ride it down, wear it out, and then turn to another seven days' wonder for a fresh folly.'[279]

Even twentieth-century authorities have persisted in identifying a specifically national tendency. The American historian of the English press seeks explanations for the 'traditional lack of openness in British politics.' One French historian quoting another can still cite the English as the 'most candid and the most hypocritical'.[280] A German historian identifies 'a primitive conception of the undifferentiated will; which is at the bottom of the cant which the foreigner has always noted as his special characteristic'. This undifferentiated will went back to the primitive belief of the Anglo-Saxon peasant, that as tiller of the soil he was not only pursuing his own interest but sustaining the community. The English concept of common sense precisely embodied this confusion between morality and self-interest. More sophisticated, less insular societies succeeded in distinguishing the two.[281] Englishness would not be Englishness without its inherent taint of ancient barbarity.

CHAPTER THREE

DECENCY

BARBARITY

*O*NE of the prejudices that the English encountered on their Continental travels was an irritating assumption that they were latecomers in the history of European civility. This was the basis for diagnosing a variety of faults, or vestiges of barbarism, in the national make-up. Some, such as 'roughness of manners' and 'want of taste', were taken to be remediable. Others were more problematic, suggesting moral weakness, even depravity. The most disturbing was said to be a tendency to disproportionate and gratuitous violence. Disowning such violence was a high priority for those who defended the character of the Englishman. This was not always easy. In England itself there was a patriotic tradition of glorying in this reputation. In the 1690s the Huguenot Misson remarked 'Any Thing that looks like Fighting is delicious to an Englishman.'[1] Nearly two centuries later, the Victorian Lord John Manners could still insist that fighting was 'the natural occupation of Englishmen', and something not to be sacrificed to the arts of peace.[2]

French opinion, which in a Francophone European culture was difficult to confute, held that the English were by nature cruel and heartless. A neat couplet expressed the conventional wisdom, linking the atrocious enormity of the regicide to the casual cruelty of the peasant.

> Oh barbares Anglois, dont les cruels couteaux
> Coupent le tête aux rois, et la queue aux chevaux[3]

Neither the docking of horses' tails nor the decapitation of kings was in reality a uniquely English practice, but various kinds of evidence could be cited by way of corroboration. Complaints of the cruelty of English warriors, both by land and sea, were long-standing. Belief in the addiction of English authorities to harsh physical punishment also had a lengthy history. And, not least, there was the well-known brutality of the lower class, expressed in numerous ways, and scrutinized by foreign visitors.

Much of the inhumanity of English war-making could be explained away as natural and even legitimate for an island people. It was cruel only because others had not found it necessary. Privateering, the obvious means of combat for a seafaring nation confronting the superior might of its oceanic neighbours, had led to numerous complaints during Elizabeth's war against Spain, by no means all of it from Spaniards. In the seventeenth century it became common practice, and in the eighteenth a normal accompaniment to commercial and colonial wars, involving every seaboard state of western Europe. Britain's interpretation of the rules of maritime warfare continued to be controversial, provoking Leagues of Armed Neutrality during the War of American Independence and the Napoleonic Wars, and contributing to the outbreak of the Anglo-American War of 1812. But by then the debate had become one of legal technicalities, few disputing that trade was a legitimate target for warring parties.

The alleged cruelty of the English warrior seems to have had more to do with his rare appearances on the Continent in the sixteenth and seventeenth centuries than with a proven record of brutality. To the extent that atrocities were laid at the door of any nationalities, it was newcomers from the eastern rather than the western fringe of civilized Europe,

notably Hungarians and Croats, who in successive conflicts from the
Thirty Years War onwards acquired a name for ruthlessness. On the
other hand, enough of the older prejudice against English troops
remained for patriotic Englishmen to insist on their humanity as characteristic.[4] In particular they proclaimed themselves masters of 'the art of
bringing men to the ground without absolutely killing them'.[5] Yet few
would have wanted to deny that an Englishman armed was an implacable foe. The safest option seemed to be to concede that magnanimity
was late in coming but all the more complete when it came. This was
Hazlitt's judgement: 'The character of English generosity is not sufficiently understood. It only begins to operate when all power of resistance
on the part of an enemy ceases.'[6] Some even thought that it resulted in
excessive indulgence. 'England's false generosity oftentimes proves detri-
mental to her real interests.'[7]

   Treatment of civilians was the decisive test of humanity in the military.
The findings, both at home and abroad, changed over the years. In its
infant phase under Charles II and James II the English regular army had
a grim reputation among its own people. No doubt some of this stemmed
from its use by popish monarchs in furtherance of unpopular causes, but
the complaints that inundated the Privy Council from the localities where
garrisons were stationed are too circumstantial to leave room for doubt.
In terms of ethnic virtue, the only comfort seems to have been that Irish
and Scottish troops employed by the Stuarts had an even worse name
than their English hosts.[8] After the Revolution of 1688 the standing army
gradually shook off its reputation for lawlessness, mainly, one suspects,
because Parliament instituted an effective regime for procuring quarters
and supplies, the two traditional sources of conflict between civilian and
military.

   In the eighteenth century the worst accusations concerned the behaviour of English forces not within England itself but still within the British
Isles. Two rebellions gave rise to them, those of Scottish Jacobites in 1745
and Irish Jacobins in 1798. For the brutal suppression of the former, it
was convenient to blame the German-born Duke of Cumberland, the
'Butcher of Culloden'. Yet the carnage that followed Culloden was
approved by many English generals and politicians, convinced that they
were extirpating at best a sinister popish rebellion, at worst a race of
savages, 'barbarians, enemies to all civil society'.[9] Others succeeded in

dissociating themselves altogether. A legend grew up around Wolfe, who later fell heroically and victoriously at Quebec, to the effect that he had been ordered directly by Cumberland to shoot a wounded rebel on the battlefield but had refused to do so.

In the case of Ireland shifting responsibility to another nationality was trickier, though when Scots were involved they attracted a disproportionate share of opprobrium. It was a maxim of the English military that while both Scottish and Irish troops had admirable qualities, they were not displayed when the two came into contact, whether they were serving together in a British force or pitted against each other in Ireland. The fact that in Ireland as in Scotland rebellion was in the nature of civil war as much as civil uprising made it easier to confuse the issue of ethnic guilt. The Irish militia in 1798 were not less hated than the rest of the loyalist army. Cornwallis, the Viceroy whose job it was to stabilize the situation, was accused of undue favour to Irish rebels against loyal Irishmen as much as the reverse, for instance when he showed his anger with a jury exonerating a Protestant who had shot a pardoned rebel in cold blood.[10]

Recent history was cited in support of English humanity, though not without a certain awkwardness at times. One of the longer visits to the Continent by a British army occurred during the Peninsular War of 1809–13. At the height of this conflict in 1813 Wellington publicly informed his troops that 'discipline had deteriorated during the campaign, in a greater degree than he had ever witnessed, or ever read of in any army'.[11] It was argued in defence that the main sufferers had been a considerable number of Spanish pigs and that Wellington's concern was with the unreliability of regimental officers rather than with the brutality of their charges. His, and his country's, enemies put a different gloss on the affair.

None the less, Continental opinion was inclining to the view that a British occupation was less brutal than most of the alternatives. English troops were rarely accused of plunder. Marlborough's army on the Danube march of 1704, which culminated in the victory of Blenheim, made military history not least by winning 'the goodwill of the local inhabitants because the soldiers paid their way'.[12] During the Seven Years War the British Commissariat in Germany acquired a reputation for reliability without parallel among Continental armies. And when the

French population was itself exposed to invasion by an English army, the same that Wellington had commanded in Spain, it was startled to receive payment for its produce.[13]

There was apparently something about the English serving man that was less intimidating than his Continental counterparts. The Allied occupation of France at the conclusion of the Napoleonic Wars provided numerous examples, all the more interesting because the French were used to occupying rather than being occupied and the novel experience lent a certain piquancy to their revision of old assumptions.

Some of the credit that English forces gained at this time derived from the contrast with the Prussian troops that served alongside them. In retrospect the comparison seems less than fair. Franco-Prussian enmity already had a history, and there were many on duty in Paris in 1815 who could recall what Napoleonic forces had done to Berlin in 1807. Even so, it was claimed that fundamentally different attitudes could be seen among the occupying nationalities. In a quarrel with a native Frenchman the Prussian was likely to draw his sabre, the Briton to lay aside his weapons and put up his fists.

Stories of Gallic surprise and appreciation abounded. The journalist Cyrus Redding provided one. 'The populace showed their feeling towards the Prussians most unequivocally; and blood would have been shed but for the activity and incessant watchfulness of the police in keeping order. One specimen of John Bullism I cannot forget. An English dragoon, on guard at his officer's quarters near the Place de la Pucelle, was insulted by a carter smacking his whip at him, under the idea that the soldier could not move from his post. Depositing his sword and gloves in the sentry-box, the dragoon went up to the fellow, and gave him a severe drubbing with his fists, and then resumed his duty. The people wondered he did not punish the affront with the flat of his sabre. The story flew all over the city. The boys came up, squaring their fists in a ludicrous way, "Vous boxie, Monsieur Anglais."'[14] Ironically, when opinion did turn against the British it was because the Allied commanders employed them for sensitive operations in which it was deemed unwise to let the Prussians loose. One of the most difficult was the crowd-control required when the horses of St Mark's, plundered by Bonaparte in 1798 and restored to Venice in 1815, were removed from the Place du

Carrousel. Nobody alleged misbehaviour by officers or men, but mere
association with so unpopular an act of retribution was sufficient to cause
a revulsion of popular opinion.[15]

Improving the image of the martial Englishman was made easier by
explaining the legal and social framework in which the armed forces
operated. Foreigners who had the opportunity to observe the English in
their native habitat were intrigued, given the success of British arms
around the world. The dislike of standing armies, the role of a citizen
militia, above all the system of law which put a soldier on the same footing
as a civilian, these seemed highly distinctive. Some of the most telling
anecdotes were those that revealed the way professional warriors not only
accepted these constraints but gloried in them, as part of their own tradition. It seemed strange to see a line of troops, marching in formation
on the streets of London, step aside to let civilians pass.[16] Such deference would have been unthinkable in Paris or Berlin. And where were
the off-duty uniforms that were so visible in the cafés and on the streets
of other European cities? No sooner did an English officer return from
barracks to London than he donned the regulation costume of an ordinary gentleman.[17] There were admittedly surges of militarism in British
life, particularly during the wars which followed the English Revolution
of 1688 and the French of 1789. But these were not sustained and not
comparable with what could be witnessed on the Continent, where the
prominence, status, and influence of the military were of a different order.
In no European capital of any size was civil society as civil as it was in
London.

This emerging picture of a domesticated military was far from earlier
images of bloodthirsty barbarians. What had not been lost, however, was
belief in insular bravery. In fact some, like the Baron Pöllnitz, thought it
was 'sturdiness in battle' rather than savagery that instilled fear.[18] Hazlitt
offered an ingenious elaboration of this argument. Cruelty was precisely
not what characterized English courage. 'I think the reason why the
English are the bravest nation on earth is, that the thought of blood or a
delight in cruelty is not the chief excitement with them. Where it is, there
is necessarily a *reaction*; for though it may add to our eagerness and
savage ferocity in inflicting wounds, it does not enable us to endure them
with greater patience. The English are led to the attack or sustain it
equally well, because they fight as they box, not out of malice, but to show

pluck and manhood. *Fair play and old England for ever!* This is the only bravery that will stand the test.'[19]

None the less, common impressions of English life fitted with the confusion of bravery and brutality. Beef-eating came under close scrutiny. Philosophers argued that meat-eating peoples were naturally cruel. The Tartars, who did not cook their victuals at all, were 'the very hardiest of men'.[20] Thomas Jefferson opined, 'it must be the quantity of animal food eaten by the English, which renders their character unsusceptible of civilization. I suspect that it is in their kitchen, and not in their churches, that their reformation must be worked, and that missionaries from hence would avail more than those who should endeavour to tame them by precepts of religion or philosophy.'[21]

Before Jefferson's time, assumptions about religious practices had in fact strengthened such claims. Flesh eaters, it was said, with Protestant confidence, would always beat the Lenten men.[22] Sir William Temple noted how Prince Maurice of Orange had called 'for the *English* that were newly come over, and had (as he said) their own Beef in their Bellies, for any bold and desperate Action'. Temple himself considered that it was probably a deterioration in diet that explained the decline of Dutch courage, a phenomenon much noticed in the late seventeenth century.[23] The difficulty here was that they were believed to have preserved their cruelty while losing their bravery.[24] In fact Dutch brutality was a favourite English stereotype, generated by the rivalries of the seventeenth century, and revived when commerce and empire expanded into South Africa and the East Indies. The British empire saw itself as teaching Dutch colonists something of its own humanity.[25]

When English abolitionists drew up comparative tables of slave treatment in the late eighteenth century, Dutch planters were accorded the place of dishonour as the most callous of masters. Unfortunately, third parties often awarded it to the English themselves. The conventional French view was Diderot's, that they owned 'the unhappiest of slaves. The Englishman, tyranny's foe at home, is the most ferocious despot abroad.'[26] Americans of the half-century that followed independence often agreed, rolling a range of domestic and foreign activities into one overwhelming indictment. 'If you wish to learn their real character, look at their bloody code of laws, read their wars with Wales, with Scotland and with Ireland. Look at India and their own West India Islands.'[27]

Great interest attached to corporal punishment. Diverse peoples were puzzled by the English liking for it. The Chinese, for instance, were shocked by 'too much flog' and 'too much fight'.[28] Campaigns to abolish flogging in the armed forces, commenced during the Napoleonic Wars, attracted much attention outside Britain. What seemed astonishing was not the vigour with which it was employed but the discovery that there were so many Britons prepared to endure it. Corporal punishment seemed not to be thought degrading in the way it was elsewhere, though its educational use was not uncontroversial. Flogging was a recurrent theme in criticisms of public schooling throughout the eighteenth and nineteenth centuries and condemned by some distinguished victims well-placed in later life to influence opinion at home and abroad. Not all of them were known for their liberal views. Southey, who had been expelled from Westminster for his indiscretions in a magazine entitled the *Flagellant*, never retracted his criticisms. Significantly, his target had not been the cruelty of the master so much as the ethos of violence to which it gave rise, 'till the hall of learning becomes only a seminary for brutality'.[29]

That violence was endemic seemed to be demonstrated by the fact that even aristocrats took it in their stride. Heinrich Heine claimed to have seen jockies lashing gentlemen out of the way, and lords cudgelled without any loss of face.[30] This is not easy to credit but it belongs with a rich fund of stories about English gentlemen who were content to submit to plebeian chastisement. The favourite among such anecdotes concerned the fourth Duke of Bedford, who on a famous occasion was said to have been horse-whipped at a race-meeting. There was some truth in the story in that Bedford had been attacked by a Jacobite mob at Lichfield in 1747. Foreigners found it extraordinary that Bedford went on to hold numerous offices of state, and even to appear as British ambassador at Versailles. What other country could bear the thought of being represented at the capital of courtesy by a nobleman who had permitted himself to be publicly humiliated in this way?[31]

Tales of this sort reflected interest in an aristocratic caste that was prepared to pay for its rule by accepting correction from its inferiors. The nobleman who exposed himself to the 'humours of an election', or engaged in fisticuffs on the streets of Tom and Jerry's London, was a stock subject for the satirist. But such images also had a bearing on the national propensity to 'barbarous' practices. For if the English aristocrat was somewhat brutalized by his commerce with the English plebeian, perhaps the English plebeian was somewhat civilized by his commerce with the English aristocrat.

Certainly this was a standard explanation of features of English crime that were otherwise difficult to understand. Tyburn and the grisly code of capital punishment that it symbolized could be displayed as part of a culture of gruesome but paradoxical physicality. Foreigners were shocked by the spectacle of an execution, which seemed rather to resemble a carnival of death than a solemn exaction of civil penance. On the other hand, they were impressed by a legal process that presumed innocence rather than guilt and took pains to ensure that only the guilty suffered. 'Must you not conclude with me,' enquired the abbé Coyer, 'that humanity dwells among this People?'[32] Here was a curious mixture of civility and brutishness, both in those who exercised authority and those who suffered under it.

The English criminal was credited with a certain sense of generosity and chivalry, at any rate by comparison with his brethren elsewhere. The favourite example was the 'gentleman of the road', 'le gentilhomme de grand chemin'.[33] Why were highwaymen so cruel in France and so genteel in England? It was a subject much debated. One explanation was that the efficiency of the French police prevented such men from mingling in society, turning them into outlaws who dwelled brutishly in forests and wastes. In England it was possible, so to speak, to be a part-time brigand, even a gentleman. The upper class was as immoral as the lower but less cruel. Its manners might rub off on the most unlikely material. This was the duc de Lévis' thoroughly aristocratic (and French) view.[34]

The English themselves were at least as fascinated by the doings of the genteel highwayman as their visitors, but generally attributed it to a deep-seated humanity. Even the English footpad, it was said, was rarely the murderous thug that he would have been on the Continent. Defoe described an '*English* way of Robbing generously, *as* they called it, without Murthering or Wounding'.[35] But this was not an exclusively English view. Visitors found robbers less cruel than what they endured at home.[36] Some believed that chivalry was truly at the core of the most humble Englishman. Quarrelsome as he might seem, in his quarrels there was always a generosity at work. 'A bloody Nose, or black Eye, are usually the worst Consequence of a Fray among the inferior Sort.'[37] And horrid and barbarous though the Gordon Riots undoubtedly were, no woman had been molested. The most drunken and abandoned of the rioters had not threatened the female sex, even when they were known to be of the Catholic faith.[38]

Something had to be done about brute creation in England, however. Gratuitous cruelty seemed a distressing feature of the native attitude towards animal life. This was a source of embarrassment to self-consciously civilized Englishmen. Steele devoted an issue of his *Guardian* to the subject, quoting Montaigne to the effect that the English liked watching animals fight but not play: 'I am sorry this Temper is become almost a distinguishing Character of our own Nation'.[39] The native addiction to cock-fighting, bear-baiting, and bull-baiting provided obvious examples. These were time-honoured recreations which many considered an ingrained part of English life. They were still being staunchly defended well into the nineteenth century. Others were so barbaric that they found fewer defenders. Pitiless slaughter, such as the duck-hunt on the Serpentine, which set water spaniels on captive birds with pinned wings, was not calculated to give tourists a refined picture of the Londoner's amusements.[40]

Cruelty to animals was a target for the gathering sensibility of the eighteenth century. Few of the arguments deployed were new, but the wide measure of acceptance that they achieved was.[41] A national Society for the Protection of Animals and formal legislation against diverse forms of cruelty had to wait until the nineteenth century, and it has been claimed that 'the connection between Englishness and kindness to animals was forged' during the early years of the Society's existence, in the 1830s.[42] This perhaps underrates the growing desire to establish such a connection earlier. Public debate and pressure were considerable by the 1760s and 1770s, as numerous foreigners observed. Assessments of the results varied. Alberti thought the English kind to animals, his countryman Wendeborn the opposite.[43] What all agreed was that in Britain the moral climate was increasingly unfavourable to their exploitation and ill-treatment. Foreigners were naturally influenced by the resulting preoccupations. A recurrent theme was mistreatment of the huge herds of cattle that were marched long distances to the capital and then, with increasing visibility, through the crowded streets of the City. Visitors had not noticed it in the early eighteenth century, but they frequently did so when it was becoming a cause for concern to enlightened opinion in London in the last decades of the century.[44]

Like most fashionable commodities sensibility did not recognize national frontiers. English travellers and journals found much to condemn in the way foreigners abused their fellow creatures, repaying with interest the moral superiority which the French expended on English cruelty. A plausible riposte was that in Britain there seemed to be more concern with suffering animals than with suffering people. Adolphe Blanqui pointed out that this was after all the country that favoured hulks for prisoners and flogging for free subjects.[45] The most magnificently extravagant of such attacks on English hypocrisy was that of René-Martin Pillet, a French general imprisoned in Britain during the Napoleonic Wars. He took revenge on his captors by listing the inhumanities that he claimed to have witnessed there. In fact most of them seem to have been his version of sensational items reported in the press, suggesting that if nothing else the much abused prisoner of war had enjoyed a ready supply of London newspapers. They ranged from widespread parricide and infanticide, via systematic abortion in young ladies' academies, to the brutal vivisection of animals by children in the streets.[46] Pillet's book gave rise to a minor diplomatic crisis between the British and French governments, demonstrating if nothing else that the old image of what its author called 'a naturally cruel nation' remained in the collective European memory.

By this time, the context for such judgements had been transformed by the French Revolution. Older analyses of the relative civility of the different nationalities of Europe had clung fast to one certainty, that Frenchmen as a race were the standard-bearers of European civility, in this matter of everyday human decency, as in others. The traditional image of the English was steadily revised between the middle of the seventeenth and the middle of the eighteenth centuries but it did not shift this assumption. There was, it was thought, an underlying quality of forbearance, even softness, that marked Gallic civilization. No French frondeur was capable of the beastliness of an English leveller, no Parisian to be likened to a Londoner. During the initial stages of the Revolution, this fund of ancient wisdom and self-restraint apparently stood the French in good stead. As late as July 1791, when the Birmingham Church and King mobs appalled even their sympathizers by their brutal assaults on reformers and dissenters, the contrast held good.[47] As the Prussian musician Johann Friedrich Reichardt noted, it was remarkable, that after centuries of absolute rule, and in the turmoil of revolution, the French had not resorted to the barbarities of the peasants' war in Germany or the cruelties of the Civil Wars in England.[48]

Reichardt made this remark, unhappily for his own reputation, in 1792, shortly before the September Massacres. If anything could put paid to the notion of innate French non-violence, it was this. The shock inflicted on the European mind by the Terror makes sense only against this background. Similar events in St Petersburg, or Prague, or even Naples, would have had nothing like the same effect. One of the tenets of contemporary civilization had been shattered by the nation that had been its unchallenged exemplar.

The new barbarity of the Frenchman at the very least suggested the wisdom of re-examining the old barbarity of the Englishman. Grand Tourists had traditionally been impressed by the manners of Parisians. After the Revolution they came expecting to find them offensive, as Lady Brownlow noted. 'Often have I driven through excited English mobs, but they were mild and amiable in their appearance when compared with the ferocious demeanour of these French specimens, who were apparently capable of any atrocity.'[49] Thereafter it was all too easy to associate any sign of plebeian resentment with malignant aggression. As Charles Henningsen put it, to observe the look on the face of a Parisian artisan as the carriage of a capitalist passed him on the street, was to 'be tempted to imagine that you saw one of that pitiless multitude who, in the saturnalia of oppression overthrown, tore the Princess of Lamballe limb from limb'.[50]

FAIR PLAY

Controlling the innate violence of the English moved steadily up the domestic agenda in the eighteenth and nineteenth centuries.[51] The cult of sportsmanship is often located within a project to distance genteel lifestyles from vulgar.[52] But its early advocates seem to have been more concerned with limiting plebeian boisterousness than with snobbery as such. Michel Angelo, the champion of sportsmanship in hockey in 1776, made the connection very clearly. 'There is a wide difference in *merely* playing this game, and playing it genteely. Some boys are of such an eager, warm disposition, that they care not whom they hurt, or whose skin they break, so that they get at the kockey; but this is the mark of a bad player. A right sportsman is always cool, and ready to take any advantage that offers, without having recourse to unfair proceedings. This may be done without much violence, or any hurt. I have played at this game for half a day together, without giving or receiving the least cause for complaint.'[53] Making 'sportsmanship' a national rather than an aristocratic asset did much to define a distinctive English civility.

Continental interest in the physical recreations of the English, especially the English lower class, was long-standing. At least until the mid-seventeenth century the tendency was to assume that they constituted yet more evidence of a race barely emerged from barbarism. Foreigners were dismayed by their brutishness. They attributed love of barbarous sports to the permanent impact of Roman rule, or to the enduring taste of a Germanic people for its ancient pastimes.[54] In Continental societies such energy had either been refined into *fêtes champêtres* fit for a seigneurial audience or diverted into competitions of marksmanship serving the military needs of the State. Spontaneous combat of the kind witnessed at a Cornish parish wake or indeed on the streets of London must be a survival of pure Gothicism. Its most obvious feature seemed an inherited delight in disorder. Wrestling and boxing revealed the Englishman's addiction to mindless brawling; football was merely an excuse for breaking windows and coach glasses, 'very troublesome and insolent', as the Swiss Muralt put it in 1726.[55]

Voltaire did not say a great deal on this subject but what he did say transformed the way in which it was viewed. English pugilism was 'a species of honour not known in any other part of the world'.[56] By the late eighteenth century foreigners seem to have found it obligatory to describe a boxing match, whether the impromptu kind to be witnessed on the streets or the more organized variety categorized as 'prize-fighting'. In either case the emphasis was on strict adherence to unspoken and unwritten rules, binding competitors and spectators in recognition of the necessity of fair play. This was a peculiarly English rite, and one as fascinating to the English themselves as to their guests. It changed. By the time of Pierce Egan's 'Fancy', in the early nineteenth century, boxing had become highly commercialized, featuring national championships, mass audiences, and sensational publicity. Even so, it remained received wisdom that it was in essence a superior form of lower-class duelling, wise, humane, philosophical.[57]

The laws of honour were the common inheritance of Christian Europe. Their continuing appeal at a time of rapid change is intriguing. It is possible to view the phenomenon as evidence of sustained aristocratic hegemony in the commercial states of western Europe. Yet it depended on the desire of bourgois families to ape the social customs of their betters.[58] To this extent the duel survived by virtue not of its aristocratic lineage but its egalitarian potential. Fighting, in theory at least, was permitted only between equals. To offer a challenge was to assert one's parity with the challenged. To refuse a challenge was to deny such parity; unfortunately it was also to run the risk of being thought a coward. The resulting conflict of feelings could be experienced at all levels of British society, regardless of the weapons employed. As a schoolboy, James Stephen was advised by his friends to refuse the challenge of a pugilistic gardener's labourer, just as a gentleman would take a horse-whip to an inferior rather than suffer the shame of duelling with him. But in a society in which it was increasingly difficult to distinguish social frontiers miscalculation and disrepute were obvious dangers. In fact Stephen insisted on fighting his plebeian challenger, just as numerous noblemen recognized the necessity of duelling with marginal gentlemen.[59]

This delicate balance between social pretensions and egalitarian tendencies rested on the assumption that the rules of honour had the assent of all classes. There was general agreement that Continental Europe offered no parallel. Where plebeian systems of honour did seem to prevail regardless of Church and State, as in Italy and Spain, they were associated with inherited tribal enmities, a vengeful mentality, and brutally underhand forms of combat. An English traveller in Sicily could be guaranteed to delight in the manly morality even of his humblest countrymen when confronted with the horrors of the vendetta.

Gratifying though it might be to reflect on the superiority of English honour, it was not easy to prove that it went with ethnicity. Successive generations of travellers testified to the failure of emigrating Englishmen to take it with them across the Atlantic. Rank bad sportsmanship was one of the commonest complaints about Americans; for them, winning the game was what mattered, playing it not at all. Various reasons were assigned, the most common the prejudices of their Puritan ancestors, those pious opponents of the Book of Sports, who had shunned ungodly amusements in their native country and fled to one where they could avoid them all together. In fact ball games had a continuous history in New England, but within a framework of communal earnestness and discipline, making them rather a variety of business than recreation.[60] The theory went that the American tradition of sport evolved in a spirit quite foreign to English ways, as a cynically mercenary form of competition in which the manner of winning counted for nothing.[61]

Yet there seemed to be more to this than ancient denominational prejudices. The American South boasted English genteel manners but not English plebeian honour. Observing a quarrel that developed at the races in Virginia in the 1820s, Basil Hall noted a significant divergence from English custom.

In merry England, 'a ring! a ring!' would have been vociferated by a hundred mouths—seconds would have stepped forward—fair play would have been insisted upon—and the whole affair finally adjusted in four or five minutes. One or other of the combatants might have got a sound drubbing, and both would certainly have been improved in manners, for the remainder of that day at least. It was quite differently settled, however, on this occasion. Several persons rushed out of the crowd, and instead of making them fight it out manfully, separated the disputants by force, who, nevertheless, continued abusing one another outrageously. Not content with this, each of the high contending parties, having collected a circle of auditors round him, delivered a course of lectures on the merits of the quarrel, till, instead of a single pair of brawlers, there were at least a dozen couples, interchanging oaths and scurillity in the highest style of seaport eloquence.[62]

Hall was considered by Americans a hostile witness, but numerous travellers commented on the strange codes of conduct that characterized low life across the Atlantic, especially in the south. The descendants of the English in the slave states of America were notorious for their gouging, butting, and kicking, all practices which would have been banned by an English mob. In a travesty of sporting admiration of honourable competition, to be 'a fine gouger' was high praise in the back country.[63] This became a sensitive point for republican patriots. In 1794 the geographer Jedidiah Morse associated the practice with the tyrannical nature of imperial government and claimed, rather prematurely, that since Independence it had largely been eradicated. 'How quick, under a mild government, is the reformation of manners.'[64] Others blamed the native inhabitants of the Continent for infecting European newcomers with their bestial ways. The cruel and implacable spirit of the Kentuckians in particular was attributed to their living among Indians.[65] More objective observers had their doubts. As Charles Janson put it, 'these barbarities appear not to have been the genuine growth of American soil. No such practices would have been endured by an English mob; no such disgraceful revenge ever entered the breasts of a Creek, a Cherokee, or a Kicapoo Indian.'[66] In fact Indians seemed to possess a sense of sportsmanship which resembled that of home-bred Englishmen. Their liking for ball games suggested that they might even have something to teach the public schools of England.[67]

Removing the lower-class Englishman from his own environment evidently had the effect of loosening his moral moorings. In Australia a strong case was made for encouraging cricket as 'the *one* truly game of England' on precisely these grounds.[68] In Canada, where American and British influences overlapped and often collided, codes of sporting conduct proved hard to reconcile. Schoolteachers found themselves having to cope with tactics euphemistically described as 'American realism with regard to competitive athletics', while teaching the traditional fairness enjoined by 'British moral theory'.[69] In both Australia and Canada there remained sufficient loyalty to English institutions and traditions to provide relative immunity to the supposed cynicism of American life.

Assuming that the English did possess a plebeian code of honour, what did contemporaries seek to conclude from it? First, though it might flourish only under genteel influence, it was not a mere imitation of chivalry or aristocratic honour, but a deeply entrenched ethic with its origins in national character. It derived from custom not instruction. The rules of honour were the rules of English children, as numerous newcomers recorded, many of them from other parts of the British Isles. The memoirs of the mariner John Nicol include a revealing tale of his experience as a youth transplanted from his native Scotland to London. 'Once, in passing near the Tower, I saw a dead monkey floating in the river. I had not seen above two or three in my life. I thought it of great value. I stripped at once, and swam in for it. An English boy, who wished it like-wise, but who either would or could not swim, seized it when I landed, saying, "He would fight me for it." We were much of a size; had there been a greater difference, I was not of a temper to be easily wronged; so I gave him battle. A crowd gathered, and formed a ring. Stranger as I was, I got fair play. After a severe context, I came off victor. The English boy shook hands, and said, "Scotchman, you have won it." I had fought naked as I came out of the water, so I put on my clothes, and carried off the prize in triumph—came home, and got a beating from my father, for fighting, and staying my message; but the monkey's skin repaid me for all my vexations.'[70] Stories of this kind occur frequently in the autobiographies of young Britons, as well as in the reports of foreign visitors.

From this instinctive or at least early imbibed faith in the rule of law derived a pronounced belief, at its best high principle, at its worst priggishness, in 'fairness'. Everyone from the lord to the coachman seemed to know 'what is fair', remarked Henri Meister in 1790.[71] Institutions, especially those that could be traced back to the juridical legacy of the Anglo-Saxons, might both express and reinforce this sense of natural justice, but they did not create it. Moreover, fairness was a collective concept, either subsuming or overriding all other values and principles. By the first quarter of the nineteenth century, the Englishman's most celebrated achievement, the British Constitution, was thought incomprehensible if not viewed in this light. Remarking on the parliamentary code that permitted outgoing ministers to spend three days vilifying their opponents and then advise the Queen to summon them, Trollope remarked 'There is nothing like it in any other country,—nothing as yet. Nowhere else is there the same good-humoured, affectionate, prize-fighting ferocity in politics.' America might possess similar institutions, but it lacked the same spirit. 'There the same political enmity exists, but the political enmity produces private hatred.'[72]

The public itself, wrote Hazlitt, could be envisaged as 'the most tremendous ring that ever was formed to see fair play between man and man'.[73] Earlier commentators, particularly those from the absolute monarchies of Europe, had emphasized English libertarianism and individualism; now 'fair play' provided a framework of social consensus which made it easier to distance the Englishman from the abstract doctrines of rights that flourished in an age of revolutions. It also explained his divergence from the less abstract but equally alien individualism of his transatlantic cousins. The American was unrestrained by anyone or anything, the Frenchman restrained by governments which became more despotic the more democratic they seemed. The Englishman obeyed his inner sense of what other Englishmen would tolerate. This was a tightly textured community, unrent by Revolution and unravelled by migration. Fair play was not merely a rigid adherence to rules, a mechanical adjustment to the requirements of social living. It was the expression of a deep devotion to communal activity. The characteristics to which it gave rise were the essence of Englishness.

First among these was magnanimity. The English were proud of their lack of vindictiveness. 'No man is more remote than an Englishman from the doggedness of long-lasting, and indelible revenge', it was said in 1655. 'England is the onley Indies where this bottomless Mine of pure Gold is to be found.'[74] Again this was traced back to childhood, as the artist Joseph Farington, a century and a half later, noted. 'An Englishman learns from His Youth to depend upon His unarmed personal valour, and to spare His antagonist when conquered and at his mercy.'[75] Even the most degraded shared in this quality, as was claimed on behalf of the convicts of New South Wales. 'Such are the noble principles and habits which the Government of free and merry England engenders, even in the lowest of her sons, that with all their faults, *magnanimity of soul is an essential part of their nature.*'[76]

The implications went beyond national pride. For the English the most savage war seemed a kind of patriotic game. Perhaps this explained their lack of interest in their own history, despite its richness. Other nations were thought to have a stronger sense of their past identity. All Italians remembered their distant Roman and Renaissance greatness.[77] Where national grievances were concerned, the contrast was still more striking. The American sense of injustice, accompanied by a vivid recollection of their sufferings, contrasted with British ignorance of their own past, both rights and wrongs. It was Hall again who wrote, 'I never could convince them that such vindictive retrospections, which it is the avowed pride and delight of America to keep alive in their pristine asperity, were entirely foreign to the national character of the English, and inconsistent with that hearty John Bull spirit, which teaches them to forget all about a quarrel, great or small, the moment the fight is over, and they have shaken hands with their enemy in testimony of such compact.'[78] Similar reflections were customary when relations with Ireland were considered. For Irishmen the wrongs of the past were ineradicable, but for the English forgetting and forgiving must be synonymous.

There were obvious rejoinders. For one thing, there was a sense in which the English did not seem neglectful of their past. On the contrary, they appeared incapable of conceiving of their rights and liberties without treating them as history. Moreover, what they chose to forget of their own doings in America and Ireland might take on a different complexion if they had experienced it in their own land at the hands of others. Yet England was a much conquered country. Perhaps magnanimity had been learned from successive humiliations under successive waves of invaders? These were difficult questions to adjudicate. What seemed incontrovertible was that the English propensity for 'shaking hands and making up' was a prized part of the national psyche. If self-congratulation on the subject of Britain's relatively painless withdrawal from empire is any guide, it is as firmly lodged in the collective consciousness of the late twentieth century as it was in that of the late eighteenth.

Magnanimity is expressed by the victor. But fair play is not only about the manner of victory, it is about the nature of the game itself. The underlying human quality, of which magnanimity is only one expression, is something more comprehensive. In the English self-portrait it is good nature. This was not a new discovery but it certainly received growing attention from foreigners. They had not noticed much of it in the sixteenth and seventeeth centuries. Moreover, even its English champions tended to admit that it had to be sought below the surface. Arbuthnot's John Bull was 'choleric', as indeed was his contemporary Sir Roger De Coverley. Bad temper and good nature are not obvious bedfellows. It took some effort to give the latter the leading place in the Englishman's make-up.

If any individual put English good nature firmly in the treasure-chest of European virtues, it was probably Henry Fielding. Many educated visitors to Britain of the middle and late eighteenth century had read him in one form or another, and came expecting to find eccentrically lovable and benevolent Englishmen. Thereafter there was no stopping the literary stereotype. From the Vicar of Wakefield to Mr Pickwick, and no doubt beyond, he was a universal favourite. Foreigners were fascinated by 'good nature'. Only a few dared to challenge its English provenance, Rousseau predictably one of them. In *Émile*, he remarked that the English called themselves good-natured but nobody repeated it after them.[79]

Many saw in the philanthropic activities of Britons a practical expression of this instinctive feeling. It was noted that they took especial pride in the epithet of 'the generous nation'.[80] Public subscription as the basis for financing all kinds of charitable activity was considered a characteristically English invention, depending as it did on the free and voluntary participation of the ordinary citizen. Much ink was spilled on its unique merits and also on its implications for assessing English virtues. There was, however, an alternative view, popular with Anglophobes, to the effect that English benevolence was yet another form of English ostentation, and that the object of a public subscription was self-advertisement.[81] The fact that like many other public activities it seemed inseparable from gluttony did not improve matters. 'The new subscriber returns home more than half tipsy, to swear at his servants, beat his children, make his wife unhappy, and congratulate himself on his growing humanity.'[82] Nor was this merely a matter of printed subscription lists in the newspapers and names read out at a charity dinner. It seemed shocking that the walls of English churches were decorated with the trumpeted philanthropy of local families.[83]

Perhaps there was still something to be learned from the lay orders of Catholic Europe, which required 'personal modest work. There are no names in newspapers, no orders, no public distinction to be acquired. Every one helps unknown, unseen, and lost in the multitude, and not with money, which is often little valued, but with personal expense of rest and comfort.'[84] It was pointed out by way of rejoinder that as many as one-seventh of publicized donations in Britain were in fact anonymous.[85] Even so, modesty and anonymity did not sound very English to a

Continental ear. What could be done to make them flourish in an insular setting?

PROPRIETY

Fair play, magnanimity, good nature; these reinforced, and perhaps required, a deeply rooted moral sense. At the very least, fairness provided a framework of discipline within which common humanity could express itself. But the way in which this system worked also had about it an aesthetic quality. It concerned what was 'fitting', 'suitable', 'appropriate', in the sense of taste as well as virtue. Propriety and decorum were preeminently English characteristics, to be witnessed in many settings. As Fenimore Cooper put it, 'England is a country of proprieties. Were I required to select a single word that should come nearest to the national peculiarities, it would be this. It pervades society from its summit to its base, essentially affecting appearances when it affects nothing else. It enters into the religion, morals, politics, the dwelling, the dress, the equipages, the habits, and one may say, all the opinions of the nation.'[86]

Public life at its highest levels was expected to conform to this priority, and was generally judged to do so. The dignity of Parliament by contrast with the assemblies of other nations struck many commentators. The House of Lords was decorous to the point of dullness. Lord Grey likened a debate there to 'speaking to dead men by torchlight'.[87] The Commons was scarcely less dignified. When the French acquired comparable institutions during the Revolution, it was predictable that an aristocratic Briton like the Earl of Mornington would be shocked by the manner in which they conducted debate and made laws.[88] But even a republican enthusiast could find Westminster superior. 'Accustomed as I was to the tumult of our National Assembly,' wrote Henri Meister, visiting London, 'you may judge if I was not surprised to find in the House of Commons such decency, solemnity, and silence.'[89] Radical Francophiles who travelled in the opposite direction were dismayed. Martha Russell, daughter of Joseph Priestley's friend William Russell, found nothing but noise, confusion, and vulgarity among these new rulers of a nation famed for its politeness. 'In short, the whole scene excited in my breast a degree of disappointment, disgust, and astonishment scarcely to be imagined.'[90] English visitors to America were not much more impressed. Daughters of the Mother of Parliaments the legislatures of the United States might be, but they had not inherited its maternal dignity.[91]

The majesty of English law also owed much to this sense of decency. London's lawcourts, an obligatory sight for tourists not bent on mere recreation, were admired for the good order that prevailed in them. But where English law was practised by others it significantly lost this quality. Travelling in Ireland, Sir John Carr was intrigued by the atmosphere which obtained in the courts there. They had good humour, familiarity, even justice, but not decorum. This was a national trait. The Irish were incapable of solemnity.[92] So, it seemed, were Americans. The English traveller Thomas Hamilton, observing a trial in New York, remarked that 'No one seemed to think, that any particular decorum of deportment was demanded by the solemnity of the court.'[93]

The same applied in less weighty manners. English dress sense lacked flair and panache but it had a kind of solidity. Understatement, unobtrusiveness, uniformity, were its hallmarks, at any rate by the late eighteenth century, partly because male dress itself became markedly more sombre, partly because the French Revolution made the sartorial gulf seem even wider. The artist Joseph Farington, who, like many other Britons, used the Peace of Amiens to obtain a first-hand impression of what the Revolution had done for the Frenchman, decided that it had released the full force of his characteristic exhibitionism. All sense of station and status had gone. 'The word propriety must not be thought of in France.'[94]

This inborn propriety was something of a discovery. The traditional image of the English was of excess and exhibitionism. Decorum in dress had been for others, above all for grave Spaniards and Italians. The English and their admirers were aware that there had been a shift in this respect. They recalled well-established literary images: Gervase Markham describing 'an ordinary tapster in his silk stockings, garters deep fringed with gold lace, the rest of his apparel suitable, with cloak lined with velvet'; Thomas Nash, deriding 'England, the players' stage of gorgeous attire, the ape of all nations' superfluities, the continual masquer in outlandish habilaments'. From the standpoint of the early nineteenth-century traditionalist Washington Irving this seemed remote indeed. 'John Bull was then a gay cavalier, with a sword by his side and a feather in his cap; but he is now a plodding citizen, in snuff-coloured coat and gaiters.'[95]

A new conservatism in dress was a more obviously, if not exclusively, male than female tendency. But women, too, in other ways contributed to the evolving image. A certain kind of womanliness was claimed as a peculiarly English achievement. As Cooper, an American conscious of his Old World inheritance, put it, 'There is a softness, an innocence, a feminine sweetness, and expression of the womanly virtues, in the Anglo-Saxon female countenance, that is met with only as an exception in the rest of Christendom.'[96] But it was not only men who lauded English women. Maria Williams, the republican authoress who exiled herself to France during the Revolutionary Wars, thought the verdict universal. 'An English woman!—that appellation of which the heart is proud!—Yes—on the continent of Europe, amidst all the bitter and rancorous feelings excited by long hostility with England, the name of English woman, connected with the idea of pre-eminence in every milder virtue, the attribute of her sex, of that exalted observance of every domestic duty which arises from purity of soul, from sensibilities chastened and corrected by all the unvarying habitudes of modest rectitude, "the thousand decencies that daily flow from all her words and actions,"—the name of English woman is never pronounced by foreigners without an emotion of esteem, compared to which all other homage is degradation.'[97]

The decency of Englishwomen had much to do with sexual mores. It was not only visitors from sun-drenched lands of love who were struck by insular idiosyncrasy in this respect. Englishness passed into the German language as a synonym for prudishness, as the visiting Englishman Henry Crabb Robinson was intrigued to discover. 'Englanderei', he recorded, was 'what we should call puritanism in language and excess of delicacy in matters of physical love.'[98] Foreign authors could expect to have their works sanitized for an English readership.[99] Tourists came to England expecting to be chilled, or even to be excited, by the sexual frigidity of Englishwomen.[100] This seems not to have been a matter for comment before the late seventeenth century, though from that time there was increasing interest in it.

Sociability itself was thought to be the major casualty. 'Madame Bull has certain stern principles, national adherence to stiff proprieties, cold looks and defensive gravity, which astonish without pleasing, and estrange without meriting blame.'[101] English wives in the mass, for example attending the Congress of Vienna, made a bad impression.[102] Even in polite London society conversation was often rendered barren for foreigners by the prudery of women and the deference that men paid it. Conversely, Englishmen who travelled were enchanted by the unembarrassed manner and charming warmth of French women. Much of the delight of Paris was simply the relative freedom of social intercourse, rather than the actual availability of sexual intercourse, which in reality was at least as ready in London.

On the other hand, increasing numbers of Englishmen professed to be shocked. In parts of the world where English and French norms could be compared, there were obvious opportunities for criticism. Travelling in the French West Indies George Pinckard was dismayed by the expressions he heard from from the lips of women: 'I am Gothic enough to regard many of the refinements of our Gallic neighbours, as indecent and unbecoming, and my English feelings often lead me to think the conversation of French ladies such as ought never to escape from female lips.'[103] For this it was normal to blame the indecency with which French men customarily addressed not only married but single women.[104] It was indeed one of the boasted aims of English educators to bring up girls away from the contaminating influence of worldly men and women, so that they might be taught to 'reverence themselves'. Mixing with society from an early age, as in France, had a cheapening effect. 'The mind gradually loses a sense and perception of delicacy and virtuous conduct, when it is habitually accustomed to levity; and we soon cease to respect that woman who forgets to respect herself.'[105]

If Pinckard hinted at the Gothic origins of the male attitudes in which female propriety was rooted, others were more explicit about it. Charles Henningsen's own origins led him to hail the English as the natural inheritors of Norse chivalry. Their 'most rude and brutal expressions are filled with delicacy compared with the objugatory epithets and bestial oaths common to the French, Spaniards, Russians, Italians, Portuguese and Orientals.'[106] English women who became accustomed to living abroad, surrounded by such profanity, lost all sensitivity in such matters and with it their 'very English blush'.[107] Those who married foreigners were the 'most audacious in the license they assume'.[108] And the sacrifice that the English bride must make was far from superficial. It extended to her mental well-being. 'Before, she had that collected demeanour, that true dignity, which is imparted by habits of communion with one's own mind.' Afterwards, her thoughts ran only 'upon the events of the past evening, or of the future week'.[109]

The readiness of French women to admit to feelings which were never discussed and rarely expressed in England seemed shocking. Lady Louisa Stuart's reading led her to discern a crucial difference between English and French womanhood. 'The smallest grain of *amour physique* poisons the whole, renders it literally and positively *beastly*, for it is describing the sensations of a brute animal. And here lies the difference between even *bad* English books and the French ones, which everyone reads without blushing. Mrs. Bellamy and Mrs. Baddely, two women of the town, whom I remember as actresses, wrote their Memoirs. They painted their first false step either as the effect of seduction, they were victims to the arts employed to ruin them, or else they had been led away by their *affections*; they had conceived a violent passion for such and such a man, whom they took pains to paint as formed to captivate the *heart*. Madame Roland, one of the heroines of the French Revolution, a *virtuous* woman, so far as chastity goes, writes her Memoirs and tells you what were her *sensations towards the other sex in general* (without any particular object) at 14 or 15 years old.'[110] Not admitting to carnal thoughts or activities seemed to be an English speciality. The French lawyer Charles Cottu was startled by a country house practice which led the ladies to retire to bed at a signal from their hostess, leaving their husbands to follow them later. 'Their modesty would be assailed if they were seen reentring their bedroom with a man who would remain in it until the next morning.'[111]

The Englishness of 'English strictness, delicacy and reserve' was something that had to be explained to many outsiders. In 1805 Lady Sarah Napier lectured her French educated Anglo-Irish cousin Lady Charleville on the difference between Irish and English modes of speech. 'The most recherché word in Johnson (however pedantic) would have a better chance than the slightest expresssion that wont bear the severe scrutiny of even absurd delicacy; and used as your eyes have been first to French indelicacy, next to Irish freedom, and lastly to the licentious style which Ld Charleville thinks (very erroneously) *that all Women like*, it would be no wonder if you should accidentally seem to understand

and laugh at freedom of conversation. In France you know that what is called *le ton animé* (in contradistinction to *mauvaise honte*) is approved of; yet the *latter* is the favorite foible of every English breast, and to deviate from it on system is a crime in England.'[112]

English propriety had to be defended in many other contexts. The dance-floor was one. London ballrooms were not known for their daring. Most Continental fashions did eventually accommodate themselves but usually by degrees and with difficulty. The most enlightened Englishman was startled by the sight of a waltz, with its amazing rolling, turning, and close physical intimacy.[113] Viewed in Paris it seemed a fair prediction that 'if its introduction ever should take place, it must certainly be pruned of those lascivious movements, which are here considered as the most delightful part of the exercise'.[114] In its Anglicized version, indeed, it never attained the sensuality of the original. A genuine waltz could hardly be performed at arm's length, as it was in Britain.[115]

Admittedly, the English had their own country dance, which was famous in its own right and exported throughout western Europe by the mid-eighteenth century. Moreover, female dancers were admired. There was about an English woman an impressive vigour, a wholehearted spirit of participation, which brought colour to her cheeks, lent animation to her statuesque beauty, and charmingly expressed the natural vitality of 'the sex' in its insular setting. Coleridge argued that the very restraint normally expected of wives and daughters accounted for this: 'The fondness for dancing was the reaction of the reserved manners of English women; it was the only way in which they could throw themselves forth in natural liberty.'[116]

Yet even those who were delighted by the sight generally admitted that in English dance there was a want of sexual magic, an impression of wholesomeness rather than excitement, let alone lasciviousness. English dance manuals and conduct books were uncompromising on the point, and the most modish dancing master was expected to import French modes without French immorality. 'The jetting short Step in Dancing, the wanton turn of the Head, the leering Look, the flirt of the Fan, and the disagreeable Motion of the Hips', these were almost lovingly described before being condemned.[117] Englishwomen themselves were dismayed by the overt sexuality expected of French girls learning to dance. The authoress Mrs Stothard thus described a master instructing a girl to turn her eyes to the ceiling as she pirouetted. 'But what, thought I, can a dancing-master have to do with the eyes of his scholar; a plain Englishman would not have carried his instructions beyond the management of the feet, or the arms, at most; but in France the effect which the execution of a thing is to produce, is as much considered as the thing itself: so I imagine, therefore, the management of the eyes is of no small importance in the art of dancing. I was confirmed in my conjecture; for the master dismissed his little pupil with the encouraging exclamation of "Allez vous-en, jolie mignonne, tu seras coquette un jour." '[118] French coquetry and English modesty were wholly incompatible.

MODESTY

When female modesty was discussed, much attention was focused on the social conventions. Kissing in public as a form of salutation was replaced by bowing in England as it was elsewhere, with predictable approval from the *Spectator*.[119] But the substitution seemed to imply more than it did in other societies. In Britain there had not been the distinction between social and sexual kissing that seemed to be well understood on the Continent. In the sixteenth and seventeenth centuries to kiss on the lips was considered decent where it would have been thought excessive elsewhere.[120] Thereafter social kissing was remembered only in rather dated courtesy books and remote communities.[121] Among men it became almost unthinkable. Between men and women it was increasingly restricted to the family circle.

The result was paradoxically that kissing came to seem more cold and formal in Paris than in London, where the way was now open for it to become a purely sexual activity, implying only one kind of intimacy.[122] Foreigners were often shocked by the passionate nature of a stage kiss in England, 'lips to lips, audibly'.[123] Conversely, English travellers elsewhere, not least in the outlying parts of the British Isles, found it difficult to look upon the welcoming embrace as mere courtesy. The Englishman Edward Topham was struck by the contrast between England and Scotland in this respect, and, recalling that Erasmus had described kissing English girls, reflected on the pros and cons of the

change in manners which must have occurred in England since the sixteenth century. On the one hand, the gain in terms of female modesty was
manifest, and perhaps English men could sleep more secure in their beds
when they were assured that the sexual sensibility of wives had not been
precociously stimulated by frequent kissing in adolescence. On the other
hand, there was no denying that married life had become less stimulating. 'Consider also, you who are blessed with every conjugal endearment,
how languid and insipid must be the marriage bed, when incapable of
deriving pleasures from this source?' Was there not even a danger that
men would be driven to unspeakable perversions, replacing the loss of
one pleasure by resorting to others?[124] Of course, all of this might have
been an Englishman's exaggeration of the sensuality of Scottish saluta-
tions. French visitors observed the discrepancy between English and
Scottish greetings, but seem to have considered the Scottish embrace as
ritualistic as the Continental.[125]

From the standpoint of a predatory foreign male, female costume
provided the clinching evidence of female frigidity. Stays were one of the
most characteristic features of English civilization, defying the otherwise
unbreakable laws of fashion, until in the mid-nineteenth century they
conquered the West as a whole and thereby ceased to be English. By
the standards of other countries, they were worn too frequently and
too close. Outsiders were repelled by them, both metaphorically and
physically. Henri Meister admitted their efficacy in the preservation of
female chastity but denounced the visual effect of 'these abominable
stays, which are absolute breast-plates, that destroy this beauty, whilst
they serve the purposes of concealment and defence. How often has
virtue been preserved in this world, by its being enabled to resist the first
onset!'[126]

Even among foreigners whalebone à l'anglaise was not without its
defenders. Grosley credited its unique design with preserving the 'ease
and beauty of the shape' of an English woman's breasts.[127] Unsurprisingly the English of both sexes seem to have adapted their ideal of feminine beauty to take account of stays. Thomas Nugent was disgusted by
the staylessness of Hamburg's women.[128] Mariana Starke thought Italians
of her sex equally ill served. 'The women are of middle stature, and, were
it not for bad stays, would be well made.'[129]

Yet the English did not take stays with them wherever they went. In India, where the heat made them less bearable, sexual relations seem not to have deteriorated.[130] In Virginia the appearance of an English governess in stays 'almost to her Chin, and swaithed around her as low as they possibly can be, allowing her hardly Liberty to walk at all' merely gave rise to mockery.[131] For the visiting South Carolinian Peter Manigault in the 1770s, to 'see the Bristol Women, as crooked as Cow's Horns' was to 'lament that man, or rather Woman, should attempt to mend the works of God'. He warned his own daughters against all attempts at imitation of transatlantic fashion.[132]

Foreign challenges, such as the polonaise, were stoutly met with a modesty handkerchief, the German-born Queen Charlotte heroically leading the charge. But stays and prudery were not in all respects synonymous. Foreigners were often startled by the revealing dress that Englishwomen wore, particularly in the evening. Harriet Beecher Stowe was one. 'The ladies were in full dress, which here in England means always a dress which exposes the neck and shoulders. This requirement seems to be universal, since ladies of all ages conform to it. It may, perhaps, account for this custom, to say that the bust of an English lady is seldom otherwise than fine, and develops a full outline at what we should call quite an advanced period of life.'[133] Moreover, in the language of male self-titillation, stays were much resorted to:

> With Hat awry, divested of her gown,
> Her creaking stays of leather stout and brown,
> Invidious barrier, why art thou so high,
> When the slight covering of her neck slips by?
> Disclosing to th'enraptured gazer's sight,
> Her full ripe bosom, exquisitely white.[134]

Not only stays puzzled foreigners. The extreme fastidiousness of English womanhood where natural functions were concerned seemed strange. The marquis de Bombelles observed that in the country, when a woman needed to relieve herself, her husband moved the men away, everyone knowing what was going on. In France a woman could do so without anyone taking any notice. He was equally surprised that it was considered offensive to speak of a woman's pregnancy.[135] In fact to talk at all of bodily matters was considered tasteless. Male tourists in London sometimes fell headlong into this trap. Voltaire was one of those who gave offence to English gentlewomen by his brutally frank remarks on physical ailments.[136] Others were merely mystified. If, enquired Joseph de Gourbillon, legs had to be called feet, breasts chests, and bellies stomachs, how did doctors communicate accurately with their female patients about their complaints?[137]

The English abroad were appalled by the Continental woman's lack of inhibition in public places. It was the lavatorial aspect that seems to have been most disgusting of all. Nothing shocked English travellers more than public urination and defecation, especially when those involved were females. The conclusive proof of the filth of Flanderkins for the far from prudish Philip Thicknesse was the sight of 12-year-old girls relieving themselves in the street.[138] Dr William Maton, in France in 1826, thought that the French had somewhat improved in this respect, thanks to the English example, but was taken aback at Beauvais by 'the situation of a young female under the walls of this church within sight of numerous passers-by'.[139]

All kinds of practices which on the Continent seemed uncontroversial were offensive to an English eye. Male servants changed bedclothes for their mistresses and female guests, 'and would do every office of a maid servant, if suffered'.[140] Horace Walpole's sister was dismayed, asking for a bedpan, when 'the footman of the house came and showed it her himself, and everything that is related to it'.[141] It was not only employees who had to be kept at a distance. The bedroom, a centre of sociability in other countries, had ceased to be so in England, and by the eighteenth century the notion of entertaining in bed was shocking to English ladies. Foreign men were warned that 'The lady's bedchamber is a sanctuary which no stranger is permitted to enter. It would be an act of the greatest possible indecorum to go into it, unless the visitor were upon a very familiar footing with the family, or did it upon some very urgent occasion.'[142] Their womenfolk were not less startled. It seemed odd that even in inns it was unthinkable to use the bedroom for anything but sleeping.[143] The discovery that an English lady would rather make her bed herself than have it made by a stranger was positively baffling.[144] Henri Meister thought it was the sanctity of the bedroom that accounted for the Englishwoman's reputation for chastity. 'The greatest difficulty is not always to persuade an Englishwoman to suffer you to carry her off, but to find a convenient opportunity for telling her you wish to do it. Amiable and modest as they are, there is less art and good fortune required to bring the love adventure to a successful conclusion than there is to open it.'[145]

Yet there were discrepancies. Joseph Fievée discovered that whereas English women foiled his attempts to visit them in their bedroom, they saw nothing shameful in rushing to the window to watch half-naked boxers flexing their muscles and displaying their masculinity. In France this would have been unthinkable.[146] The fact that English women considered 'it indecent to shew themselves at the window' made this all the more striking.[147] It was also thought strange that English women were quite prepared to travel atop a coach where the combination of speed and breeze were guaranteed to disarrange their dress and provide onlookers with a view of their legs.[148]

Female hypocrisy intrigued the German feminist Fanny Lewald, who was disturbed to see tourists viewing old masters in the art galleries of Florence. 'Elegant women, English ladies, who shudder at the sight of a frog, and cannot hear the word "shirt" pronounced without blushing, stand before entire walls covered with those martyrs, and examine things and scenes, with their eye-glasses, from which a healthy mind must turn away with disgust. They slide about on tip-toe, and lisp out their false delight of which they ought to be ashamed.'[149] Later, when she got to England, she was still more astonished by the interest with which bourgeois women inspected the specimens of physique to be viewed on stage. These were mothers who taught their daughters that actresses and ballerinas were shameless, and who went to extraordinary lengths to protect them from even the sight of a naked Apollo or Venus. They would have been appalled if their husbands had praised the breasts or the legs of any woman, on or off the stage. Yet they were avid ballet spectators and made no attempt to conceal their fascination, opera glasses at the ready, with the exaggerated sexuality of the performers.[150]

Modesty, however, was more than embarrassment about bodily functions, prudery where sex was concerned, and fastidiousness in matters of personal deportment. It was, like true gentility, a certain *je ne sais quoi* and on that account fascinating to foreigners of both sexes. To men it was especially intriguing, for it could be viewed in rather different lights. It might be the natural virtue of an Englishwoman, vestiges of which could be retained by the most abandoned of her sex. On the other hand, it might be sheer hypocrisy, the tribute paid by vice to virtue. It might even be what was necessary to stimulate the sexual taste of the repressed English male. John Milford was charmed but not seduced by the easy manners of Spanish girls: 'Yet how contrasted does this facility of acquaintance appear to one who has been accustomed to the superior pride of the English fair; that soft retiring modesty, which, though it may border a little on reserved stiffness or formality at first, gives but a fresh zest to a nearer acquaintance.'[151] And at the Cape the naval memoirist 'Billy' Pitt was first delighted then disturbed by the familiarity of Boer 'Africandas'. 'A young lady, divested of delicate feeling, becomes an easy prey to the libertine; and stripped of modesty, she is deprived of her richest ornament.'[152] He was not the only English globe-trotter hovering between sexual greed and sexual guilt in such circumstances.

For foreigners a chaste expression and manner were an integral part of English beauty. Such apparent innocence, however misleading, had a certain appeal for foreign roués. To vice, wrote the Prince de Ligne, 'the English women lend the charms of candour. I have taken the girls of Vauxhall and Ranelagh for the most virtuous women in Europe and America.'[153] Meister offered a similar judgement: 'The lowest order of females, those who are reduced to offer their charms, or more properly their favours, to the first person who solicits them, observe a decency and degree of modesty not to be found amongst the same class in any other country.'[154] He attributed this peculiar kind of moral sensibility, uncontaminated by the grosser sensibility of the French, to the presence in the air of coal smoke.

Whatever the cause, those who actually sampled these delights were generally appreciative. Stendhal, in London after a disappointment in love, sought something other than the cynicism of the bordello and found it in a terraced house in the suburbs, where three young girls, tender, frail, and timid, charmed him with their seemingly unaffected innocence.[155] Others were rather shocked. A Scotsman in London for the first time asked: 'Do not many of these strumpets seem modest? and are not many of them even of an angelic form? But alas! it is plainly nothing else but outward semblance; within all is vice and rottenness!'[156] Like most things English, much depended on context, especially commercial context. At Vauxhall or in a Clapham villa the market was 'sensible'. Elsewhere, on the streets, it was often less refined. The Swede Geijer was distressed by the shamelessness of London's lowest streetwalkers. The English could not 'practise vice with decency'.[157]

It was pointed out that whores were naturally, and often by profession, actresses. A demure prostitute was mimicking the froideur of her less corrupted countrywoman. Moreover, in explaining the unresponsiveness that underlay modesty, it was helpful to resort to the boasted centrepiece of Englishness, a long tradition of liberty. Sexual frigidity was the price of feminine freedom. 'Taking liberties' with a woman was, after all, a phrase which gave sexual interference a highly political tone. English women enjoyed unusual freedom but preserved it only by allowing their menfolk the minimum of latitude.

A crucial weapon in this form of warfare was ingrained female restraint. The dancing-master and self-appointed moral instructor John Essex commended 'a strict Reserve' to his female readers as the surest antidote to the poison of men's flattery.[158] It was not, of course, a uniquely English preoccupation. Moralists of all nations emphasized the value of female reserve as tending to the preservation of sexual morals.[159] It was generally recognized, however, that English women peculiarly embodied it. In them it constituted a natural part of modesty, something that was not narrowly sexual in meaning. The contrast with France was marked. 'Women of all ranks in France are destitute of that native self-respecting dignity of appearance and manner, claiming respect and attention as a right, rather than soliciting them as a boon.'[160] Even from a French perspective no women could match the English for modesty. Madame de Staël, whom nobody ever accused of excessive modesty, distinguished carefully between the German variety, which looked superficially similar, and the English. German women were admittedly modest, she noted, yet never reserved in the way their English counterparts were.[161]

Such shyness had surely to be inculcated. Some thought it ethnic, but evidence from distant places influenced by English settlement suggested the contrary. English stock across the Atlantic soon lost the bashfulness that characterized it in the mother country. Divested of the 'blushing modesty of the country girls of Europe, they will answer a familiar question from the other sex with the confidence of a French Mademoiselle'.[162] This was the verdict of the English traveller, Charles Janson. Yet Europeans did not find American girls unchaste. On the contrary, they were described as making pure mothers.[163] What was in question was their reserve not their virtue. Elsewhere the consequences were more serious. The white women of the English West Indies were thought prone to lose their shame along with their modesty.[164]

In England female reserve was instilled at an early stage. Comparing two premier girls' schools of London and Paris, respectively the Queen's Square Academy and Saint-Cyr, Sophie von la Roche gained quite different impressions. The French girls exhibited an obvious sense of fun and also of obstinacy, the English girls a quiet pride bordering on coldness and reserve. Never again would she disbelieve in a 'national cast of feature', she observed.[165] Others also noted the peculiar behaviour of an English maid. Coming across a party of schoolgirls in Worcestershire, Blanqui remarked: 'They look at the passers-by out of the corner of the eye, without turning the head, in a quite singular manner.'[166] Avoidance of eye-contact or even a frown were characteristic 'girlish bulwarks of defence'.[167]

With such an upbringing how could an Englishwoman not make a frigid lover? Iron control could only be exerted at the expense of wholesome passion. Balzac constructed one of the most forceful females in European literature from such materials. His Lady Dudley, supposedly based on the real-life Lady Ellenborough, had so encased herself in fortifications of steel that when she gave herself in love she resembled rather a mechanic than a human being.[168] Her creator could not resist adding that only a Protestant country could have given birth to such a freak.

Female modesty was as interesting for what it implied about men as what it revealed about women. It was a standard claim by foreigners that in the strictest sense there was no such thing as gallantry in England.[169] The social space for sexual flirtation did not exist. The effect was either to inhibit men in the presence of virtuous women or to drive them into the company of immoral ones. As Louis Simond put it, 'There are many men in England who are libertines out of modesty or rather *mauvaise honte*, unable to control their awe of modest women.'[170] This was indeed the point of Goldsmith's play *She Stoops to Conquer*, in which a tongue-tied young man of fortune, incapable of conversing with well-born women and sexually confident only with whores, had to be reformed by a gentlewoman posing as a serving girl. But more than personal morality was at issue. Amazonian discipline had its disadvantages. It trained women in a form of social self-defence and discouraged men of less than commanding assurance. Men frequently fled even from occasions nominally designed for both sexes. The baron d'Haussez remarked that women did not regulate English society. In France their power to censor and educate young men was crucial. English men were not house trained.[171] Female reserve led inexorably to male unsociability.

English travellers generally thought this price worth paying. The Continental institution that perennially presented them with proof of their own superiority was that of the Italian *cicisbeo* or *cavaliere servente*, a source of endless fascination and some sarcasm. 'The English women are particularly shocked at it, who are allowed to hate their husbands, provided they do not like any body else.'[172] No travel book was complete without a discussion of its merits. The Italian defence was a simple one. Such a practice merely recognized reality, and gave to all parties the right to contract out of the disagreeable features of marriage without destroying it as a necessary social institution. For the English this violated all 'morality of decorum'. But for the Italian decorum was hypocrisy. Did not the English respect candour and frankness? Yes, came back the answer, but this was not true frankness and sincerity. It was 'total disregard of public opinion'.[173] True candour meant submitting to the prudery required by a nation obsessed with public standards of behaviour.

Public opinion was not only an English invention; its peculiar force was inconceivable in any other but an English context. The notion that individuals should take upon themselves the defence of the community's collective morality as they did in societies for the reformation of manners and prosecution of vice, seemed very strange. The duc de Lévis thought it impressively public-spirited. He could not conceive of the apparatus of moral reformation working at all in France.[174] If neither State nor Church found grounds for acting, it seemed almost beyond belief that individuals might do so. His countryman Amédée Pichot agreed but was less impressed. 'In France such an institution would soon sink under the shafts of ridicule.'[175]

There was a price for this form of high-mindedness. When an individual claims to represent the public as a whole he exposes his motives to scrutiny and his conduct to censure. The least deficiency in either respect lays him open to the charge of hypocrisy. When a whole society loses the capacity to see that its public virtue is a mask for private vice all become implicated in a gigantic act of self-deception. This was what William Cobbett thought had happened, not least in matters of morality, where his countrymen had seemingly exchanged real delicacy for false. What kind of people would invent such a term as small-clothes to describe their underwear while tolerating the presence of prostitutes even in their villages.[176] Similar absurdities could be found in an urban setting. Amédée de Tissot remarked that the effect of English modesty was such that a foreign tourist would find no nude statues of women in London but, renouncing inanimate marble, might choose among the 50,000 or 60,000 prostitutes who paraded their wares openly.[177]

This tendency to invest relatively minor matters of social regulation with moral profoundity, while winking at moral enormities, came to be seen as particularly, if not uniquely, English in the early nineteenth century. De Tocqueville thought he had made a profound discovery to this effect when he noted that public bathing aroused no anxiety in Ireland yet gave rise to acute controversy in England. This was despite the fact that the illegitimacy rate seemed to be far lower in Ireland than England.[178] He concluded that the English preoccupation with decency had more to do with manners than morals.

De Tocqueville's observation was not as original as he perhaps supposed. Fenimore Cooper made much the same point when he remarked that 'The great mistake is the substitution of the seemly for the right.'[179] Their impression coincided with that of many contemporaries, by no means all of them foreigners. In retrospect it may seem easy to relate such an attitude to the massive surge of moral revival that originated with the Evangelical awakening and culminated in what we think of as Victorianism. But viewed as part of a project for national regeneration, it might be seen to have diverse, if interlocking, origins. One was plainly the desire to demonstrate the 'domestic purity' of the British elite in a time of widespread social upheaval.[180] Another was the hope that a nation once notorious for its ferocity and brutality could claim to have become, as the Englishman by naturalization, C. F. Henningsen, put it, 'thoughtfully humane'.[181] And above all there was the assumption that the moral character of the English, not least as exemplified in its model of womanhood, could be shown to have an ethical fibre that set it apart from others. The essence of English self-esteem was the assumption that moral superiority was at bottom based not only on rightness but on honesty. Rendering an entire nation more polished, more humane, and more decorous was certainly not meant to have made it less upright.

CHAPTER FOUR

TACITURNITY

By Order

SILENCE

'*SILENCE* is golden' runs the proverb. It is, however, a Swiss rather than an English proverb, popularized in England by Thomas Carlyle, whose Germanic learning evidently struck a chord with Victorians. No collection of English proverbs before his time includes it, though the sentiment seems to have been common enough in various forms, most of them implying that silence was not so much a virtue in its own right as one appropriate to inferiors, especially those of the female sex. That girls should be seen but not heard was axiomatic by the fifteenth century. In the seventeenth the injunction was extended to all women, and in the nineteenth to all children.[1]

The gender politics of speechlessness aside, part of the appeal of the proverb as Carlyle rendered it may have been that it endorsed what seemed a patriotic truth. The English, men as much as women, had a reputation for being a silent people. Even foreigners who thought inconsistency the essence of Englishness made an exception for taciturnity, one constant characteristic of an Englishman.[2] It was true that this was sometimes difficult to distinguish from another characteristic, reserve with strangers. But observant visitors noticed that even among friends the English were less loquacious than their Continental neighbours. As the Swiss Bonstetten reported: 'It is remarkable to see the silence that generally prevails in the social circles of England amongst persons knit together by the strongest ties of friendship. In that lowering climate sentiment and thought, always self-concentrated, seem to be void of language.'[3] To the Hamburg reformer Caspar Voght, the reluctance of English parents to engage their children in conversation even in the family circle appeared particularly telling.[4]

No other nation was so fearful of 'wasting words', a revealing phrase. In England bureaucrats seemed determined to communicate as briefly and simply as possible, something that puzzled those more familiar with Continental bureaucracies.[5] In polite society it was easy for foreigners to be caught out by 'an infinity of these little conventions for dispensing with speech', such as placing one's teaspoon in one's cup, as a way of indicating that no more tea was desired.[6] Even drawing-room furniture seemed to take account of its native users' uncommunicative nature. What other people could have invented the 'immense and heavy *fauteuils*, which appear calculated to produce sleep rather than conversation'?[7] Moreover, from those who waited upon them, the Upper Ten Thousand expected the same silence that they desired among themselves. English servants were thought astonishingly noiseless by Continental standards. It was said that a French lackey could not have emulated them had the King himself ordained it.[8] Even for the Francophile Fenimore Cooper, returning from the Continent to England, the silent service to be found there was an enormous relief.[9]

Servants were considered no different from the rest of the class they came from in this respect. The English labourer seemed as wordless as the English gentleman, whether at work or play. Continental critics of industrialization sometimes attributed the muteness of machine-minders to the severity of the regime they lived under and the barbarity of a new class of capitalist masters.[10] Yet such observations went back far beyond the era of the factory system. Comparisons with plebeian Irish folk who chattered cheerfully whether on their home ground in Ireland or in the colonies they established in London, drove home the lesson. Nor was this a matter of rank. To go aboard an Irish steamer, even on the quarterdeck, was to find twice as much conversation as on board an English vessel.[11] And the Irish gentry themselves were well aware that to succeed in London the toast of Dublin must curb his tongue.[12] It was perfectly possible for a talkative and sociable race to withstand the mists and mournfulness of the British Isles. Anglo-Saxons presumably lacked the temperament to do so.

Nothing seemed likely to draw them out. Close proximity and confinement made little difference. Travelling in a packed stagecoach was in England a quite different experience from elsewhere. Ludwig Wolff reckoned that he heard not more than a hundred words during the entire journey from York to Leeds in 1833 in company with five other passengers. This would have been barely possible in Germany and inconceivable in France. Among the English it was the norm.[13] Nor did their famed attachment to animals move them to speech. English drivers were rarely observed to talk to their horses, as did their French counterparts.[14] Surely liquor must loosen tongues. Apparently not. It merely made the English violent. Taine attributed the necessity for a temperance movement to this.[15] He was not the first commentator to note that the verbal warfare which characterized Mediterranean life was rarely to be heard on the streets of London. 'When two Englishmen quarrel, actions mean more than words. They say little but repetitions of the same thing, clinching it with a hearty "God damn you!" Their anger boils up inside them and soon breaks out in violence.'[16]

Famous Englishmen were not usually remembered for their garrulousness. It was recalled that Lord Burley had never used his tongue, when a movement of his head was sufficient.[17] Talking too much was an unforgivable sin for the English, and virtually the definition of a bore. Famous foreigners were not exempted. Grotius was said to have been disregarded in London for holding forth overmuch.[18] It was axiomatic that silence went with a wise mind and a modest manner. The corollary was that talkativeness implied ignorance and egotism. In France, wrote Mercier, 'the art of keeping silence is not regarded as a merit. A Frenchman is not more easily known by his countenance and his accent than by the legerity with which he talks and determines on all subjects; he never knows how to say, "I understand nothing of that."'[19] The English language itself had a rich range of derisive expressions for useless talk. 'Jabber, babble, chatter, patter, blabber, prattle, tattle, blather' suggested something of the contempt in which the English held speech undirected towards a specific object. Such terms were readily applied to the discourse of those inferior to the English male: women, children, and foreigners of all kinds. In other languages frivolous chatter was permitted a measure of appeal, as Walter Savage Landor recorded in the 1820s. 'What we, half a century ago, called to *banter*, and what, if I remember the word, I think I have lately heard called to *quiz*, gives no other idea than of coarseness and inurbanity. The French convey one of buzz and bustle in *persifler*; the Italians, as naturally, one of singing, and amusing and misleading the judgment, by *canzonare*, or, as Boccaccio speaks, *uccellare*.'[20]

These linguistic differences extended beyond the use of one's tongue to any kind of noise. In English silence came to have a distinctive metaphorical power. Abnormality could be registered in decibels. A flamboyant colour or a tasteless style of dress was described as 'loud'. The habit spread to other languages but significantly required more emphasis on the extreme nature of the offence to express the same meaning. What it was sufficient to describe as loud in English had to be 'criant' in French, 'schreiend' in German, 'chiassoso' in Italian.

The Swede Geijer called the English 'an amazingly quiet nation'.[21] By his time, at the end of the eighteenth century, the foreigner's amazement was increased by the unlikely circumstances in which absence of noise prevailed. London was the most dynamic city in the civilized world. Yet its inhabitants maintained a degree of calm and quiet which baffled the denizens of other European cities. To walk from Cornhill to the Strand through Cheapside was to process in an endless column of men and women who combined an air of activity with an unreadiness to engage in conversation.[22] This mixture puzzled many visitors. Some connected it with the gloom which seemed to be a characteristic of Londoners. The Napoleonic propagandist Joseph Fiévée was so depressed by the silence of the streets that he said he felt perpetually as if he ought to rush up to Englishmen and condole with them for some disaster which might explain their want of animation.[23] The English themselves were conscious that it was not to be found elsewhere, even among America's Anglo-Saxon descendants. Recalling that George Washington was remembered for his serenity and silence, Matthew Arnold remarked that 'some of the best English qualities are clean gone; the love of quiet and dislike of a crowd is gone out of the American entirely'.[24]

Businessmen, however bustling, were no noisier than others. The Royal Exchange, famous for the quantity and complexity of its commercial dealings, struck visitors to London by its pervading calmness. The same was true of the metropolis of the industrial north. William Cooke Taylor, who toured the manufacturing districts of Lancashire in the 1840s, was intrigued by the composure that characterized the Manchester Exchange, even in the most trying circumstances. 'Very much is done and very little is said. Transactions of immense extent are conducted by nods, winks, shrugs, or brief phrases, compared to which the laconisms of the ancient Spartans were specimens of tediousness and verbosity. There is a kind of vague tradition, or rather remote recollection, that a man was once seen to gossip on the Exchange: it was mentioned in the terms one would use if he saw a saraband danced in St. Peter's, or Harlequin playing his antics at the Old Bailey. For my own part, I felt my loquacious tendencies so chilled by the genius of the place, that I deemed myself qualified to become a candidate for La Trappe.'[25]

Places of recreation where the English might have been expected to let their hair down seemed subdued by Continental standards. Madame du Boccage was put off by the silence of Vauxhall and amused herself by envisaging the hubbub her countrymen would have made in such a place.[26] At a famous Thames-side tavern, frequented by as many as two thousand people enjoying its gardens and bars, Giacomo Beltrami was equally startled. 'I heard no noise but the trampling of the feet of those who came in or went out'.[27] Coffee houses, in their nature dedicated to sociability, were strangely noiseless. Ferri di San Costante complained that he had to speak in whispers if he wished to talk in an English coffee house.[28] Amédée Pichot reported a typical scene thus: 'enter one of our coffee-rooms, and you will probably find two Englishmen seated silently in a corner, instead of entering into conversation with each other. If, by chance, one of them, throwing off some of the national reserve, should venture to address a question to his neighbour, the latter will put on a grave look, and return at most a dry monosyllabic answer, for two talkative Englishmen seldom meet under the same roof.'[29]

In clubland itself clubbishness did not generate the buzz of conversation. Flora Tristan found only a sepulchral silence and utter boredom. 'There is nothing more comical than the sight of a hundred or so men disposed about the enormous rooms like so much furniture.'[30] Even in the Travellers, founded specifically by and for cosmopolitans, Talleyrand observed 'une taciturnité tout anglaise'.[31] And most bizarre, there was the stunning quiet of an English brothel, fittingly supervised by an imperturbably grave English waiter.[32] The best bagnios, like the best clubs, were quietest of all. Wealth and tranquillity evidently went together in England, and not only in the most exclusive settings. When London's streets were macadamized the resulting silence under foot and under wheel was much appreciated, albeit at the price of making pedestrian life somewhat more hazardous. Abroad, the English traveller's contempt for wooden shoes, long a mark of Continental inferiority, was heightened by the clatter that they made.[33] There was a paradoxical symbolism to be observed here. The poverty of absolutist States made for disagreeable racket. The freedom of the plebeian English expressed itself in reassuring calm.

Orderliness and silence seemed to be synonyms in England. After visiting a Manchester penitentiary, the German J. G. Kohl reported: 'I was particularly struck by the perfect silence pervading the assembly, which was carefully guarded by a few vigilant overseers who walked among them, everywhere maintaining order and stillness. No one was allowed to speak above a whisper. I was told that this strict silence was absolutely necessary to prevent quarrels and disturbances. It seems that the English silent system is maintained in other places than the prisons. Such a system would be looked upon in some countries, in France for instance, as the very height of tyranny.'[34]

That so much of the evidence of English silence was gathered in large cities seemed all the more surprising. Conversation was urban. As Madame de Staël pointed out, it presupposed a society committed to the town as a form of social organization. The French mal de pays was not so much a love of country as a horror of the countryside. In Louisiana French settlers would travel six hundred leagues to New Orleans to escape the longueurs of rural life, and 'causer à la ville'.[35] By the early nineteenth century the English were the most urban people on earth in terms of population distribution. Yet whatever they wanted from their towns, it did not seem to be conversation.

Conventional wisdom located English taciturnity in a broader framework which associated it with racial characteristics. The Gothic peoples
of the sunless north were given to introverted brooding forced on them
by their domestic isolation in an adverse climate. The Latins of the south
suffered no such constraint; their alfresco manners went with a social
existence. For English travellers one of the first impressions upon entering any city south of the Alps was the volume of man-made noise. Robert
Bakewell, touring on the Continent in the 1820s, gave the palm to Savoy
when he was awakened at the hour of 4 a.m. 'No cause can be assigned
for opening the shops at so very early an hour, unless it be to enable the
inhabitants to discharge a portion of the talking fluid, which may have
accumulated to a painful excess during the silence of the night. The
Savoyards are certainly the greatest talkers in Europe.'[36]

By these standards the English plainly belonged with other northerners. Philosophical travellers were quick to point to certain common
features of the phlegmatic temperament to be found north of the Alps.
An account of the gloomy quiet which prevailed in a Dutch tavern or
a German inn might seem very like that in an English tavern. Yet the
English case could not be assimilated in all respects. After all, the stillness of English life was as striking to Germans as it was to Frenchmen
or Italians. When Germans gathered together in the streets they had none
of the orderly calm which made an English mob strangely impressive. It
seemed precisely a characteristic of English phlegm that it was exerted
as much in the mass as in individuals, whereas its German counterpart
proved fragile when subjected to the pressure of collective emotion.

Impassiveness was increasingly associated with the English speaking
manner, especially in polite society. The social climber had to give up
appearing 'decisive and lively' and speak 'in the toneless whisper of some
of the English grandees, with deliberate utterance and unvarying
languor'.[37] The art of understatement also had to be mastered. Why,
asked a German visiting the Great Exhibition, did anything worthy of the
highest commendation have to be described as 'nice'? 'Anyone who dares
to describe a woman as beautiful or even as bewitching demonstrates
only that he is not yet at home in the highest circles.'[38]

Above all, there was the matter of physiognomy. Not moving a muscle
while speaking was a prime characteristic, one which the French actor
Joly, who spent some time in London to acquire a knowledge of English

manners, turned to delightful effect both with foreign audiences, and with those of the English prepared to laugh at themselves, including King George IV.[39] An English wit was expected to avoid facial movement, as Maria Edgeworth's pen portrait of Thomas Grenville recognized: 'saying in a low drawling English gentlemanlike sleepy tone the drollest and keenest things without moving his head to the right or the left or changing a muscle of his countenance'.[40] Facial composure was maintained in the most unlikely circumstances. Grosley, like many Frenchmen, was impressed by the warmth with which Englishmen shook hands on meeting, sufficient, he remarked to dislocate one's shoulder. 'There is no expression of friendship in their countenances, yet the whole soul enters the arm which gives the shake.'[41]

This was not merely manly affectation. Englishwomen were considered to have immobile features, contributing to their reputation for statuesque beauty.[42] There were evident aesthetic implications. The English proficiency in portraiture was thought to owe much to the faces of those portrayed. More particularly was this the case in historical painting. West's portrait of Nelson reminded the onlooker that the English face was naturally calm, even heroic, more so than the French, more like ancient heroes. This was said by a Frenchman, not an Englishman.[43] On the other hand, the French countenance might be considered correspondingly more expressive of character than the English.[44]

Similar reflections were prompted by the English horror of gesture, beyond what even fellow northerners thought natural. In Parliament gesticulating orators invariably met with disapproval.[45] In ordinary conversation 'want of action and of expression' was the norm. [46] As Giacomo Beltrami put it, 'whether they court you or storm at you, whether they praise you or abuse you,—their countenance, tone of voice, and gesture, are the same'.[47] In Britain, it was only the Irishman who 'speaks with every part of his body'.[48]

For their part, the English were often amused or irritated by the contrary manners they encountered elsewhere. The propensity of the Continental clergy to employ theatrical gesture in the pulpit seemed indecorous as well as comical.[49] This was equally true of Catholics and Protestants, prompting John Locke to conclude in France, that ' 'Tis possible this way here best suits with the Customs and Manners of the People; who are all Motion, even when they say the easiest and most intelligible Things.'[50] At home the English clergyman was expected to avoid 'too much action'. Sydney Smith got into trouble on this account but had no doubt that the customary manner of his brethren in the established Church was conceding an advantage to more demonstrative Dissenting preachers. 'A clergyman clings to his velvet cushion with either hand, keeps his eye riveted upon his book, speaks of the ecstasies of joy, and fear, with a voice and a face which indicate neither, and pinions his body and soul into the same attitude of limb, and thought, for fear of being called theatrical and affected.'[51] Foreigners regarded the resulting effect as stiff and unappealing.[52] On the other hand, it was hard not to concede that it had the advantage of a certain modesty which contrasted with the instinctive exhibitionism of a French preacher.[53]

Interestingly, the great exception was the stage. Visitors found London actors surpisingly, even bizarrely, expressive in the use both of gesture and facial movement.[54] A few English players, for example Charles Mathews and his son Charles James, were admired on this account.[55] But in general this paradoxical English excess did not please foreign theatre-goers. The verdict of the Parisian printer Crapelet, when he saw a production of Colman's comedy The Jealous Wife in 1816, was typical. 'I am sure that if an actress, at the Théâtre Français, emitted such piercing cries as Miss O'Neill, made so many contortions, outrageous gestures, prancings, she would not appear a second time. Different tastes like the countries.'[56] Certainly, Eliza O'Neill's technique was more successful with Englishmen. It brought her marriage to a wealthy MP, the title of Lady Becher, and promotion from the demi-monde to the beau monde.

In polite society the ex-actress was expected to play the part of a high-bred lady, in which a quiet manner and a serene countenance were de rigueur. But English breeding was supposed to build on ethnic tradition, not renounce it, and patriotic commentators liked to associate such poise and equanimity with an inborn mental strength and durability. There were also foreigners who were prepared to connect impassivity with temperamental steadiness. The Prussian statesman Friedrich von Gentz thought 'a certain calm' the ruling characteristic of the whole nation when he visited Britain after the Peace of Amiens and placed it high among the manifold virtues that he professed to find there.[57]

Orderly tranquillity was admitted to be a peculiarly English state of affairs. But this tranquillity was more than mere insensibility, such as

characterized the Dutch. It signified a capacity to control the most powerful feelings, something which figured much in English legal doctrine
as well as the observed behaviour of the Englishman.[58] As the French
Anglophile Adolphe Esquiros put it, 'the force of passion concealed by
a species of solemn and imposing calmness is a national trait'.[59] Esquiros
attached significance to cricket, a game which required exceptional
resources of self-control. No foreigner could achieve such mastery,
however assimilated. 'This game marks, to some extent, the limit of practical naturalization.'[60] But the implications went far beyond a mere game.
'Unflappability', which was something more than the old aristocratic ease
and assurance of the man of civility, something more because it was something sterner, was a much later term but as a concept it was already well
established, and enshrined in the uniquely English simile, 'as cool as a
cucumber'.

CONVERSATION

If the English proneness to silence and solemnity was not without advantages, it remained a worrying national trait. Its implications in the context
of sociability were particularly serious. Taciturnity virtually disabled the
Englishman from participating in a modern culture. Civility was inconceivable without conversation, the mark of a society at once rational and
polite. Self-conscious sensibility and humanity could not be maintained
without the capacity to articulate and communicate. Sympathetic discourse provided a framework of reference for philosophical maxims,
literary models, and moral principles. The eighteenth century's faith in
social progress depended on it.

It was all the more distressing then that attempts at conversation in a
social setting seemed feeble, even in self-styled Society, with its celebrated Season and its round of London entertainments. For most Europeans, eating together meant talking together. But the tedium of an
English dinner party was a recurrent complaint.[61] Even those who shared
the language were sometimes disappointed. The first United States
ambassador in London, John Adams, decided that the dinner party
'ruins the true American sociability'.[62]

Such judgements seemed the more surprising because England was famous for its dining tradition, both public and private. Nowhere else, it was thought, did so many dine so well and so frequently. Corporate feasting was a common feature of public bodies as well as private associations, providing English satirists with staple matter. Theodore Hook called dining in company 'the universal employment of our countrymen'.[63] Foreigners were intrigued and often impressed. Emerson thought dinner, rather than trial by jury, the capital institution of the English nation.[64] His countryman Nathaniel Hawthorne was startled by its almost spiritual quality. 'How tenaciously this love of pompous dinners, this reverence for dinner as a sacred institution, has caught hold of the English character.'[65] Others went further still. Charles Lyell recorded a remarkable tribute at the Geological Society in 1823: 'Professor Oersted, of Copenhagen, pronounced the following eulogium of our scientific dinners of which, as it was spoken in English, you may imagine the ludicrous effect. "Your public dinners, gentlemen, I do love, they are a sort of sacrament, in which, you do beautifully blend the spiritual and the corporeal!!" '[66] Englishmen might find such compliments fanciful but they certainly concurred that an English dinner had a uniquely agreeable quality. Exposed to prandial practices abroad their response was likely to be that of Henry Matthews, author of *Diary of an Invalid*, when entertained to a succession of Neapolitan banquets. 'Dinner is not here, generally speaking, the social feast of elaborate enjoyment, which we are accustomed to make it in England.'[67]

But if an English dinner was a social feast it did not follow that repartee was on the menu. The contrast with France was especially striking. There, for all the regard paid to cuisine, it was primarily the accompaniment to a display of conversational skill. In the 'oratory of the table' wit and wisdom could flourish.[68] In England they could hardly exist at all given the absence of general conversation. 'The conversation never extends beyond your next neighbour, and it would excite attention to make a speech across the table.'[69] The exceptions proved the rule. Sydney Smith was well aware that his own success resulted from his insistence on totally ignoring it. 'Most London dinners evaporate in whispers to one's next-door neighbour. I make it a rule never to speak a word to mine, but fire across the table.'[70]

Conversation in England did not accompany dinner, but followed it,

at any rate so far as men were concerned. 'Frenchmen are very loquacious at table, and during the act of eating; the Englishman enjoys the
conversation over his dessert and wine.'[71] But even then there were distinctive features. The American ambassador Richard Rush, a thoroughgoing Anglophile who delighted in the opportunity to mix in high
society, noted that self-expression at an English dinner party depended
paradoxically on a marked sense of restraint, 'a disciplined forbearance,
under the golden requisition of which none talk too much'.[72]

Moreover, dining in the English manner was a social occasion only by
appointment. When the English were eating in public, in restaurants or
hotels, they seemed as withdrawn as ever. In such establishments tables
were normally set apart from each other in boarded or curtained booths.
Even when there was an opportunity to open up, they avoided taking it.
London eating houses were gloomy places in which a stranger stood no
chance of striking up a friendship with the natives. The contrast with the
Continental table d'hôte could not fail to strike travellers in both directions. Young Englishmen on the Grand Tour were notoriously nonplussed at having to hold their own in a motley assembly of casual
acquaintances for whom eating was synonymous with conversing. When
women travellers proliferated in the early nineteenth century they were
equally startled. Anna Bray's first experience, on holiday in Normandy,
led her to reflect on the oddity of this kind of sociability. 'Conversation
seemed as much the object of attention as their repast; the whole party
spoke together, and made a most unceasing voluble noise.'[73]

Tables d'hôte were not unheard of in England. In boarding houses
they were unavoidable, if only for reasons of domestic economy, and even
in the better establishments in some fashionable resorts, they prospered.
This was especially the case at Harrogate, Buxton, and Matlock, where
there were few private lodgings, and where, as an aristocratic visitor
remarked, 'everybody dines at a *table d'hôte*, and nobody can choose their
next neighbour'.[74] Even so, they were not known for generating the easy
atmosphere of Continental inns. Disputes about social precedence in
such an open setting sometimes drove genteel visitors to dine not very
comfortably in their own chambers in pursuit of 'quiet meals'.[75] Deliberate attempts to create a comparable experience were not notably successful. The young Scotswoman Catherine Sinclair was disappointed by
one such at Cheltenham in 1833. Expecting the feast of wit and soci-

ability of which she had read in Continental travels, she prepared herself with care for dinner in a renowned Cheltenham hotel. 'The door flew open, we entered, and found—such a failure! Two old gentlemen belonging to the last century, with a lady apparently of similar date, who seemed habitués of the house, were seated at dinner, all prodigious eaters, and not much given to conversation; as every word spoken they addressed to "Thomas," the waiter.'[76]

Informal gatherings did not seem much better, even in the most refined society. The standard form of social mixing in private homes in the West End by the end of the eighteenth century was the 'rout'. Continental visitors noted that in essence it was an imitation of the Italian *conversazione* but without the ease which Italians practised so effortlessly.[77] In fact it resembled nothing so much as a gigantic crush, as one of the expressions coined to describe such gatherings, 'squeeze', implied.[78] The gentility of these evening meetings, 'so much in vogue among all ranks of the community, from the dowager countess in May-fair, down to the substantial tradesman's wife in her rural retreat at Hackney . . . is to be estimated by the difficulty of breathing and moving about!'[79] The mêlée semed more appropriate to a boxing match.[80] Archibald Alison called it 'corporeal and mental torture' and noted the irony of invitation cards to an '"At Home." That any set of rational men and women should volunteer into such service as this, is really inconceivable: Yet such is the modern notion of the perfection of English society; and not content with this, they have denominated this unnatural convocation, this scene of all that is rude and jarring, by that hallowed word of Home, which has so long connected itself with far different scenes—scenes of pure, tranquil and unobtrusive enjoyment.'[81]

What did people do at these parties? enquired Blanco White. 'Why, the same as at a funeral in Seville: they put in an appearance. The host stands at the door of the drawing-room and spends two or three hours shaking the hand of those who manage to reach them through the throng, "very pleased to see you" and hoping you will go as soon as possible.'[82] Conversation was not to be expected beyond an enquiry after one's health and a remark on the weather. Play was not an aid to repartee but a substitute for it. 'In such assemblies as I have just described, cards usurp the place of conversation; from which all rationality is banished. Here a crowd, who cannot get even the accommodation of a temporary seat, squeeze past each other in dull rotation from room to room; and, having compleated the scrutinizing stare over each other's dress and person, repair to a succession of similar scenes till some favorite air at the end of the opera or the ballet calls them to the theatre, where the buzz and bustle of the coffee-room concludes the pleasures and amusements of the night.'[83] On all such occasions a distinctive etiquette seemed designed to minimize the chances of enjoyable intercourse. In polite society it was a dire breach of good manners to address a person to whom one had not been introduced by a third party. French visitors considered this highly inconvenient, especially where ladies were involved. The English shyness of large groups could also be inhibiting. One of the virtues of the famous hostess, Lady Blessington, was that she had 'the peculiar and most unusual talent of keeping the conversation in a numerous circle *general*, and of preventing her guests from dividing into little selfish *pelotons*'.[84]

'Une conversation à l'Angloise' was considered by foreigners as simply a long silence.[85] The stage Englishman in both France and Italy was a ludicrously tongue-tied buffoon. In England itself, charitably disposed foreigners put the kindest possible gloss on this trait. The German immigrant Wendeborn tried to make it seem an eccentric but not objectionable interruption in the flow of sociable discourse. 'It now and then happens in English companies, that after much conversation and pleasantry, a sudden pause is made for some minutes, during which they look at one another with serious attention. They know that this is peculiar to them, and call therefore this short silence, *an English conversation*.'[86] The Swiss Muralt noted a resulting oddity. He was initially puzzled by the tedious 'How d'ye do's' with which the English punctuated the long silences of their conversation, but decided it must be a form of politeness. The object was simply to remind one's collocutor that one was listening and that silence did not betoken inattention.[87] This shortcoming was a source of embarrassment to cosmopolitan Britons, especially when they encountered French 'facility of expression', as Anna Bray put it. She was intrigued by the complete absence of any of the conversational devices observed by Muralt. 'Nor do they, as it sometimes happens in England, snuff the candles, stir the fire, or have recourse to "It's fine weather," or "I wonder what's o'clock," as a help to fill up the dead pause of conversation, where all have the faculty to hear, but none the talent to speak.'[88]

Other British commentators were more scathing still. Hogarth's 'Midnight Modern Conversation' belonged in a self-mocking genre that portrayed complacent, inebriated inarticulateness as all too typical of a sociable evening. Celtic satirists could hardly miss this target. Arthur Murphy designed 'An Englishman in Paris' to appeal to the xenophobia of the London theatregoer, but he was confident that his audience would share the joke when he had his Jack Broughton, returning to London after a sojourn in Paris, announce: 'this is an English Visit, and I'll sustain an English Conversation. (He continues silent for some time, looks at Mr. Quicksett and at last addresses him) How do you do? How do y'do? What News? A very dull day.'[89] The Scottish belletrist Henry Mackenzie also traded on the taciturnity that prevailed south of the border, sarcastically offering the axiom that 'conversation spoils good company'.[90]

Was this a matter of preference or inadequacy? The English themselves often admitted that they lacked confidence when it came to holding forth. The French gift was for conversing freely with friends, in the presence of strangers, without displaying or causing unease.[91] To watch an Englishman attempting conversation was to observe not so much witlessness as timidity. Cowper memorably described the

> bashful men, who feel the pain
> Of fancied scorn and undeserved disdain,
>   And bear the marks upon a blushing face
> Of needless shame, and self-imposed disgrace.
>   Our sensibilities are so acute,
>   The fear of being silent makes us mute.
> We sometimes think we could a speech produce
> Much to the purpose, if our tongues were loose;
>   But being tied, it dies upon the lip,
> Faint as the chicken's note that has the pip:
>   Our wasted oil unprofitably burns,
>   Like hidden lamps in old sepulchral urns,
> Few Frenchmen of this evil have complained;
> It seems as if we Britons were ordained,
>   By way of wholesome curb upon our pride,
>   To fear each other, fearing none beside.[92]

What could account for this pusillanimity? The philosopher of counter-revolution, Joseph de Maistre, believed that it was rooted in a sense of intellectual inferiority. The English preferred to be thought boors rather than simpletons, and opted for silence in dread of saying something that might seem foolish.[93]

Whatever the cause, some distinctive features of domestic life made sense when interpreted as part of a national strategy for overcoming this horror of self-exposure. Descriptions of domestic interiors reveal various arrangements intended to promote conversation. The books of caricatures and prints to be found on drawing-room tables had a social, not an aesthetic, function. 'Those unfortunates who cannot be got to talk, or are nervously reserved, are usually set by the hostess to find entertainment, and become social over a portfolio of ludicrous scenes in which celebrated personages have acted with more or less success.'[94] On the walls, framed conversation pieces, whether in oil or mezzotint, served a similar function. Even here, though, it was noticeable that the English made this a rather distinctive art form, for it was rarely a depiction of conversation at all, except in the older sense of the word, as human contact and sociability.[95] Its subject was rather the status, character, and manners of those portrayed. The contrast with the French genre, in which the conversation took place on the canvas, uniting viewer and viewed, was striking.[96]

The use of furniture not to enclose space but to fill it, and thereby to encourage social contact, was a late eighteenth-century trend commenced in Britain and resisted by high society elsewhere. Closely related was the longer-standing centrality of the hearth in an English home. Georgiana Chatterton offered a systematic analysis of this subject, provoked by her experience of Continental sociability.

The English have not by nature sufficient sociability in their dispositions to do without a visible fire. A cheerful blaze is necessary to thaw their innate shyness and reserve, and to form a central point of union. . . . They cannot converse comfortably with their hands unemployed. Some excuse must be found for idleness; some reason for being in one part of the room in preference to another. The slightest appearance of formality terrifies them beyond measure, because it reminds them of their own defects . . . All manner of contrivances are employed to break the bug-bear *form*. In summer, ottomans, albums, and windows, supply in some measure the loss of the darling fire, and enable English men and women to try and talk to each other. At first sight, society abroad often appears formal to English taste, because the houses are not crammed as full as they can hold, and people do not sit in all parts of the room. But foreigners do not feel under any particular restraint because they are sitting in a circle. They all talk away to each other with the greatest ease, and never feel the slightest scruple in traversing the empty space if they wish to converse with any one on the other side. The English are well aware of their own innate formality of disposition, and therefore seek, by outward arrangements, to remedy the defect. But all this will not do; unless they feel at ease, they will never be able to impart that feeling to others.[97]

Significantly, when the English did succeed as conversationalists, it was their confidence as much as their wit that seemed to distinguish them from their countrymen. Fenimore Cooper thought the renowned 'Conversation' Sharp living proof of the point. He found him more a gossip than a conversationalist, but 'rather more disposed than usual to break the stiff silence that sometimes renders an English party awkward, and may have become distinguished in that way'.[98]

Sharp was prominent in a campaign to improve English conversation at the turn of the eighteenth century, when prolonged warfare kept potential Grand Tourists at home and self-conscious literary improvement was in vogue. The result was the celebrated King of Clubs based at the Crown and Anchor in the Strand. In retrospect it is the contrived nature of its proceedings that seems most striking. The custom was to keep ledgers of witticisms employed, not so much for purposes of record but rather to avoid repetition in the same company.[99] The club's two leading lights were James Mackintosh and Sharp himself. According to the poet-businessman Samuel Rogers, Mackintosh 'sacrificed himself to conversation, read for it, thought for it, and gave up future fame for it'. Accounts of Sharp also suggest choreographed rituals rather than eruptions of spontaneous wit. 'There is a story of Richard Sharp having one day seen on the desk the notes of the conversation in which his partner Boddington was to join in the evening. Sharp was to be of the party, and he committed to memory the prepared impromptus of his friend, assisted him to lead the conversation in the right direction, and then forestalled him with his stories and clever things.'[100]

It was this want of spontaneity that left some judges unimpressed. The young Francis Horner, fresh from the conversational vigour of Edinburgh in its heyday as the Athens of the North, thought the King of Clubs lacking in 'intellectual gladiatorship', and found too much 'assentation' between Sharp and Mackintosh.[101] Much the same point could be made about attempts by polite society to incorporate the spirit of the King of Clubs. Mid-Victorians often looked back to the Regency and Reign of George IV as a golden age of table talk. But the more candid among them admitted its carefully calculated character. Recalling conversational dinners featuring Thomas Moore, Samuel Rogers, Henry Luttrell, and Sydney Smith, Frances Lady Shelley remarked that they were 'invited especially to give the *ton*, and to lead the conversation, whose brilliancy had often been prepared with as much care as a fine lady bestows upon her Court dress. The conversation was seldom impromptu . . . yet everyone accepted its charm without scrutinising too closely the manner of its "get-up".'[102] In effect, this was turning conversation into a performing art, as the wife of a United States ambassador shrewdly concluded. 'The English habit seems to be to suffer a few people to do up a great part of the talking.'[103]

Experiments such as the King of Clubs were often cited in conduct manuals directed to improving English conversation and elocution. Whatever it did to keep up the income of those who published, lectured, and tutored in the subject, its practical effect was often doubted. The *Quarterly Review* employed some effective sarcasm on this subject. 'It is this doctrine we are most anxious to protest against. There may be no great harm in encouraging young ladies to kiss their hands from balconies or young gentlemen to eat gooseberry pie with a spoon, and we apprehend little danger from the threatened inroad of silver forks and napkins into regions hitherto unconscious of them; but we deprecate all attempts to extend the breed of village Jekylls or convert our mute inglorious Sheridans into talking ones.'[104] The *Quarterly*'s rival, the *Edinburgh Review*, was equally scathing, even when the authority was as learned as that of Oxford's William King. King had recommended daily memorizing a page of one of the English classics for young men at university. This assumed, the *Review* pointed out, that the deficiency was one of education, whereas it was actually a national 'shyness composed of mixture of timidity and pride'. 'We do not put forth our force in conversation; we are ashamed of turning sentences; we dislike attracting the attention of others to our manner of speech, by seeming to make it the object of our own.'[105]

Englishmen embarrassed by their inadequacy as a nation often believed that good conversation had existed in the past. Successive generations found reasons for explaining a decline in this respect. Marlborough, the victor of Blenheim, believed that in his lifetime the rage for cards had destroyed the art of conversation.[106] Later, Burke thought he observed towards the end of his life a reaction against the mid-eighteenth century's obsession with correct taste. 'Great disgust at the pedantry of the last age in some of the higher Classes produced at last an insipid Languor in conversation very distressing now to general society.' The result was a veritable system of Terror in London as in Paris, but directed at conversationalists rather than counter-revolutionaries.[107] Later still, in the nineteenth century, successive generations of self-made plutocrats were blamed for mistrust of verbal brilliance and wit.[108]

By this time a talent for talking was indeed a prized component of literary tradition, as the vogue for 'Table talk', 'Wit and Wisdom', and 'Ana' suggests. But memorable sayings are not synonymous with interesting conversation, and when the English looked back on their literary history they found it difficult to come up with examples of intellectual giants whose authority was matched by a reputation for a ready tongue. Most of the available evidence suggested quite the contrary. Addison, the father of modern English politeness, was no conversationalist, admitting with a characteristically commercial metaphor that he could draw a bill for a thousand pounds but had not a guinea in his pocket.[109] Other celebrated writers were thought no better at communicating their wit and wisdom in person. Charles Churchill was one such with 'little to say in company'.[110] Dr Johnson, of course, was famed for his skill in disputation. But was he a conversationalist? His form of dialogue was not so much exchange as combat, its conclusion the defeat of an adversary, not the shared triumph of eirenic discourse.[111] His contemporary Gibbon was much admired for his wit, redolent of the French salon, yet as the politician James Burges remarked, his 'mode of discoursing' did not encourage the exchange of ideas, or even permit a reply.[112]

Similar doubts were expressed about the sages of the following age. Coleridge, Sydney Smith, Macaulay, and Carlyle were all charged with monologue rather than dialogue. They were not so much conversationalists as conversation-hoggers.[113] As Mrs Trench remarked of the conversation of another celebrated talker, Joseph Jekyll, it 'hardly consists in reciprocal communication. Jekyll talks; others applaud, excite, and listen.'[114] The contrast with some equally famous foreigners was stark.

When tourists visited Voltaire at Fernay they knew they were in the presence of outstanding civility as well as remarkable wit. To be in his presence and record his conversation was to participate in a whole culture. English parallels were hard to find. Wordsworth, the recipient of numerous visitors, was venerated for the genius that he exuded rather than for what he said. Many literary tourists expressed their delight at meeting him. But while they were inspired by his presence and 'moral elevation', they rarely recorded his 'mots'.[115]

In this matter at least, foreign travel was not notably liberating. Distinguished Britons were often lionized in Paris, the capital of civilized discourse, but they rarely shone. Was there something about English as a first language that simply disabled its speakers in this respect? Burke, like Gibbon, made little impression. Perhaps even the Francophile Scot David Hume, a renowned campaigner for the value of conversation, had been more contaminated by his English experience than he liked to admit. Madame d'Épinay's disappointment in his powers as a conversationalist, confirmed by the experience of placing him between two of the prettiest women in Paris and finding him utterly inarticulate, does not suggest that he was very good at practising his own precepts.[116] Nor does Horace Walpole's remark that 'Mr. Hume's writings were so superior to his conversation, that I frequently said he understood nothing till he had written upon it.'[117]

Where justification failed, mitigation was attempted. Much attention was paid to the relationship between English speech and the English language. Worries about the unsuitability of English for classical eloquence were long-standing.[118] In an essay that was later read widely by foreigners, in translations of the *Spectator*, Addison himself pointed out that the English tendency was always to contract speech to the minimum. This process had shortened the past participle of almost all English verbs by a syllable, so that 'drowned' had become 'drown'd'. It had replaced the suffix 'eth' as in 'sayeth' with a terminal 's' as in 'says' and thereby rendered English a strangely hissing kind of language full of sibilants. It had generated elisions of a kind which baffled foreign students of the language: 'can't' for 'cannot', 'won't' for 'will not', and so on. It had even led to the commonplace shortening of proper names, with unpleasing effects. Nicholas was inelegantly truncated to 'Nick', whereas Italians made it more graceful by the addition of a syllable: 'Nicolini'. All this Addison thought had ruined English as a language. On the other hand, as he put it, 'I have only considered our Language as it shews the Genius and natural Temper of the *English*, which is modest, thoughtful and sincere, and which may perhaps recommend the People, though it has spoiled the Tongue.'[119]

Foreigners agreed that the English seemed to speak in monosyllables, but sometimes offered less complimentary associations.[120] Samuel Sorbière remarked that they were 'great admirers of their own Language; and it suits their Effeminacy very well, for it spares them the Labour of moving their Lips'.[121] Sexual and conversational frigidity went together, as the Spaniard James Salgado implied when he described the Englishman speaking 'for fear his Mouth catch cold, Like Lady small-mouth'.[122] Even without the innuendo foreigners found English enunciation very peculiar. Viewing a Roman actor taking the role of an Englishman in 1760 Christopher Hervey noted the care he took 'to speak with his teeth always shut, which is the principal fault attributed to us, when we talk southern languages'.[123]

The Russian Karamzin made a similar judgement. 'It seems as though either the mouths of the English are gagged or there is a heavy tax for opening them. The people here scarcely unclench their teeth; they whistle, suggest, but do not talk.'[124] The abbé Coyer in 1779 confessed himself defeated by this peculiar whistling. He suggested one might understand the English better by looking at their expressions than listening to their words.[125] Half a century later the duchesse de Dino remarked that 'ears are less busy than eyes here' but admitted that at least the near silence of the English was restful.[126] Others were more critical. Heine described what he called the 'Zischlaute des Egoismus', the 'hiss of egoism'.[127] Even the English, when abroad and accustomed to other languages, might be struck by the 'lisping sounds' of compatriot voices.[128]

Syntax was also at issue, not least among orators themselves. Burke was one of those who 'complained of the discord and intractability of our language'.[129] His friend Lord Charlemont was struck by the contrast with the French, 'a nation endued with great advantages for public speaking. They are totally free from any degree of mauvaise honte. They rise for the first time to speak in the assembly, with more confidence than our oldest debaters. Added to this, they have an inconceivable fluency of language. They never hesitate; having the idea, it seems to clothe itself in expression. Perhaps the nature of their language may account for this. It is a language of phrases. There are scarcely two ways of expressing the same idea with equal propriety. The man who speaks correctly has little room to choose. Habit makes the phrase present itself with the turn of expression, and instead of casting about as we do for language, the moment he thinks, it offers itself spontaneously.'[130] In the following generation Lord Houghton made a similar comparison when analysing the deficiencies of parliamentary debate at Westminster.

Nor is our language one that lends itself to frequent and ready speech. I have attended public debates in France, Spain, and other foreign countries, and I never witnessed abroad anything like the hesitation, the haggling, and the difficulty of finding words which prevail in our House of Commons. Englishmen always seem to say what they must say, while Frenchmen seem to be able to say anything they choose. The truth is, that the composite nature of the English language produces in the mind of a speaker hesitation as to the best construction and the best word to employ; and thus some of our best public speakers hang, as it were, on a precipice for the choice of a word, and bring down the acclamations of their audience when they happen to hit upon a right one.[131]

There were simpler and less complimentary analyses. Fenimore Cooper remarked, not without malice, that 'The French, in this respect, have the advantage of us, their language having no emphatic syllables. A Frenchman will often talk an hour without a true argument or a false quantity.'[132]

Defenders of the English language retaliated by blaming foreigners for its stunted form and stilted enunciation. As the philologist Samuel Henshall put it: 'our slow-speaking ancestors always annexed ideas, or common sense, to their words, and this nation, happily, has retained the language that can convey them; but the Norman and French innovators, "talking like popinjays," have so apostrophized, abbreviated, or cut short our Mother Tongue, to give volubility to *their tongue*, that labour and penetration are necessary to discover the Parent-Root from the altered Form of the Off-spring.'[133] This was a linguistic version of the Norman yoke. Old English, like the Ancient Constitution, had been undermined by foreign innovations.

Henshall's was a self-consciously 'Little England' standpoint. Many of his compatriots were more concerned with the language of cosmopolitan politeness. For them it was embarrassing that English as a tongue should be so far adrift of the Continental mainstream. Theirs was not the only regressive language in this respect, but it did seem uniquely ill-favoured. French enjoyed undisputed supremacy as the language of sociable intercourse. Other Latin languages received honourable mention. Germanic tongues were generally derided. It was a common-place point that German itself was ill-adapted to conversation. A language in which each sentence had to be completed for its meaning to be certain was not one which lent itself to the thrust and counter-thrust of repar-tee. Unfortunately English seemed to have gone to the opposite extreme. Where Germans conversed badly, the English were ceasing to converse at all.[134]

There was a certain convenience in blaming the English language for the deficiencies of English conversation. Unfortunately, it was not clear that the blame was fairly apportioned. For one thing, not all English-speakers seemed inadequate as conversationalists. There was, it was reported, no 'shyness of conversation' across the Atlantic.[135] The young British diplomat Henry Addington described it as 'prosy and verbose'.[136] Harriet Martineau similarly found American English 'prosy, but withal rich and droll' and after initial dismay at its seeming long-windedness, grew to relish its picturesque and informative qualities. She also noted that Americans considered English conversation 'hasty, sharp and rough'.[137] It was indeed claimed by American authors that the Addison-ian tradition had denied the potential of English as a language, with its relentless quest for a severely classical, rational discourse. Literature, manners, and public oratory were all affected in England by a tendency to 'push simplicity to affectation' whereas across the Atlantic the richness of English vocabulary and syntax were vigorously exploited.[138]

Closer to home Celtic speakers of English were admitted even by the English to have certain advantages. Edinburgh was a 'talking town', and the Scots a 'people of talkers'.[139] Historians brought supporting evidence from ancient accounts of the 'bold and ready eloquence' of the Britons.[140] This was not necessarily a matter of compliment. To concede that Celts, especially the Irish, possessed the 'gift of the gab' savoured as much of accusation as admiration on an Englishman's lips. It granted a superior-ity whose real value was not to be admitted, except perhaps in those whose upbringing provided a measure of linguistic discipline. 'The gift of the gab is the property of the populace, circumlocution that of the middle rank, and eloquence the portion of the educated Hibernian.'[141] Even then there were unfavourable connotations. The anti-Irishness of the London press, often at the expense of Irishmen whose trade was words, in Parliament or on the stage, depended on the assumption that they talked too much, and often without sincerity. The Welsh frequently suffered in the same way.

For their part, Celtic critics believed that the English failing was deeply rooted. Giraldus Cambrensis, the 'malicious Welshman' as Gibbon called the chronicler, could be quoted for his claim that it was Norman subjugation that had rendered the Anglo-Saxons permanently speechless.[142] The *Edinburgh Review* attributed it to an underlying surliness. 'There is nothing which an Englishman enjoys more than the pleasure of sulkiness,—of not being forced to hear a word from any body which may occasion to him the necessity of replying. It is not so much that Mr Bull disdains to talk, as that Mr Bull has nothing to say. His forefathers have been out of spirits for six or seven hundred years, and seeing nothing but fog and vapour, he is out of spirits too; and when there is no selling and buying, or no business to settle, he prefers being alone and looking at the fire.'[143] The Irish novelist and hostess Lady Morgan was slightly less withering but still more damning, deciding that native stolidity rather than misanthropy was at issue. 'I have seen the best and the worst of English society; I have dined at the table of a *city trader*, taken tea with the family of a *London merchant*, and supped at Devonshire house, all in one day, and I must say, that if there is a people upon earth that understand the *science of conversation* less than another, it is the English. The quickness, the variety, the rapidity of perception and impression, which is indispensable to render conversation delightful, is *constitutionally* denied to them; like all people of slowly operating mental faculties, and of business pursuits, they depend upon *memory* more than upon *spontaneous* thought.'[144]

ORATORY

Lady Morgan's testimony is interesting not only because she was Irish but because she was a woman. It was received wisdom, that the Fair Sex

were, in Hume's words, 'the Sovereigns of the Empire of Conversation'.[145] However, they manifestly needed a certain degree of freedom to
be able to enforce this sovereignty. Saint-Évremond put the theory in its
simplest form when he argued that in unliberated countries such as
Spain, where women were often sequestered from men, the essence of
romance was to gain physical access to them. Latin lovers were men of
action, because it was action that gained them the company of women.
Where the female sex was free, as in France, the emphasis was on wooing
with words. Women in a position to choose required more than mere
passion. Their currency was conversation. It followed that the wit and
wisdom of the salon was the surest test of female independence.[146]

English women failed this test. Pöllnitz observed that they have 'but
little Talk, and their chief Conversation is the Flutter of their Fans'.[147]
Perhaps the most devastating of all indictments came from Madame de
Staël. Her Corinna thought an Italian convent full of life compared with
an English drawing-room, and in translation her account of the tedium
of tea-table talk stung successive generations of English women who read
it.[148] Visiting foreigners generally considered it not unjust, excepting only
the conversational ease that might be found within a confined family
circle.[149] Significantly, the contrast was not only with Mme de Staël's
countrywomen, but with the Celtic inhabitants of the British Isles. Irish
women especially had a notable 'vivacity of conversation'.[150]

It seemed odd that the societies with which the English did apparently
have something in common in this respect would have been thought
highly regressive by comparison with Britain. In Brazil, for instance, it
was noticed that men and women in social settings tended to segregate
by sex, with damaging consequences for the art of conversation.[151] Yet
this was precisely the criticism made of English society by foreigners. 'In
parties, the ladies always keep together, and beyond certain prescribed
formalities, are treated with perfect indifference.'[152] In a typical drawing-
room it was a common sight to see women talking in one group and men
in another. The same behaviour applied in ballrooms. Men seemed
incapable of conversing with women, especially with more than one
woman at a time. Confronted with the female sex in a body their reaction was to engross the attention of one of its number. Hence, so it was
said, the peculiar English custom at a ball, by which gentlemen dancers
made themselves responsible for entertaining their partner for a whole

evening. Women who did not find an escort at the outset were likely to spend the evening on their own, an expectation which must have intensified the female anxiety and competitiveness that preceded a ball.[153]

Again there were societies within the British Isles that provided a contrast. Edward Topham in 1776 described practices in Edinburgh which seemed very unlike what happened south of the border. 'Whenever the Scotch of both sexes meet, they do not appear as if they had never seen each other before, or wish never to see each other again: they do not sit in sullen silence, looking on the ground, biting their nails, and at a loss what to do with themselves; and, if some one should be hardy enough to break silence, start, as if they were shot through the ear with a pistol: but they address each other at first sight, and with an *impressement* that is highly pleasing.'[154]

The new sensibilities of the eighteenth century implied constant reassessment of the place of women in social life. None the less, conventional English wisdom continued to censure or ridicule female eloquence. The *Spectator*'s noble desire to provide suitable subjects for the tea-table has often been lauded for its precocious feminism, yet running through Addison's discourse with his women readers was a continuous thread of misogynism. The assumption was that female conversation depended at best on superficial wit and included no place for argument.[155] Numerous eighteenth-century works, including *The School for Scandal*, derived their success from the theme of the malice and unenlightenment of ladies' *conversazioni*.[156]

Didactic literature left still less room for doubt in this zone of social intercourse. Samuel Richardson, whose novels were for some readers the equivalent of conduct books opined that 'there are very few topics that arise in conversation among men, upon which women ought to open their lips. Silence becomes them. Let them therefore hear, wonder, and improve, in silence.'[157] In the succession of moralizing advice to daughters, instructions to young women, and so on which proved so marketable in the following years the point was made repeatedly, reinforced by the claim that for an Englishman female speechlessness was a significant element in sexual attraction. 'Will not her very silence interest?' enquired James Fordyce.[158] Such attitudes are entrenched in the social commentaries of the eighteenth and early nineteenth centuries, not least those recorded by women themselves. It was the socialite Lady

Charlotte Bury who remarked of a female friend that 'she is very agreeable, and, I think, has much natural cleverness; but it is all wasted in
eloquence in conversation'.[159]

A corollary was English suspicion of the French salon. Some, like the
actress Fanny Kemble, thought it inimitable. 'The intimate, easy, constant
intercourse of a French *salon* is not to be obtained in England, the antisocial temper and formal habits of our people being ill adapted to it.'[160]
Attempts at imitation, by such as Lady Holland, Lady Cork, and Lady
Blessington, the last two incidentally Irishwomen, were not altogether
successful. Lady Cork set out to create a Parisian atmosphere but succeeded only in acquiring a reputation for eccentricity. Lady Blessington's
assemblies were regarded as rather raffish affairs, frequented by rakes and
foreigners. Charles Greville's indictment was devastating. 'There is a vast
deal of coming and going, and eating and drinking, and a corresponding
amount of noise, but little or no conversation, discussion, easy quiet
interchange of ideas and opinions, no regular social foundation of men
of intellectual or literary calibre ensuring a perennial flow of conversation, and which, if it existed, would derive strength and assistance from
the light superstructure of occasional visitors, with the much or the little
they might individually contribute. The reason of this is that the woman
herself, who must give the tone to her own society, and influence its character, is ignorant, vulgar, and commonplace.'[161]

Lady Blessington could doubtless have responded in kind. She seems
to have regarded herself as a polite colonist in a land of barbarism. The
barbarians were the men rather than the women. Insular ideals of masculinity certainly associated the virtue of silence more particularly with
men. 'If we speak little, it is because we are taught that women are made
to babble and men to think.'[162] This was the observation of a Francophile
Italian, seeking to put himself in the position of a rational Englishman
defending his taciturnity. It was not, however, the only defence available
to the English male. Indeed, by and large, when the English wanted to
deride French facility in conversation they did not resort to the German
tactic, which was to assert that the French were a talking people, whereas
the Germans were a thinking people.[163] They preferred to claim that
talking must have a publicly defensible function. It must have a purpose
beyond mere sociability and exhibitionism. The point was sometimes
well taken by their neighbours. Madame Roland conceded that the

French were 'no good at discussion. They have a sort of levity; they skip from subject to subject without proper order and never pursue anyone's thesis to a conclusion. They are not good listeners.'[164] The challenge was to offer a coherent and convincing alternative. Constructing a model of English capacity in the science of communication, one that took full account of national character without conceding its inferiority, was an important part of the vindication of Englishness being mounted in the late eighteenth and early nineteenth century.

Politics was central to this process, unsurprisingly given a strong, and steadily strengthening, parliamentary tradition. It provided the staple of everyday conversation. Kielmansegge described an encounter among strangers in England as a deep silence, followed by some circumspect remarks on the roads or weather, before political topics were broached.[165] It was also noticed that politics was the only subject on which the most taciturn Englishman was liable to become suddenly animated and eloquent.[166] This could, of course, be considered in very diverse lights. From the standpoint of outsiders it was not necessarily something to boast of. Indeed, the Englishman's political sophistication might be an impediment to his polite progress. A recurrent complaint about what passed for English conversation was its obsession with parochial concerns. These were often political in the narrowest sense, and for the rest political in the sense that they concerned the way English people managed their 'business', especially the business of public affairs and the business of commercial transactions, as Johanna Schopenhauer concluded.[167]

The English possessed the virtue of practicality with its attendant vice of pettiness. They were incapable of breadth and generality. A learned American, Benjamin Silliman, was dismayed on his visit to England in 1805–6 by the 'personal and local' character of conversation, even in circles which might have been expected to be capable of a more elevated tone. The peculation of Lord Melville and the merits of the wine were the nearest things to general topics at a Liverpool dinner party.[168] Not only merchants were thus constrained. Aristocrats were unlikely to be interested in trade, but for them the alternative to politics was not more enlightened. Prince Albert complained that 'the English nobility in general could talk of nothing but horses, dogs, and politics'.[169]

Women were also affected by such preoccupations. In a London conversation about politics, 'the women put in a word and almost always with much sense and subtlety'.[170] A taste for politics was essential to freeborn Englishwomen, if only with a view to catching a freeborn Englishman. So reasoned Archenholz. 'This passion is actually among them an inducement to marriage. A husband who can talk of nothing but public affairs, is always sure to find in his wife a person with whom he may converse concerning those topics which interest him most. He has no need to go abroad, to satisfy his appetite for this darling subject.' But not only marriage was in question. Archenholz also repeated a well-known story that the Frenchified Irishman Lord Tyrconnel, who visited England for the first time when he was 30, vowed not to do so again when he found that even at a bagnio it was impossible to stop women prostitutes talking about Parliament and politics.[171]

Critics of English conversation frequently traced its deficiencies to this obsession with politics. Maurice Rubichon remarked that 'England may be the country of Europe in which least is said, yet it is that in which most ineptitudes are uttered'.[172] When Niebuhr visited in 1798 he found conversation, but thought it heavily formulaic.[173] Self-conscious improvers of conversational skills were also aware that politics was a problem. One author helpfully provided a *Dictionary of Conversation* to give a nation whose vision had been permanently narrowed by this preoccupation a guide to the alternative subjects that they might consider.[174] It might have been supposed that a country with so rich a literature would not be short of elevating topics. But the rejoinder was not difficult to find. A high proportion of what the English read came in the form of periodical pap. Newspapers were filled with the novelties and trivialities of the moment. They also provided their readers with ready-made opinions. In Continental cities with a less flourishing press there was more scope for originality, less repetition of what the newspapers said.[175]

Could there be a positive side to this? If so, it must be in that public arena where the highest common factor of communal life prevailed, and where the tendency to practicality and pettiness, properly directed and disciplined, could be turned to good account. Englishmen were trained in oratory, the art of haranguing one's fellow countrymen in Parliament, or at a public meeting, rather than the art of conversing with them. The baron de Staël-Holstein claimed to have met an extreme case in real life.

'I know a man, whose timidity in company is scarcely equalled by that of a girl of fifteen, who in a drawing room would not answer the simplest question without blushing and confusion, yet if invited to give his opinion at a public meeting would rise without hesitation, and speak for more than an hour in an easy and copious style before thousands of his fellow citizens.'[176] Trollope's Pallisers, in Lady Glencora's words, were 'non-talkers. That doesn't mean that they are not speakers, for Mr. Palliser has plenty to say in the House.'[177] It could be argued that oratory and conversation were indeed incompatible skills. Even in France, when the Revolution came, the traditional art of conversation was thought to have suffered, as Frenchmen turned from debate in private to disputation in public.

It was precisely the nature of English eloquence that it was about talking at people, not talking to them, a matter of political tradition more than social skill. In effect, this was not sympathetic communication but a form of demonstration. It exhibited power even when it aimed at persuasion. Louis Simond noticed that in the House of Commons the principal gesture was striking down a clenched fist; in France it was an outstretched hand.[178] Vigour, even violence, often characterized the most effective speakers. Not the least of Gladstone's rhetorical weapons was his physical dynamism, especially his habit of banging a fist on an open hand.[179]

Making a virtue of necessity, it was possible for foreigners to disparage parliamentary rhetoric as futile garrulousness on the part of the English, 'who think that the essence of liberty consists in babbling'.[180] But it was the aristocratic Freiherr von Riesbeck who offered this judgement and at the time he made it, in 1776, it was far from the common one. In fact in the late eighteenth century British oratory enjoyed a considerable vogue on the Continent. From the 1770s parliamentary speeches were not only available in the English press but widely reprinted in the journals of Continental Europe, providing aspiring politicians with much material. In Frankfurt where she was startled to find Germans discussing English politics for want of any of their own, Ann Radcliffe was moved to protest at this most English of masculine preoccupations. 'The faculty of making a speech is taken for the standard of intellectual power in every sort of exertion; though there is nothing better known in countries, where public speakers are numerous enough to be often observed, than that persons may be educated to oratory.'[181]

English schooling in oratory was certainly impressive. Public debating societies were a favourite subject of comment. By the 1770s they had become a standard means of experiment and exhibition for young men with political ambitions but no obvious means of expressing them. The fact that many admitted women as spectators and some permitted female participation added to the interest of these proceedings.[182] They also seemed intensely English. The attempted suppression of such societies in the loyalist reaction of the 1790s was described by the radical John Gale Jones as a 'Degradation of the National Character'.[183]

Faith in formal oratory survived such trials. If anything, its status in public schools increased, as schoolmasters appealed more and more consciously to parents hoping for a distinguished public career for their sons. The universities were rather slower to provide a matching service. Lord Normanby, who received instruction in public speaking from his father, Lord Mulgrave, had to attend a town debating society in Cambridge to develop his skills while at university after the Napoleonic Wars.[184] For the next generation the Oxford and Cambridge Unions provided a more genteel setting, enabling gown to dispense with town.

Whether such experience equipped the Ciceronian tyro for life in either House was another matter. Lord Byron took pains to prepare himself for the part of patriotic statesman but abandoned his attempt to shine in the role in Parliament at an early stage.[185] He was not the only one to find that oratorical training at public schools and debating societies took little account of the practical requirements of parliamentary life. Wellesley remarked in 1829 that the smartly turned phrase of the practised Union speaker irritated rather than impressed ordinary backbenchers.[186] A related point was offered at the time of the 1832 Reform Act by Charles Watkin Williams Wynn, 'who made a very good observation on the young orators coming forward ready formed from debating societies, instead of learning their trade in the House of Commons, which he says makes them rhetoricians, and not business speakers'.[187] The distinction was telling. After all, the English flair was meant to be for business, not high-sounding talk, and if oratory savoured more of the latter than the former, it lost its prime purpose. The Russian traveller

Karamzin, like others before him, was struck by the similarity between the Exchange and the House of Commons. Each revealed intense application to business in a consensual, almost collegiate spirit, within loose but effective rules of procedure. In the one the British gave laws to themselves; in the other they gave law to the entire world, at any rate the world of commerce, which was coming to seem pretty much the same thing. If Karamzin had scrutinized more closely how much of the Commons' own business was concerned with the concerns of exchanges and marts, he would have been even more persuaded of the similarity.

CLUBBABILITY

The paradox here was that the mode of debate required for the conduct of business seemed to require qualities that were lacking in a social context. Parliamentary discourse struck foreigners as distinctly conversational. It was intimate, direct, unpretentious. It lacked form and formality. Over-polished contributions of the kind offered by the future Prime Minister Lord Liverpool as a young man in the House of Commons, were dismissed as 'speechifying'.[188] Written preparation of speeches in Parliament and indeed in other assemblies was frowned upon, something that struck the baron de Staël-Holstein as peculiarly English. 'To speak in public and to speak extempore, are synonymous terms.'[189] Members were by and large good-humoured. The notorious English spleen did not characterize parliamentary proceedings. Debate was in the nature of a continual exchange of views, with constant interruptions, interjections, interrogations. The rules of parliamentary procedure made the delivery of set speeches virtually impossible, unless the speaker commanded the respect to quell challengers and hecklers. Parliamentary oratory seemed notably lacking in the traditional techniques of rhetoric. In short, ordinary debate seemed like nothing so much, in Louis Simond's words, as 'an argumentative and uninterrupted conversation'.[190] Very similar comments were made about the Upper House. The peers debated by way of conversation, not oratory.[191] The sense of continuous interaction between speaker and audience sometimes shocked Americans, whose own legislators were not used to interruption.[192] For their part, the British were apt to counter with Lord Lyndhurst, son of the American painter J. S. Copley and a Tory Lord Chancellor, that 'debates' took place in Parliament and 'speeches' in Congress.[193]

Many of those who knew the Commons concurred. The parliamentary reporter Edward Whitty described Commons debating as 'elegant conversation'.[194] Sir James Mackintosh, who as a schoolboy in Aberdeenshire had delighted in acting out the oratorical performances of Fox and Burke, as reported in the *Aberdeen Journal*, found the reality far from oratorical.[195] He 'characterised it by saying, that "the true light in which to consider it, *was as animated conversation on public business*"; and, he added, that it was "rare for any speech to succeed in that body which was raised on any other basis."' George Canning agreed, remarking 'that their speaking must take *conversation* as its basis, rather than anything studied, or stately. The House was a business-doing body and the speaking must conform to its character; it was jealous of ornament in debate, which, if it came at all, must come as without consciousness. There must be method also; but this should be felt in the effect, rather than seen in the manner; no formal divisions, set exordiums or perorations, as the old rhetoricians taught, would do. First, and last, and everywhere, you must aim at reasoning; and if you could be eloquent, you might be at any time, but not at an appointed time.'[196]

There were, of course, different kinds of parliamentary conversation. Bagehot believed that Canning was one of the last representatives of an aristocratic tradition that submitted to a more utilitarian order in the 1830s. 'The House was composed mainly of men trained in two great schools, on a peculiar mode of education, with no great real knowledge of the classics, but with many lines of Virgil and Horace lingering in fading memories, contrasting oddly with the sums and business with which they were necessarily brought side by side. These gentlemen wanted not to be instructed, but to be amused; and hence arose what, from the circumstance of their calling, may be called the class of conversationalist statesmen.' Canning was 'like the professional converser, . . . so apt at the finesse of expression, so prone to modulate his words, that you cannot imagine him putting his fine mind to tough thinking, really working, actually grappling with the rough substance of a great subject. He was early thrown into what we may call an aristocratic debating society, accustomed to be charmed, delighting in classic gladiatorship. The old delicate parliament is gone, and the gladiatorship which it loved. The progress of things, and the Reform Bill which was the result of that progress, have taken, and are taking, the national representation away from the university classes, and conferring it on the practical classes. Exposition, arithmetic, detail, reforms—these are the staple of our modern eloquence.'

For Bagehot, Peel epitomized the new middle-class eloquence which suggested not the profound thinker but the business gentleman.[197] Others agreed that the decline of oratory was due to a contempt of 'fine speaking' and a 'commercial, calculating spirit'.[198] But it was not only a commercial background that could breed such a mundane rhetoric. Lawyers, a large and growing element in the House of Commons, were also accustomed to prosaic discourse, as foreigners, used to a more declamatory style of pleading, noted. Amédée Pichot, who conducted a detailed comparison of contrasting modes of argumentation distinguished the English Bar, 'which is simple, devoid of ornament, and reduced to the dry discussion of facts', not only from its Continental counterparts but from those in Scotland and Ireland too. The result was remarkably uninspiring: 'the pretended London school presents no example of eloquence worthy to be distinguished in a literary point of view'.[199]

In truth, it was not common for the English to think either of the law-courts or the legislature from a literary point of view, though the public appetite for the doings and debates of both lawyers and lawmakers grew enormously, generating a highly specialized form of journalism to cater for it. But among politicians and newspaper editors it was widely accepted that the printed word often bore little resemblance to what had been said in either setting. Not much more faith was expressed in the volumes of 'Speeches' that came to be expected of every great parliamentarian from the time of Fox, Burke, and Pitt onwards. Naturally the public wanted to believe and was frequently reassured that what it read was what its representatives in Parliament had heard. It suited all parties to play down the gulf that separated the close political culture of the House of Commons from the open arena of newsprint. Yet in the last analysis those who hoped to succeed at Westminster had to address themselves to the former. Learning the requirements of this unique audience was the first and chief priority of the trainee statesman. It was for this reason that Wilberforce remarked that men seldom succeeded in Parliament if they entered it after 30 years of age. 'In order to apprehend the humours of so mixed a body, and to be in some sort of harmony with it, the quick impressibility of youth is required, and its powers of ready adaptation.'[200]

Certain oratorical styles faltered in all periods. The Scots Mackintosh and Brougham were both renowned speakers, but neither was altogether at his ease in Parliament. Hazlitt thought that they had too much of the northern college and lecture room to excel. Their instinct was not so much to take a side, or at least express an opinion, the very essence of conversation, but to state a question.[201] Declaimers of any kind invariably failed, even when, as in the case of the elder Pitt's friend William Beckford, they had notably patriotic credentials.[202] Hume believed that it was English distrust of rhetoric that accounted for an otherwise surprising phenomenon, the relative absence of famous English orators in a country whose history might have been supposed to favour formal eloquence.[203]

Hume's was perhaps the last generation that might have thought it desirable, even necessary, to match the style of parliamentary debate with the classically approved models of oratory. A few speakers, including the elder Pitt and Edmund Burke, were likened to Demosthenes or Cicero, and some set-piece occasions, such as the impeachment of Warren Hastings, unquestionably drew on ancient rhetoric. But the everyday business of a British Parliament was generally of a humdrum kind, lending itself to a less formal mode of delivery. In this respect the impression conveyed to a wider audience could be misleading. As reported in the press, both at home and abroad, parliamentary debates featuring long orations by leading speakers encouraged the reader to draw classical parallels. Foreigners who actually attended such debates at Westminster found the truth less impressive. The duc de Lévis thought the House of Commons deficient in point of classical technique, and notably unsystematic.[204] Burke's appearance astonished him. He expected, he wrote, a noble and imposing orator, almost dressed in a toga. But Burke wore a brown suit, distressingly crinkled and creased, and his tiny wig made him look more like a village beadle than a Roman senator. Slightly stooped, somewhat nervous, even humble in manner, arms crossed as if he were addressing a huddle of neighbours, he spoke in low tones, almost mumbling, so that it was not easy to hear him. Lévis found it difficult to believe that this was the British Cicero. Where were the classical periods, and measured eloquence; where the evident self-confidence and sense of superiority; where the grand manner of a great orator? None the less Lévis continued to listen and ended deeply moved by Burke's ability to awake the emotions of his hearers. But the way this effect was achieved owed nothing to rhetoric as traditionally understood.

When the French invented their own senatorial tradition in the 1790s, the resulting contrasts enhanced the distinctiveness of Westminster. Newspapers were necessarily an imperfect record of debates, but with Londoners and Parisians both enjoying access to an extensive periodical press, they clearly revealed the gulf that separated an English orator from his French rival. Verdicts varied. The classical scholar Thomas Twining considered English speeches as they appeared in the newspapers decidedly inferior and subscribed to a cosmopolitan coffee house specifically to read the French debates.[205] But few of his contemporaries agreed, and most of those who had an opportunity to attend French parliamentary sessions in person found their proceedings tediously theatrical and long-winded.

Even some French observers admitted the force of such criticisms. Chateaubriand compared French debaters to marionettes.[206] The comparison seemed an instructive one. Significantly, on the stage, where the arts of rhetoric were at least as important as in Parliament or on the hustings, the English were not thought of as appreciating self-conscious oratory. The long speeches and narratives that were so much relished by French audiences had no appeal at Drury Lane or Covent Garden. The dramatist George Colman the younger observed: 'I can only account for this paradox by their considering, as a light people are apt to do, their amusement to be matters of the utmost importance; and that they look upon every play as a subject for grave study, while we go to see them chiefly for relaxation.'[207] But perhaps more was at issue. English taste generally seemed to place high value on immediate relevance and directness, and it was this which seemed such a feature of political discourse. 'The imposing effect of the English House of Commons by no means lies in externals; it lies in the thought of the results to England, nay, to the whole, from words thus unartistically and negligently uttered'.[208] As the Russian Napea summed it up, 'in France every particle glistens, all is blandishment; in England all is utility, but no glitter'.[209]

The corollary was that manifestly inferior speakers could succeed if they possessed the knack of appealing to this peculiar audience. Plain language and simple manners made up for much. Throughout the eighteenth and early nineteenth centuries there were country gentlemen who were highly regarded on these accounts. What seemed to be implied was that they enjoyed a certain representative status, as mouthpieces of the nation. The outstanding case was perhaps that of Samuel Whitbread, significantly a landowner whose money had been made in brewing, and who was not ashamed of his origins. As the Scot Francis Horner remarked, he had limited education and knowledge of affairs 'but he must always stand high in the list of that class of public men, the peculiar growth of England and of the House of Commons, who perform great services to their country, and hold a considerable place in the sight of the world, by fearlessly expressing in that assembly the censure that is felt by the public, and by being as it were the organ of that public opinion which, in some measure, keeps our statesmen to their duty'.[210] English commentators also thought he personified the national character. Joseph Farington described him as 'quite *English* in plainness and directness to the subject'.[211] Hazlitt said he 'spoke point-blank what he thought, and his heart was in his broad, honest, English face . . . he was the representative of the spontaneous, unsophisticated sense of the English people on public men and public measures'.[212]

Such men were not confined to the role of back-bench Cassandras. Lord Althorp, a Whig entirely lacking in the metropolitan sophistication of Whigs of the Holland House kind, proved highly successful when entrusted with the task of piloting through the Commons the Great Reform Bill, the most controversial of all measures. Althorp, better known for his horsemanship than his political leadership, appeared the quintessential Northamptonshire squire. Yet his seeming slowness and dullness were not disadvantages when it came to managing the Commons. Bagehot offered an explanation. 'No doubt the slow-speeched English gentleman rather sympathises with slow speech in others. Besides, a quick and brilliant leader is apt to be always speaking, whereas a leader should interfere only when necessary, and be therefore felt as a higher force when he does so. His mind ought to be like a reserve fund—not invested in showy securities, but sure to be come at when wanted, and always of staple value. And this Lord Althorp's mind was; there was not an epigram in the whole of it; everything was solid and ordinary. Men seem to have trusted him much as they trust a faithful animal, entirely believing that he would not deceive if he could, and that he could not if he would.'[213]

There were perceived losses as well as gains, of course. The preoccupation with pragmatic debate in a parliamentary setting disadvantaged more elevated varieties of discourse. Bulwer Lytton attributed the declining quality of English life in this respect to the separation of wits and statesmen, which had seemed unthinkable in Addison's day, but which had come to be taken for granted by the early nineteenth century. The late hours of Parliament he thought particularly damaging. What prospect was there of social mixing between the political classes and the literary classes in such circumstances? But Lytton was not very representative in this respect, and the tendency was to treat the apparent deficiencies of parliamentary debate as cause for self-congratulation rather than shame. Emerson observed that 'a kind of pride in bad public speaking is noted in the House of Commons, as if they were willing to show that they did not live by their tongues, or thought they spoke well enough if they had the tone of gentlemen'.[214]

This readiness to glory in something which to some at least in an earlier generation would have been a matter for apology, went generally with a patriotic insistence on the unique character of the British legislature, one that might distance it from the ideologically disturbing claims of newer sovereign legislatures in France and in America. In this as in other ways the claim made for Parliament was that it was truly representative, not in a measurably democratic sense, but in that it embodied the national character. Interest in the ethnic implications of the Gothic revival and in the historic credentials of Anglo-Saxon institutions buttressed this readiness to view Westminster as owing its legitimacy primarily to its place in English folk tradition, something that had no parallel elsewhere in the civilized world, except perhaps in the last vestiges of lower Saxon self-government that Justus Möser's immense and learned study of the medieval institutions of Westphalia identified. Of course, foreigners were at liberty to scoff that this was the final proof of British barbarism, helpfully suggesting that the proper comparison with Parliament was not with counterparts in Paris or Washington but with the practices of primitive peoples, such as the 'savages of America'.[215] But from the standpoint of Englishmen at war with revolutionary ideas, this organic conception of the place of public bodies in national life fitted well with an appeal to the customs of Englishmen rather than the rights of man.

The logical conclusion was that Parliament was simply the supreme English club, in which the manners and prejudices of ordinary Englishmen were fully displayed. This may have been obvious to its members but came as something of a surprise to foreigners. When the Italian poet Alessandro Verri first encountered clubs and Commons on a visit to London in 1767, he found what seemed the same strange mixture of drinking, cheerfulness, and serious debate in both.[216] With the establishment of some London clubs on a more formal footing at the end of the century, the resemblance grew stronger still. The Commons was not, of course, a dining club, though at times it had the odour and appearance of one. Members were forever wandering in and out of Parliament's own eating house, famous in the 1780s and 1790s for the quality of its veal pies, steaks, and chops.[217] It was not unknown to find members themselves cooking their meat in the Commons kitchen when the cooks were fully occupied.[218] And in the formal life of Westminster dining had important functions. To eat with the Speaker in his chambers below St Stephen's was a much treasured privilege of all members, not at all inferior to dining with Cabinet Ministers and courtiers. Unsurprisingly, gastronomic metaphors were often employed when speaking of Parliament and its relationship with the nation. Debates were the 'unique aliment' of English conversation.[219] A tedious speaker, as Edmund Burke eventually became in the belief of a younger generation of MPs, was a 'dinner bell'.

There were, naturally, social activities that one could not practise within the precincts of Westminster, either in the chamber or the dining-room. But they tended to be things—gaming and dancing, for example—which were normally conducted in the presence of women and about which full-blooded Englishmen were extremely ambivalent. The effective exclusion of women from the Strangers' Gallery in the late eighteenth century had a significance that went far beyond worries about the distracting presence of women in the chamber during debates, as self-appointed reformers discovered.[220] The House of Commons was about dining, drinking, and debating, the familiar rituals of male society. The appearance of MPs in ordinary dress, and not infrequently in disagreeably sloppy dress, together with their refusal to appear professionally solemn about their presence in the chamber, their lounging, lying, and evident uninterest in statesmanlike deportment all suggested to outsiders a sovereign body whose dignity could certainly not be said to derive from its appearance.

The resulting tone made perfect sense of the conversational nature of Parliament, as the baron d'Haussez explained, when he sought to relate English clubbishness to English politics. 'Club habits have necessarily a very considerable influence on the national manners. They are a sort of initiation to political life, less by means of discussions, which are rarely entered on within their walls, than by conversations, in which the most important affairs, relating to the general interests of the country, are treated with depth and justness of view.'[221] It also explained an otherwise curious paradox. How, it was asked, could such a taciturn race behave so jovially in Parliament, where they might have been expected to be more solemn and dignified.[222] On the Continent politicians were solemn, and socialites frivolous. In England Society was dull while Parliament was notable for its levity.[223]

Heinrich Heine was one of those startled, but also strangely impressed by the tone of parliamentary debate when matters of gravity were under consideration.

Let me be forgiven if I treat in a flippant style a controversy, the solution of which will affect the commonweal of England, and thence perhaps indirectly the good of the world. The more important a measure is, the more merrily it must be treated. The bloody carnage of battles, the shuddering sound of the whetted sickle of death, would be unendurable did there not resound more loudly the deafening martial music with its joyful kettle-drums and trumpets. The English know this well, and therefore their Parliament affords a gay scene of the easiest wit and the wittiest ease. During the earnest debates, when the lives of thousands and the happiness of whole countries are at stake, it never occurs to any member to pull the stiff upper lip of a German representative, or to declaim in a pathetically French manner. As is the pose of their body, so also is their mental attitude, quite unconstrained. Sport and fun, self-irony—perhaps unconscious—sarcasm, humour and wisdom, malice and benevolence, logic and verse, all sparkle in the rainbow play of colours, so that the annals of Parliament still, after long years, yield the most intellectual amusement. What a contrast, on the other hand, is presented in the empty, padded, blotting-paper speeches of our South German Chambers, whose tediousness even the most patient newspaper reader has not the power to overcome, yea, whose very smell can already scare an intelligent reader, insomuch that we are forced to believe there is throughout a secret design to deter the great public world from forming an estimate of those debates, and in spite of their publicity to smother the main points, which still remain quite secret.[224]

Heine was no admirer of England but his analysis of the style of English debate might have struck a chord with English observers. The case for a taciturn nation confronted with rivals of superior fluency and plausibility was to emphasize the priority accorded its practical-mindedness, its attention to public affairs. In the heavily protected sphere of male collegiality, combining the unifying purpose of a political assembly with the conventions of masculine conviviality, there flourished a version of sociability which, if it did not impress by its eloquence, certainly did so by its ambience. Place an Englishman at his ease in an enclosed environment where he would not encounter strangers in any number, and he became communicative, accessible, almost loquacious. If politics was truly his natural sphere it was the politics of the tavern and the billiard room rather than the politics of the salon.

In Parliament itself and in its myriad imitators, the parish vestry, the municipal corporation, the governors of an infirmary, the trustees of a turnpike or a school, the grand jurors at an assize, and so on, the conversing Englishman was likely to conceive of himself first and foremost as a kind of clubman. But viewed from elsewhere this seemed a highly idiosyncratic tradition, with nothing to teach less inhibited peoples. The essence of all such public assemblies was that they placed Englishmen in a relationship which was clearly understood, even fixed, in which all knew their place. Taken out of these secure settings they seemed to revert to type. In high society the Westminster MP was no more talkative than his less burdened countrymen. Even on the hustings, where he was talking not to his fellow members but to those who were members of other, less superior clubs, his style of speaking changed, as the more observant foreigners noticed.[225] English conversation, at any level, was possible only between those who genuinely thought of themselves as equals. For all the high-flown sentiments of patriotic statesmen, not to say of designing demagogues, it was not addressed to humanity, though it might be addressed to the humanity of one's peers.

The code of the Englishman seemed to be in large measure about silence, suspicion, and separateness. A case could be made for his skills as an orator and his affability as a clubman, but neither brought him closer to the ideals of conversational sociability which centuries of European civility had evolved. Periodic campaigns to improve polite discourse rarely made much difference. Literary men might fancy that Addison had 'given a new direction to the national character' but in the Englishman's concept of himself as treasured by early Victorians, Sir Roger de Coverley seemed to have triumphed over Sir Andrew Freeport.[226] For outsiders it was the resulting reticence that remained characteristic. As Adolphe Esquiros concluded, 'If the Englishman be the most clubbable of men, according to Johnson's expression, it is not so much because he likes to speak, as that he possesses the art of holding his tongue. He respects your silence, but he expects you to respect his.'[227] One sees the point of Emerson's remark on this subject. Given the English reputation for taciturnity, he asked: 'Was it then a stroke of humor in the serious Swedenborg, or was it only his pitiless logic, that made him shut up the English souls in heaven by themselves?'[228]

CHAPTER FIVE

XENOPHOBIA

UNPROVOKED antipathy to strangers is a sure sign of barbarism, of failure to subscribe to the basic standards of civilization. Some of the most primitive cultures take pride in their enlightened treatment of aliens, and in the history of Christian civility it has always possessed pivotal significance. Medieval visitors to Britain do not seem to have found the English wanting in this respect. However, from around the middle of the seventeenth century a growing volume of complaints testified to their failure to progress in politeness along with other European peoples. By the eighteenth century, the image of the xenophobic Englishman was well established, as educated Englishmen themselves were all too aware. In his Shandean satire, *Another Traveller*, of 1767, Samuel Paterson helpfully provided 'suppositions' concerning European countries, which the traveller could take for granted without bothering to check for himself. The 'mob full of insolence' formed part of his characterization of London.[1]

Numerous foreign impressions supported this assumption, complaints ranging from a cold or hostile demeanour to verbal and physical abuse. Stories about the mistreatment of distinguished visitors circulated long after their departure. Perhaps the most recurrent of all such anecdotes were those generated by the scientist La Condamine, perpetually followed through the streets, as he allegedly was, by a crowd 'who were drawn together by a great tube of block-tin, which he had always to his ear; by an unfolded map of London which he held in his hand; and by frequent pauses, whenever he met with any object worthy of his attention'.[2] Grosley, who was in England in 1765 soon after La Condamine, remarked that the streets of London made perfect sense of the state of nature as conceived by philosophers.[3] The mildest foreign judgements were hardly flattering. The self-conscious 'voyageur philosophe' Charles-Étienne Jordan remarked that Londoners were less 'officieux' than Parisians.[4] The very term was revealing. 'Officious' in English came to have an unfavourable connotation.

Because so much British propaganda was devoted to encouraging patriotic zeal, it was easy for foreigners to connect stories of individual ill-treatment with a more systematic tendency to insular prejudice and aggression, something that might be related to various aspects of English life and history but which remained a matter for condemnation at the bar of European civility. Any English claim to superior manners and morals required that such charges should be confuted or at least placed in a less embarrassing context.

One tactic was to point out that a certain relativism governed common assessments of English distinctiveness. The shock of it was greater for visitors who had crossed the Channel rather than the North Sea. The Swiss Muralt remarked in 1725 that the reserve and coolness ('retenue' and 'sang froid') of which travellers complained seemed considerably less striking to Frenchmen who came to England via Holland.[5] German travellers, however they arrived, were less disturbed by it than were their French or Italian counterparts.

It was also possible to claim that whatever the hurt to foreign feelings, English law was comparatively favourable to immigrants. Huguenots, if they sometimes suffered from the prejudices of English workers, none the less found lawyers prepared to assert the principle that 'Strangers are entitled to justice as much as our neighbours are.'[6] A standard criticism of French practice, by contrast, was the custom which permitted the Crown to seize the effects of foreigners who died on French soil, a telling criticism because France had an ancient reputation, despite the Revocation of the Edict of Nantes in 1685, as a refuge for migrants.

On the other hand, there was some evidence that latent xenophobia held back the kind of toleration that was possible in some other societies. Attempts to make foreign naturalization easier and thereby permit the large-scale immigration of fellow-Protestants, whether at times of persecution or economic crisis, met with a backlash of patriotic sentiment strong enough to obstruct more liberal legislation. Britain's reputation as an asylum for political refugees of all kinds was effectively a creation of the 1790s and after when a succession of revolutions and reactions on the Continent sent generations of emigrants to shores that had rarely been troubled with them in the past.[7] Nor was it universally approved. The Alien Acts passed from 1792 to control such influxes were unoppressive more by accident than design. And it was Palmerston who shocked fellow liberals by seeking further to limit control of immigration after the Orsini Plot in 1858.[8] By and large the fairest judgement was perhaps that of the well-inclined Emerson, who thought most of English tolerance attributable to the balance-sheet mentality. 'Shop-rule' hospitality could be traced back to Magna Carta. It offered only what was necessary to oil the wheels of trade and brought no 'sweetness to unaccommodating manners'.[9]

From time to time attempts were made to explain away the evidence of English xenophobia. Bishop Sprat's response to Samuel Sorbière's remarks on the subject of the incivility which Frenchmen had to endure as soon as they set foot on English soil was to point out that the offenders cited by Sorbière were schoolboys. It was surely unfair to confuse the indiscipline of Dover School with the attitude of an entire nation.[10] Another tack was to argue that the xenophobia of the English was in truth the xenophobia of Londoners. The starting point for such discussions generally began where the mistreatment of foreigners most obviously began, on the streets of the capital. It was pointed out that London itself, as a great emporium, received the least desirable elements of other nations, giving the English an understandably low view of foreigners.

Alessandro Verri found the Italians that he met in England the dregs of his nation. 'This is an island on the edge of Europe, where every rogue in search of a fortune washes up.'[11] Englishmen had often seen things this way, speaking of foreigners 'continually emptying and discharging themselves into this grand Reservoir, or common-Sewer of the World'.[12]

In rural areas complaints of a hostile reception were much rarer. On the other hand, commercial and manufacturing cities in the provinces were even more repellant than London. Luigi Angiolini found Birmingham people considerably ruder, especially to foreigners, than Londoners. 'Their manner resembles the hardness of the metals which they handle.'[13] Whatever peculiar forces might explain the legendary rudeness of the Cockney, it remained an example of the rule rather than an exception to it.

Some attention was focused on politics. In a relatively open system where people of all classes were encouraged to have an opinion and had diverse ways of expressing it, it was easy for the preferences of the State to translate themselves into popular prejudices. The subject of an absolute monarchy was expected to provide cannon fodder without any incentive stronger than terror of his commanders. In a free society a more determined hostility towards one's enemies was required. National antipathies certainly corresponded well with the priorities of government. During the recurrent Anglo-French warfare which occupied so much of the period between the reign of Louis XIV and the reign of Louis XVIII, xenophobia might be viewed simply as Francophobia.

Visitors from the Continent offered supporting evidence for this view. Oloff Napea found that Russians like himself were readily mistaken for Frenchmen but when they revealed their nationality, were much liked.[14] The same experience was recorded by numerous Germans. Conversely, French-speaking Swiss, at no point at war with Britain and in many instances good Protestants to boot, were none the less liable to be thought French in England and suffered accordingly. As for the French themselves, even those who emigrated permanently to England continued to complain. The fate of a Frenchman unfortunate enough to marry an English maid was to undergo a lifetime of torment from his new countrymen.[15]

Some of what passed for inhospitality could be explained as part of a tradition of equality and independence. Irreverence for rank and dislike of foreigners were not readily distinguished. The testimony of visiting Americans on this point is valuable, partly because they were not as easily told apart from English people as Continental Europeans, partly because in America they were well acquainted with a highly egalitarian society. It was an axiom of democratic politics that artificially deferential manners resulted from the constraints inevitable in despotic governments. Americans prided themselves on their unceremonious, blunt, and even offensive behaviour.[16]

Even so, they were often startled by the ordinary Londoner's sturdiness in this respect. The Bostonian Lydia Smith, in London in 1805, was dismayed by the humiliation which she underwent: 'It appears to me that the lower class in England [are] the most barbarous set of beings on earth, they scarcely ever see a lady in the streets (it is most customary for the genteel class to ride thro these places) and when they do they stare and gape at them as at a raree-show. I was never so heartily ashamed as in my promenade thro Fleet Street. I had dressed myself *toute à la mode* for the Park, having on all my new finery and as I pass'd along I was mortified by being look'd at by all the idlers and refuse of society and when I enter'd Clementi's there was a half a dozen fools stop'd at the door to look at me.'[17] A foreign woman might have taken this for xenophobia, but it was plainly nothing of the kind. When Henri Decremps wrote his guide to London in 1789 he made this clear. To dress flamboyantly in the streets was asking for trouble. But this was because flouting the sartorial conventions of the people was like speaking ill of the sovereign elsewhere. In London the people was sovereign.[18]

Insularity also explained much. Horace was quoted to the effect that even the ancient British had been notorious for their dislike of foreigners.[19] There was, however, a difficulty about this. The Scots, Welsh, and Irish were also inhabitants of the British Isles. Moreover, they were, in ethnic terms, supposedly true descendants of those Britons. Yet, lower-class Celts were not xenophobic, at any rate by comparison with the English. They were generally considered more hospitable than their English neighbours by foreigners. Prisoners of war had particular cause to notice the difference. Those sent north of the border to Scotland found none of the plebeian brutishness by which they suffered in England.[20]

Nothing was likely to extinguish the English reputation for sourness in the face of strangers, but by the late eighteenth century something had been done to take the edge off the ferocious xenophobia so often complained of by foreigners. Numerous outsiders, both resident and visiting, testified to a significant shift in the street behaviour of the ordinary Londoner. Georg Forster, who left England in 1778 and returned briefly in 1791, had no doubt that such a 'revolution of manners' had occurred in the interim.[21] He may have been exaggerating the sharpness of this change but there is certainly a contrast between the unfavourable comments passed by foreigners on the subject as late as the 1760s and the subsequent compliments. Writing a guide to London in 1787, Louis Dutens, a Huguenot whose knowledge of Britain went back over thirty years, felt sure that there had been a notable change in the treatment of visitors.[22] Another witness whose evidence carries weight was the Saxon Heinrich von Watzdorf, who was favourably surprised by his reception in 1784. Expecting incivility he found politeness and refinement.[23]

Quite why such a change should have occurred at this time is not clear. It may have resulted from an increasingly urbane urban environment. In numerous British cities, but most of all in London, the reign of George III saw the creation of a new townscape more orderly, spacious, and hygienic than the clutter and squalor traditionally associated with a great city. It has also been argued that the period witnessed a certain 'softening of manners' thanks to the influence exerted by an increasingly market-oriented middle class.[24] On the other hand, compulsion cannot have had much to do with this process. London was thought underpoliced compared with other European capitals even after the introduction of a new metropolitan police force in the 1820s. Servants, disproportionately numerous in the West End, perhaps acted as conductors of middle-class mores to lower-class families. Perhaps, too, especially after the French Revolution, the genteel classes were more ready to join in a common street culture of civility that made mutual respect rather than social distance the keynote.

Whatever the cause, those who dwelled in England concurred that behaviour had changed, not only as it affected foreigners. The American painter Benjamin West observed in 1805 that 'he had traced a growing refinement and humanity in the manners of the people. Formerly, every young gentleman was obliged to learn boxing to defend himself against the insults of the mob, which he was sure to receive in walking the streets;

but now, there is universal decorum and civility in the manners of the
lower ranks.'[25] As for Londoners themselves, there seems to have been a
notable lessening of concern on the subject. The radical Francis Place
thought it one of the most significant changes that had occurred since his
childhood in the metropolis in the 1770s and 1780s.[26] By the 1820s the
principal encroachers on 'the laws of civil society in pedestrian excur-
sions through a crowded Metropolis' were not boorish plebeians but
tradesmen whose barrows, drays, pots, pails and trays sometimes made
progress difficult.[27] Against this background it is less surprising that
stories of foreigners beset by brutal mobs diminished.

The cessation of hostilities on the streets did not of itself signify very
much. Increasingly, it seemed desirable to distinguish between outright
xenophobia and a certain lack of grace, something that reflected national
character rather than national barbarism. Nothing occurs to the traveller
in a foreign land more readily than a sense of the amenability of the
people among whom he travels. Civility seemed to come naturally to
some peoples, and equally to be alien to others. The contrast between
the French and the English in this respect was particularly obvious. The
English were entirely lacking in bonhomie, and indeed significantly possessed no word for it. Their famed 'good nature' was in French 'bonne
nature' or 'bon naturel' which entirely lacked the expansive social quality
found in France.[28]

English authorities were less analytical but not necessarily of a different mind. Confronted with the kindness of a peasant near Rheims in 1771
Joseph Marshall could not help contrasting it with what would have
occurred at home. Had 'I carried a letter to a little farmer in England
(supposing him able to read it), he would look at my shoes half an hour
before he asked me to go into his hovel, and have a surly reserve about
him throughout the whole visit. But a Frenchman reads the occasion in
a minute, thinks himself honoured, has a flow of spirits in a moment,
which you catch, in spite of yourself, and are as much delighted with him
as he seems with you.'[29] When William Hazlitt reflected on supposed
changes in manners he decided that violence had been internalized rather
than eradicated. 'There is always much "internal oath", preparatory
knitting of the brows, implied clenching of the fists, and imaginary
shouldering of affronts and grievances going on in the mind of an
unsophisticated Englishman.'[30]

HOSPITALITY

Moderating the rudeness of an English mob and modifying the resulting image of Englishness were evidently feasible tactics, and if there remained a certain unsociability and even hostility, it was easy enough to make allowances for uneducated and insular plebeians. But as Burke remarked, the traditional perception related to the people of England as a whole. Their reputation was that of 'a sullen, unsocial, cold, unpleasant race of men'.[31] Holbach was one of those who considered supposedly polite and propertied people only marginally better than their inferiors when he saw them in 1765, condemning simultaneously 'the polite who are sad, cold, haughty, disdainful and vain, and the vulgar who are coarse, insolent and barbaric'.[32] Even the more open-minded of his countrymen, such as Édouard de Montulé, in the 1820s, could be exasperated by a coldness which, he bitingly remarked, combined the theatrical hauteur of the Neapolitan with the severe pride of the Prussian.[33] And later still, in 1840, Guizot was put off by the 'air of disdainful and caustic reserve' that he found in English society.[34]

The surest test of sociability was taken to be the readiness of people to offer hospitality and reciprocate hospitality. It was the claim of some visitors that if the English were admittedly reserved in public, in private they behaved quite differently. The natural historian Audubon noted 'how perfectly an English gentleman makes a stranger feel at home'.[35] Others thought the initial reception even in the home somewhat forbidding. A *mise en scène* of 1783 described the reception of a French visitor at a bourgeois household in Buckinghamshire. His welcome was 'a glacial look' from the mistress of the house and 'an appearance of irritation' from her two daughters. Only after some hours of acquaintance did he feel any lessening of the constraint.[36]

There were in any case others who denied that the English were capable of warmth even when they were trying to be hospitable. The Season in London was famous throughout the Continent for its parties or 'routs', but newcomers were startled by the want of grace and affability in those who hosted them. The comtesse de Boigne believed that such coldness in West End hostesses would simply not have been tolerated in Paris.[37] Departure was as comfortless as arrival. Guests were not seen to the door. 'English politeness confines its duties on this occasion to a pull of the bell, as a notice to the servant who is entrusted with the duty of doing the honours of the ante-chamber.'[38] The English themselves contrasted the 'constant ingress and egress from ten till one, as at a London assembly' with the more orderly conventions and predictable acquaintance to be found in high society on the Continent.[39] This peculiar form of entertainment had a marked affect on town house design, as the architect Isaac Ware pointed out in 1756. 'We see an addition of a great room now to almost every house of consequence. The custom of routs has introduced this absurd practice. Our forefathers were pleased with seeing their friends as they chanced to come and with entertaining them when they were there. The present custom is to see them all at once, and to entertain none of them; this brings in the necessity of a great room.'[40]

It was often noted that some of the common forms of polite life, observed in all civilized countries, were taken by the English to their logical extreme. Letters of introduction constituted an international currency, but in England they acquired a distressingly precise and limited value. They were disliked because they threatened the Englishman's independence, presuming on his complicity.[41] On the other hand, they represented a convenient medium of social exchange, extending but limiting social commitments.

As the American scientist Benjamin Silliman put it, 'a letter of introduction to an Englishman is generally little more in effect than an order to this purpose: "Sir,—Please to give the bearer a dinner and charge the same to yours, etc." '[42] Something of the same kind occurred with the visiting card. As Robert Southey remarked, 'The name dropt by a servant, [was] allowed to have the same saving virtue of civility as the real presence'.[43] This seemed a clear example of a device designed in theory to ease the process of sociability but used in practice to protect the English host from mixing except on his own terms and with those he chose. It was employed to repudiate unwished-for social obligations, not to discharge them. Genuine sociability had to be achieved by other means, not to be found in guides to etiquette. The Prussian Baroness von Riedesel, in London during the American War of Independence, was at first puzzled by the English custom of requesting favoured guests to return by means of a whispered word on parting, but quickly cottoned on to it, finding it 'very convenient, because it enabled one to choose those people with whom one liked best to associate'.[44]

It might have been supposed that the English when abroad would adopt something of the Continental attitude towards hospitality. Evidence that this happened was unfortunately slight. Lady Caroline Fox noted in Paris in 1763 that men especially were more agreeable to women, because, she supposed, they found they needed their company more than they did at home.[45] The same does not seem to have applied to women themselves. When numbers of English women became accustomed to touring on the Continent, after the Napoleonic Wars, charges of unsociability if anything increased. Unfavourable comparisons were made with the women of other nations. William Jacob, in Italy in 1819, was intrigued by the extent to which German women in Italy mixed with locals in contrast with their English cousins.[46]

Such incivility was a recurrent complaint about tourists, 'that erratic English community, which, like the gipsy tribe, is governed in all its wandering by rules and regulations of its own, mixing as little as possible with the natives of the soil'.[47] When present in strength, the English were often charged with congregating to the exclusion of their local host society. In Madeira, where a substantial English community established itself in the early nineteenth century, much ill will was caused by its reluctance to entertain the Portuguese.[48] Wherever the English assembled for their health they brought with them a kind of social infection, ruining the healthy manners of other societies. Montpellier, a celebrated watering spot for the English, was thought a striking instance.[49] To some extent the same was true of those long-standing colonies of Englishness generated by networks of trade. As Strang observed in his *Germany in 1831*, the merchants at Hamburg 'herded together', retaining their national manners, prejudices, and mode of life over entire generations, each as little disposed to mix with the natives as its predecessors.[50] The effects of such conduct might be serious. Cosmopolitan Britons like John Moore, the Duke of Hamilton's travelling tutor, were highly critical of 'our taking no trouble to conciliate the affections of foreigners'. In Austria during the American War of Independence he was convinced that much of the delight taken in the humbling of the British empire was 'that reserve which keeps Englishmen from cultivating the friendship of foreigners'.[51]

Among themselves, the English had a reputation for social feuding which was at least as marked on foreign soil as at home. As the Victorian painter William Archer Shee remarked, 'the "English colony" in a foreign city possesses all the worst characteristics of a small country town in England. The same jealousies and backbiting, the same cliqueism, the same assumption on the part of those who have no claims to assume, the same struggle to make distinctions and maintain them among a set of people between whom there is, socially speaking, nothing to choose.'[52]

Henry Swinburne, a genteel traveller well-placed to appreciate such idiosyncrasies, noted this propensity much earlier, touring Italy in the 1770s. At Rome disputes about who could visit whom were legion. At Florence the British envoy, Sir Horace Mann, celebrated for his genial hospitality, kept open house and thereby succeeded in minimizing 'feuds, . . . opposition sets, which, among the English, is too often the case'.[53] Even when they were not bickering, English travellers tended to follow their own social rules and observed them with great rigour in foreign cities where there were sufficient English residents or passers-through to make it viable to do so.[54] In such places the best that bemused foreigners could hope for was to be entertained on terms devised for London rather than Rome or Geneva. They found it particularly hard to understand the rules of female warfare, when for instance, ladies of doubtful status in London presented themselves in Continental cities where West End society was well represented. Lady Blessington's Italian tour in 1828 taxed even the diplomatic resources of the French and Austrian ambassadors to the Vatican.[55]

Complaints were not restricted to the Englishman's inhospitality where strangers were concerned, nor to his stand-offishness when travelling. It was also said that he would not repay at home the hospitality that he received abroad. 'The English who disembark at Dover are not the English who were at Paris and in Italy,' wrote Alessandro Verri.[56] Anecdotes on this subject came to constitute something of a genre. Typical is a story of the Neapolitan diplomat Caracciolo. Caracciolo was a bosom companion of Lord Malton, heir to the Marquessate of Rockingham, as a Grand Tourist in Italy in the 1740s, and when he later visited England as envoy, he naturally expected a warm reception. Instead, encountering his former companion, now a senior politician, at court, he met only 'cold, formal politeness'. He got his own back in due course when he found himself dining in the company of Rockingham with a royal prince, the Duke of Cumberland. On this occasion it suited

Rockingham to demonstrate his Continental connections by reminding Caracciolo of their acquaintance in front of Cumberland. Caracciolo responded by remarking that he could only recall a young nobleman of the name of Lord Malton.[57]

There were, indeed, English people who virtually admitted their own difficulty on this account. Back at home, Lady Sarah Lennox ingenuously wrote: 'You cannot think how French I'm grown, for I liked being one of the very few English women taken notice of at Paris, it flatters one's vanity, and of course one thinks the people very *sensible* that like one. It's a little troublesome here tho', for I'm obliged to see them more here than I wish, and London abounds in French.'[58]

Various excuses were offered. Crabb Robinson, who spent some years in Germany and knew his countrymen's reputation, attributed it to insularity rather than active unkindness.[59] Others pleaded the pressure of public life in England compared with the Continent. Thus Louis Dutens, who as a diplomat at Turin had done many services for English visitors, summarized it: 'Their defence is, that the neglect arises from their modes of life. No sooner are they returned from their travels, than they are immersed in public business.'[60]

One clue was the fact that the foreign complaints made about the English resembled provincial complaints made about London. It was alleged that Londoners cheerfully availed themselves of rural hospitality on country visits but declined to reciprocate when their hosts appeared in the capital. Hunting counties close to London, such as Northamptonshire, were said to be considerable sufferers as a result. Even an acquaintance made in Bath could be disowned in the capital, if an anecdote of the wit George Selwyn is to be credited. Selwyn was supposed to have cultivated an elderly gentleman in Bath to kill time and then, at the height of the following season in St James's Street, passed by him without acknowledgement. ' "What, don't you recollect me?" exclaimed the *cuttee*; "we became acquainted at Bath, you know." "I recollect you perfectly," replied Selwyn, "and when you next go to Bath I shall be most happy to become acquainted with you again." '[61]

London, of course, was a place where it was easy to escape the embarrassment of encountering someone to whom one had incurred obligations, and where the consequences of evading one's social responsibilities could be ignored or at least minimized. The capital promoted sociability, but only of a certain kind. The intimacy of its fine ladies, it was remarked, in reference to the pleasure garden, was 'Ranelagh deep'.[62] London friendship yielded 'nothing more tender than a visiting card'.[63] On a town visit it was possible to guess the composition of the company by scrutinizing the footmen waiting at the door. 'If you saw the livery of any one you did not like, you would pass on, but if they belonged to people you wished to see, you would call likewise.'[64] In such surroundings the entire currency of social relations could be, so to speak, devalued, and even recognized responsibilities were liable to be discharged at the minimum going rate. The tractarian Thomas Mozley told the story of a hospitable Gainsborough man who always entertained a London friend on business tours and was shocked on going to London not to be asked to dinner. Mozley's conclusion, with only a hint of irony, was that a visitor from London relieved the dullness of country life whereas a country cousin did nothing to amuse a Londoner. The social terms of trade fairly reflected the difference.[65]

London was the hub of commercial development as well as of social life and it was easy to argue that the two were closely connected. Progress required a more mercenary view of relations with strangers than had been possible in the close world of feudal society. It permitted the entrepreneurial provision of facilities which had to be supplied by every household in a more primitive world, not least the more primitive worlds of England's neighbours in the British Isles. Foreign appreciation of the hospitality they received in such quarters needed placing in this context of relative economic backwardness.[66]

Mrs Piozzi, herself a Welshwoman, did not think the much-vaunted Celtic reputation for hospitality at all deserved. It had nothing to do with ethnic character, everything to do with the mundane realities of life. In Scotland, Ireland, and Wales there were few of the inns and hotels to be found in England. Accordingly, the old hospitality persisted. In England it had simply ceased to have any function.[67] The most systematic justification of English practice on these lines was perhaps that offered by Georg Forster, better known for his scientific researches and explorations than for his Continental travels, but an indefatigable inquirer after curiosities in Europe as elsewhere. The English, he admitted, had abandoned the ancient practice of hospitality but put in its place a commercialized version, to be seen in the unusual politeness of English shopkeepers and innkeepers, both renowned among Europeans for their ingratiating manners with customers. In a society where money could buy anything it could certainly buy courteous manners. This might be distressing to some, but to Forster it seemed encouragingly egalitarian. On the Continent innkeepers and shopkeepers were impressed by rank rather than money, by privilege rather than buying power. England's was the way of the future.[68]

Forster has support from the historian of early modern hospitality who argues that the tendency to treat sociability in highly commercial terms had begun unusually early in England.[69] It had also subverted the English notion of what hospitality might represent. To confront the real thing was to be embarrassed rather than comforted. One traveller in southern Italy complained in print 'of the necessity of accepting the hospitality of private gentlemen, instead of the accommodations afforded by inns; describing the overstrained attentions of persons whose habits and modes of life are so opposite to ours as irksome and oppressive, and inconsistent with that degree of liberty and independence which constitute so much of the charm of travelling'.[70]

Differing experience of inns and hotels certainly came to seem a kind of litmus test for the purpose of assessing modernity. As always the Celtic 'fringe' merely confirmed the impression of English superiority. In Ireland 'the Assiduity of the Landlord' and 'the Alacrity of the Attendants' was far below English standards. In Wales the same was true, except, significantly, on the major post roads.[71] Elsewhere, English visitors judged Continental politeness by the demeanour of innkeepers. The Gothic novelist Ann Radcliffe was appalled by her reception at German hostelries. 'When your carriage stops at an inn, you will perhaps perceive, instead of the alacrity of an English waiter, or the civility of an English landlord, a huge figure, wrapt in a great coat, with a red worsted cap on his head, and a pile in his mouth, stalking before the door.' The very best inns, she discovered were worse than the halfway houses between London and Canterbury, the lowest of all such establishments in Britain. 'Even when you are satisfied, his manner is so ill, that he appears to consider you his dependent, by wanting something which he can refuse.'[72] Unfortunately, the exceptions merely proved the rule. Robert Gray, later the bishop whose palace was burnt down in the Reform Bill riots at Bristol, had a gratifyingly polite reception at an inn near Zurich in 1791. It turned out that the proprietress was the daughter of a Palatine officer in English service who had learned polished manners abroad. When she returned with her husband to his Swiss birthplace they were so dismayed by the social graces of their neighbours that 'they set up the inn merely to enjoy the company of such strangers as pass through the village'.[73]

In England itself, a telling symbol of the transition from the old to the new hospitality was the country house turned road house. Confusing the two would have been unthinkable on the Continent but Goldsmith's *She Stoops to Conquer*, in which two young men of fashion mistook a manor house for a hostelry, did not seem absurdly implausible to contemporaries. In the real world, Petworth under the eccentric third Earl of Egremont, had a reputation for hospitality which made it appear 'consequently like a great inn'.[74] Mansions situated close to turnpiked trunk routes were increasingly commandeered for commercial purposes. One was the 'vastly grand and commodious' Talbot Hotel at Malton in Yorkshire, formerly the residence of the Stricklands. Even more palatial was the Castle at Marlborough on the Bath Road, the historic seat of the Dukes of Somerset and by the 1770s renowned as the finest inn on the finest road in the world.[75] A French visitor wrote in 1785, 'The service is magnificent—the porcelain, the silver tea-pots, canteens, bread-baskets, beer-tankards, flagons, a beautiful tea-urn—in a word, everything one could wish for in the house of a great lord: in truth it seemed almost as if we were staying with the duke of Somerset.'[76]

Travellers abroad judged that even the better Continental hotels could not provide the 'tasty, genteel Air' of their British counterparts.[77] The social function of a good English hotel was precisely that it made guests feel as if they were being entertained as gentlemen, even though they were paying for the experience. Modern country house owners have taken this principle further by putting up the wealthy specifically to give them the purchased experience of gentility. In the eighteenth century foreigners were impressed by the luxury of an English inn but puzzled by the mentality involved. The servants who contributed to the aura of unforced, ungrudging politeness were themselves ruthless entrepreneurs. It came as a shock to many guests to discover that they were not only not paid for their services, but themselves paid substantial sums to obtain their posts. They were capitalists investing in their own labour. In the great coaching inns, in London's most favoured taverns, and above all in the great gentlemen's clubs, hundreds of pounds might be involved. The result was to make such servants patronizing and contemptuous when encountering foreigners not disposed to spend on a grand scale.

The expense of an English inn made deference appear an overpriced commodity. One noble Florentine 'set up his quarters comically enough at the waggoners full Moon upon the old bridge at Bath, to be quit of the *schiavitu* [slavery], as he called it, of living like a gentleman, "where," says he, "I am not known to be one." '[78] Foreigners found the English inn hard to understand in this respect. The owner of the best inn at The Hague in the 1760s, who named it 'The Parliament of England', was displaying his ignorance. However much he revered the parliamentary tradition, no English innkeeper would have made the mistake of associating his house with democratic manners. He was much more likely to adopt a motif with royal or noble associations, frequently appropriating the arms of the most prestigious local house. To visitors it seemed strange that common taverns should bear noble arms.[79] But these snobbish connotations were precisely what the customers wanted. On the Continent, in due course, the Earl of Bristol was to provide a suitable name for attracting English travellers.

Making a public house resemble a private one was an essential part of the innkeeper's art. At an English inn the proprietor would advance to welcome his guests, his wife standing at the door ready to conduct ladies to their rooms, while he did the honours for the gentlemen. Continental practice varied but never resembled this. In France and Italy, the honours were done by servants; no attempt was made to preserve the fiction of homely hospitality. In Germany it was the rank of the guest that determined the nature of the reception. Even in English colonies or former colonies it was difficult to find matching standards. If Germans grovelled only to the great, Americans grovelled to nobody. English visitors to the United States found innkeepers intolerably intrusive and boorish. Even in the less republican atmosphere of the British West Indies something of the same sort applied. The Scot Janet Schaw, visiting Antigua in 1774, was intrigued at her lodging in St John's to be 'received by a well behaved woman, who welcomed us, not as the Mrs of a Hotel, but as the hospitable woman of fashion'. At dinner, this lady 'presided at the head of her table, (very unlike a British Landlady)'.[80] This was not the offensive, democratic familiarity of the Americans but it was familiarity none the less, and a reminder that the Englishness of the English was a peculiarly insular condition, not an ethnic inheritance. A polite welcome *à l'anglaise* was not the same as a familiar reception.

It seems likely that English attitudes hardened in the era of Revolutionary manners. After the Wars of 1793–1815 and the resulting restrictions on Continental touring, English travellers were unprepared for the familiarity of French landlords suggesting 'the remnant of the revolutionary rust which time had not yet polished off or removed'.[81] Eighteenth-century benevolence had earlier elicited a tolerance which went against the English grain but was embarrassing not to concede. William Coxe's response to an innkeeper at Garis in 1780 is revealing. 'Our host is an open-hearted honest Swiss: he brings his pint of wine with him, sits down to table with us, and chats without the least ceremony. There is a certain forwardness of this kind which I cannot bear, when it apparently is the effect of impertinent curiosity, or fawning officiousness; but the present instance of frank familiarity, arising, as it evidently does, from a mind conscious of its natural equality, and unconstrained by arbitrary distinctions, is highly pleasing to me; and I prefer the simple demeanour of unsophisticated nature, to all the false refinements of artificial manners.' In America at the same time and in Switzerland later Coxe would surely have been less tolerant, but in 1780 genteel correctness was relatively expansive and even in the English permitted a certain complaisance.[82]

Was commerce then the key, as Forster argued? There were evidently some discrepancies. Commerce did not seem to have quite the same effect elsewhere. In America and Antigua it produced forms of civility which diverged from their English origins. In the Netherlands it did not seem to produce anything that could be called civility at all. Dutch innkeepers were notoriously 'brutal and surly'.[83] Was there then some component that marked English commercial hospitality, something perhaps more English than commercial? Significantly, travellers on foot did not share the impression of the superiority of the English inn. Moritz's sufferings in this respect were particularly poignant, inflicted as they were, on one who greatly admired English ways. Even when he was accepted without evidence of having his own transport, the result was distressing. 'They served me like a beggar, . . . but charged me like a gentleman.'[84] Moritz evidently did not fully comprehend the commercial mentality of an English innkeeper. Money was certainly the object but in money matters as others it was essential to take the long view. The guests of a fashionable hostelry must not only be wealthy, but be seen to be wealthy. A pedestrian in outdoor dress, however rich, could only put off more modish visitors.

Innkeepers shared their reputation for modern manners with shop-keepers. The ordinary London salesman, the 'counter-coxcomb', was ridiculed for precocious breeding by satirists as diverse as Ned Ward and Robert Southey.[85] Foreigners were more likely to regard him with awe. Even Parisian shopkeepers, despite their natural advantage of French complaisance, could not match him. As the émigré vicomte Walsh remarked, whereas people of rank everywhere had learned their manners from the salons of Paris, the shopkeepers of France had had to learn the 'bon ton du comptoir' and the *bonnes manières* des magasins' from England.[86]

Innkeepers and shopkeepers were polite because they sold commodities which in England were in ready supply and the subject of intense competition. They came to embody one of the most noted features of English life, its supposed indifference to rank. The ease of such men in relating to all classes, including the highest, was something to boast of. 'A city shop-keeper, behind his counter, looks as if he and his customers were persons exchanging civilities.'[87] The Russian Napea noticed some interesting ethnic distinctions. 'London shopkeepers, who are Englishmen, receive their customers of rank, as if they were equals, and the transactions between them mutually beneficial; those who are Irish, stare at such until their eyes nearly burst. Scotch shopkeepers cringe to their customers, much as ours do; and while they bend to people who stand higher in the world than themselves, exact obedience from those below them with an iron hand.'[88] Still greater was the contrast with France, where the genteel and pseudo-genteel of the *ancien régime* strenuously resisted such familiarity. 'Thus an upstart lady of quality (an imitator of the old school) would not deign to speak to a milliner while fitting on her dress, but gave her orders to her waiting-women to tell her what to do. Can we wonder at twenty *reigns of terror* to efface such a feeling?'

Perhaps it was the case that in England the commercial salesman enjoyed a freer relationship with his blue-blooded customers than elsewhere. Even so, there remained an assumption of dependence that was nearly as marked as in a more traditionally hierarchical relationship. In a Continental context this sense of something innately demeaning about the giving and receiving of what elsewhere would simply have been an act of hospitality looked very English. The resulting conflicts of values produced instructive anecdotes, especially in Mediterranean societies where traditional forms of hospitality were deeply entrenched. A typical story was that recorded by Sir John Carr, on his travels in Spain during the Napoleonic Wars. Carr was struck by generosity to strangers in a land where 'My house is yours' was a commonplace form of greeting. In an ice-house or 'neveria' it was impossible to converse with a Spaniard without his insisting on paying the bill. On one occasion he observed the contretemps which an Englishman embarrassed by such courtesy could cause. A naval lieutenant was startled to find that his bill had been paid for him and chased after the departing Spaniard to remonstrate with him. 'He continued, with an oath, that he had never been treated so before, that he had never, hitherto, been under an obligation to any one, and would not put up with it. He then told the waiter, through an Englishman who spoke Spanish, that he insisted upon paying for his punch; the waiter refused to take his money, he remonstrated, the other still refused, and, doubtless, thought him mad, upon which the worthy, blunt, but mistaken lieutenant threw a dollar into the bar, and ran out of the house, declaring, much as he liked a Spaniard, he would be d—d before he would be under any obligation to him.'[89] Tales of the anger aroused by Englishmen insisting on their right to pay for hospitality came to seem characteristic.

FAMILIARITY

The preservation of an equal relationship, averting any fear of contempt on one side or resentment on the other, was a boasted English merit as much as a touring inconvenience. Foreigners did not dissent when they saw it in action. The Swede Geijer, in England during the Napoleonic Wars, observed: 'This politeness between higher and lower, this outward recognition of mutual rights is an interesting point in English manners;

there are few places where one meets with so universal a sense of right and obligation as here.'[90]

Equal rights dictated a degree of caution. Hence the Frenchman's 'fawning, cringing, interested politeness; less truly respectable than the obliging civility of the common people in England'.[91] A certain distance was implied. Failure to keep it was to fall into a dangerously un-English 'familiarity'. Familiarity presupposed a right to intrusive conduct, especially questioning. It was the way people expected other members of their family, or alternatively intimate friends, to behave. This made for recurrent English complaints about foreigners, though in the nature of things these were somewhat lessened by linguistic obstacles. Objectionable cross-examining loses much of its sting in a barely comprehended language, partly because questioners are liable to give up the attempt at familiarity if their questions are not understood, partly because the questioned can hardly take offence at such cryptic assaults on their privacy. Where the language happened to be English there was more room for annoyance. American unawareness of the 'pleasures of privacy' was the despair of British diplomats in Washington.[92] Nothing seems to have more consistently irritated Englishmen visiting the United States in the early nineteenth century than this. Mrs Trollope placed familiarity of address high among American impertinences.[93] So did her generally better-inclined countrywoman, Fanny Kemble: 'I constantly sit thunderstruck at the amazing number of unceremonious questions which people here think fit to ask one, and, moreover, expect one to answer.'[94]

Even Americans generally considered that they were exceptionally unreserved on personal subjects, something which was taken to be the result of the long distances that often separated settlers in a new country. In any event, the manner in which strangers were molested and badgered for information would have been unthinkable in England.[95] The most anodyne enquiry could seem offensive there. The Victorian radical George Holyoake recalled that when rambling around the country in his youth he had often been taken for a foreigner, perhaps, he thought, 'from my freedom of manner and speech. Most English persons go without information rather than ask it of strangers.'[96] Grand tourists were aware that they paid a price in this respect. 'I have the English pride and shyness about me so strong', wrote Charles Burney, on his Continental voyage of musical discovery in 1770, 'that I abominate the thought of asking the way.'[97] What he and his countrymen did not always appreciate when abroad was that their very shyness gave offence, not least in other English-speaking societies. The traveller George Thompson, in South Africa, defied his instincts and took to volunteering information about himself. 'This communicative system is so much more popular and preferable in every respect to the morose and dogged silence which many English travellers resort to when pressed by the familiar but good-natured interrogations of the colonists, that I often adopted it to a considerable extent.'[98]

Sociability as non-interference was an intensely English concept. The English manner was described as setting a kind of ring around everyone, within which it was possible to feel at ease.[99] Privacy was the most marketable of all commodities and pleasurable occasions were frequently defined in terms that measured its presence. George Canning's ideal of breakfast was one at which it was possible to eat 'as silently and shortly and sulkily as you please, without interfering one with another'.[100] The relationship between eating and privacy was often remarked on. Significantly, Englishmen travelling on the Continent and bent on curing the *mauvaise honte* that made them so notorious abroad, were advised to make a point of attending table d'hôte dinners with a view to joining in the friendly openness that seemed natural elsewhere though highly objectionable at home.[101] But the table d'hôte of Continental inns was a mark of inferior accommodation in England, associated at best with commercial hotels.

This touched a point of great sensitivity in English life. Dining was customarily a discrete if not clandestine activity or alternatively it was a rite with elaborate rules. To eat in private, either in a separate room or within partitioned spaces, was considered essential for people of any pretension. Travelling abroad it was shocking not to have the opportunity to do so. Particularly in the United States the blank incredulity that met requests to dine alone was perplexing in the extreme, as even the occasional French visitor admitted. To be told by an innkeeper that Washington himself would not have dared ask such a thing was unanswerable but baffling.[102]

Collective eating was respectable only when one knew the kind of company one would keep, a college, a club, a corporation. English dining was more than socializing. It constituted a kind of public legitimacy. 'In

England, every thing is done by a dinner.'[103] A charitable society, it was even claimed, could be defined as 'a number of people whose highest pleasure is eating'.[104] Much the same might have been said of less formal associations. 'Ordinaries', to employ the traditional term, were for professional men such as clergy or lawyers, or for any body of men who had occasion to meet for business and required sustenance afterwards. Assizes when lawyers gathered, or commercial gatherings that brought merchants and manufacturers together spawned many such. In London, taverns came to specialize in ordinaries for the men whose work lay near by. The Eagle in the Strand famously brought together newspaper men and Somerset House employees on almost a daily basis. They were governed by conventions that included the choice of a president and vice-president and ensured a fair division of cost.[105] In the gentleman's clubs of the early nineteenth century a communal dining table was standard though by this time it was more polite to describe it as a 'table d'hôte' than an 'ordinary'.

Crucial to these rituals was the social equality of those present. This was understood by all ranks. In the army, if the troops desired to honour a commander, they invited themselves to a dinner and him to drink with them. He was not expected to sit down.[106] In civilian society the requirements of rank might seem less oppressive, but similar pains were taken to observe proprieties. Masters and servants might join in certain social activities when the conventions of high life permitted, usually in a country setting where remembered traditions of communality had to be occasionally honoured. But dining together was not desired or required. It went without saying that women were generally excluded from this male ritual. At grand civic or corporate dinners they might be present as observers but not as diners.

What was so startling about the Continental table d'hôte was precisely its neglect of distinctions that were generally more inflexible than those in England. In France after the Revolution it was perhaps unsurprising that it might resemble 'an ill-regulated kennel of foxhounds'.[107] But Germany was thought of as having the most rigid of all social demarcations. Even so, in a German inn noble men and women found no difficulty in joining in the conviviality of a 'table d'hôte' open to all who wished to eat.[108] At Baden-Baden in 1818 it was noted that the Englishman absolutely refused 'eating at the same convivial board with those of inferior rank, though he is almost certain to meet with others of equal and superior station to himself; for all etiquette of this nature is waved,—the Prince and the untitled hero mix in social converse; the waiter, who generally carves each dish at the sideboard, also assigns your place at the table, from the date of your arrival.'[109]

More than national preference might be involved. It was in the nature of commercial progress that it made individual comfort in isolation more attainable. Perhaps it was English wealth that promoted private travelling, private dining, private drinking. Those who made such connections were also aware that privacy often seemed to imply a retreat from social contact, primarily on the part of the privileged. The easy accusation was that this was mere snobbery. But snobbery was not a monopoly of the English. A more plausible explanation required closer scrutiny of the peculiar nature of English conditions.

The most amenable testing ground for theories about social relations was often taken to lie within relations between masters and servants. There was much debate about the treatment of servants by different nations. The overwhelming consensus, from very diverse sources, was that the English model was unique, in that it offered servants relatively generous terms and conditions at the expense of human warmth and interdependence.

The ease with which Continental masters behaved in the company of their servants was a source of awe to English travellers. In 1818 Marianne Baillie had only to cross the Channel to Boulogne and make her first encounter with a maid to appreciate the difference. 'In short, her manner was something quite peculiar to the French in that class of society. An English maid servant who had kept up this sort of badinage would most probably have been a girl of light character; but servants in France are indulged in a playful familiarity of speech and manner which is amusing to witness, and seldom (if ever) prevents them from treating you with every essential respect and attention.'[110] By the time she reached Portugal the young novelist was aware that the further south one went, the more marked this phenomenon grew. 'The extreme familiarity of this people with their domestics strikes an English person at first sight in a forcible manner; and it is somewhat difficult to reconcile such a mode of conduct with their inherent arrogance of birth. In the present state of society in England, a similar behaviour would be attended with considerable inconvenience; yet I certainly think, that even there, greater benevolence and kindness of manner between master and servant would be more consonant to the dictates of liberal policy, and true Christianity.'[111]

This emphasis on 'extreme familiarity' occurred in countless English tours of Spain, Portugal, and Italy. It applied equally to both sides of the relationship. Employers used endearments that would have been unthinkable bestowed on an English domestic. On the other hand, they tolerated language that would have been considered the grossest insolence in England. In these societies domestics were seemingly regarded as members of the family. In England the use of the term 'family' to describe an entire household rather than the blood relationships at its centre was obsolescent, though it lingered on until the middle of the eighteenth century, and in places beyond.

Time and again foreigners noted the unusual austerity of the master–servant relationship in England. Some were impressed, especially when they were able to compare customs elsewhere in the British Isles. J. G. Kohl reported: 'In England, where servants are kept at a proper distance, it is seldom that they venture on the familiar impertinence of which I saw frequent instances in Ireland.'[112] But the general conclusion was that if the English on both sides displayed close attention to duty, they showed little human feeling. Here was strict propriety but no real attachment. As the comte de Melfort put it, 'I do not know any country where one is served with so much respect, with so much silent attention, as in England; nor where the distance between master and servant is more strictly marked: and yet this is not accompanied on the part of the latter by any baseness of demeanour, nor is it the effect of compelled servitude; but the servant shows that in his capacity he respects himself, and that familiarity would be no more to his taste than to that of his master.'[113] In this respect it was significant that there was no difference between a domestic servant in the home and one in the tavern, the inn, or the eating house. Visitors who thought they could purchase amiability as well as efficiency were disappointed. Washington Irving noted the 'taciturn obedience' generally of servants.[114] Holbach complained of being served well and promptly, yet without affability, by waiters.[115]

At bottom, what was taken to be at issue was the presumed power of people who were nominally in a position of dependence. Continental servants were treated so familiarly precisely because they lacked the privileges of the English lower class. The extreme case was that observable in eastern Europe, where servants were privy to all kinds of secrets; since they were no better than the property of their masters, it was unthinkable that they could ever use such liberties as a form of subversion.[116] French and German servants were not to be compared with Polish helots, but they were sufficiently dependent to be treated as if their opinions carried no consequences. In England matters were very different. Consciousness of rights affected the behaviour of masters as much as servants. They could not afford to patronize men who were entitled to enter a polling booth alongside them. Only in England could an employer say, as Samuel Parr said of his manservant, that he was 'a good fellow, but we have the misfortune to differ in politics'.[117] Servants did not need to abase themselves before masters whose legal equals they were. It was even claimed that they might have to give characters to gentlemen wishing to hire rather than the other way around.[118]

Perhaps it was this which made servants so suspect in England. The assumption was that loyalty could only be found where the relationship was one of shared experience, and that was taken to be far more marked on the Continent. It was often observed that English servants were kept increasingly at a distance whenever possible. Visitors' attendants found themselves left outside where in the past they would have been welcome inside the house.[119] Servants themselves preferred not to be offered shelter from the rain rather than be exposed to the embarrassment of association with their betters.[120] Even within a household, the continuing presence of a servant in the same room as the family was a source of shame. It signified insufficient wealth to heat servants' quarters apart.[121] In English houses, aristocratic and bourgeois alike, there was a growing tendency to remove them as far as possible from contact with the family they served, except when they actually had to present themselves face to face. Hence the gloomy corridors, the poky backstairs, the dingy basements and garrets designed even in quite humble middle-class homes for the servants. Hence too the desire to protect their employers' conversation and social intercourse from their long ears and prying eyes, on occasion exploited by enterprising foreigners. Merlin von Lüttich made his living in England designing labour-saving devices which would have this effect, and which greatly impressed some of his visiting countrymen.

Sophie von la Roche was particularly intrigued by a mechanical tea-table equipped with foot pedals.[122]

The most commented on of all such inventions was the dumb-waiter, which made its appearance around 1780. The advantages in point of sociability were obvious, permitting 'the full flow of confidential inter-course'.[123] In fact, deaf waiter would have been a less hypocritical name, for it was the absence of ears that counted rather than the absence of tongues. The dumb-waiter made an important contribution to a notable English institution, the waiterless breakfast, a curious affair of congeal-ing dishes and cooling tea, unattended by servants and served by the breakfasters themselves, or at best by the ladies of the house.[124] The sheer inconvenience of this arrangement was much commented on by foreign-ers and often lamented by the English themselves. A few tried a differ-ent approach. Lady Lansdowne employed a Milanese servant to wait at breakfast, and thereby won over the initially sceptical Maria Edgeworth. 'I am a convert which I thought I never should be to this system,' wrote Miss Edgeworth. 'Conversation goes on delightfully and one forgets the existence of the *dumb waiter*.'[125] The custom did not catch on, however. Privacy counted for more than comfort.

Dr Johnson took pleasure in urging Catherine Macaulay, whose republican politics were well known, to instruct her servants to join them at table.[126] Yet it was on the supposedly much more status-conscious Continent that the British were likely to find themselves uncomfortably close to their servants. Sharing a room with them, when necessity arose, was a humiliation. Perhaps the most famous of all British travellers on the Continent, the Earl of Bristol, was dismayed by one such experience in 1766: 'We have been oblig'd to drink our wine and eat our bread and butter in the same room with our Postillions, blacksmyth and Laborers who almost strove to drink out of the same glass not contented with doing so out of the same bottle.'[127]

British servants were understandably amused by the discomfort of their masters in such circumstances. The Scottish footman John Mac-donald told a story of his journey with his employer between Liège and Spa: 'At the half-way house my master went into the parlour, and ordered dinner, and we servants remained in the kitchen. Soon after, a Dutch gen-tleman, his lady, and daughter, came to the inn. They went in with our master to dinner, and we sat at dinner in the kitchen with their Dutch footman, in a coarse livery and a large Dutch hat. He would not sit with us nor take off his hat, but cut some of the meat and put it on his bread, and went into the parlour and eat it, and kept speaking to his master and the ladies, with his large hat on his head, about the roads, the postilions and the country. When his meat was done he came out for another slice, and then went in again. Henry and I laughed till we were like to split our sides, to think our master was dining with the footman; for Mr Crauford was so proud that he would not let a servant ride in the chaise with him, but would rather be at the expense of a horse. The gentleman in the parlour was in full-dress, in black silk clothes, and wore a dress hat under his arm. His lady was in a riding-dress; and the daughter, one of the finest young ladies I ever saw, in a riding-dress, most richly trimmed with silver. They seemed as much pleased with their footman's behaviour as if he had been a prince.'[128]

To foreigners it was shocking that even the English sense of chivalry had to give way to the English desire for apartness. Henry Matthews noted an intriguing example in Italy after the Napoleonic Wars. 'In the course of our route to-day, we saw a chariot at a distance advancing towards us. The ladies clapped their hands together and cried out, *Eccolo! Eccolo! inglesi! Inglesi!* I asked them how they knew at such a distance to what nation the carriage belonged, when they laughingly pointed to the female domestic on the box. They cannot see the propriety of the distance which is preserved between English masters and their domestics—especially female domestics. The sight of a *female* posted on the outside of the vehicle shocked their notions of the deference and courtesy due to the sex—all considerations of rank out of the question—and was considered by them as an unpardonable act of high-treason against the divine right of womanhood; nor could I make them understand that the Abigail was probably better pleased to accompany her fellow servant on the box, than to be admitted inside, subject to the constraint arising out of unequal association.'[129]

The underlying development was the growing contractualism of terms of service. Even in France, by the 1780s, Mercier thought that servants were losing their status as members of the family and becoming mere employees.[130] The extraordinary sensation achieved by Beaumarchais's highly independent Figaro and the fact that he virtually killed off the French servant as a figure on the French stage, testify to sensitivity on this point.[131] Yet there remained differences. French ease and familiarity were famous. The same class which was to suffer so severely from the social levelling of the 1790s was the boast of Europe before the Revolution for its easygoing attitude to mixing with inferiors. French women were used to undressing in front of their servants, and also, more doubtfully, in front of their confessors. It was high society women who continued to carry off the latter, shocking the bourgeoise Madame Roland.[132] But the principle was the same. There could be no shame in revealing oneself before one's dependants.

Among men, even somewhat unlikely inferiors might be treated as companions. In the army French officers were noticeably less starchy and formal with men in the ranks than was the case in other forces.[133] The sight of them chatting and joking together even in the midst of a grand review was a startling one to an Englishman.[134] The same applied in Spain, where it was possible to see officers and their men exchanging cigarettes.[135] This was also held to apply in some measure to relations with slaves. In the West Indies George Pinckard found that 'the French are more in the habit of conversing, as companions, with the slaves, than is common among the English and the Dutch; and that the females, employed in the house, are treated more in the manner of the filles de chambre of Europe. From this circumstance, together with the slight gradations of shade, or the many links forming the chain between the Europeans and the Africans, and from the great number of people of colour, who have obtained their freedom, it is extremely difficult to ascertain where the line of slavery commences.'[136] In New South Wales the belief was that the circumstances of a newly founded colony, one in which criminals and the control of criminality were prime elements, had given the first generation of Australians a quite excessive dose of Englishness. By the 1820s it was being stated that 'A better and more liberal race of men are now come to the Colony; and we doubt not but the next generation will be less English in regard to their treatment to their servants and animals here, and adopt the French kindness towards inferiors.'[137]

The comparison with animals was rather revealing. It was a French visitor to England before the Revolution, Lacoste, who noted that the English did not, as French masters did, treat their servants like useful domestic animals.[138] From a British standpoint it was possible to argue that the French master's failure was indeed a failure either to fear or respect his own servant and that it had had fatal consequences. Lord Dunstanville even believed that the French Revolution could be traced to this source. 'The free intercourse they had with their servants who heard their sentiments propagated the most dangerous opinions. At table his Lordship sd. He had heard such immoral things said as were shocking, but were smiled at or unnoticed.'[139]

It did not follow that the English were incapable of something that could be described as familiarity. There were certain concessions that some inferiors were well placed to extort. 'The art of being affable to farmers without appearing proud' was invaluable for country landowners, whether it was their financial or their political well-being that they had in mind.[140] This made the genuinely 'condescending' nobleman a useful member of society. As Joseph Farington put it, recording a conversation with his fellow artists: 'there were many persons in high situations in life who never excited apprehensions in the minds of persons of any degree'. Lord Lonsdale, the late Earl of Dartmouth, and the late Marquis of Thomond were 'persons of such affability as to make the meeting them a certain pleasure'.[141]

Hume in his *History of England* attributed to the Duke of Buckingham what he called 'English familiarity', as if this were some specifically national characteristic.[142] Hume was not often charitable about the English, still less about Buckingham. He seems to have had in mind a kind of vulgar bonhomie that might be contrasted with the easy but genteel politeness of true breeding. Other outsiders noticed certain exceptions to the seeming coldness of the English. Moritz was startled by the familiarity of an English greeting. 'As I passed through a village shortly before sundown I was greeted by various people with the words, "Fine night" or "Fine evening". Some greeted me with "How do you do?" to which the answer is "I thank you". This form of greeting must seem very unusual to a foreigner, coming from a man he has never seen before in his life and asking all at once what he does, or how he finds himself.'[143] This was, however, the reflection of a literal-minded German, for whom disregard of rank was in itself striking. French travellers rarely found an English greeting either familiar or warm by their standards.

INTIMACY

How much of all this had to do with a stunted capacity for human relationships? Was there some emotional chemical missing in the English make-up? The subject was much debated, not least in the context of relations between men and women. To some visitors it seemed that the English gentleman took the sociability even out of sexuality. Madame d'Avot remarked that in public he admired himself, and in private his mistress. For women in general he was dead.[144] This was generally taken to be one of the defining differences between English and Irish gentility. Madame d'Avot's contemporary John Gamble remarked that any woman must prefer the latter. 'A woman is an Englishman's wife, his mistress, his friend even, but she is seldom his companion. Even from women of the town, when the passion is satisfied which brings him to them, an Irishman does not fly, as an Englishman does. He remains with them, he accompanies them to places of public resort, he takes an interest in their welfare. This soothes their feelings, wounded by so often finding themselves the object of brutal lust only.'[145]

High society itself seemed predicated on the assumption that mixed company, however desirable, was the exception rather than the norm. One of the commonest observations of the social round in London concerned the extent to which women took the absence of men for granted. Female shopping expeditions, female visiting, female promenading, all were conducted to an extent and with a degree of independence that was not to be found in other capital cities. A German visitor in 1851 noted what he took to be an unstated contract. Women set the rules of etiquette in England but men had to submit to them only between the hours of two and four in the afternoon, or in the evening.[146] The ultimate accolade for a West End hostess was to ensure an adequate representation of men at her entertainments. A standard line in cattiness was that exemplified by the young Lady Anne Wentworth's remark in 1734: 'Lady Harcourt has her assemblies this year but they are as female as ever.'[147] Things had not changed fifty years later. Describing a ball in 1785, Lady Louisa Stuart noticed hardly 'a man, I verily think, more than twenty years old, and a great many much younger, all boys from Oxford'.[148] At the same time, visiting Hanover, the young Melesina Trench was startled to find more men than women at a fashionable ball, 'having been accustomed to see seven women to one man in London'.[149] Not that even the English could not be converted in the right circumstances. For an aristocratic Englishwoman, one of the unexpected attractions of colonial life in Calcutta was that husbands and wives were commonly to be found in the same place of an evening.[150]

Perhaps manly virtues shone only in male company. Englishmen often asserted and foreigners sometimes admitted that while the English were slow to make friendships, once made they proved loyal and lasting. 'They are allowed to be fast friends, but uncertain acquaintances', it was said, or 'they are friends instead of only appearing to be so'.[151] If this were the case, unsociability might be considered merely reserve, that is reluctance to be the first to strike up an acquaintance. The semantics were significant. In French this was, rather pejoratively, *mauvaise honte*. In English it was shyness or bashfulness, not necessarily implying a want of human warmth, only a fear of self-exposure. The far from retiring wife of an English Prime Minister, Elizabeth Grenville, called it 'a strange English awkwardness', analysing her own unease when confronted with strangers and more especially foreigners.[152]

The seeming stolidity of the English temperament also suggested a lack of superficial responsiveness, which might be taken for coldness and insensibility, not least in a religious setting, as Archenholz noted. 'It is easy to perceive from the *phlegm* with which the English perform their duties of their religion, that they are very little impressed by a sense of its awfulness. Even in a collegiate church, when they are *chaunting* in full choir, the cold, inanimate, and sometimes irreverent manner in which they acquit themselves, shocks the feelings of a stranger.'[153] Yet the same people seemed oddly susceptible to gusts of evangelical enthusiasm and even charlatanism. How, wondered Adolphe Blanqui, could so grave a nation be so vulnerable to a preacher such as Edward Irving?[154] Others were able to reconcile this seeming contradiction, as the Quaker Caroline Fox remarked of her friends the Bunsens, who occupied the Prussian embassy in London during the 1840s. 'Their first impression of the English was that they were a formal and heartless people, but this got itself corrected in time, and they now value the forms as all tending to lead to something better—as a safety-valve, or else a directing-post for religious feeling when it comes, which is just what they think the Germans lack.'[155]

A horror of emotional display was not thought of as a particularly English phenomenon between the mid-seventeenth and late eighteenth century, though the subject figured in the literature of gentility to which the English made a notable contribution. But by the early nineteenth century, not only had the English model of the gentleman come to reveal an almost overwhelming preoccupation with composure, impassivity, and self-control, but the national character itself was taken to embody it. This was not merely an insular ambition but a foreign perception. Princess Lieven, that sympathetic but hard-headed observer of high life in London concluded firmly that 'England is not the country of emotions'.[156] In patriotic discourse this was generally taken to be a matter for pride, especially to the extent that it suggested a rationality and commitment that lay deeper than the superficial feelings of lesser beings. Occasionally it was admitted that in the suppression of emotion the English were depriving themselves of a useful weapon, not least when they were travelling abroad. Fear of making a scene placed the English at the mercy of innkeepers, who could impose on them with little risk of a contretemps.[157] Even if this could be borne with, it was irritating. 'Travelling in Italy is not a good thing to improve one's temper, for it is absolutely necessary to *blow up* constantly and to *appear* at *least* in a violent passion—one gets no attention otherwise.'[158] By and large, however, the working assumption was that emotional display was best left to others.

Discussions of this kind were affected by cultural fads and fashions. In the 1760s and 1770s the 'man of feeling' was an English aspiration every bit as much as a Continental one. Thereafter the cult of manliness made it easier to incorporate reserve into prevailing values. Rejecting the language of sentiment and sensibility, it was possible to relegate feeling to the realm of weakness, preferably Celtic or Continental weakness, as a famous story about Madame de Staël revealed. She 'was regretting to Lord Castlereagh that there was no word in the English language which answered to the "*sentiment.*" "No," he said, "there is no English word, but the Irish have one that corresponds exactly, 'blarney'."'[159] Like all the best stories this generated different versions. Another featured the celebrated wit Joseph Jekyll. '"Why, for a single word," said Jekyll, "perhaps not; but I think we have a *phrase* that will do: All my eye, Betty Martin."'[160] It was perhaps not without significance that by the end of

the eighteenth century the word 'sentiment' itself came to be employed
in English for the meaningless formality of dinner party toasts.

Feelings are hard to distinguish from thoughts, and were rarely discussed without consideration of the cast of mind that was thought to
be characteristically English. Their supposed practical-mindedness suggested a preference for the mundane and the material, both implying
reliance on calculation rather than instinct. It did not go without notice
that in English feeling was indeed often identified with opinion rather
than sensation. If 'l'English feeling' was an appropriate expression to
describe public opinion, was it because the English preferred feeling
to thinking, or because they did not know the difference.[161] Either way,
regularity was everything to an English mind.

The cultural consequences were much discussed. A common French
claim, expressed for instance by the Breton antiquarian Jacques de
Cambry, was that even when they sought to appreciate the fine arts the
English did so with reflection rather than feeling.[162] On the other hand,
the outburst of creative energy associated with the Romantic poets gave
rise to English dismissals of the French capacity to feel. Henry Matthews,
author of *The Diary of an Invalid*, believed the French 'eminently deficient in sensibility, imagination, and enthusiasm; when they attempt to
be sentimental, they do but talk it'. He doubted whether any translation
of the *Pleasures of the Imagination* could ever make its meaning intelligible to them. They confused mere sensation with true sensibility. 'A
Frenchman cannot rise out of the mire of sensuality.'[163] This viewpoint
was not narrowly insular. Heinrich Heine, no champion of England,
remarked that the French, seeking sensibility, achieved only sentimentality. 'Sentimentality is the doubt of the materialist, who, unable to be in
all to himself, dreams in an indefinite manner, abortive manner of some
better sphere.'[164]

That there might be such a thing as an English sensibility was not necessarily disputed. But serious attempts at analysis distinguished between
diferent kinds of feeling. The standard arguments presumed a spectrum
of emotional capacities to be identified with music at one extreme and
poetry at the other, with fine arts ranged uneasily between. Few foreigners were prepared to recognize the Englishman as a natural musician.
Most accepted him as a poet. As an artist he was harder to place, though

from the late eighteenth century there was at least an assumption that there might be something to place. Such perceptions inevitably reflected English anxieties and speculations on these matters. It is worth noting that the most stalwart champions of Englishness frequently took their place alongside sceptics. Hazlitt was one of these, classifying signs of excellence in the arts as 'excrescences on the English character'. Poets, he remarked, did not have to be encouraged with premiums and institutions. They alone naturally expressed the English capacity for feeling that was essentially internal, not external, reflex, not organic. Words, not pictures, were the hard-headed Englishman's only means of responding to a world of impressions.[165] The result was that for the illiterate and the uneducated there was little hope of cultivating the finer feelings at all. The contrast between the philistinism of the lower orders at home and the instinctive cultural awareness of those abroad was something on which numerous Grand Tourists commented. 'The comparative barbarism of our population' occasioned much head-shaking on the part of artists such as the Victorian President of the Royal Academy, Sir Martin Shee.[166]

This emphasis on the introverted character of English sensibilities could be readily linked to the peculiar nature of English sociability. The most plausible case for the latter was that it flourished primarily as an extension of the domestic, the familiar, and the enclosed. In some analyses the attachment of English men and women first and foremost to their own homes was treated as necessarily subversive of sociability. When the French Revolution led to a reduction of the political influence of aristocratic women, it was claimed the French were following suit. 'The French', wrote William Jerdan in 1818, 'are now (what they once threw as a shade over the character of the English) cold, repulsive, unsociable.'[167]

At the very least, the magnetic power of the family helped explain the constricted nature of social life. As 'home-power' became the supposed basis for so many British achievements, this line of analysis grew increasingly attractive. The tendency to retreat into the smallest group possible in any situation was considered characteristic. At any kind of gathering it constituted a standing impediment to sociability in the Continental sense. The London hostess Lady Cork even fixed her drawing-room chairs to the floor to prevent her guests pushing them into small circles.[168] Holiday resorts conformed with this tendency rather than broke with it, as even the more independent-minded English admitted. 'Bournemouth', observed Grantley Berkeley, 'seems made for social enjoyment, and to waken the heart to genial sympathy; yet the visitors apparently shrink within themselves, remaining in their lodgings or hotels, or secreting themselves in the cover afforded by the neighbouring bushes.'[169]

'Domestic affections' themselves could be considered revealing of a preference for the enclosed and the small-scale. It was even argued that the English proficiency in the division of industrial and entrepreneurial labour resulted from it. 'Each man shuts himself up with a species of scrupulousness in the circle of his attributes and acquirements. There are in the United Kingdom very few universal minds, but you find there are many special talents.'[170] Regarded as a social phenomenon this tendency explained much. Given a choice, any self-respecting Englishman or woman would opt for a small circle of acquaintance and a clearly defined context within which it would operate: hence, as Fenimore Cooper put it, the fact that London had much company but no society, and Paris much society but no company.[171]

Numerous examples could be cited, but that most commonly identified by the early nineteenth century was the gentleman's club, an institution so quintessentially English that when imitated by Anglophiles in other countries it remained elusive. It is tempting to see the rise of the gentleman's club as a classic example of that retreat from the public world of enlightened sociability which seems so characteristic of the late eighteenth century. But this is rather misleading. It depends on treating the coffee house of the eighteenth century as an open forum of lively sociability, the club as a closed world of tedium and retreat.[172] The first portion of the premiss will not hold. By Continental standards English coffee houses were always dull places and not sociable at all. They were frequented day in day out by the same groups of people, often serving as a kind of common room for business and professional men. In short, they were in effect clubs, and many of them operated formally as such albeit in the premises of a private entrepreneur. In fact the early histories of Georgian clubs are tantamount to lists of coffee houses and taverns.[173] If Baudelaire was right to describe the English life of the clubs as the 'death of the heart' then he was at least as right about the eighteenth century as his own time.[174] The contrast with Continental coffee houses, whose sociability extended readily to visiting foreigners, was striking, from at least the mid-eighteenth to the mid-nineteenth century.[175] The notion of a stranger walking off the street into the vital world of eighteenth-century sociability is far removed from the reality of the coffee house in England.

By the English clubs were often praised for their unique social virtues. 'The word', as their chronicler Charles Marsh wrote, 'is untranslatably English. In spite of the long standing calumny, that our habits are uncommunicative, an Englishman's club is one of the types of his moral constitution, which is essentially gregarious.'[176] The point could be widened to include a range of voluntary associations, from the purely recreational to all kinds of useful collective endeavour. Surveying two centuries of such activity, the Victorian novelist George Gissing made an eloquent case for their value. 'Take the so-called sleepy market-town; it is bubbling with all manner of associated activities, and these of the quite voluntary kind, forms of zealously united effort such as are never dreamt of in the countries supposed to be eminently "social". Sociability does not consist in a readiness to talk at large with the first comer. It is not dependent upon natural grace and suavity; it is compatible, indeed, with thoroughly awkward and all but brutal manners. The English have never (at all events, for some two centuries past) inclined to the purely ceremonial or mirthful forms of sociability; but as regards every prime interest of the community—health and comfort, well being of body and of soul—their social instinct is supreme.'[177]

Yet to foreigners this seemed a strange kind of gregariousness. J. G. Kohl observed that without a specific object, 'a community of tastes, a peculiar tie, which draws him nearer his fellow-men', the Englishman saw no point to society.[178] Flora Tristan found it depressing that the real object might be to 'obtain the material advantages from association. There is something frightening about this spiritual inertia, this social materialism.'[179] And even where such a motive was hard to identify, Alphonse Esquiros asked himself 'whether the success of British Clubs is really based, as people say, on a footing of sociability' and concluded that it was not. The real object was to identify and fix a group of friends and companions who made no demands on an Englishman beyond what he chose to recognize. 'Without being deficient in politeness—at least the politeness of his own country—he can isolate himself in a crowd, attend to his business or pleasures, or come and go exactly as he likes.'[180]

At the end of the day almost every inquiry into English sociability concluded that after all it was, by the standards of other nations, an unsatisfying thing. Even polite society was in the view of outsiders rendered disagreeable by the Englishman's basic distrust of contact and communication. Pückler-Muskau wrote: 'What contributes much to the "dullness" of English society, is the haughty aversion which Englishmen . . . show to addressing an unknown person; if he should venture to address them, they receive it with the air of an insult. They sometimes laugh at themselves for this singular incivility, but no one makes the least attempt to act differently when an opportunity offers.'[181] Some Englishmen indeed deplored as well as laughed. John Stuart Mill's judgement was devastating. 'Everybody acts as if everybody else were an enemy or a bore.'[182]

Very diverse visitors agreed. The Russian Karamzin observed in the 1790s: 'To live here for the enjoyment of social life would be like seeking flowers in a sandy desert. All the foreigners in London with whom I have become acquainted and talked agree with me.'[183] A few years later, the Napoleonic consul Joseph Fiévée, remarked that if civilization 'is the art of making society sweet, easy and aimable the English are the least civilised of all European nations'.[184] After the Napoleonic Wars the prestige and influence of Britain made reserve seem more worthy of imitation, but it remained controversial. In France, attempts to imitate it by the *jeunesse dorée* produced complaints that in them it merely seemed like sullenness and insolence ill becoming the French character. It could not profitably be transplanted from its native land.[185] None the less, especially in societies south of the Alps, as many English travellers testified, to be 'proud and reserved as the English are supposed to be' was a sure sign of the Anglomaniac.[186]

Even those variants of polite and professional society that might have been expected to value the easy exchange of ideas and opinions proved disappointing. When Giacomo Beltrami visited Oxford he was 'very much struck by the reserve prevalent here, among the members of the respective colleges. The fellow by whom I was accompanied appeared everywhere a greater stranger than myself; and he was no less reserved with me; for all my *fiscalisations* on this great manufactory of learning, morals, and politics, were nearly without success: all I could obtain from him was, what I least cared for, a good dinner.'[187]

Few doubted that this was indeed a question of Englishness not Britishness. The superior politeness of the Scots, Welsh, and Irish constitutes one of the most hackneyed themes in the travel literature of this period, ever more incontestable as growing numbers of foreigners ventured not only beyond London but also beyond England itself in the late eighteenth and early nineteenth centuries. The common judgement on Scots, Irish, and Welsh was that their most lowly representatives had a degree of politeness not to be found among the English. Edward Topham was startled to find the ordinary folk of Scotland 'infinitely more civil, humanized, and hospitable, than any I ever met with'.[188] Angiolini found the Scotsman 'more urbane, more self-possessed, more obliging than the Englishman'.[189] Scots themselves were excusably patriotic on this score. Mrs Grant of Laggan, who spent portions of her life in North America and England, and enjoyed a huge audience for her works in England, proclaimed her native country 'the land of social life and social love' untainted by the 'cold and close attention to petty comforts and conveniences which absorbs the English mind'.[190] It was a boast of Edinburgh society that it largely avoided the London obsession with rank, allowing gentry and the professions to mix freely.

In Ireland, too, visitors thought they were in the presence of a superior tradition which could not simply be attributed to outdated modes. Sir John Carr, in his tour of 1805, found a certain politeness which existed at all levels of society and which had little of the English about it. He defied his reader to attend an Irish ball without being struck by 'the spirit, good-humour, grace, and elegance, which prevail in it: in this accomplishment they may rank next to the animated inhabitants of Paris'. But this was no monopoly of the middle class; the most degraded of the peasantry seemed to have it. 'Their native urbanity to each other is very pleasing; I have frequently seen two boors take off their hats and salute each other with great civility.'[191]

Similar comments were made about the Welsh, especially when the Welsh tour became fashionable in the late eighteenth century, giving travellers an opportunity to observe what the poet Samuel Rogers called a 'very joyous social people'.[192] And the Cornish, too, could recall that they

were descended from Celts who had once traded with the whole of the
civilized world and been recognized for their social skills. G. B. Worgan,
in his report to the Board of Agriculture in 1811, boasted that 'From the
peer to the peasant there is a mildness and complacency of temper, an
urbanity, hospitality, and courteousness of manners, a noble frankness
and liberality of heart, extremely conciliating to the stranger; and what is
peculiar to the Cornish, morning, noon, or night, they greet the traveller
with an appropriate gracious salutation. This is no novel character of
them, but stands recorded as anciently as the times of Augustus Caesar,
and is attributed by Diodorus Siculus, to that frequent intercourse with
merchants of foreign countries, which the traffic for their tin could not
but occasion.' For good measure Worgan added Queen Elizabeth's testimony that 'the Cornish gentlemen were all born courtiers'.[193]

Nor was Celtic sociability only to be found in Celtic society. On
English ground Scots and Irish were considered to retain their native
manners. The American Benjamin Silliman, entertained to dinner in
Liverpool, was anxious, when he found Liverpudlian gentlemen less than
forthcoming, to explain that this was an English not a Scottish characteristic. 'Before dismissing this dinner, I ought to observe that the reserve
and coldness which marked the manners of most of the gentlemen were
strongly contrasted with the polite and attentive hospitality of our host,
(a Scotchman,) who suffered no one of his guests to remain unnoticed.'[194]
Foreigners noted that where the Irish were present in numbers, as at
Bath, the effect was greatly to enliven social life.[195]

Open-minded Englishmen sometimes admitted the Celtic advantage
in this respect. To say as the actor-manager Tate Wilkinson said of Hull
that it was the 'Dublin of England' was to praise the liveliness of its
society.[196] Irish sociability was generally conceded though usually with
offsetting qualifications. Scots were regarded slightly more favourably.
But compliments to either the Scots or the Irish were likely to be of the
backhanded variety. No self-respecting Englishman would actually have
wanted to emulate them. He merely confessed that there were frivolous
arts in which other nationalities were more accomplished precisely
because they were more frivolous. And more than frivolity might
be involved. Polite though the Welsh might seem when one was touring among them, their inquisitiveness would become a nuisance on
more extended acquaintance.[197] The Irish were still more suspect. The

'flattery and attention' encountered in Ireland were things 'we have no notion of showing to anybody in England, let them be foreigners of ever so high a rank'.[198]

Even Scots were doubtful about the Irish. To the politician Francis Horner the famous Sheridan seemed 'rather too attentive to strangers, though his manners certainly are very polished; but this courteous notice of one looks as if it had a purpose, though it may not'.[199] And it was a daughter of that much abused Scotsman, the Earl of Bute who replied smartly to an Irish lady boasting of the natural affinity of manner that promoted amicable relations between the French and the Irish. ' "I am not at all surprised at it," replied I, and I own I thought many traits of the French Revolution and the Irish Rebellion afterwards served to prove the truth of her observation in a manner she would not have been pleased at.'[200] John Bull's reserve as a form of immunization against democracy had additional appeal in an age of revolution.

EXCLUSIVENESS

Explaining the irreducible minimum of reserve that even defenders of English sociability conceded and doing so in a way that need not be attributed to native misanthropy required some ingenuity. An early clue was provided by Mrs Piozzi when she had the opportunity to compare the customs of her own country with those of her Italian husband. 'Our government has left so narrow a space between the upper and under ranks of people in Great Britain, that if our persons of condition fail even for a moment to watch their post, maintaining by dignity what they or their fathers have acquired by merit, they are instantly and suddenly broken in upon by the well-employed talents, or swiftly-acquired riches, of men born on the other side of the thin partition, whilst in Italy the gulph is totally impassable, and birth alone can entitle man or woman to the society of gentlemen and ladies.'[201]

Heinrich von Watzdorf similarly thought English reserve the consequence of an absence of legal privileges. Noblemen who lacked formal rights must attempt to preserve their status by means of a certain stiffness.[202] Foreign noblemen certainly found English irreverence when confronted with rank startling. The Russian Prince Kurakin planned to use an assumed name when he visited Britain, as he did elsewhere in Europe, only to give up the practice when it was explained to him that his hosts took no interest in titles however grand.[203] Such revelations helped explain the peculiar burdens which systems of manners had to carry in England. Social superiority could only be maintained by the cultivation of subtle distinctions that might be felt but not described. There was something about English gentility that was inimitable. Whatever sustained it was either inborn or required long training. If it often went with rank it was far from synonymous with it.

This explained something puzzling about the French relationship between masters and servants. It was not just that French servants were more dependent on their masters, and lacked the power to challenge them. The fact was that French servants actually behaved more like their betters than did their counterparts in England. This was said to be one reason why French actors found it easier to take upper-class parts, such was the essential similitude of manners, as the travelling companion of the young Duke of Hamilton, John Moore, observed. 'There is not such a difference between the manners and behaviour of the people of the first rank, and those of the middle and lower ranks, in France as in England. Players therefore, who wish to catch the manners of people of high rank and fashion, do not undertake so great a task in the one country as in the other. You very seldom meet with an English servant who could pass for a man of quality or fashion; and accordingly very few people who have been in that situation ever appear on the English stage: But there are many *valets de place* in Paris so very polite, so completely possessed of all the little etiquettes, fashionable phrases, and usual airs of the *beau monde*, that if they were set off by the ornaments of dress and equipage, they would pass in many of the courts of Europe for men of fashion.'[204] Actors and actresses who could hit off people in high life were particularly prized on the English stage. Mrs Abington achieved such success in this speciality that she was even consulted by upwardly mobile ladies about tasteful dress and accomplishments.[205]

What was at issue was a question of class, or rather of the difference between rank and class. Rank guaranteed recognition, class craved it. Snobbery, as Lionel Trilling remarks, is the vice not of aristocratic societies, but of bourgeois democratic societies. It arises from the insecurity

of the individual who seeks pride in status but lacks pride in inherited
function. In any social setting he asks 'Do I belong? Do I really belong?
And does he belong? And if I am observed talking to him, will it make
me seem to belong or not to belong?'[206] Rank, in theory at least, solved
this problem, for it represented a relatively fixed state of affairs. Class
depended on status determined largely by wealth, and visible wealth at
that. This was not something readily judged, though commerce might
make men competitive and calculating. A stranger was in the first instance
a commodity whose worth needed weighing. As the American William
Austin put it, the English repulsed strangers because for the commer-
cially minded 'the first maxim should be to know nobody by whom they
are not likely to profit'.[207] His judgement needs to be located in the contemporary debate which was raging in his own country, where commerce
and the manners it brought were feared as solvents of democratic
integrity. It also needs some refining to explain the attitudes of gentlemen
who were at pains to distance themselves from tradesmen and who
claimed to prefer the subtler advantages that wealth ultimately bought to
its material advantages. None the less, it does focus attention on the
crucial phenomenon, the judgemental wariness which individuals show
when confronted with people of whom they have no personal knowledge.

The argument took on additional sophistication and force in the
hands of de Tocqueville, who also analysed 'this English avoidance of
English people' in terms of the difficulty of estimating social status, particularly in a relatively egalitarian culture that punished unjustified
assumptions of superiority severely.[208] But this was a merely negative
conclusion. It said nothing about how to make oneself agreeable in a
more positive sense. Unfortunately, estimating the wealth and therefore
the status of people below the rank of a peer of the realm and above the
level of the labouring man, was extremely difficult. Traditional courtesy
literature attached much significance to the way one should treat superiors and inferiors. But this assumed that one knew pretty clearly who
were one's superiors and inferiors. In other countries the cringing
manners of the peasant or the servant, on the one hand, or the overbearing familiarity of a great magnate or a rich bourgeois on the other
told their own tale. Englishmen, being both free and equal under the law,
had no occasion to give away their status. Appraising each other accordingly became a complicated, nuanced task. Small wonder, as the novelist

Robert Plumer Ward remarked, that the 'greatest distress of Englishmen and Englishwomen' was 'the fear of one another'.[209] And smaller wonder that outsiders saw this as a national malaise. Keeping those below in their place was, wrote the American Calvin Colton, 'an hereditary vice of this community'.[210] Nobody was free of its contamination.

This sense of the difficulty of evaluating any social situation did not have to be put either critically or apologetically, however. In fact the growing tendency to conceive of gentility in high-flown moral terms made a merit of necessity. Reserve in this form made the English gentleman one of nature's Aristotelians, an instinctively patient interpreter of the extraordinary complexity of life. Wisdom lay not in instant reaction and instant judgement, let alone instant agreeableness. First impressions were often wrong. Self-respect and respect for others, alike, would fit naturally with an Englishman's reserve, far more naturally than with complaisance, a foreign word which lost its appeal and gradually fell out of use in the late eighteenth century. In a mid-Victorian gentleman's sensibilities, reserve was a sign of the gentleman's superior wisdom. 'His awareness of what it takes to understand and be understood by others will inhibit him from speaking to everyone as he does to friends.'[211]

Reserve in this form became a civic virtue and one that represented something of a shift from the older concept of civility. The semantics were telling. In the cult of courtesy, mien, or demeanour, was an essential department of civility. It was the face presented to the world, a sociable face. That is what it meant in early eighteenth-century English as it did in other languages. But by the end of the century 'demean' had come to signify something less agreeable. To demean oneself was to abase oneself. It was noticed at the time that the usage had begun with the 'lower people' though Richardson had helped give it genteel currency.[212] Perhaps only in England could the art of pleasing be considered a form of self-abasement, but so it was. In German, in French, and in Italian there were quite different words for the two things.

Some Englishmen used such arguments to lessen the odium of their reputation for unsociability. One contention was that the pressures of commercial growth and social instability had actually transformed the natural character of the English. It seemed they were not really antisocial at all, but 'being in fact socially disposed, were obliged to be stiff to strangers, because all were trying to hang upon and be pulled up by the

skirts of those above them'.[213] Others rued their sacrifice of communality to modernity. Thus the poetess Caroline Norton reasoned in 1841: 'I
am not sure that in the overeducating of the classes who never can have
our *leisure*, what ever else they may obtain that is ours, we have not
destroyed all our companionship with them; they stand too close for our
comfort or theirs; they climb just close enough to our level to prevent
their looking up to us; they elbow us, and we have no longer room to
stretch out our hand in fellowship with them!'[214] In a country where the
liberty of all took precedence over the authority of the few, some stiffen-
ing of the social fabric was essential. This artificial framework, as the
artist Joseph Farington expressed it, could only be provided by manners.
'Where the distinctions of rank are most positive and where one part of
a community, are in most subjection to those above them, personal
freedom is often allowed in a *great* degree. He who can be crushed at the
will of a power may be permitted to approach very near. In England the
case seems to be otherwise. Rights being equal, and the laws effective,
manners alone can preserve that subordination which is allowed to be
necessary.'[215]

Many of Farington's generation believed that class was a burden which
England had shouldered manfully, even necessarily, but not willingly. His
contemporary Henry Taylor relished the escape to a less forbidding
social landscape. In France, he found, 'the great relief is from the jeal-
ousy of classes, which forms so many knots in the English people and
obstructs the free circulation of a good fellow-feeling. I, for one, never
have the good feeling towards an English mechanic, being a stranger,
which I have towards dogs and horses, being so. But the moment I came
amongst the French I had it. Oil seemed to have taken the place of rust
in the mechanism of society.'[216]

Many thought this rust of recent origin. There existed a belief that
from around the 1770s social competition had intensified as an expanding middle class sought recognition of its genteel status and as the
topmost layer of society itself became more obsessed with the preservation of its superiority. For the lawyer John Adolphus, looking back from
the 1840s on his youth in the 1780s, the 'reserve of modern days' had significantly diminished the 'scene of society' he had known then.[217] The
recognition of Society with a capital 'S' was itself a sign of insecurity. It
was not that aristocratic life had been less snobbish or exclusive before,

only that it seemed increasingly necessary to mark off the resulting privileges, traditions, and rights.

There was a growing emphasis on the language of exclusion—the term the 'Exclusives' was itself only one example. The 'cut' as a weapon of social warfare was invented in the 1770s. The word 'snobbery', originally aimed at those seeking admission to the elite rather than those within it, came soon after. The fact that social warfare within high life was as bitter as that on its frontier with low life merely accentuated this sense of crisis. 'Why is the present English social system like the Ptolemaic system of astronomy?' it was asked. 'Because it is full of circles which *cut* one another.'[218] The language of 'set' and 'cut' was by no means a nine days' wonder. A German visitor to the Great Exhibition in 1851 thought it revealing of the state of English society.[219] There was general agreement that it was unique. In the United States in the 1820s the young Henry Addington remarked that 'the art of cutting especially, a filthy bud of English growth and nourished by the insolence of Aristocratic pride, is unpracticed and unknown across the Atlantic, as indeed every where but in England alone'.[220]

Whether there was truly more social competition would be hard to decide and in a sense does not matter. What is significant is that contemporaries believed there was and adjusted their attitudes accordingly. The change was reflected in the models and templates of gentility offered in the etiquette of the late eighteenth and early nineteenth century. The ideal early eighteenth-century gentleman had been the man of ease, condescension (in the eighteenth-century sense), and affability. His successor was a somewhat sterner figure, displaying manly reserve, decorum, and propriety. It was easy for self-appointed critics of high society to allege, as Lady Charlotte Bury did, that 'the most prominent folly of London, and the most in vogue amongst the first classes in the metropolis, is the system of exclusiveness'.[221] Sydney Smith summarized it still more simply. Fashionable society in England was 'high table-land, very flat and cold'.[222] A high table-land was intended to be inaccessible. Fenimore Cooper explained it in terms that put the emphasis on the threat from the social climbers below. 'In a country where wealth is constantly bringing new claimants for consideration into the arena of fashion . . . those who are in its possession contrive all possible means of distinction between themselves and those who are about to dispute their ascendancy.

Beyond a doubt what is called high English society, is more repulsive, artificial and cumbered, and, in short, more absurd and frequently less graceful than that of any other European nation.'[223]

The point featured in an extended analysis in 1822 by Francis Jeffrey in the *Edinburgh Review*. It examined what Bonaparte had called the 'Morgue Aristocratique' of the English, 'the sort of sulky and contemptuous reserve with which, both at home and abroad, almost all who have any pretensions to *bon ton* seem to think it necessary to defend those pretensions'. The reason was 'a considerable drawback from two very proud peculiarities in our condition—the freedom of our constitution, and the rapid progress of wealth and intelligence in the body of the nation'. This was not a new phenomenon but rather one that had operated with decisive effect during the early years of George III's reign. 'So many persons now raised themselves by their own exertions, that every one thought himself entitled to rise; and very few proportionally were contented to remain in the rank to which they were born; and as vanity is a still more active principle than ambition, the effects of this aspiring spirit were more conspicuously seen in the invasion which it prompted on the prerogatives of polite society, than in its more serious occupations; and a herd of uncomfortable and unsuitable companions beset all the approaches to good company, and seemed determined to force all its barriers.' There had resulted an 'incredible increase of forwardness and solid impudence among the half-bred and half-educated classes of this country'. The piece ended with a pious hope. 'The extreme facility with which it may be copied by the lowest and dullest of mankind,—the caricatures which are daily exhibited of it in every disgusting variety,—and the restraints it must impose upon the good nature and sociality which, after all, do *really* form a part of our national character, must concur, we think, with the alienation it produces in others, speedily to consign it to the tomb of other forgotten affectations.'[224]

Others also defended national character but were more doubtful of the prospect of improvement. If the underlying problem was modernity, of, as Constantine Phipps put it, 'the diffusion of knowledge, wealth, even fashion, in fine of every profession or endowment that can give one man or set of men superiority over another', then matters could only get worse and augured ill for less advanced societies bent on imitation. 'Walk our streets, enter our saloons; there is mistrust in every face, and even in the

greeting of every friend there lurks a reserve behind the show of friendship, that is chilling to the heart that cares for aught beyond itself.'[225]

Offering plausible explanations for what looked like English unsociability doubtless did something to salvage national pride. But at best it
was a defensive measure, and one that smacked of desperation. It did
nothing to conceal the shift in external perceptions, which had once portrayed the English as a nation of cheerful libertarians, verging on barbarism, no doubt, among the lower sort, but healthily unreserved and
relaxed in its everyday social relations. Such a nation had offered a vision
of politeness that allowed Anglomaniacs to subvert the supposed artificiality and stiffness of aristocratic manners elsewhere. But by the end of
the eighteenth century and increasingly as the nineteenth century wore
on, a less cheering picture had to be painted, one of social unease and
even conflict, engendering a cold exclusiveness on the part of the great
and a grudging civility among their inferiors. The fact that the resulting
stereotypes were sufficiently unifying to make it easy to speak of an
underlying character intensified the resulting dismay. At its worst,
English gentility had ceased to offer a model of social progress for other
nations and become little more than a mask for incorrigible national
unsociability.

CHAPTER SIX

Eccentricity

LIBERTY

*T*HE freeborn Englishman was not only a favourite invocation of the English themselves but an enduring, if less treasured, image of their European neighbours. However, both at home and abroad it meant different things at different times, subtly responding to the requirements of new generations and reflecting the changes that occurred in English and Continental life. A seventeenth-century Frenchman might be inclined to see it as an interesting remnant of the barbaric culture that it was the historic mission of Latin civility and Gallic culture to tame. His successor of the mid-eighteenth century was taught to consider it altogether more refined and ennobling, something that might profitably be employed to polish the increasingly tarnished absolutism of the Bourbon monarchy. And a century on again he was coming to consider it an idiosyncratic feature of an inimitable society, something that in its undemocratic form was no longer in the vanguard of progressive thought yet which in England at least contributed to the unique stability of British institutions.

There were some continuities. A high proportion of foreign commentaries throughout the period concerned matters of law and constitution. Some of the results, notably what Montesquieu alluded to in the *Esprit des Lois* and what de Lolme more systematically described in *The Constitution of England*, helped to propel two waves of Anglomania in France and prepared the way for a third in Germany. This emphasis on the legal and institutional framework as products of historical forces was congenial to the taste of the mid-eighteenth century. It was also compatible with modes of thought which figured prominently in England itself. The litany of liberties rooted in English history was rich indeed: trial by jury, habeas corpus, Magna Carta, the Petition of Right and Bill of Rights, taxation by means of elected representatives, the restriction of monarchical powers within a tightly controlled executive, the parliamentary franchise and frequent parliamentary elections. Three constitutional victories associated with the Revolution of 1688, the winning of freedom of worship for Protestant Dissenters under the Toleration Act, the effective assertion of parliamentary authority over the army indicated by the Mutiny Acts, and the liberation of the press by the lapsing of the machinery of censorship in 1695 completed this tableau of a free people accustomed to assert its rights.

Even when admiration for these achievements was at its height there were other views. Some French sceptics thought of this liberty as an interesting anthropological specimen rather than a pointer to the future of mankind. Parliament might be the foundation of English liberty but not everybody considered it a sign of superior civilization. The duc de Lévis took advantage of its primitive roots in Germanic society sarcastically to point out that similar councils were found among the savages of America.[1] Lévis certainly knew his savages of America, but as Montcalm's successor in command of a defeated army in Quebec, his analysis was not, perhaps, impartial.

Others wondered whether the English enjoyed true liberty. Once the first flush of Voltairean enthusiasm was passed, an increasingly critical perspective was brought to bear. Rousseau's celebrated observation that Englishmen were only free once in every seven years, at general elections, was one consequence. Much attention was focused on the electoral process. Foreign commentators before the reign of George III had been prone to overrate the size and independence of the electorate. Thereafter they became increasingly well informed about the erratic distribution of the borough franchise, the extent of electoral corruption, and the techniques of oligarchical control. They learned these things from the English themselves. It is often remarked how little successive generations of reformers actually accomplished in the way of concrete change. But one of their less trumpeted successes was certainly to weaken Continental faith in the virtues of the British constitution. John Wilkes spent an important part of his career in France, in exile in the 1760s, and the interest that he generated there was scarcely less than the controversy that he created in Britain. He could readily be seen as a representative English figure, asserting the ancient rights of Englishmen against an authoritarian monarchy. But like other radicals, Horne Tooke, Christoper Wyville, and Sir Francis Burdett, he confirmed the impression that English liberty was now being contested on its home ground. By the 1780s it was a common perception outside Britain, commoner indeed than inside it, that this contest was being lost by the libertarians.

Oddly enough, one of the undisputed victories of the reformers enhanced this impression. In the 1770s Parliament effectively lost control of the publication of its own debates. Thanks to the readiness of even the most oppressive regimes on the Continent to permit the reprinting of London news, Opposition speakers such as Burke, Fox, and Sheridan found themselves addressing newspaper readers not only in Britain but as far afield as Rome, Copenhagen, and Vienna. Continental opinion could hardly be expected to contextualize their rhetoric as British opinion might. The accusations of corruption hurled across the floor of the House of Commons at the ministers of George III were more likely to be believed abroad than at home. For loyal supporters of government, a foreign tour provided opportunities to correct the resulting impressions, as Patrick Brydone did in Sicily, where he was at pains to point out to his hosts that what they heard was 'only the voice of the most abandoned and profligate wretches in the nation, who, taking advantage of the great freedom of the press, had often made these newspapers the vehicles of the most detestable faction'.[2] Counter-propaganda of this kind seems to have had little effect.

Apart from the corrosive effect of corruption on parliamentary representation, other shibboleths were questioned. Freedom of the press itself was not seen as a boon by every foreign commentator. Carlo Denina blamed the extraordinary quantity of meretricious literature published in England on it.[3] Even those who admired freedom of expression worried about the way it was used. The intrusiveness, licentiousness, and heart-lessness of English journals took Continental readers by surprise. Marshal Pillet, whose imprisonment in the hulks during the Napoleonic Wars embittered him for life, was evidently not prevented by his captors from reading English newspapers. His notorious work *L'Angleterre vue à Londres et dans ses provinces* consisted largely of episodes trawled from the gutter press and reproduced as evidence of a decadent national character.

It was arguable that decadence was itself part of the social cost of a free constitution. Light policing had its disadvantages. One often cited by visitors to London was the State's lack of interest in regulating the capital's morals. The result was the right of the freeborn whore to make large parts of the city unendurable for respectable men and women, and to spread veneral disease far and wide without submission to public inspection and medication.[4] It was also alleged that the almost instinc-tive favouring of private right over public duty had ingrained in the English certain practices that were highly objectionable. One of the most commented on was the all too visible vandalism that society tolerated. English parks were notorious for the resulting damage. 'Any place thrown open to the English was sure to exhibit traces of their visitation in the initial names and ribaldry carved in every piece of woodwork, and scratched on every patch of glass, or to be marked by the mutilation and destruction of pictures, and statues, furniture, flowers, shrubs, beasts, and trees.'[5] To visit public buildings or parks in France or Germany was to be struck by the respect that was shown them.[6] The English them-selves often admitted the fundamental difference in such matters. One such was the Victorian travel-writer Lady Chatterton, who admired the Germans for the orderliness which made it practicable for their govern-ments to provide wayside seats for strangers without fear of destruction. 'They possess none of that sort of indescribable propensity which will be sure to make some Englishmen walk on the part of a road destined for equestrians or ride on the footpath. This same spirit, if carried a little farther, would make him tear up the flowers, and break down the seats, and then rail against the government which has kindly arranged it all.'[7]

Another line of attack was to argue that English liberty was less com-prehensive than some of its champions claimed. Naval impressment was subjected to close scrutiny. How could Englishmen boast of their famous habeas corpus when it did nothing for the victims of a brutal press-gang? Was the plight of a freeborn British seaman in reality any better than that of a conscripted peasant on the Continent? Gentlemen, of course, were not likely to be inconvenienced by the 'press'. Yet the civil law was considered by many as great a threat to genteel liberty. Imprisonment for debt was difficult to reconcile with the notion of personal liberty. Since it figured so much in English literature, usually in an unmistakably critical context, it is unsurprising that so many foreigners were disturbed by it.

A frequent observation was that English freedom, however praise-worthy in principle, did not make for the happiness of those who did not happen to be free. Slave-owners of English stock were generally considered to be harder masters than those of other nations, with the possible exception of the Dutch, themselves, of course, bred in a republican tradition. The point became increasingly controversial in the late eighteenth century, partly because the abolitionist movement was stronger at home in England than anywhere else, partly because the English were considered in other respects an unusually humane and philanthropic people. Modern authorities make the accusations plausible, if only in the sense that the constitutional rights enjoyed by English colonists in the West Indies permitted them to frame their own slave regimes, whereas those of other European states might be regulated by Continental governments readier to recognize the unwisdom of ill-treating slaves.

A related point concerned the rights of women, a favourite topic from the mid-eighteenth century, when enlightened treatment of 'the second sex' was considered one of the marks of a modern society. As arguably the most modern society of all, England was subjected to particular scrutiny, with mixed results. That English women enjoyed unusual freedom of movement and action, especially by comparison with the unmarried women of Continental societies, was generally conceded, though there were sceptics such as Joseph de Gourbillon, in 1817, who thought 'it confined to their ability to promenade a few hours in the morning in certain parts of the town, meeting places of the first classes of both sexes'.[8]

It was also believed that women enjoyed a surprising degree of choice when a partner was under consideration. As Victor Hennequin put it, an English girl married 'not because she is eighteen, not because she knows the names of the kings of France, not because she can tap a piece of Herz on the piano, not because she has a fortune equal to his, but because she loves and is loved'. Hennequin evidently had a rather romanticized view of such matters. The freedom of an English girl's upbringing was, he thought, visible in every step she took or gesture she made. 'That is why, if ever you see an Englishwoman descend from a post-chaise in order to walk on the glaciers of the Alps, you see her in a white dress, fresh and gracious as if she were lost under the trees in Kensington Gardens.'[9]

Whether this in practice did very much for female rights was another matter. Many thought that in this so-called 'paradise of women' the laws of marriage were harsh, especially to the extent that they deprived the married woman of control of her own property, a view supported by modern analysis.[10] Moreover, there seemed to be little give and take in the English idea of domesticity. Pückler-Muskau contrasted a 'lighter kind of slavery' imposed on wives by English husbands with the 'reasonable liberty' which they would have enjoyed on the Continent. 'Women are grateful to be trusted, and far more obedient to the man who gently leads them than the brutal one who only knows how to command.'[11] Pückler-Muskau's contemporary Beltrami was impressed by feminine fortitude more than female rights. 'The character of Englishwomen is masculine and resolute, and they pique themselves on a sort of conjugal heroism, which is the more noble and virtuous, as it is not always either deserved or requited.'[12]

However, Englishwomen did not themselves necessarily concur. Sarah Austin, who was to find herself translating the works of Pückler-Muskau, thought his countrywomen far worse off than her own. At Bonn in the 1820s, at the very time that Pückler-Muskau was touring Britain, she remarked, 'we are apt to think we are worse treated by our *natural legislators* than any of our continental sisters, but "come here a bit" (that is German) and you shall see'. In Dresden she was even more shocked by the contempt with which German women were treated. 'My English blood boils at seeing myself so degraded. We in England are *oppressed*, but not condemned.'[13]

Whatever the truth, the common Continental view, well-established since at least the 1760s, was that of Pückler-Muskau rather than Sarah Austin. Even the English did not deny that the women of fashionable society in France, especially, enjoyed more political and intellectual influence than those in London. An obvious explanation was that such variations depended very much on political systems. When government was the prerogative of the court, women shared with men relative political insignificance and gained a certain equality in point of comment and protest. When government was the prerogative of the male, women could hardly enjoy comparable status. The French Revolution, ironically by some blamed on the excessive politicking of French women, ended by confirming this notion. The effect of inventing a legitimate public role for ordinary Frenchmen was precisely to generate the kind of domestic seclusion and preoccupation for women which had been long confined to England. Liberating men was synonymous with enslaving women, as the Swiss littérateur Charles Bonstettin, put it.[14] His assertion has since become a commonplace of feminist historiography.

Gender aside, events lent force to the swelling volume of doubt about the reality of English freedom. The two great revolutions of the late eighteenth century, the American and the French, threatened Britain's monopoly of political wisdom and tested the English vision of liberty almost to the point of destruction. Even Anglomaniacs were dismayed by the sufferings of the American colonists. The abbé Coyer was genuinely puzzled. How was it that the Corsican patriot General Paoli, whom he met in London, could be idolized as leader of one set of colonial insurgents while another set across the Atlantic were being driven to open rebellion?[15] The obvious response was that Paoli was resisting the French, Washington the British, but Coyer seems to have been too polite to suggest it. Others were less restrained. It seemed a reasonable conclusion from the events of the 1770s that English liberty had migrated across the Atlantic leaving behind it only a monumental hypocrisy to conceal its absence.

There was an alternative hypothesis, though one which had implications for the English themselves, forcing them to define their own traditions rather more cautiously. The American challenge might be seen not as a symptom of liberty at all, but of licence. Americans were Englishmen, perhaps, but Englishmen who had lost their bearings, descending first into democracy and no doubt eventually into anarchy. This was not just a matter of constitutional analysis. The British had shown little interest in the make-up of American society while the thirteen colonies were part of the empire; after 1783 they showed a great deal of interest, and there sprang up a flourishing market for pictures of American life and manners. The resulting, highly unfavourable images can easily look like the sour grapes of defeated English gentility. Americans were paraded as crude, ill-mannered, unhelpful, intrusive, materialistic, things which had formerly been said of plebeian Englishmen. But in all this metropolitan snobbery there was a serious point, namely that American liberty was antisocial, enfranchising the individual at the expense of his social relations, leaving other idividuals no privacy, no precedence, no pride. English liberty was an altogether more sensitive thing, part of an organism which had been nourished in insular security by the descendants of Hengist and Horsa. Americans might have continued these traditions even in a vast new Continent, and in a few rather isolated regions, for example Virginia, some of them did so. But by and large 1776 represented a great caesura in the history of the Anglo-Saxons, one which left English opinion with increasingly few regrets that it had occurred.

The response to French liberty was still simpler. It was a charade, a frightful carnival of horrors which caricatured liberty without ever attaining it. The terrible tyranny of the Jacobins, the orgiastic corruption of the Directory, the military despotism of Bonaparte, merely demonstrated how profoundly the French had misunderstood the nature of liberty. They had grasped at English ideas as it were in a social void. Moreover, bringing to the enactment of liberty characteristically French concerns, they had revealed how enervating centuries of absolutism had proved. Men who went to France in 1801, when the Peace of Amiens brought a temporary halt to the revolutionary wars, were fascinated to observe a society which had torn up its own roots, and artificially recreated itself. This Frankenstein could not be compared with the freeborn Englishman.

The desire to distance English liberty from these alternative models and thereby to make it a more orderly, less turbulent, more domesticated, and less public force, was a central preoccupation of the late eighteenth century. Even before the French Revolution the Wilkite mobs, the radical protesters against the American War, and the Gordon Rioters helped provoke anxieties about the disruptive potential of an English crowd. If any doubts were left in the minds of those prone to worry about the threat to authority they were removed in the 1790s by revolutionary theories at home and revolutionary practices abroad. Increasingly the English tra-

dition of liberty was placed in a heavily loyalist, even conservative framework that permitted full expression of the authoritarian impulse of the
early nineteenth century.

Disputing the possession of the holy grail of liberty was no new activity, though the claims made by infant republics in America and France
certainly gave this rivalry additional zest. Republicanism was not demon-
strably a guarantor of the ordinary citizen's freedom. Indeed a favourite
cause of self-congratulation to Englishmen and women on the Grand
Tour was the manifest decay of Italian city states and the resulting
absurdity of their boasted laws and traditions. Public buildings which
bore inscriptions or emblems advertising such claims were much derided
by progressive eighteenth-century travellers, who were aware of the
mixture of oligarchy and tyranny which characterized some of these
states. Genoa seemed a particularly offensive case, Lucca and Venice
scarcely less so. The Revolutionary republics of the late eighteenth
century were not necessarily more impressive in this respect. The wilting
poplar trees of Paris made it easy to mock the superficial liberty conferred
by the Revolution. And the symbolism of Washington's neoclassical
architecture often left early visitors unimpressed.

Part of the assumption was that the English were not supposed to have
time for symbolizing, apostrophizing, and idolizing liberty. Rather it was
a personal possession, something somehow private. They did not think
in terms of the liberty of the public but in terms of the liberty of every
individual who composed it. This confirmed the impression that there
was something oddly personal and instinctive about the freeborn
Englishman's freedom. Heinrich Heine observed that English liberty had
a strangely domestic quality, unlike French and German concepts. An
Englishman loved freedom as his lawful wife, a Frenchman as a bride
with whom he was infatuated, a German as his old grandmother.[16]

INFORMALITY

As interesting as the growing preoccupation with the patriotic loyalty
and even authority of English traditions, was the emphasis on the loose
texture of life which made liberty something not to be reduced to mere

politics. For travellers especially the most promising laboratory for the testing of English liberty was that which they were able to observe with a minimum of special expertise or previous experience, social life itself.

Among Anglomaniacs it was precisely the freedom of English mores that was so attractive, especially when it took a form that could be imitated elsewhere without formal recourse to government. Dress was the obvious case. The Frenchman of quality dressed always for the public as if he was dressing for the court; the Englishman dressed as informally as he dared. The loose frock coat, adapted to every occasion and permitting freedom of movement whether on foot or on horseback, an English fashion which was to sweep Europe, was seen as an emblem of the British constitution. When it reached France in the 1780s it distressed those who believed that it was the duty of Frenchmen to maintain dignity, if necessary at the expense of comfort.[17] Mercier, in his futuristic fantasy *Memoirs of the Year Two Thousand Five Hundred*, predicted that by then modern loose-fitting dress would have become the norm in Paris.[18] Head-wear was also in question. The freedom to wear one's hat where one wished was considered an English innovation, one of those 'manières grossières' which polite Frenchmen of the old school were shocked to see infiltrating French life.[19]

They were equally dismayed by the informality of an English salutation. A form of acknowledgement, which amounted to little more than a nod of the head or a slight gesture with the hand, struck newly arrived foreigners as distinctive.[20] Body language implying deference was evidently not liked. The deep bows of the Continent were anathema to an English gentleman. It was noted that bowing had been reduced to a minimum earlier in England than elsewhere; shaking hands was for long considered a specifically English form of greeting. The perfunctory character of an introduction or a meeting in London could readily be seen as the expression of a society of equality and mutual self-respect.

As the mark of English politeness, lack of formality was doubly significant. It expressed the modernity of Europe's most forward-looking nation and created a model of 'natural' behaviour that was one of the most cherished ambitions of the eighteenth century. Liberty implied the avoidance of 'artificial' forms and ceremonies. Lack of ceremony was often considered synonymous with Englishness, and before the revolutions and republics of the late eighteenth century, almost uniquely so.[21] As the Swiss Zimmermann, in an influential tract on national pride, put it, the effect 'resulting from the idea of freedom, which is the chief glory of a certain great nation in Europe, is the neglect of ceremony, and the opinion that the dictates of good breeding need not be further followed, than as they are consistent with our own convenience, or our own inclinations'.[22]

Ceremony, as a means by which relationships of power are expressed and reinforced, was frequently analysed in political terms. The tendency was to assume a fairly simple correlation between concentration of power and elaborate protocol on the one hand, and the diffusion of power and free and easy manners on the other. The crippling etiquette of Spanish and German courts, not to say the bizarre rituals encountered in oriental despotisms, could be contrasted with the informality that reigned in English high society, not least at the court of St James's itself.

The British monarchy was considered one of the least hidebound in Europe. Foreigners were impressed by its accessibility and visibility. George II was not thought of as a popular monarch, yet tourists were surprised to see him and his Queen walking among the crowds in the park with only half a dozen yeomen of the guard to attend them.[23] The royal family lived a more public life than it would have elsewhere, frequently emerging, as it seemed, from the protective shell of the court, to appear before and among the people. When Continental monarchs appeared in public they were exhibiting their private life rather than leaving it for a more open one. The great rituals of royal households, which gave subjects the right of viewing their rulers in the bedchamber and the dining hall were still sufficiently common in the late eighteenth century to heighten the contrast. Sophie von la Roche noted that although it was no longer permitted to view the English royal family eating in public, it was quite unremarkable to see them at the theatre.[24] At times English lack of interest in royalty almost reached what would now be thought of as Scandinavian levels. Georg Lichtenberg was astonished at Kew in 1775 when a crowd watching an impromptu boxing bout completely ignored the King and Queen as their phaeton drove past.[25] It was natural for foreigners to conclude that this was the way of the future: the British offered a model of semi-republican royalty suitable to the needs of a liberated society.

It seemed significant that the most popular monarchs, George III and William IV, were those who went out of their way to avoid unnecessary pomp and circumstance, especially when they were not on parade, at Windsor Castle or Buckingham House.[26] For foreigners it was remarkable that a court so domestic could none the less attract such respect and devotion.[27] The impression made by George III and his Queen was particularly lasting and perhaps permanently redefined the role of the monarchy, as British subjects who survived them recollected for the benefit of Victoria's subjects. 'A Drawing room in the last reign seemed an epitome of the country. All was quietly cheerful; and an air of freedom, a something which reminded one of a land of liberty, was blended with the whole arrangement. The King and Queen were as parents surrounded by their children. They kept no state.'[28]

The highest praise that could be bestowed on a royal house of German blood was its naturalization in such matters. Princess Charlotte was mourned on her death in childbirth in 1817 as 'a true genuine Englishwoman; natural, frank, open'.[29] And if lack of ceremony was found in a Continental court it was easy to look for an English presence, as Mirabeau did at Brunswick, when he attributed it to the Duchess of Brunswick, who, he noted, was 'wholly English, as well in her inclinations and her principles as in her manners'.[30]

More generally, wherever informal manners were to be found it seemed plausible to attribute them to English influence. Hanover was an absolute monarchy but such was the infectious nature of English liberty that, as the Duke of Hamilton's travelling tutor John Moore put it, 'the English manners and customs gain ground every day among the inhabitants. The genial influence of freedom has extended from England to this place. Tyranny is not felt, and ease and satisfaction appear in the countenances of the citizens.'[31]

Naturally, not everyone was impressed by English freedom of manners. The Prince de Ligne called it the liberty to piss at dessert.[32] It was not, however, only male refinement that suffered. Lack of ceremony could look very like inhospitality and inattentiveness, as the Saxon Anglophile Heinrich Watzdorf regretfully conceded.[33] It was also easy to argue that sociability more generally was the casualty of the English love of liberty. If the celebrated parties or 'routs' of West End hostesses were the height of fashion, they were marked rather by reckless individualism than true civility. 'The routs', wrote the émigrée comtesse de Boigne, 'increased my admiration for our good and useful police, and invariably put to flight my love of liberty.'[34] It seemed a rout was a kind of scrum in which any chance of refined conversation and delicate gallantry was out of the question. In fact to a French participant the obvious comparison was with the ordinary Englishman's love of physical combat rather than the Frenchman's of polite intercourse. Significantly, when Parisian Anglomaniacs tried to import it in the 1760s, they turned it into a kind of civilized salon or café.[35] The rout was unexportable.

An obvious conclusion was that the English were indeed free but that their freedom was, as history suggested, a remnant of their Gothic barbarity, preserved by the accident of insularity. There was, however, another school of thought, one which looked beneath the surface of English social life and discerned evidence of some organic tendencies which did not fit traditional perceptions at all.

English unceremoniousness was not found everywhere. In the travel accounts of the late eighteenth century and early nineteenth century there was a growing emphasis on the paradoxical mixture of energy and order of English life, especially in London. The metropolis had always startled visitors by its size and vitality. But increasingly this went with a sense of composure, discipline, and order, which it was difficult to define but which made it seem unlike other European cities nominally more controlled and policed.

In retrospect this can look like the deadening effect of urbanization in a recognizably industrial society, the arrival in history of the modern metropolitan crowd, deprived of the public sociability of its pre-modern predecessors.[36] To contemporaries it was a phenomenon. Other Europeans were getting used to the impact of London fashions and London manners, and early signs, for instance, of the urban dress that was later to prevail throughout the western world, notably the dark blue or black coat worn by London's professional, commercial, and even serving classes, were already the subject of comment as representing a novel uniformity. But the colourlessness of an ordinary street scene remained surprising when it was encountered in England. Even the Dandy of the Regency was palely imitative by comparison with the Macaroni of the 1770s. England was the home of self-consciously picturesque scenery, but it seemed to lacked the variety of picturesque human figures.[37]

The monochrome quality of London's human landscape was end-lessly fascinating to foreigners. But was it just colour? The duc de Lévis was startled by English dress. It all seemed to come from the same fabric, to have been cut by the same tailor.[38] Travelling Englishmen were either amused or offended by sumptuary legislation, which still controlled dressing habits in much of Germany and Italy. Yet the force of fashion in a commercial society was engendering a far more regimented people. To the Saxons who accompanied their king on his visit to Britain in 1844, the attention to sartorial appearances seemed strange. 'In a country pos-sessing such great political freedom, there is in these, as well as in many other human things, no freedom at all.'[39] The French historian Michelet, visiting London in 1834, was equally struck by the orderliness of dress and behaviour that it displayed. He likened it to an immense convent.[40] Flora Tristan thought this an apt simile, but broadened the point to the entire range of everyday existence. 'There is no other country in Europe where fashion, and prejudice exert such monstrous tyranny. Life in England is encumbered with a thousand absurd, puerile, excessively tire-some rules, like a monastic order.'[41] The results seemed highly idiosyn-cratic. Rules of visiting, for example, existed all over Europe, but the English practice was extraordinarily elaborate, moving Southey to admit that 'The system of visiting in high life is brought to perfection in this country.'[42] The English were quick to deride the fearful formality of Court life in European capitals, yet foreigners found West End life almost as rule-bound. Friedrich von Gentz, who certainly knew his diplomatic protocol, was impressed by the practice of visiting in London as a kind of State affair.[43] It did not go unnoticed that the language of visiting made it seem a duty rather than a pleasure. In what other language could one 'pay' a visit, as if in discharge of a debt?[44]

The truth seemed to be, as Johanna Schopenhauer pointed out, that the English were not given to informality at all. They seemed to her an etiquette-ridden nation. In private and in public they sought routine and ritual. All the way from family life to the supreme social challenge of the spa, she remarked, they felt and were from birth taught to feel, deeply uncomfortable without this sense of regimen and predictability.[45] Few foreigners came to close quarters with a family, but many confirmed her view of the spa, as displaying the surprising degree of social restraint which freedom-loving Englishmen imposed on themselves.

Bath, the quintessential expression of English social life, was highly regulated. It was ruled with a rod of iron by a Master of Ceremonies whose powers would never have been tolerated in a king or a minister. What was English about it was not its unconstrainedness, but the fact that neither the Court nor government had any authority within it. The Master of Ceremonies was freely elected by those who patronized his assemblies, by a process that was a microcosm of English public life.[46] At any rate the result seemed very strange, strangest of all perhaps to young French noblemen like the marquis de Bombelles. 'The English, so fanatical about liberty, so licentious at the theatre, like sheep obey a pollicon who after misconducting himself elsewhere comes seeking a job which every other man of good society would decline.'[47]

Not only Bath was liable to criticism on such grounds. It was Epsom, in the early days of the English spa, that had a late seventeenth-century official called 'The Governor'.[48] And at fashionable Cheltenham in the early nineteenth century, the Master of Ceremonies received strangers with what was described as the 'most anti-English officiousness and pomposity'.[49] Yet this was a very English kind of order. On the Continent there were less intricate and sometimes more objectionable forms of regulation. At Spa, where swords were not permitted, the military guard of the Prince of Liège kept the peace.[50] Not that an English resort lacked a certain sense of martial authority. As the young La Rochefoucauld noted in 1785 the 'very strict rules of behaviour' seemed to derive from the fact that Masters of Ceremony were often military men who commanded the dance floor in much the same way they commanded the parade ground.[51]

This kind of authority could be exercised by oligarchies as well as elective monarchies. At Almack's famous assembly in London it was entrusted to a group of women whose word was law and described caustically by Marianne Spencer-Stanhope in her novel of the same name. 'Almack's is a system of tyranny,' she wrote, 'which would never be submitted to in any country but one of such complete freedom that people are at liberty to make fools of themselves. No government would ever have had the effrontery to suppose that people would, on their knees, crave permission to pay their money to a junto, self-elected, whose power exists but by courtesy; who make laws, and enforce them too, without any sort of right. A cabal may attempt a monopoly, *that* I can understand;

but that submission to it should be considered as a subject for congratulation, is indeed past my comprehension.'[52]

Ultimately what sustained the power of such coteries were the sanctions that they were in a position to inflict. Social excommunication was a peculiarly English weapon, according to Prosper Mérimée. 'The terrible interdiction of the popes, in the Middle Ages, is scarcely more to be feared than the anathema of the beau monde in England.'[53] This power was personified in a stage character who passed into the language as a byword for pedantry and ruthlessness in the pursuit of etiquette. 'Mrs Grundy' was appropriately not among the dramatis personae of Thomas Morton's play *Speed the Plough* of 1798; she never appeared on stage but was constantly evoked as a guide to correct behaviour by the other characters.

Even home life exhibited signs of this slavishness to custom. The round of country visits made by the diplomat Philipp von Neumann in 1819 provided him with startling evidence of the absence of the informality that he had expected to find. A typical example occurred at Lady Granville's Wherstead in Suffolk, when Lord Charles Fitzroy 'came at 11, but did not put in an appearance, not wishing to change so late. This seemed to me a striking example of the formality of English customs, which do not allow of one appearing after a certain hour in clothes which are appropriate to another period of the day. Everything here has to give way to convention, even the dearest affections and sentiments; but in a country where liberty and licence are so allied it is only by such restrictions that one can prevent them overlapping.'[54]

Neumann was speaking of the highest reaches of society, but others noted the same tendency throughout the social scale. His contemporary Giacomo Beltrami connected it with a certain innate tendency of the English. 'I have had the good fortune of being admitted into society of all, or nearly all classes, and I have remarked that etiquette and precedence are observed in so rigorous a manner, as could only arise from inveterate and habitual aristocracy of feeling and opinion. In the most humble cottages, every one takes the place assigned him by his respective class, and with a suitable deportment . . . an English house, whether of the great or the humble, may be considered as the most venerated sanctuary of aristocracy, and the English as its most pious devotees.'[55] Whether this greatly benefited the better-off was, however, a debatable point. For an American employing English servants the rules seemed principally to work to the advantage of the latter. 'Everything here', wrote the wife of the American ambassador in 1847, 'is as inflexible as the laws of the Medes and Persians, and though I am called "Mistress" even by old Cates with his gray hair and black coat, I cannot make one of them do anything, except *by* the person and *at* the time which English custom prescribes.'[56]

There were diverse ways of regarding the tyranny of custom. In an illuminating aside, Fenimore Cooper remarked that 'The effect of a promiscuous assemblage any where, is to create a standard of deportment; and great liberty permits every one to aim at its attainment.'[57] English liberty might be considered in terms of the rules which English people freely adopted for their own confinement. As Alexander Herzen observed, 'On the Continent people are powerless before authority: they endure their chains, but do not respect them.' In England the chains were self-imposed and consisted of the prejudices of society, not the prerogatives of rulers.[58] This made sense, so far as foreigners were concerned, of the paradoxes which seemed to govern so much of English life. The parallels with law and politics were obvious. If a Berkeley Square rout might be likened to a Wilkite mob, then a Tunbridge Master of Ceremonies might be considered a Chairman of Quarter Sessions. Perhaps the freedom of the press and the tyranny of the press-gang were less irreconcilable than they appeared.

Consideration of the complex social conventions by which the English conducted their daily intercourse made for a more sophisticated analysis of their liberty. In the 1790s Henri Meister suggested that in point of behaviour, the French had long enjoyed far more real liberty than the English. The former behaved as individuals confident of their capacity to master their own fate, whereas the latter operated under a strong sense of personal restraint; though subject only to laws which they had broadly consented to themselves, they remained less individualistic than their neighbours.[59]

French visitors were indeed particularly struck by this phenomenon. In 1817, one suggested a set of castors as an appropriate metaphor for a society in which individuals had an evident will of their own and yet could readily be induced to pull in one direction.[60] Later on, de Tocqueville was also much intrigued by the Englishman's seemingly contradictory love of association and independence. He concluded that it was precisely the extreme individuality of the English character that heightened the sense of getting and wanting to get things that could often be done only by clubbing together.[61] And to this day Gallic interest in this subject continues. A distinguished French historian has recently referred to it in admiring terms. 'What in practice is particularly original about English individualism is that it combines the recognition of an almost unlimited liberty for the individual with the habit of voluntary association, that is the possibility of enjoying all kinds of groups and societies: hence a myriad of small communities where one finds oneself accepted instead of feeling isolated and abandoned.'[62]

The point did not escape the English themselves. Hazlitt, too, argued that it was unsociability that explained association. 'The English join together to get rid of their sharp points and sense of uncomfortable peculiarity. Hence, their clubs, their mobs, their sects, their parties, their spirit of co-operation, and previous understanding in every thing.'[63] The gentleman's club of the early nineteenth century did indeed seem the ultimate expression of what had emerged as the crucial characteristic of the English, their curious ability to imprison themselves within a cumbersome framework of rules and constraints while retaining their apparent freedom of action. A regime of ballots, black balls, committees, annual general meetings, chairmen and agendas, rule books and so on, imparted an air of almost Teutonic gravity to what was intended, after all, to be a centre of recreation. But Alphonse Esquiros urged his readers not to be misled. 'There are other nations quite as sociable as the English, and yet with them aggregation speedily degenerates into serfdom. The Englishman possesses the extreme advantage of remaining himself in the midst of a group of friends or companions, and there is no reason to fear that he will ever sacrifice his liberty for any consideration.' The Club-man was a thoroughgoing example of the power of the voluntary association, 'the great counterpoise of British personality'.[64]

By this time the social genius of the English seemed almost to have obscured their celebrated liberty, especially when their stature as the new leaders of the world was at issue. Even sceptical Britons found it hard to resist the resulting hubris. The journalist Cyrus Redding, no narrow-minded patriot, positively revelled in it. 'The unaccountable, cold, proud, exclusive, money-making, prejudiced, tasteless Englishman, is lost in the magnitude of the effect produced by united action. It is here that he stands with his majestic front, a giant among the inhabitants of the earth, an indomitable creation viewed by his achievements, by his spoken language, by his extent of dominion.'[65]

ORIGINALITY

Individualism was too strong a tradition to be forgotten, however. Emerson caught the essence of this tradition when he described the English as 'a nation of humourists'.[66] The Scottish historian John Millar had used the same phrase half a century earlier.[67] A humourist in this sense is one who carries his particular temper or humour to the point where he becomes a source of merriment to those around him, though not, as modern usage implies, self-consciously so. He does not set out to be funny. Even by Millar's time, however, 'humour' had become ambiguous. An alternative term was originality. The English were a nation of originals. That they gloried in being so was itself revealing. In French 'quel original!' was said with horror rather than admiration.[68]

There were thought to be certain significant features of this form of individualism. First, originality had nothing to do with status, class, or rank, though foreigners often associated it with blue blood. They generally approached Englishness through English literature in the first instance, and the kind of literature that they read, especially the novel, gave disproportionate space to aristocratic life. They were constantly on the watch for living examples of enchanting oddity. English travellers must often have been tempted to live up to these expectations. Madame d'Épinay was delighted to come across a real-life version of a character invented by Samuel Richardson when she was in Geneva in 1767. 'I received a visit yesterday from a gentleman of eighty years of age;' she wrote. 'We are both in love with each other. I call him Roland Meredith, because he resembles him. He is an original, but his originality is very piquant, and always accompanied by an inexhaustible fund of kindness; anyone can see this in his face.'[69]

Sir Roland Meredith was meant to be a Welshman but in their search for suitably quixotic Englishmen, well-read French ladies were unlikely to worry about such distinctions. In any case the kinds of travellers with whom foreigners generally came into contact were of relatively high social standing. Even when they were not it was easy to assume that they were. Indeed, according to Prince Pückler-Muskau in the 1820s, it was precisely because British tourists were generally parvenus pretending to be aristocrats, that many of them gained a reputation for oddity. Their maladroit behaviour was interpreted as charming English eccentricity by people who took them for 'milords' when they were nothing of the kind.[70] This explanation is not altogether convincing. The Earl of Bristol, most celebrated of all eccentric tourists, was nothing if not a nobleman, and Pückler-Muskau himself was not a reliable guide to what might be thought of as good form in any country.[71] On the other hand, the intricacies of English class were certainly beyond most Continental Europeans and there must have been many bourgeois Blunderheads whose gaffes might be seen for what they were in Bath but which might mislead the populace of Spa or Aix-la-Chapelle.

Even without such foolish pretensions the English traveller might appear eccentric, if only by virtue of his disposable wealth. In poorer societies, Switzerland for example, conspicuous expenditure could itself look like ridiculous folly. The impression was doubtless heightened by the British practice of treating a European tour as itself a form of education, whether directed by a travelling tutor or experienced in a military academy. The 'stupid and capricious pranks' that startled the Grand Tourists' hosts might seem a predictable consequence of sending young men abroad after a prolonged period in a boarding school, but to those who witnessed them they suggested undisciplined manners and barbarous singularity.[72] It could not go unremarked that these boys were, or certainly considered themselves, 'gentlemen'. There were, admittedly, colonies of British merchants or tradesmen on the Continent, and English commercial travellers as well. But they were neither numerous nor ostentatious enough to outshine the Grand Tourists. The kind of corrective that a lower class of tourist might have provided to the prevailing impression of English visitors was largely missing until later, with predictable results for the Continental perception.

Within England itself a different perspective was possible. Originality was thought to be as marked among ordinary, lower-class Englishmen as among their betters. As Richard Steele reminded readers of his *Guardian*

in 1713, Shakespeare had been in no doubt that it was a national char-
acteristic. The gravediggers in Hamlet, who were to be considered
Englishmen rather than Danes, were no less originals than was Sir John
Falstaff himself. 'This National Mark is visible amongst us in every Rank
and Degree of Men, from the Persons of the first Quality and Politest
Sense, down to the rudest and most ignorant of the People.'[73]

The English had seemingly long treasured an affectionately self-
mocking image of their own waywardness. The self-characterization of
the sixteenth-century physician Andrew Boorde was often quoted. 'I
have suche matters rolling in my pate, That I wyl speake and do, I canot
tell what.'[74] A readiness to carry such self-will into relations with one's
betters was a prized part of this tradition and generated numerous historical anecdotes of droll, plebeian Englishmen, who confronted their
superiors with their homespun wit. Stories which featured a diver who
wittily contradicted the Duke of Buckingham in front of Charles I at sea,
or a waterman who taunted George II on the bank of the Thames are as
interesting in retrospect for the evident desire to keep them alive as for
their intrinsic humour.[75] And from the standpoint of outsiders, these
images reinforced long-standing assumptions. As Hazlitt sarcastically
remarked, 'An awkward Englishman has an advantage in going abroad.
Instead of having his deficiency more remarked, it is less so; for all Englishmen are thought awkward alike.'[76]

By the eighteenth century much thought was being given to the origins
of English originality, invoking a predictable range of explanations, ethnic
and environmental, natural and artificial, trivial and profound. Foreigners were well placed to offer a fresh if not necessarily unbiased perspective. Perhaps the simplest analysis was that of one who came to England
to rule it, the Hanoverian George II. According to Sarah Churchill, 'he
said he believed the reason the English people were such strange Creatures was, that they had not been whipt, and this was before a whole
Room full of English People. I made no reply, tho' I had a strong Inclination to have said, that I believed his Royal Highness had been often
whipt, or he could not have been so very *polite*.'[77]

Less privileged visitors were rarely so outspoken and many resorted
to explanations which might have commanded English agreement. Predictably, the climate figured much in such speculations. A country in
which it was impossible at breakfast time to forecast the weather for the

rest of the day was not one in which stability and consistency were likely to be much prized. 'Good-day' was a common enough greeting among English-speakers in sunnier climes, North America and New South Wales, for example. But in England 'Good-morning' was as much as could safely be ventured.

This was not meant to be a superficial observation. It was an old axiom that English politics were as variable as English weather.[78] Both were 'freeborn'.[79] It seemed logical enough to extend the point to all kinds of behaviour. Despite the English pride in certain kinds of steadiness of temperament, notably in battle, stability was not thought of as charac-teristic, even by the English themselves. 'We are a *moody* people', wrote an opponent of Junius in 1770. 'This is our character; and it is one so sin-gular, there is not in any other language a word to express it.'[80] The satirist Louis-Antoine de Caraccioli claimed to have heard an innkeeper declaring 'We are as inconstant as the element that surrounds us.'[81] This seemed all the more striking when it was reflected that the ethnic cousins of the English in northern Europe were generally noted for their phlegm and stolidity. The Dutch presented a remarkable contrast with English changeability.[82] In the nineteenth century, the racial implications seemed even more surprising for those who believed that 'enthusiasm and inde-pendence' were to be found above all in the 'true, unadorned England' north of the Trent, where the 'pure Saxons' survived, supposedly un-contaminated by close contact with conquered Celts or conquering Normans.[83]

The commonest explanation of unpredictability was historical but not racial. In Steele's own analysis originality was the natural and necessary outcome of the legal and political rights which Englishmen enjoyed. Elsewhere, singularity had to be repressed for fear of the consequences. In England it was protected by 'the Ease of our government, and the Liberty of professing Opinions and Factions, which perhaps our Neighbours have about them, but are forced to disguise, and thereby may come in time to be extinguished'.[84] Ruthless conformity was incom-patible with the English tradition. A nation that had the power to change its government whenever it liked would naturally assume that it could change everything else.[85] The English reputation for ungovernability persisted into the eighteenth century and coloured Continental assump-tions beyond that. The German Uffenbach was told in 1710 that the reason he could see so few forts in England was the rebellious spirit of a nation which rendered it unwise to afford any rallying places.[86] Insubordination on this scale made quixotic social behaviour all the more understandable.

Many visiting foreigners fully accepted this argument. As the Russian Karamzin put it: 'This unbounded freedom to live as one wishes, to do whatever one desires on every occasion, provided it is not contrary to the welfare of others, has produced in England a great number of peculiar characters and a rich harvest for the writers of novels. Other European countries are like well-laid-out gardens where the trees are all of the same size, the paths straight, and everything uniform. The English, on the other hand, grow up, morally, like wild oaks, according to the will of fate. Though they are of one stock, they are all different. Fielding did not have to invent characters for his novels. He had only to observe and describe.'

Karamzin linked with English liberty another English characteristic commonly associated with originality. 'Is it not spleen that also produces the numerous English eccentricities, which in some other place would be called madness, but here are called only capriciousness or whim? A man who has lost the taste for the true pleasures of life invents false ones and, when he cannot charm people by a display of his happiness, he tries to astonish them with something out of the ordinary. I could copy from English newspapers and magazines scores of strange anecdotes—how, for example, one rich man built himself a house on a high mountain in Scotland and lives there with his dog; how another, by his own admission hating the earth, made his home on water; how a third, having an antipathy for light, leaves his house only at night and sleeps during the day or sits in a dark room by candlelight; how a fourth, denying himself everything except the bare necessities of life, every spring gives his neighbours a sumptuous feast which costs him almost his entire year's income. The British take pride in the fact that they can make fools of themselves to their heart's content without accounting to anyone for their caprices.'[87]

One advantage of this kind of analysis was that it brought into focus a subject of much puzzlement to foreigners, the Englishman's sense of humour. The fact that the term itself was changing in meaning did not help matters. By the beginning of the eighteenth century 'humorous' was already sufficiently synonymous with 'comical' to provoke Congreve to protest.[88] Charting the progression from the black comedy of the seventeenth century to the benevolent whimsy of the eighteenth made a certain kind of literary sense. Uncle Toby was no Volpone.[89] It also had interesting implications for originality, opening the way to a less antisocial, more good-natured concept of eccentricity. But it did not lessen the perceived uniqueness of the English spirit. In fact the notion of the English humorist as a comic character was peculiarly inaccessible to foreigners, who confronted it most commonly on the English stage. It was not mere burlesque, the stylized clowning of the pantomime tradition, popular though that might be in England as elsewhere. On the other hand, it was certainly unsubtle. Moreover, the English showed their appreciation of comedy in curious fashion. Seated in the theatre-pit or standing before a printshop window they would appear engrossed without any evident signs of amusement, until, as if from nowhere, sudden gusts and guffaws of laughter were heard. There seemed to be nothing between a dourly serious appreciation and tasteless hilarity. Who else could have invented the 'horse-laugh'? [90]

It was generally agreed that 'humour' had no equivalent in other languages. 'Bon mot', 'plaisanterie singulière', and 'einfall' were unsatisfactory; all savoured of conversational wit, not characteristic humour.[91] Wit was not English for it shunned the sarcasm and buffoonery that, in Pichot's words, stood 'in lieu of wit among a nation whose manners are devoid of elegance'.[92] Moreover, this substitution of 'irony and slang for gay wit and happy humour' was not to be found among the Scots or the Irish. Humour in the sense an Englishman understood it was unique.[93] Georg Lichtenberg, one of the most sensitive observers of Englishness during the early years of George III's reign, came closer to understanding it than most, but eventually abandoned the attempt to express it in German. It was untranslatable and inimitable.[94]

CHARACTER

The 'humours' tradition, and the national reputation for originality that went with it, seemed such natural parts of English life as to need no apology. Yet they were far from unproblematic in terms of the perceived priorities of the eighteenth century. For one thing, it was precisely this tendency to peculiarity of behaviour that made it so difficult to characterize the English as a nation at a time when doing so possessed a certain patriotic priority. Others, the Danes, for example, were celebrated for their uniformity and 'evenness of character'.[95] Frenchness was thought to be so unifying a force that it quickly turned foreign settlers in France into Frenchmen. Even countries marked by strong regional characteristics, Germany, Italy, and indeed France itself, were thought none the less to possess a high degree of common identity, ultimately based on submission to widely accepted values and norms of behaviour. And the supreme paradox was that the young United States, which combined ethnic diversity with a large cultural debt to England, in some ways appeared the most uniform of all. The fervently patriotic American Fenimore Cooper and the highly critical Englishman Charles Dickens agreed on that.[96]

Anything like a national character required at least some degree of conformity and it was conformity that seemed so alien to the English spirit. As Joseph Priestley put it, 'The English, they say, have least of an uniform national character, on account of their liberty and independence, which enables every man to follow his own humour.'[97] The point had been made much of by Hume,[98] and was repeated by those who read him, sometimes with interesting variations. Kant, for example, linked originality with xenophobia, and believed that it actually concealed a common characteristic, that of 'arrogant rudeness' to others. The Englishman's 'affectation of a character is precisely the common character of the people to which he himself belongs, and this character is contempt for all foreigners, primarily because the English think that they alone can boast a respectable constitution that combines domestic civil liberty with might in external affairs. . . . The Englishman behaves insolently toward everyone else because he thinks that he is self-sufficient, that he does not need anyone else and so can dispense with being pleasant to other people.'[99] Originality was merely a by-product. The Englishman, 'easily becomes an eccentric not out of vanity but because he concerns himself little about others, and does not easily do violence to his taste out of complaisance or imitation'.[100]

Kant was offering one way of solving the problem of English

individuality, but at a cost too high for English self-regard. In any case the difficulty of sustaining a concept of national character while rejecting the desirability of conformity was not the only problem presented by originality. Independent thinking and wilful conduct could hardly be considered compatible with the superior social manners on which Augustan Britons wished to congratulate themselves. The Anglophile Archenholz remarked that 'no polished nation was ever so free as the English are at this day', an assertion that begged the uncomfortable question: how polished were the English? Pointing out, as he did, that the mentally unstable Christian VII of Denmark had preferred London to Paris on this account, was not altogether reassuring.[101]

Courtesy literature condemned singularity, on diverse grounds. One was that it violated good taste, of which politeness was itself a form. Singularity, like all bad taste, was ridiculous. But the objection was not merely aesthetic. Indulgence of individual idiosyncrasy was by definition antisocial. The function of civility was to eliminate potentially irritating oddities of behaviour in the interest of communal life. This heightened the sense of uncertainty that attended much discussion of English improvements in manners. On the one hand, the champions of politeness were disposed to argue that the Englishman's originality was a remnant of a more barbarous age, one which must be extinguished in the name of progress. On the other hand, opponents, especially those who had foreign models in mind, doubted whether politeness had anything to be said for it if it ran counter to the prevailing temperament of the nation. The interminable debate about upper-class manners, especially Francophile manners, took on additional sensitivity in this respect. Cosmopolitan politeness would be especially threatening if it tended to transform the gentry into carbon copies of *petit maîtres*, alienating them from their own countrymen.[102]

Could modern civility be rendered compatible with ancient originality? Many doubted it. The fact that this worked in both directions reinforced the point. Excessively polite Grand Tourists lost the individuality that was essential to an Englishman in his own country. Equally, French Anglomaniacs merely irritated their countrymen with their imported manners. Reviewing the attempts of fashionable Parisian 'jockeys' to imitate English originality, Mercier concluded that they stood no chance of altering French attitudes. Even if they incidentally promoted some desirable habits, they would be derided for their folly and stupidity by conventional society.[103]

In England itself the contrast between provincial and metropolitan manners prompted similar reflections. For foreigners London might be all too original, but from an English perspective it was losing its originality. Some were pleased. The artist Benjamin Haydon was struck on a visit to Devon by the difference between the kind of conversation he found there and the kind which prevailed in London. In Devon the talk was of local people, with the emphasis on their foibles and eccentricities. Good humour abounded but there was also a kind of barbarity, a certain brutality and ignorance, which permitted much unthinking cruelty.[104] Others were less sure that London's way represented progress. The elder D'Israeli considered that metropolitan modishness merely installed monotony in place of individuality and dissipation in place of energy. 'When the national character retained more originality and individuality than our monotonous habits now admit, our later ancestors displayed a love of application, which was a source of happiness, quite lost to us. Living more within themselves, more separate, they were therefore more original in their prejudices, their principles, and in the constitution of their minds.'[105]

Such was eighteenth-century interest in all things British that English originality was truly a subject for general concern, not something that could be left to the introspection of an insular people. Foreign admirers might be charmed by its whimsicality but none the less found its antisocial potential disturbing. They devised various means of softening its force. For instance, French Anglomaniacs, in their writings, gradually transformed the conventional portrait of their English heroes and heroines, rendering them increasingly anodyne and amenable. In effect they stripped the English of their *singularité* and replaced it with *sensibilité*.[106]

Gentle correction was also supplied by German Anglophiles. A minor literary genre grew up, based on stories of eccentric Englishmen taught by more socially self-conscious foreigners to curb their individuality. Typical of the resulting 'anecdotes' was one concerning the English tourist whose delight in hunting was foiled by ill health and bad weather when he took rooms in a German country house. With characteristic single-mindedness he turned his apartment into a veritable forest, complete with flora and fauna. His fantasy hunting was unfortunately so boisterous and noisy that it seriously inconvenienced a German scholar who lodged above him. When he remonstrated, the Englishman merely retorted that he could do whatever he liked in his own home, however temporary, and if he chose to hunt, anyone who objected might find himself being hunted. The sequel pitted the German's sense of responsibility against the Englishman's self-will. One morning the latter was astonished to find water pouring through his ceiling into his chamber. Rushing upstairs to confront his fellow lodger, he threw open the door to find him seated with a fishing rod, surrounded by water. 'If you can hunt,' cried the scholar, 'I can fish, and anyone who objects may find himself on the end of my hook.' The Englishman's anger turned to amusement, they shook hands, and became fast friends. An original Englishman had been taught the virtues of social collaboration.[107]

Continental observers were endlessly fascinated by the English preoccupation with originality of character. Serious consideration of the virtues and vices of English theatre, a subject brought to the fore by Voltaire's notorious condemnation of Shakespeare, and kept there by successive generations of German enthusiasts for the Bard, dwelled much on the merits or otherwise of characterization. At least until Stendhal the most favourably inclined of French commentators on English drama admitted that in its attachment to the development of character, especially character detached from the moral framework of classical drama, it had gone too far.[108] German Anglomaniacs rarely had such reservations, but whatever the conclusion, there was agreement that character was crucial.

It was a simple matter to link this with English prowess in other spheres, for example prose fiction, satirical caricature, and the art of portraiture, all supposedly revealing English fascination with individual identity. And when foreigners plunged into the more commonplace literature of the English, as distinct from the works which found their way readily into foreign languages, they were even more impressed by the obsession. Biography seemed to be *the* English form, as prominent in the trivia of newspaper reporting as in the systematic 'lives' which formed so large a proportion of published works. Nowhere else did it command such a readership.[109] It did not go without notice that the Victorian cult of the great man gave additional impetus to this tendency, not least because it could be made to reflect national character, or even influence it. Of the Duke of Wellington, it was asserted, 'he, more than any man who ever lived, has contributed to stamp a character upon our nation'.[110]

Observers believed that these literary evidences were part of a deeply entrenched cultural tradition. English education appeared revealing in this respect. It was thought that English educators were obsessed with the development of character rather than the inculcation of knowledge or the development of vocational skills. Young Frenchmen were taught the skills of polite life: dancing, horsemanship, fencing, conversation. Young Germans were instructed in the learning essential to intellectual and spiritual life. Young Englishmen were hardly taught at all. They were reared in self-reliance and self-expression. Character in the sense both of moral worth and of individual self-reliance was the essence of English schooling, especially public schooling, on which growing attention was focused by the early years of the nineteenth century.

None of this entailed uncritical admiration of the English system even among the English. On the contrary, it gave rise to much criticism. But even denigrators saw its central advantage, among them the Duke of Wellington himself. 'Speaking of men's education, he observed that they learnt nothing at a public school and less at college, but that English public schools were chiefly valuable as forming the habits and feelings of a *gentleman* and giving a knowledge of the world, and an independence and *originality* of character rare to be met with abroad. "You will find every Frenchman cast in the same mould, but every Englishman has a distinct character." '[111] Significantly, one of the worries about the mounting interest in the needs of the young displayed by public school reformers during Wellington's lifetime was that in the process they might obliterate this quality. The German tourist C. A. G. Goede, who came to England during the Napoleonic Wars, thought he saw signs of this happening, as did Charles X's minister the baron d'Haussez.[112]

Any suggestion of State intervention certainly aroused this concern among the English themselves. Even the modest educational grants of the mid-nineteenth century, exiguous though they were, promoted fears of a professional, clerical influence, 'increasing the servility of the National mind and destroying its healthy spontaneity'.[113] The ultimate object of schooling was after all precisely to entrench that independence of spirit which every parent sought to inculcate from birth. 'The first lesson he has received from his father, and the first lesson which he transmits to his son, is that independence is the inheritance of an Englishman. He is proud of being *himself*; of thinking, feeling, and acting *for* himself. Hence that variety of character which is in England, and which is not to be found in any other country in the world.'[114]

Linguistic evidence of the extent of English individualism was much collected and analysed by outsiders. Why did the English, uniquely, resort to a capital for the personal pronoun 'I'? This question intrigued many Britons, too. Southey remarked that it said much about the way the English regarded themselves. 'An Englishman does think himself some-body, and has good reason to think himself so:—our great *I* is in charac-ter.'[115] In protest the Scottish antiquary John Pinkerton compelled his printer to use lower case throughout his published work.[116] Compound words with 'self' seemed either to be much commoner in English or at any rate to signify something beyond the reflexive function of their equivalents in other languages. To the Florentine Luigi Angiolini the word 'selfish' had a revealing significance. It had no equivalent in Italian and signified a degree of egotism unparalleled elsewhere.[117] Isabelle de Charrière was similarly intrigued by it.[118]

The word 'egotism', however obvious its derivation, was coined by an Englishman, Addison, though he sought to blame it on the French fathers of Port-Royal and observed that 'the most eminent Egotist that ever appeared in the World' was another Frenchman, Montaigne.[119] In fact it is generally Stendhal who is credited with successfully carrying it into the French language. He did not consider it the only example of an idiosyncratic English preoccupation with self. Indeed Stendhal employed a private language of his own for use on his manuscripts, in which English featured heavily. 'Mr Myself et la self-importance' had a particular fascination for him.[120]

It would have been easy to deride and denounce the unique egotism of the English, and certainly many of their neighbours indulged the temp-tation. But thoughtful observers were generally more cautious. Even the arrogance that Kant thought he discerned often aroused admiration, not least for the self-confidence and self-assurance with which it imbued the English character. Goethe called it 'eigenwüchsigkeit' and envied it in the literary travellers he encountered at Weimar.[121] Underlying such reluctance to condemn there seem to have been two distinct beliefs. One was the reflection that, after all, it would have been absurd to suppose that the English as a nation had been provided with a larger share of original, selfish sin than other nations, however superficially impressive the evidence to the contrary. The other was the charitable but telling observation that English awareness of self seemed to consist of a want of consciousness of others rather than an active malice towards them.[122]

Moreover, megalomania did not seem to be an English disease. A preoccupation with character was not necessarily as egotistic as it might sometimes seem. Shaftesbury, who was as much read on the Continent as he was in England, had offered an analysis of genius as a divine spark which placed its holder second only to God. But the concept had less appeal in England than in Germany, where Herder took it up,[123] and whence in due course it was to return via Carlyle. Genius had a worryingly un-English association with purely intellectual capacity or alternatively with superhuman qualities. About the English character there was nothing superhuman, and not much that was coldly intellectual. It was precisely the essence of English character that all should possess it or at least aspire to it.

English character had evidently moved a long way from its Continental counterparts. As Mrs Piozzi, herself the author of a much read biography of Dr Johnson, noted, the very term 'a character' was an English expression.[124] At least by the 1740s, perhaps earlier, the common English usage was close to the modern concept of 'personality', if not in its awareness of complex psychological forces, at least in its sense of wholeness, of an organic being uniquely defined by certain qualities of mind. That definitive corpus of Enlightened thinking, the *Encyclopédie*, discussed character extensively and in numerous contexts, without ever embracing this concept, even when, for instance in the abbé Mallet's consideration of literary character, it might have seemed difficult to avoid. Significantly, Mallet not only ignored Fielding and the English novel, but all prose fiction, preferring to concentrate on heroic drama.

Character, in the prevailing contemporary sense on the Continent,

meant typically human predispositions or tendencies. Their interest
did not derive from the resulting individuality of their possessors, but
from their interaction with the forces of good and evil.[125] This was the
traditional meaning of the term, one which remained recognizable in
England itself.[126] But as was often noted by cosmopolitan Englishmen,
the idea of 'caractère' as a kind of heroic superiority could not be simply
translated into English.[127] Epic heroes were meant to represent their
entire society. In England heroes were celebrated as winners, and villains
as losers, not representatives of the virtue or vice present in all.[128] Prince
Albert's mentor Stockmar thought this explained the Englishman's
apparent devotion to slander and libel. 'One of the things which
the English best understand is the art of calumniating. For inasmuch
as a "character" is in England considered as something positive and
tangible, every effort is made to destroy it.'[129] Less weighty matters could
also be affected. Continental observers were amused that the English
treated masquerades as an opportunity to multiply fancy dress characters of their own invention rather than parade the stock figures author-
ized by tradition.[130]

There were some meeting points between English and Continental
practice, though these gave rise to much confusion. Character in one
sense signified primarily the identity which an individual was granted by
his community, in short his public standing. In 1789 Henri Decremps,
seeking to guide tourists through the perils of mutual misunderstanding
had to explain that the English 'character' was best translated by the
French 'réputation'.[131] By this time this represented an obsolescent
version of character in England. It applied only in certain very specific
contexts. Servants were still being given 'characters' at the end of the
eighteenth century, though the terminology was dying out. Diplomatic
language, still dominated by French usage, continued to treat the formal
standing of diplomats as 'character', something granted by a head of state
to the representative of another state. This was perhaps the most extreme
example of a quality which had nothing to do with the individuality of
the character in question, being bestowed by convention.

The notion of character as something granted by others had, of course,
an English provenance, however outmoded by the end of the eighteenth
century. The common law drew heavily on it. But there were significant

changes taking place which showed how much pressure was being placed on the old assumptions. Anciently juries had been as much concerned with the previous record of the accused as with his guilt. Hence the overwhelming importance of testimony on the point of character. Such evidence continued to count, but increasingly in mitigation of the sentence rather than in determination of guilt.[132] The laws of evidence emphasized the probability of criminal responsibility on the basis of the circumstances of the crime rather than the known character of the accused, to the point where evidence one way or the other of his previous character could be considered positively an impediment to the discovery of truth.

A dynamic, less fixed concept of character focused attention on the more self-defining and self-projecting aspects of individual behaviour. Not everyone was enthusiastic about pursuing this course to its logical conclusion. The conservative argument, forcibly expressed by Leibniz, was that character was fixed by God or nature, and that the seemingly unpredictable contingencies in which it expressed itself were equally predetermined. Fielding, who did as much as any Englishman to bring to the attention of foreigners the peculiar nature of the English idea of character, seems to have been reluctant to abandon this kind of divine determinism.

There were alternative views, making character amenable to direction from within and pressure from without. Flexibility and variety were both essential to the emerging notion of character. Many of the generation that succeeded Fielding's grew up doubting the presence of original sin in any but a metaphorical sense, and convinced that innate ideas did not exist. The result was a stronger sense of the complexity of human psychology and a clearer notion of the richness of human experience. Personality became less, not more explicable, and much harder to judge definitively, more prone to delicate and uncertain distinctions. Increasingly it was individual choice that counted in place of divine agency or inherited types and humours.

Character in this sense could itself be a synonym for virtue, not in the sense that it was a moral implant but in the sense that an individual who chose the path of virtue could be said to possess it. What it did not permit was the possibility of character as dependent on the perceptions of others. It was still possible to have a good or bad reputation, a good or bad name, a good or bad record. But none of these things was synonymous with character. Character was increasingly the possession of the individual. Early in Boswell's *London Journal* there is a passage in which the author assesses the impact of London life on his own behaviour, concludes that it is hastening his progress in gentility, and revealingly adds 'I have discovered that we may be in some degree whatever character we choose.'[133] This sense of empowerment over one's own personality was a feature of the prevailing mentality of the 1760s. But it did not stop there. Before very long all kinds of curious evidence was to be consulted as to the nature of that character, from quirks of handwriting to bumps on the cranium. Anything, it seemed, was to be trusted in preference to the collective 'presumption' or 'prejudice' of other people.

In time, Continental fashion caught up on the English concept of character. But the gap was big enough to sustain a strong sense of diversion from the European norm and one which heightened the tension implicit in English originality. What was required was a kind of character that could accommodate the needs of politeness and sensibility, without detaching Englishmen from their patriotic moorings of liberty of thought and action. A potentially anarchic tendency had to be subordinated to the demands of a disciplined national character, without sacrificing that 'energetic individualism' which, according to the apostle of Self-Help, Samuel Smiles, 'has in all times been a marked feature in the English character, and furnishes the true measure of our power as a nation'.[134]

How could this be done? In a word, by turning the original into an eccentric. The change of terminology is significant. Originality in the ancient sense did not signify departure from a norm, rather it treated norms as irrelevant or at least secondary. But eccentricity was by definition an exception to the norm, an abnormality. The original was an individual who knew not how to make the transition from private to public. In society, in his family, in his study he behaved the same. His individualism was potentially disruptive in a world of change and improvement where the fixed institutions to which he might at least pay some obedience were being replaced by various kinds of public allegiance. But retrained as an eccentric he was more serviceable, providing an engaging diversity without threatening conformity.

ECCENTRICS

Eccentricity is considered a familiar feature of the English character as perceived both by foreigners and by the English themselves. In fact the term is no older than the 1770s, and did not come into vogue until the 1790s. Originality in its old sense gradually withered at this time, leaving the way clear for its use in the modern sense, as representing novelty or inventiveness. Synonyms for eccentricity there were, none very complimentary, though none as potentially disturbing as originality. The changes were rung on whim, caprice, singularity, folly. Eccentricity was the mildest and most anodyne of these. It was also the only one that necessarily implied some recognizably desirable norm, some 'centricity' from which the eccentric had deviated.

The literature which introduced the eccentric or rather displayed the original in his new role as eccentric was of very different kinds. There were eccentric magazines, eccentric biographies, eccentric caricatures. And in the plays, novels, and memoirs of the period eccentrics of various sorts, fictitious and actual, proliferated. The result was permanently to affect the language and the imagery of Englishness. In fact nearly two hundred years later both the word and the concept remain very much what they then became.

The point needs emphasizing because it is possible to envisage alternative lines of development. There were usages which would have given eccentricity a meaning quite different from that which it has acquired. For instance, some of the hack biographers who cashed in on the cult threatened to make the word a synonym for any form of celebrity or notoriety. Mere historical fame qualified some eccentrics, and incidentally introduced foreigners, who were problematic in a number of ways for the English concept of eccentricity. In any event, Alexander the Great and Oliver Cromwell, whatever their personal oddities, did not readily fit in a gallery of eccentrics. The power to inflict real harm, let alone the inclination to do so, are alien to eccentricity, the essence of which is a degree of amiability. An eccentric cannot be sinister or malign. In fact, even in the most trivial matters, eccentricity seems to have a connotation of virtuous rather than vicious absurdity. One of the most famous of all English eccentrics, the second Lord Rokeby, gained his place by an obsessive attachment to constant bathing, turning the axiom that cleanliness is next to Godliness into a pathological obsession.

Another usage deserves more attention, if only because it was adopted by Fanny Burney, whose delineation of the values of her day was so carefully considered. In *Camilla*, published in 1796, she painted portraits of some much loved fictitious characters. She also sketched that of the young Mrs Berlinton, a woman who had been brought up in a household of exceptional neglect and extreme sensibility. As a result she had mistaken enthusiasm for religion, sentiment for feeling, romance for reality. 'Brought up thus, to think all things the most unusual and extraordinary, were merely common and of course; she was romantic without consciousness, and excentric without intention.'[135] The clear implication was that an eccentric could be so by intention, and in fact two of Fanny Burney's most celebrated characters, the highly unconventional Mrs Arlbery, who delighted in flouting social etiquette, and the grotesquely foppish Sir Sedley Clarendel, were certainly eccentrics by intention. Burney's aim was to contrast what she called traits of character with 'traits of excentricity', in order to display the moral superiority of the former. If she had had her way the harmless eccentric would not have materialized. He would merely have been a self-conscious exhibitionist, and it is essential to eccentricity that self-conscious exhibitionism should not be at the bottom of it. The eccentric must appear to others unconscious of his own absurdity or wrong-headedness, a victim of delusion or obsession, not a perpetrator of a confidence trick. The latter could certainly not have been incorporated in the avowedly patriotic concept of national character. In the history of English characterizations, exhibitionism is often pictured as an alien characteristic, especially a Latin one. The extent to which outsiders agreed is striking, though some were more sceptical. Amédée de Pichot dismissed 'the whimsical humours' of the English as 'for the most part merely a trick to engage public attention. The man who pretends to brave public opinion is often a slave to it.'[136] But by and large foreigners preferred to assume that the eccentric was guileless.

Eccentricity, then, had to be intrinsic, rooted in a fundamental misapprehension of the real world. It was not insanity, though defining the line which divided eccentricity and mental instability would have been difficult. One way of drawing it was to note that the eccentric was only permitted to give expression to his eccentricity within a certain range. As Fanny Kemble put it, 'It is curious how much minor eccentricity the stringent general spirit of formal conformity allows individuals in England.'[137] The eccentric was allowed to be obsessive about one thing, his hobby horse, his bee in his bonnet, or about trivial things. The tension between gentlemanliness and originality is particularly telling in this respect. English gentility, as it settled into its nineteenth-century pattern brought together two traditions, both of which spurned obsessiveness of any kind. One derived from classical ethics and Renaissance courtesy; it emphasized the virtues of general knowledge rather than minute learning, social skills rather than technical instruction, amateur accomplishment rather than professional proficiency. The other combined the life of the Tudor Books of Policy with the new political circumstance of the post-1688 world, and portrayed gentlemen as a leadership class, administering, judging, governing, legislating. A social system which made the acquisition or retention of gentility of overwhelming importance, naturally placed a strain on the single-minded pursuit of special expertise, learned or not. But eccentricity permitted a certain divergence from the norm, a kind of safety valve for pursuits that might be plausibly tolerated. This is not to claim that all eccentricities were in fact useful or indeed genteel. Some were both useless and vulgar, such as, for example, the taste for carriage-driving and pugilism in which some late eighteenth-century gentlemen revelled. But it was precisely the function of genteel eccentricity to permit any kind of individuality that could be classified as harmless. This may have lent a rather amateur air to many preoccupations; yet it also gave them space to thrive.

More appealing still was the kind of oddity which resulted when certain well-known features of Englishness were pushed to extremes. The artist Joseph Farington was something of a collector of such specimens. One was the chronic shyness of Sir Henry Harpur Crewe of Calke in Derbyshire. Crewe was so fearful of his servants that he communicated his instructions to them by letter. He kept a pack of hounds yet declined to hunt, and relied on his huntsman's reports for vicarious sportsmanship. His eccentricity seemed all the more amusing and lovable because it was in fact an extreme form of a trait generally considered eminently defensible in the Englishman, his innate reserve. A closely related case was that of taciturnity. The supreme example at the end of the eighteenth century was said to be Lord Moira, who was admitted 'to have great pleasure in being surrounded by Society, but it is remarkable that though he is a ready and in some degree an eloquent speaker in public, his taciturnity when at his own table is such that unless it is to ask a person to drink a glass of wine, He seldom speaks, and will sit for Hours silent, but His manners are courteous in the highest degree.'[138] Again, though taciturnity of this order was exceptional, it was merely an extension of a well-known English characteristic. A no less revealing example was misogynism. Considering the pains taken to bring English males up with extreme caution where women were concerned, it is unsurprising that some of them abandoned all attempts to deal with the female sex. A celebrated aristocratic scientist, Henry Cavendish, was one such. The elaborate architectural alterations made in his household, including the erection of a second staircase in his Clapham villa, to prevent him coming face to face with a female member of his staff, were thought peculiar but not altogether incomprehensible.[139]

Few people would have defended any of these qualities as such: unsociability in the face of both male and female company conflicted with every dictate of civility. But this unsociability was considered by foreigners notably English and admitted by the English themselves as such, especially contrasted, for example, with the impertinently sociable, incessantly talkative, alarmingly libidinous Frenchman. Crewe, Moira, and Cavendish served as warnings, perhaps, but the kind that helped reinforce national stereotypes, enjoyed an only half-condemned notoriety, and ultimately served to sustain certain values. The eccentric was an original whose faults were on the right side.

These three were all aristocrats, but similar characteristics were noted in much the same way for all classes. There were also others which reveal an ambivalence about contemporary values. One of the commonest eccentrics to figure in early nineteenth-century literature was the miser, genteel or not. No doubt his popularity was owing partly to the quantity of anecdotes that it could generate, as individual examples of bizarre meanness accumulated. The most famous was John Elwes, landowner and MP, who ended by living in a garret and letting his handsome town house for profit. Elwes was the subject of a full biography by the newspaper publisher and man about town Major Topham. However, he was only the most prominent of a considerable corps of misers. At the other extreme, spendthrifts were rarely treated as eccentrics. The exceptions were those whose misspending seemed not only absurd but ultimately harmless. One such was John Mytton, who gambled away an immense inheritance in eighteen years. Yet it was difficult to condemn him; much of his money was spent on his friends or in extraordinary hunting exploits, one of which featured his naked pursuit of a duck. Most spend-thrifts wasted their substance on vices that ruined others as well as them-selves. Miserliness was less objectionable. It was the exaggeration of a much trumpeted virtue, good husbandry. Moreover, it could amount to philanthropy. Thomas Cooke, the pinchpenny sugar baker of Pen-tonville, would pretend to have epileptic fits to attract the compassionate alms of passers-by. Yet the fortune of over £120,000 that he accumulated was largely left to charity.[140]

The most common form of eccentricity of all was one that could be seen as another exaggeration of Englishness, its innate conservatism. This was a kind of misplaced conformity, which it was certainly possible to admire. It was not a new phenomenon. Satirizing conservatism in the cause of modernity has always been difficult in England, as Addison and Steele found when they created a character, in Sir Roger de Coverley, more appealing than his supposed superior, Sir Andrew Freeport. But a century later John Bullism positively gloried in it. Perhaps the common-est kind of eccentric was he, or for that matter, she, who preserved the dress of his or her youth. This was conformity, though the mistaken con-formity of adherence to canons no longer approved. So gentlemen who preserved a portion of the manners of an older age were always allowed some latitude, particularly when confined to a country setting where their habits were unlikely to annoy polite people. The 'last of the old-English gentlemen' was a type much resorted to.

In short the eccentric was not a threat. The French historian Émile Boutmy was fascinated to observe that England could 'number so many original characters, and not one revolutionary spirit'.[141] An eccentric was not and could not be a revolutionary, for a revolutionary is one who by definition is hostile to eccentricity. He is the advocate of a code, not the bearer of a character. This is not to say that political diversity was frowned upon. Political views themselves might be strange provided they were, like Crewe's bashfulness, or Moira's taciturnity, or Cavendish's misogynism, offset by strict conformity in other respects. Generations of so-called radicals were treated with latitude because they were social conformists. The celebrated Major Cartwright, for all his democratic enthusiasms, endeared himself to many by his genteel manners.[142] John Wilkes did so too, as did John Horne Tooke.[143] The kind of man who would make an engaging dinner companion could not be really menacing, however distressing the political sentiments he espoused.

Political eccentricity was indeed much more within the English tradition than some other kinds. Religious enthusiasm was certainly not. For one thing, the religious enthusiast, at any rate in his English Evangelical form, was by definition a menace to the peace of mind of others. As Richard Graves demonstrated in his novel *The Spiritual Quixote*, whimsicality might take such a form temporarily, but eventually the contradiction would become manifest. A true Methodist would have to abandon his whimsicality. A true whimsical would have to abandon his Methodism. In Graves's very English case, the whimsy won through. Significantly, most clerical eccentrics were Anglicans of latitudinarian views whose oddity lay in enthusiasms that often seemed incompatible with spiritual earnestness: hunting parsons were favourites, as were drinking parsons and racing parsons. There remained room for the uniquely quixotic, such as the parish priest who achieved notoriety through his mania for collecting objects that would have been useful only in small numbers. At his death he reportedly owned thirty wheelbarrows, 300 pickaxes, 100 pairs of breeches. This delight in possession extended even to his servants, whom he locked up every night for fear they might disappear. He perished late one evening when exercising his dog. It inadvertently dragged him into his duck pond. The servants heard his dying cries for help but were unable to assist.[144]

Another excluded category was that of sexual eccentricity. There was no room for heterosexual libertines, let alone any other kind. Foreigners found the English attitude to sex puzzling and hypocritical. Sexual excess and abnormality seemed endlessly fascinating but not admissible as cause for innocent mirth. This was one reason why Byron could not possibly be an eccentric. He was too dangerous. It is admittedly true that

some men of dubious moral standards were considered notable
eccentrics. The third Earl of Egremont, Turner's patron, and Sir John
St. Aubyn, the formidable stage Cornishman of the Regency period, both
kept mistresses and fathered bastards. In each case, however, this was
incidental to their eccentricity of manner, not part of it. Moreover, each
was in a curious way rather conventional, living in a state of marked
domesticity with his partner, and in St. Aubyn's case eventually marrying her. Numerous celibate bachelors and spinsters have been ranked as
eccentrics, perhaps, as Edith Sitwell was to argue, because sexual promis-
cuity was in effect by definition, non-eccentric.[145]

Putting eccentricity in these terms makes it seem a rather restricted
category. To the extent that it reflected predominant concerns at the turn
of the eighteenth and nineteenth centuries, however, it could also be liberating. Roman Catholics, for example, would not have been considered
originals by Steele. But by the early nineteenth century they were unquestionably candidates for eccentricity. Quixotic loyalty to an ancient creed
came to seem increasingly English, provided one was not Irish. Catholics
figure largely in the modern annals of eccentricity, to the extent
that Roman Catholicism can be considered 'a great breeder of eccentrics
in England'.[146] In fact its recognition as such coincides with Catholic
Emancipation, and represents in a way the most telling evidence that
papists had at last established their right to be considered English.
Perhaps the first of this breed was the remarkable Charles Waterton,
traveller and naturalist. Waterton came of a long line of Yorkshire squires
who had never deserted the faith, and himself retained a lively sense of
the injustices that they had suffered for so doing. The only creature
he delighted in slaughtering was the brown, so-called Hanoverian rat,
identified for ever with the Protestant rulers it had allegedly accompanied across the North Sea. Waterton made himself famous for his
crocodile riding in South America, for his gruesome practical jokes with
taxidermy, and for turning his country estate into an early conservationist's animal reservation.

Other beneficiaries, if that is the correct term, were women. The early
nineteenth century is often perceived as weakening the status of modern
woman. Yet it was then that women decisively established their right to
be as eccentric as men, both in theory and practice. Pope had famously

denied that women could have a national character, or indeed any character at all. The view was not without its adherents a century later. As Henry Matthews, author of *The Diary of an Invalid*, put it: 'it is perhaps the highest merit in a woman, that she is without those strongly marked peculiarities which constitute what is called character in man;—for in her, to be prominent is to be offensive; and her most engaging qualities are of that unobtrusive kind, which belong rather to the sex than to the individual.'[147] Oddly enough, even in Pope's day foreigners were often clearer about the national character of women than men. However characterized, English women were thought to be recognizable by their bearing, manner, and dress, anywhere. But at home, too, there was growing interest in female character.

One of the important aspects of the increasing fascination with personality was that it made character more a matter of inner nature, less a matter of external action. As innumerable novelists, male and female, demonstrated, character in a woman was as variable as in a man, even if it had to be displayed in the context of passive response to the action of others rather than as the active voice of heroic man. If woman could be shown to be capable of character then she could be eccentric, though the emphasis tended to be different. Women were disproportionately the kind of eccentrics who dressed without regard to fashion, like Mrs 'Lady' Lewson, of Cold Bath Square, who died in 1816 at the age of 116, having preserved both the costume and furnishings of her youth in the reign of George I. Alternatively, they were notorious for engaging in extremes of feminine display. Lady Archer's penchant for wearing unsuitable cosmetics made her the undoubted queen of paint at the court of George III.[148]

None the less women appeared in numerous categories of eccentricity. Some of them, like the traveller Lady Hester Stanhope, or the supposedly reclusive Ladies of Llangollen, continue to exercise a peculiar fascination. Nor was politics excluded. Mary Wollstonecraft was not considered an eccentric, but then neither was her husband. They were both threats to an entire order. Women who operated within the existing political system, fully concurred in its underlying assumptions, and only demonstrated their individuality in particular contexts, received due recognition. The Duchess of Gordon, who raised the Gordon Highlanders and spent a lifetime of wire-pulling and wangling to get her friends jobs was a figure of fun but not of reproof. She was an authentic eccentric. One of the great male eccentrics of her day, William Beckford of Fonthill, took pride in humiliating her.

If eccentricity represented initially a rearguard action by the English original it ended as something considerably more valuable. The new uniformities and conformities generated by the industrialization and democratization of the mid-nineteenth century made many think it more important to sustain individuality than tame it. In Victorian discourse fears that conformity of all kinds posed a threat to character were recurrent.[149] John Stuart Mill pronounced that 'Eccentricity has always abounded when and where strength of character has abounded' and deplored the tyranny of opinion that might make eccentricity a reproach.[150]

The cultural consequences of this readiness to recognize that the pendulum might have swung too far against English originality were extensive. Earlier generations, all the way back to the seventeenth century, had often worried that it obstructed national progress in the arts. 'But still the English singularity will come in and have a share' regretfully wrote Roger North, distressed by his countrymen's resistance to importing the musical sophistication of Italy.[151] The refrain was a recurrent eighteenth-century one. By the mid-nineteenth century there was at least as much concern about the possibility that English creativity itself was being stifled by English developments. Dickens was one of those who confessed his 'fear that mere form and conventionalities usurp, in English art, as in English government and social relations, the place of living force and truth'.[152]

There were various ways of viewing the tension between the collective and the individual. Madame de Staël believed that originality was possible for the English precisely because they had achieved such a high degree of conformity.[153] The marquis de Custine thought, on the contrary, that having escaped despotic government, the English had submitted to two alternative despotisms, those of fashion for the rich, and custom for the poor. Each threatened diversity of character.[154] During their lifetimes the dominant trend of British life seemed to favour a degree of political authoritarianism. It was plainly no coincidence that the literature of eccentricity coincided with a growing concern for order and authority.[155] This was, after all, the period when many people preferred

to be considered Nonconformists rather than Dissenters, when reform
became preferable to revolution. If there was a time when originality
needed redefining it was this.

More important than politics was what was thought to be a deeper
commmitment to conservativism, one rooted in social and cultural forces.
It seems odd that the English had to be newly thought of as deeply
attached to their own heritage. But so it was. At least a century of
informed opinion had gone into creating the image of a ceaselessly restless and innovative people, revolutionists in politics, entrepreneurs in
commerce, improvers by instinct and conviction. It took an era of revolutions abroad to demonstrate that such characterizations were, to say
the least, misleading. Interestingly, what foreigners often harped upon is
perhaps revealing about the preoccupations of the English themselves. It
was the sense of rediscovering or recreating an ancient inheritance that
seemed so significant. The enthusiasm of English antiquarians and folk-
lorists for disinterring popular traditions threatened by extinction provided numerous examples, as did the cult of medievalism and Gothicism.
In identifying English continuities outsiders joined in with equal enthusiasm, sometimes with surprising results. It took a German journalist to
decide that the English tradition of dance and pantomime had remained
the same over centuries whereas those of the Continent had changed
repeatedly.[156] If the peculiar status of the English as the conservationists
of Europe was laboriously constructed the need fulfilled was evidently a
European as well as an English one.

Few foreigners came to Victorian England without sensing what they
took to be the extraordinary social cohesion of the English that went with
this faith in continuity. Here was a country, wrote Carus, in which 'from
the cultivator of the soil upwards, every one feels himself to be a part of
one great whole. . . . in that part of self which remains he readily adopts
or falls into a species of rough, eccentric originality, in order thus, in some
measure, to compensate for the other deficiency or loss. And this,
perhaps, is in fact the best means of accounting for many of the peculiarities, and much of the coarseness of the Englishman.'[157] Increasingly
it was the perception that Americans had taken up the baton of un-
bridled libertarianism to the extent, as Victor Hennequin put it, that they
had become caricatures of the English.[158] And Americans themselves
were frequently the most struck by the resulting contradictions in Britain,

its mixture of individuality and uniformity, self-expression and self-effacement. Henry James, for instance, was puzzled by the paradox of English conformity combined with great eccentricity in this 'land of anomalies', and wondered 'how they reconcile the traditional insularity of the private person with this perpetual tribute to usage'.[159] But perhaps there was no contradiction.

CONCLUSION

Manners and Character

*T*HE manners and character identified in this book were not dis-
aggregated attributes but rather a treasured compound which
brought to mind living Englishmen and Englishwomen. The
philosopher Herbert Spencer thus recalled his uncle, the Victorian
Churchman Thomas Spencer: 'Mr. Spencer may be regarded as having presented in a high degree the predominant peculiarities of the Englishman. He possessed an unusual proportion of that unflagging energy
which is so distinctive of the race. His modes of thought and action
leaned strongly to the "practical"—a quality by which we are nation-
ally marked. Throughout life he exhibited a great amount of that
English characteristic—independence. He was largely endued with
the perseverance which makes us as a race "not know when we are
beaten". The active philanthropy by which we are distinguished
amongst nations, distinguished him amongst us. That uprightness
in which, on the whole, we are superior to our continental and
transatlantic neighbours was in him invariably manifested. Even in
its deficiencies he represented the Anglo-Saxon nature. That
occasional *brusquerie* of manner, and that want of tact in social
intercourse for which we are complained of as a people, were
visible in him. He lacked those finer perceptions which are
needful for the due appreciation of beauty in nature and art; and

in this respect also was like his race. Above all, however, he exhibited the English type of character in the habitual recognition of *duty*. The determination to do that which *ought* to be done, simply *because* it ought to be done, is a motive of action which has been shown to be almost peculiar to Englishmen—a motive which most other nations cannot understand. This motive was with Mr. Spencer a ruling one. In this respect, also, as in so many others, he was an intensified Englishman.'[1]

With due allowance for family piety and patriotic pride, characterizations of this kind were commonplaces of the time and would have rung a bell with many foreigners. If there was any feature that sat uneasily with the rest it was Spencer's emphasis on the peculiar sense of duty that governed the English. It was not that outsiders would have refused to acknowledge the phenomenon but rather that they would have been less generous in allowing its high-mindedness. They granted that the English were a driven race, but assumed that what drove them was a unique, or at any rate insular, sense of destiny based more on arrogance than moral superiority.

The essence of the claim was not so much that the English reasoned that they were superior to others but that it genuinely did not occur to them that any rational being could suppose they were anything else. As numerous visitors noted, the highest compliment that could be paid foreigners was to regret that they were not English or even to tell them to their face that they deserved to be English.[2] Belonging to a chosen race was an implicit belief for many who would not have been interested in the theological underpinning. To be born an Englishman implied an act of divine grace that left its beneficiaries profoundly grateful. The story told by the poet Samuel Rogers of an encounter in 1815 on the streets of Paris with a countryman whose French was incomprehensible conveyed the point in humorous but telling terms. ' "Are you an Englishman?" "Thank God, I am, Sir," he answered very briskly.'[3]

Considering the significance that has been attached to perceptions of other peoples in the shaping of national identity it is intriguing that so many outsiders thought the English strangely uninterested in others. The magisterial Kant opined that the English did not despise or dislike other nations; they simply ignored them.[4] Even some Anglophiles agreed, noting that the English made little effort to inform the rest of mankind about their merits and virtues. They adopted a 'take it or leave it' attitude which was more likely to give offence than encourage emulation.[5]

For others, like Alphonse Esquiros, this indifference helped explain the tolerance by the English of insults that would have infuriated other nationalities and seemed doubly strange in a nation so noted for its patriotism. 'I have seen peoples very punctilious on the point of national honour; the least critical observation vexed them; but before an Englishman you may indicate the weak signs of British civilization and not even irritate him: he is silent, but it is the silence of contempt.'[6] It was claimed that English and French patriotism, especially, had quite different characteristics. French national pride was truly collective, whereas the English 'are vain of themselves as individual Thomsons and Johnsons, and of the English nation because it is *their* nation; not of themselves because they are members of it'.[7] It was hard to find parallels for this sense of self-sufficiency. Japan sprang to some minds, though it did not provide a perfect fit, given that the English combined sublime confidence in their own uniqueness with a readiness to impose themselves on other peoples which the Japanese did not manifest until much later.

Whether it was national arrogance or national devotion to duty, belief in a higher destiny fitted well with the hardening of stereotypes of Englishness that occurred during the two centuries reviewed in this book. The effect was to associate the distinctiveness of the English and their national triumphs with a marked degree of self-discipline and self-dedication. This did not necessarily mean obliterating older perceptions. It did, however, mean refining, remoulding, or revising them, in some instances to the point of radically changing their significance. In each case there was a tendency, conscious or not, both to protect and adapt favourite features of English behaviour in the face of the challenges posed by rapid change. Unpredictable energy could be refashioned into dependable and constructive industry. Uncompromising candour waged an interminable war with canting conformity. Natural decency had to be prevented from descending into deadening decorum. The antisocial tendency to taciturnity might be rendered compatible with the requirements of collaboration and clubbability. Rude incivility was artfully polished into a respectful reserve that served the complex requirements of a commercial society. Wayward originality was disciplined into a harmless eccentricity, which complemented rather than conflicted with the underlying cohesiveness of national life.

It is easy enough to relate these evolving characterizations to the underlying improvement in British fortunes that marked a period of economic growth, political stability, and territorial expansion. Telling a story of success, whether from the outside or the inside, gave a largely positive thrust to a process that might have been very different if the perceived circumstances had been less propitious. But beyond that, the tendency towards a stronger sense of discipline, direction, and duty, reflected some powerful campaigning causes of the late eighteenth and early nineteenth century. These included the quest for spiritual vigour reflected in the Evangelical Revival, the preservation of constitutional stability in the face of fearsome external and internal threats, and the erratic but cumulatively impressive drive to imperial expansion.

There was also the belief that there were indeed two nations, if not quite in Disraeli's sense, one which provided the essence of the national character, the other that needed some training to come up to its exacting standards. The first was a middle class which self-consciously embodied the integrity and vigour of English civilization. The second was an unconscious assemblage of those above and those below, united not by wealth but by temperamental unreliability that reflected their weaker sense of national responsibility. As the reformer Jonas Hanway put it in 1778, 'The genius of our nation is such, that those who move in a sphere *above*, and they who are below the middle rank, are with difficulty kept within bounds.'[8] Much of the unifying force that bound Englishness into a whole derived from this centripetal imperative. It was not that English aristocrats or English plebeians were considered less English than others, only that the former were less reliably so at times when Continental life offered rival models of fashionable existence, and the latter too representative of an Englishness which could be embarrassingly unconstructive in its outlook.

Whatever its origins the national character that had acquired a recognizable outline by the time of the Great Exhibition had a remarkable stability about it, all the more remarkable considering the claims that have been made for the late nineteenth and early twentieth century as 'a period which saw a particularly concerted construction of "Englishness", as part of a more general "nationalization" of English culture'.[9] These claims perhaps exaggerate the novelty of this development, which could be matched with comparable if differently configured campaigns much earlier. None the less, it is useful to distinguish between different components of what is taken to be Englishness, between the manners and character examined in this book, and the ideas, values, and causes which feature in a lively debate about the evolving nature of English and British nationalism since the mid-nineteenth century.[10] Certainly, in questions of national character the process of change was less marked. The continuity of assumptions about English character from the time of Dickens to that of 'Dad's Army' has been emphasized.[11] As recently as the 1950s, systematic surveys of national attitudes have uncovered much that would have been readily recognizable in the early nineteenth century.[12]

Even from the vantage point of a dawning new millennium it is not clear that this continuity has been permanently broken. Economic decline and imperial extinction have doubtless had their effect but not to the extent of wholly dispersing long-cherished perceptions. If focused energy has not invariably been seen as a feature of the modern workforce, there remains a considerable faith in the innate pragmatism and adaptability of the English. The paradoxical assertion of candour and hypocrisy in public life retains a certain recognizable force, as do the moral dilemmas that arise from long-standing commitments to ideals of domesticity and decency. Reserve is still thought of as a markedly insular trait notwithstanding gusts of public sentiment which prompt speculations about a new kind of English sociability. Above all, judging by the continuing market for books on the subject, the English still want to think themselves eccentric and foreigners still seem to want to grant them their wish. In all these instances, of course, it would be easy to cite exceptions that might come to be seen as the rule. But it was always thus. Throughout the period with which this book has been concerned the national character was seen as vulnerable to change, whether the viewer deplored or welcomed the predicted outcome.

Some aspects of the process that solidified in the mid-nineteenth century seem more vulnerable than others. Changes in the relative positions of the sexes make characterizations which assumed a quite different state of affairs hard to sustain. Yet many features of English manhood and English womanhood were in fact gendered versions of what was taken to be the same essential quality. Female modesty and male reserve,

for instance, were both expressions of what was supposed to be an underlying Anglo-Saxon reticence, suitably adapted to the respective roles of
women and men in the society of the day. Feminism, like other defining
orthodoxies deriving from basic principles, does not necessarily override
these tribal impulses however explicitly it may challenge them. That new
models of English womanhood are evolving is indisputable. Whether
they turn out to be any less English it is harder to say.

   Changing concepts of social equality might also be supposed to have
their effect. Gentility was central to the character that emerged in the
eighteenth and nineteenth centuries. Without the idea of the English gentleman and lady the idea of the Englishman and Englishwoman would
not have been the same. Today gentility no longer retains its potency as
an unwritten code bestowing legitimacy on people and practices. On the
other hand, its peculiar appeal and function depended much on its social
adaptability. It is conceivable that its utility is not yet exhausted. As that
most self-consciously genteel of authors, Bulwer-Lytton, remarked,
'From the petty droppings of the well of manners, the fossilized incrus-
tations of national character are formed.'[13] The manners of the later twentieth century are more democratic than those of Bulwer-Lytton's age. Yet
democracy in its modern form is perpetually subverted by the social competition that is so characteristic of the market economy. Though often
predicted, the demise of the latter does not appear imminent. National
attributes that drew heavily on the code of gentility, including self-
restraint, reserve, and eccentricity may yet derive support from the
unquenchable desire of the have-nots to acquire what they take to be the
superior mores of the haves.

   One significant feature of late twentieth-century England is perhaps
less problematic in this respect than might be supposed. The creation
of a self-consciously multiracial society, with the resulting mingling of
colours and creeds, might have startled many who sought to summarize
the English character between the mid-seventeenth and mid-nineteenth
centuries. Against this, it might be recalled that race and ethnicity were
not notably prominent in the analyses and arguments thereby generated.
On the contrary, the mongrel nature of the English breed and its ability
to adapt to new strains were often considered among its typical strengths.
The English character was indeed a character, much more than it was
ever a physical type.

There remains the ultimate joker in this pack of cards, one which can certainly transform the game. The combination of devolution at home and incorporation in the European Union abroad has made the political fragmentation of Britain not a possibility but a fact, in any sense that would have been understood by the Britons of two hundred years ago. The creation of a sovereign parliamentary state was the central element in their Britishness. There were, of course, other, earlier versions of Britishness stretching back over many centuries. But when political elites organize their language and values around a single driving concept, as they did for over two hundred years in the heyday of the Westminster Parliament, the results of superseding it are to say the least unpredictable.

Whether some other centre of gravity for a stable form of Britishness can be found has yet to be seen. What the consequences might be for those Britons who think of themselves as English is still more uncertain. On the other hand, a feature of Englishness as a historical force has been its tendency to elide the distinction between England and Britain while preserving the strong sense of identity of the former and permitting alternative cultures to flourish even in mainland Britain. In retrospect this is generally considered a matter for regret and even condemnation. Yet it apparently permitted an ethnically diverse community to collaborate in one of the more impressive projects of modern times, the establishment of a British state and a British empire. Who knows what vigour Englishness might exhibit if for the first time in many centuries the English find themselves speaking only for England?

One prediction does seem safe. Contradictions, not least in the matter of perceived character, will remain, as they did throughout the period covered by this book and indeed before. It is this after all that evoked the fascination of so many outsiders, friendly or not. In the mid-nineteenth century it puzzled Emerson, Heine, and de Tocqueville. In the century before that it puzzled Voltaire, Hume, and Kant. There never was one simple verdict, but two common responses predominated, the first a certain resigned bafflement at the irrational oddity of the English, the second a rueful recognition that the English themselves not only admitted the fact but regarded it as a sign of their own superiority. Two final illustrations may suffice. One is the remark of the poet and politician Lamartine, who last visited England in 1850, and finally concluded that among the ancient races of Europe there was none like the English.

'L'Anglais est un Anglais.'[14] The other is Emerson's recollection of his meeting with Wordsworth in 1847, when, he recorded, 'We talked of English national character.' Emerson teased Wordsworth on the subject of English philistinism, observing that if a work such as Plato's *Republic* were to be published in England as a new book it would find no readers. The great man did not deny it, '"and yet," he added after a pause with that complacency which never deserts a true-born Englishman, "and yet we have embodied it all."'[15]

Notes

All works are fully described when first cited, and more briefly identified thereafter.

Introduction ENGLISHNESS

1. *A Memoir of the Life and Writings of the late William Taylor of Norwich*, ed. J. W. Robberds, 2 vols., London, 1843, i. 195, 226.
2. James Campbell, 'The United Kingdom of England', in Alexander Grant and Keith J. Stringer, eds., *Uniting the Kingdom? The Making of British History*, London, 1995, pp. 31–47, and, more broadly, James Campbell, ed., *The Anglo-Saxons*, London, 1981.
3. Stefan Collini, *Public Moralists: Political Thought and Intellectual Life in Britain, 1850–1930*, Oxford, 1991; George Watson, *The English Ideology: Studies in the Language of Victorian Politics*, London, 1973; Kathryn Tidrick, *Empire and the English Character*, London, 1990.
4. R. Helgerson, *Forms of Nationhood: The Elizabethan Writing of England*, Chicago, 1992.
5. *Madame de Staël et J.-B.-A. Suard: Correspondance inédite (1786–1797)*, ed. Robert de Luppé, Geneva, 1970, p. 70.
6. Martin Murphy, *Blanco White: Self-Banished Spaniard*, New Haven, 1989, p. 61.
7. Norman Scarfe, *Innocent Espionage: The La Rochefoucauld Brothers' Tour of England in 1785*, Woodbridge, 1995, p. 201: 'We pass over a page of speculation on cause and effect and hypothetical national customs.'
8. Pierre-Marc-Gaston, duc de Lévis, *L'Angleterre au commencement du dix-neuvième siècle*, Paris, 1814, p. 363.
9. Charles de Rémusat, *L'Angleterre au dix-huitième siècle*, 2 vols., Paris, 1856, i. 1.
10. *An Essay on the Manners and Genius of the Literary Character*, London, 1795, pp. 176–7.
11. M. M. Cloake, ed., *A Persian at the Court of King George 1809–10*, London, 1988, p. 172.
12. Peter Mandler, 'Against "Englishness": English Culture and the Limits to Rural Nostalgia, 1850–1940', *Trans. Royal Hist. Soc.* 6th ser. 7 (1997), 155–76.
13. 2 vols., London, 1863.
14. *Sunny Memories of Foreign Lands*, London, 1855, p. 17.
15. Friedrich Wolfzettel, *Ce désir de vagabondage cosmopolite: Wege und Entwicklung des französischen Reiseberichts im 19. Jahrhundert*, Tübingen, 1989, pp. 126–7.
16. J. C. Beltrami, *A Pilgrimage in Europe and America*, 2 vols., London, 1828, i. 337.
17. Francis Hardy, *Memoirs of the Political and Private Life of James Caulfield, Earl of Charlemont*, London, 1810, p. 341.

18. David Spadafora, *The Idea of Progress in Eighteenth-Century Britain*, New Haven, 1990, pp. 304 ff.

19. *A Personal Tour through the United Kingdom*, London, 1828, p. 1.

20. George Watson, *The English Ideology: Studies in the Language of Victorian Politics*, p. 30.

21. Ralph Waldo Emerson, *English Traits*, Boston, 1856, p. 41.

22. *Memoirs of Madame de Rémusat, 1802–1808*, ed. Paul de Rémusat, 2 vols., London, 1880, ii. 160.

23. Édouard de Montulé, *Voyage en Angleterre et en Russie, pendant les années 1821, 1822 et 1823*, 2 vols., Paris, 1825, i. 11.

24. *Letters on England*, London, 1825, p. 17.

25. C. H. Phipps, later Marquess of Normanby, *The English in France*, 3 vols., London, 1828, i. 169–70.

26. *A Journey from London to Genoa, through England, Portugal, Spain, and France*, 4 vols., London, 1770, iii. 4.

27. Charles Johnston, *Chrysal or the Adventures of a Guinea*, ed. E. Baker, London, 1908, p. 296.

28. Claude-Adrien Helvétius, *A Treatise on Man, his Intellectual Faculties, and his Education*, ed. W. Hooper, 2 vols., London, 1777, i. 274.

29. Josephine Grieder, *Anglomania in France 1740–1789: Fact, Fiction, and Political Discourse*, Geneva, 1985; Jacques Gury, 'Une excentricité à l'Anglaise: l'Anglomanie', in Michèle Plaisant, *L'Excentricité en Grande-Bretagne au 18e siècle*, Lille, 1976, pp. 189–211; Michael Maurer, *Aufklärung und Anglophilie in Deutschland*, Göttingen, 1987.

30. Bernhard Fabian, 'Reception Studies: Principles and Problems', unpub. lecture at the British Academy, 25 Apr. 1998.

31. London, 1927.

32. *The Interpretation of Culture*, New York, 1973, p. 35.

33. George Heriot, *Travels through the Canadas*, London, 1807, pp. 275–6.

34. Richard Chenevix, *An Essay upon National Character*, 2 vols., London, 1832, i. 14.

35. Joseph Baretti, *A Journey from London to Genoa*, iii. 4.

36. *Burke's Works*, Bohn's edn., vii. 499.

37. Nancy Stepan, *The Idea of Race in Science: Great Britain 1800–1960*, Oxford, 1982, p. 4.

38. Patrick Joyce, *Visions of the People: Industrial England and the Question of Class 1848–1914*, Cambridge, 1991, p. 71.

39. *Self-Help with Illustrations of Conduct and Perseverance* (1866 edn.), London, 1997, p. 145.

40. De La Vauguyon, *The Truth respecting England, or an Impartial Examination of the Work of M. Pillet and of Various Other Writers on the Same Subject*, 2 vols., London, 1817, i. 22.

41. Joseph Marshall, *Travels through Holland, Flanders, Germany, Denmark,*

Sweden, Lapland, Russia, The Ukraine, and Poland, in the Years 1768, 1769, and 1770, 2nd edn., 3 vols., London, 1773, additional 4th vol., *Travels through France and Spain, in the Years 1770 and 1771*, 1776, ii. 150; William Eton, *A Survey of the Turkish Empire*, London, 1798, p. 110.

42. *Travels through Germany. With a Particular Account of the Courts of Mecklenburg*, 2 vols., London, 1768, i. 4.

43. Marianne Baillie, *First Impressions on a Tour upon the Continent, in the Summer of 1818, through Parts of France, Italy, Switzerland, the Borders of Germany, and a Part of French Flanders*, London, 1819, p. 22.

44. *A Selection of Thomas Twining's Letters 1734–1804*, ed. Ralph S. Walker, 2 vols., Lewiston, NY, 1991, i. 278.

45. *L'Angleterre et les Anglais, ou petit portrait d'une grande famille; copié et retouché par deux témoins oculaires*, trans. Joseph Antoine de Gourbillon and T. W. Dickinson, 3 vols., Paris, 1817, iii. 388.

46. *Parliamentary Portraits*, London, 1815, pp. 131–2.

47. Amédée Pichot, *Historical and Literary Tour of a Foreigner in England and Scotland*, 2 vols., London, 1825, i. 8–9.

48. C. A. G. Goede, *The Stranger in England: Travels in Great Britain*, 3 vols., London, 1807, ii. 148.

49. P. B. Granville, ed., *Autobiography of A. B. Granville*, 2 vols., London, 1874, i. 273.

50. Norman Scarfe, *Innocent Espionage: The La Rochefoucauld Brothers' Tour of England in 1785*, p. 203.

51. *Georg Forsters Werke*, vol xi: *Rezensionen*, ed. Horst Fiedler, 2nd edn., Berlin, 1992, p. 192.

52. Abbé Antoine-François Prévost, *Adventures of a Man of Quality*, ed. Mysie E. I. Robertson, London, 1930, p. 138.

53. Maurice Agulhon, *Marianne into Battle: Republican Imagery and Symbolism in France, 1789–1880*, trans. Janet Lloyd, Cambridge, 1981. The Yankee Brother Jonathan is attributed to Washington; he remained rather colourless and eventually gave way to Uncle Sam.

54. Johann Wilhelm von Archenholz, *A Picture of England*, 2 vols., London, 1789, ii. 157.

55. *Letters of a Russian Traveller 1789–1790*, trans. Florence Jones, New York, 1957, p. 261.

56. *The English at Home*, trans. and ed. Lascelles Wraxall, 2 vols., London, 1861, i. 133.

57. Eric Evans, 'Englishness and Britishness: National identities, c.1790–c.1870', in Alexander Grant and Keith J. Stringer, eds., *Uniting the Kingdom? The Making of British History*, pp. 223–43.

58. Linda Colley, *Britons: Forging the Nation 1707–1837*, New Haven, 1992, provides a thorough and positive account of this process so far as it relates to the nations of Britain itself. Irish 'Britishness' has figured less in the historiography of which her work is a pioneer.

59. Michael Hechter, *Internal Colonialism: The Celtic Fringe in British National Development, 1536–1966*, London, 1975.

60. Hester Lynch Piozzi, *Observations and Reflections made in the Course of a Journey through France, Italy, and Germany*, 2 vols., London, 1789, ii. 368; *British Synonymy; or, an Attempt at Regulating the Choice of Words in Familiar Conversation*, 2 vols., London, 1794.

61. J. Fenimore Cooper, *England*, 3 vols., 1837, i. 97.

62. Raphael Samuel, ed., *Patriotism: The Making and Unmaking of British National Identity*, 3 vols., London, 1989, i. xi.

63. Prévost, *Adventures of a Man of Quality*, p. 165.

64. Charles Le Mercher de Longpré, baron d'Haussez, *Great Britain in 1833*, 2 vols., London, 1833, ii. 68–9.

65. *A Journey from London to Genoa*, i. 44–5.

66. *Journal of a Tour and Residence in Great Britain, during the Years 1810 and 1811, by a French Traveller*, 2 vols., Edinburgh, 1815, i. 336, 185.

67. René-Martin Pillet, *L'Angleterre vue à Londres et dans ses provinces*, Paris, 1815, p. 23.

68. *Miscellanies*, London, 1770, ii. 209.

69. *An American Quaker in the British Isles: The Travel Journals of Jabez Maud Fisher, 1775–1779*, ed. Kenneth Morgan, Oxford, 1991, p. 220.

70. Patrick Joyce, *Visions of the People*, pp. 197 ff., 265 ff.

71. *L'Angleterre au commencement du dix-neuvième siècle*, p. 9; *Voyage en Angleterre et en Écosse*, Paris, 1844, p. 28.

72. J. G. Kohl, *Ireland, Scotland, and England*, London, 1844, p. 83.

73. Adolphe Blanqui, *Voyage d'un jeune français en Angleterre et en Écosse pendant l'automne de 1823*, Paris, 1824, p. 3.

74. J. Gamble, *A View of Society and Manners, in the North of Ireland, in the Summer and Autumn of 1812*, London, 1813, pp. 301–2.

75. Count Édouard de Melfort, *Impressions of England*, 2 vols., London, 1836, ii. 208, i. 153.

76. R. J. Smith, *The Gothic Bequest: Medieval Institutions in British Thought, 1688–1863*, Cambridge, 1987, chap. 3.

77. *An Historical View of the English Government, from the Settlement of the Saxons in Britain to the Revolution in 1688*, 4 vols., London, 1803, i. 59–60, 197.

78. James Howell, *Epistolae Ho-Elianae: Familiar Letters Domestic and Foreign*, 11th edn., very much corrected, London, 1754, p. 241.

79. William Carr, *An Accurate Description of the United Netherlands, And of the most considerable Parts of Germany, Sweden, and Denmark*, London, 1691, p. 81; Robert Clayton, Letters on tour, 1697–8, Bodleian, MS Eng. Lett. c. 309, 14 July 1697.

80. Thomas Nugent, *Travels through Germany*, i. 158.

81. *Travels in the North of Germany*, 2 vols., Edinburgh, 1820, ii. 258–60.

82. John Strang, *Germany in 1831*, 2 vols., London, 1836, ii. 128.

83. *An Autobiography*, 2 vols., London, 1904, i. 32.

84. *England in 1835*, 3 vols., London, 1836, ii. 81.

85. C. G. Carus, *The King of Saxony's Journey through England and Scotland in the Year 1844*, trans. S. C. Davison, London, 1846, pp. 29–31.

86. C. F. Henningsen, *Analogies and Contrasts; or, Comparative Sketches of France and England*, 2 vols., London, 1848, i. 139–40.

87. 3 vols., London, 1847.

88. Stephen Bann, *The Clothing of Clio: A Study of the Representation of History in Nineteenth-Century Britain and France*, Cambridge, 1984, chaps. 2–3.

89. *The Works of John Ruskin*, ed. E. T. Cook and Alexander Wedderburn, vol. xx: *Lectures on Art and Aratra Pentelici*, p. 41.

90. Eric J. Hobsbawm, *Nations and Nationalism since 1780: Programme, Myth and Reality*, Cambridge, 1990, p. 108.

91. *The Life of Alfred the Great*, Oxford, 1709, pp. 3–4.

92. B. Sarrans, *De la décadence de l'Angleterre et des intérêts fédératifs de la France*, Paris, 1840, p. 157.

93. *The Book of Abigail and John: Selected Letters of the Adams Family, 1762–1784*, ed. L. H. Butterfield, Marc Friedlander, Mary-Jo Kline, Cambridge, Mass., 1975, p. 111.

94. Christopher Mulvey, *Transatlantic Manners: Social Patterns in Nineteenth-Century Anglo-American Travel Literature*, Cambridge, 1990, concl.

95. Elizabeth Davis Bancroft, *Letters from England 1846–1849*, London, 1904, p. 24; Harriet Beecher Stowe, *Sunny Memories of Foreign Lands*, p. 9.

96. M. K. Ashby, *Joseph Ashby of Tysoe 1859–1919: A Study of English Village Life*, London, 1974, 1st pub. 1961, p. 65.

97. *The Works in Verse and Prose of William Shenstone, Esq.*, 3rd edn., 2 vols., London, 1769, ii. 264.

98. *An American Quaker in the British Isles: The Travel Journals of Jabez Maud Fisher, 1775–1779*, p. 228.

99. *Sophie in London 1786 being the Diary of Sophie v. la Roche*, trans. Clare Williams, foreword by G. M. Trevelyan, London, 1933, p. 290; Janet Ross, *Three Generations of English Women*, London, p. 215.

100. *Select Proverbs of all Nations*, London, 1824, p. x.

101. John Pinkerton, *A Dissertation on the Origin and Progress of the Scythians or Goths*, London, 1787, p. 92.

102. H. G. Wells, *Experiment in Autobiography*, New York, 1934, pp. 72–3; Thomas Carlyle, *History of Frederick II of Prussia called Frederick the Great*, 8 vols., London, 1897, i. 346.

103. *Journals and Correspondence of Lady Eastlake*, ed. Charles Eastlake Smith, 2 vols., London, 1895, i. 71.

104. E. M. Whitty, *The Governing Classes of Great Britain: Political Portraits*, London, 1854, p. 134.

105. Revd George Davies, *The Completeness of the Late Duke of Wellington as a National Character*, London, 1854, p. 2.

106. Rosemary Ashton, *Little Germany: Exile and Asylum in Victorian England*, Oxford, 1986, p. 67.
107. *An Essay upon National Character*, ii. 531.
108. John Mitchell Kemble, *The Saxons in England*, 2 vols., London, 1849, i. 21.
109. *Letters from London: Written during the years 1802 and 1803*, Boston, 1804, p. 173.
110. Antoine-François Prévost *et al.*, *Le Pour et contre (nos 1–60)*, ed. Steve Larkin, 2 vols., Oxford, 1993, i. 152.
111. Zacharias Conrad von Uffenbach, *Merkwürdige Reisen durch Niedersachsen Holland and Engelland*, 3 vols., Ulm and Memmingen, 1753, ii. 532 ff.
112. *Essays Moral, Political and Literary*, Oxford, 1963, p. 212. See also, p. 291.
113. *A Sentimental Journey through France and Italy*, London, 1968, p. 90.
114. *Anthropology from a Pragmatic Point of View*, trans. Mary J. Gregor, The Hague, 1974, pp. 170–7.
115. *Great Britain in 1833*, i. 54; Thomas R. Palfrey, *L'Europe littéraire (1833–1834)*, Paris, 1927, pp. 30, 32.
116. John A. Doyle, *Memoir and Correspondence of Susan Ferrier, 1782–1854*, London, 1898, p. 128.
117. *Monthly Review*, 97 (1822), 166; *Edinburgh Review*, 93 (1826), 225.
118. P. G. Adams, *Travellers and Travel Liars 1660–1800*, Berkeley, 1962.
119. *Souvenirs de Londres en 1814 et 1816*, Paris, 1817, p. 137.
120. Ethel Jones, *Les Voyageurs français en Angleterre de 1815 à 1830*, Paris, 1830, p. 21.
121. George Jacob Holyoake, *Sixty Years of an Agitator's Life*, 2 vols., London, 1893, i. 91.
122. *London Quarterly Review*, 7 (1856–7), 381–2.
123. *The Uncollected Writings of Charles Dickens: Household Words 1850–1859*, ed. Harry Stone, Bloomington, Ind., 1968, pp. 143–50.
124. Michael Duffy, ed., *The English Satirical Print, 1600–1832: The Englishman and the Foreigner*, Cambridge, 1986.
125. John Moore, *A View of Society and Manners in France, Switzerland, and Germany*, 2 vols., London, 1779, ii. 5–6.
126. Thomas Thornton, *A Sporting Tour through the northern Parts of England and Great Part of the Highlands of Scotland*, London, 1896, p. 64.
127. *The Journal of Sir Walter Scott*, ed. W. E. K. Anderson, Edinburgh, 1998, p. 789.
128. *Dunciad*, iv. 294.
129. Louis Dutens, *Memoirs of a Traveller, Now in Retirement*, 5 vols., London, 1806, i. 225–6; ii. 72–3.
130. N. M. Karamzin, *Letters of a Russian Traveller 1789–1790*, p. 140.
131. Philip Thicknesse, *Observations on the Customs and Manners of the French nation*, London, 1766, pp. 8–9.
132. Diary of unknown traveller, accompanying Kenelm Digby, 1831, British Library, Add. MS 64096, fos. 18–19.
133. Louis Dutens, *Memoirs of a Traveller, Now in Retirement*, ii. 37.

134. John Nichols, 'Tour through several Parts of French Flanders and Germany', in *Gentlemen's Magazine*, 1816, i. 486.
135. *Edinburgh Review*, 37 (1822), 287 ff.
136. Frances Ann Kemble, *Records of a Girlhood*, 3 vols., London, 1878, i. 108.
137. William Austin, *Letters from London: Written during the years 1802 and 1803*, pp. 3, 6–7.

Chapter One ENERGY

1. *England and the English*, 2 vols., New York, 1833, i. 57.
2. Peter Mathias, *The First Industrial Nation: An Economic History of Britain, 1700–1914*, London, 1969; the term was perhaps first used by Alphonse Esquiros, *The English at Home*, trans. and ed. Lascelles Wraxall, 2nd ser., London, 1861, p. 2.
3. F. W. J. Hemmings 'Stendhal: anglophile ou anglophobe?', in K. G. McWatters and C. W. Thompson, eds., *Stendhal et l'Angleterre*, Liverpool, 1987, p. 5; S. S. Prawer, *Coal-Smoke and Englishman: A Study of Verbal Caricature in the Writings of Heinrich Heine*, London, 1984.
4. Alexandre-Auguste Ledru-Rollin, *De la décadence de l'Angleterre*, 2 vols., Paris, 1850.
5. Johanna Kinkel, 1853, quoted Rosemary Ashton, *Little Germany*, p. 190.
6. *Wealth of Nations*, V. i. f. 50.
7. Michael Ignatieff, *A Just Measure of Pain: The Penitentiary in the Industrial Revolution 1750–1850*, London, 1989, p. 105.
8. *Calendar of State Papers and Manuscripts, Relating to English Affairs, existing in the Archives and Collections of Venice, and in other Libraries of Northern Italy*, iv. 289; vi. 1672.
9. William Brenchley Rye, *England as seen by Foreigners in the Days of Elizabeth and James the First*, London, 1865, p. 70.
10. *A Voyage to England, Containing many Things relating to the State of Learning, Religion, And other Curiosities of that Kingdom*, London, 1709, p. 62.
11. John Taylor, *Records of my Life*, 2 vols., London, 1832, ii. 250.
12. Gebhardt Friedrich August Wendeborn, *A View of England towards the Close of the Eighteenth Century*, 2 vols., London, 1791, i. 410–11.
13. John Carr, *The Stranger in Ireland; or, a Tour in the Southern and Western Parts of that Country, in the Year 1805*, London, 1806, p. 280.
14. E. P. Thompson, 'Time, Work-Discipline and Industrial Capitalism', in *Customs in Common*, London, 1991, p. 371.
15. *Briefe zur Charakteristik von England gehörig; geschrieben auf einer Reise im Jahre 1784 von Heinrich von Watzdorf*, Leipzig, 1786, p. 169.
16. *Briefe von einer Reise durch England, Schottland und Irland im Frühjahr und Sommer 1820*, Stuttgart, 1821, i. 49.

17. Steven Marcus, *Engels, Manchester, and the Working Class*, London, 1974, p. 213.
18. William Howitt, *German experiences: Addressed to the English; both Stayers at Home, and Goers Abroad*, London, 1844, p. 102.
19. *Sybil, or the Two Nations*, London, 1845.
20. Peter Mathias, *The Transformation of England: Essays in the Economic and Social History of England in the Eighteenth Century*, London, 1979, pp. 148 ff.
21. J. G. Kohl, *Ireland, Scotland, and England*, pp. 134-5.
22. Harriet Martineau, *Society in America*, 2nd edn., 3 vols., London, 1837, ii. 243.
23. John Armstrong, *Miscellanies*, 2 vols., London, 1770, ii. 214.
24. W. F. Mavor, *A Tour in Wales, and through several Counties of England, including both the Universities, performed in the Summer of 1805*, London, 1806, p. 41.
25. *The Querist, and Word to the Wise*, 2nd edn., London, 1750, pp. 66-75.
26. Nassau William Senior, *Journals, Conversations and Essays Relating to Ireland*, 2 vols., London, 1868, i. 46.
27. *Journal of a Tour, through Great Part of England and Scotland, in the Year 1810, performed by Alexander Dennis, of Trembath*, Penzance, 1816, p. 139.
28. W. Cooke Taylor, *Notes of a Tour in the Manufacturing Districts of Lancashire*, London, 1842, p. 49.
29. James Elmes, *Metropolitan Improvements; or, London in the Nineteenth Century*, London, 1829, p. v.
30. *Letter to a Member of the National Assembly*, in *The Writings and Speeches of Edmund Burke*, vol. viii, ed. L. G. Mitchell, Oxford, 1989, p. 334.
31. *Complete Works of William Hazlitt*, 21 vols., London, 1930-4, x. 121.
32. Ann Radcliffe, *A Journey made in the Summer of 1794, through Holland and the Western Frontier of Germany, with a Return down the Rhine*, London, 1795, pp. 47-8.
33. George Thompson, *Travels and Adventures in Southern Africa*, ed. Vernon S. Forbes, Van Riebeeck Society, Cape Town, 1967, p. 32.
34. *De Londres et ses Environs*, Amsterdam, 1789, p. 86.
35. Friedrich Ludwig Georg von Raumer, *England in 1835*, ii. 16.
36. Georg Christoph Lichtenberg, *Lichtenberg in England*, ed. Hans Ludwig Gumbert, 2 vols., Wiesbaden, 1977, i. 230.
37. Rosemary Ashton, *The German Idea: Four English Writers and the Reception of German Thought*, Cambridge, 1980, p. 99.
38. Raumer, *England in 1835*, iii. 305.
39. *The Courts of Europe at the Close of the Last Century by the late Henry Swinburne, Esq.*, ed. Charles White, 2 vols., London, 1841, i. viii.
40. *The Journeys of Celia Fiennes*, ed. Christopher Morris, London, 1947, p. 2.
41. Marc de Bombelles, *Journal de voyage en Grande Bretagne et en Irlande 1784*, ed. Jacques Gury, Oxford, 1989, p. 130.
42. P. G. Patmore, *Letters on England. By Victoire, Count de Soligny*, 2 vols., London, 1823, ii. 159-60.
43. Lévis, *L'Angleterre au commencement du dix-neuvième siècle*, p. 55.

44. Madame d'Avot, *Lettres sur l'Angleterre, ou deux années à Londres*, 2nd edn., Paris, 1821, p. 141.
45. *Great Britain in 1833*, i. 62.
46. *Tales of a Traveller. By Geoffrey Crayon, Gent.*, 2 vols., London, 1824, ii. 71.
47. *Virginibus Puerisque*, in *The Works of Robert Louis Stevenson*, vol. ii (London, 1922), p. 136.
48. Charles Dédéyan, *L'Angleterre dans la pensée de Diderot*, Paris, 1958, p. 59.
49. Haussez, *Great Britain in 1833*, i. 64.
50. Wendeborn, *A View of England towards the Close of the Eighteenth Century*, i. 412.
51. Lévis, *L'Angleterre au commencement du dix-neuvième siècle*, pp. 49–51.
52. *Reminiscences of Michael Kelly*, 2 vols., London, 1826, ii. 328.
53. *Trivia* in John Gay, *Poetry and Prose*, ed. Vincent A. Dearing and Charles E. Beckwith, 2 vols., Oxford, 1974, 'The Art of Walking the Streets of London', i. 157.
54. Cornelius Webbe, *Glances at Life in City and Suburb*, London, 1836, p. 209.
55. Béat Louis Muralt, *Letters describing the Character and Customs of the English and French Nations*, London, 1726, p. 17.
56. *The Mutability of Human Life; or, Memoirs of Adelaide, Marchioness of Melville*, 3 vols., London, 1777, i. 201.
57. *The Book of Abigail and John: Selected Letters of the Adams Family, 1762–1784*, p. 392.
58. N. M. Karamzin, *Letters of a Russian Traveller 1789–1790*, p. 270.
59. Ethel Mann, *An Englishman at Home and Abroad 1792–1828*, London, 1930, p. 155. The Englishman was John Barber Scott, of Bungay.
60. Doris Gunnell, *Sutton Sharpe et ses amis français*, Paris, 1925, p. 77.
61. Frances Ann Kemble, *Records of a Girlhood*, i. 109.
62. Louis-Antoine de Caraccioli, *Voyage de la raison en Europe; Par l'Auteur des Lettres récréatives et morales*, Compiègne, 1772, p. 248.
63. *Complete Works of William Hazlitt*, xvii. 338–9.
64. J. Michelet, *Sur les chemins de l'Europe*, Paris, 1893, p. 146.
65. *The Life and Letters of Barthold George Niebuhr*, 2 vols., London, 1852, i. 121.
66. Raumer, *England in 1835*, iii. 134.
67. Haussez, *Great Britain in 1833*, ii. 88; *The London Journal of Flora Tristan*, trans. Jean Hawkes, London, 1982, pp. 183–4.
68. *Oxford in 1710 from the Travels of Zacharias Conrad von Uffenbach*, ed. W. H. Quarrell and W. J. C. Quarrell, Oxford, 1928, p. 52.
69. Alphonse Esquiros, *The English at Home*, trans. and ed. Lascelles Wraxall, 3rd ser., London, 1863, pp. 56–7.
70. G. A. Crapelet, *Souvenirs de Londres en 1814 et 1816*, Paris, 1817, pp. 118–22.
71. Anthony and Pip Burton, *The Green Bag Travellers: Britain's First Tourists*, London, 1978.
72. Erik Gustaf Geijer, *Impressions of England 1809–10*, introd. Anton Blanck, London, 1932, p. 80.
73. *Five Years in an English University*, New York, 1852, pp. 44–5, 328–9.

74. Astolphe-Louis-Léonor, marquis de Custine, *Mémoires et voyages*, ed. Julien-Frédéric Tarn, Paris, 1992, p. 218.
75. Fanny Lewald, *England und Schottland*, 2 vols., Brunswick, 1851, i. 412–13.
76. *Journal des Dames et des Modes*, Frankfurt am Main, 5 Jan. 1801, p. 43.
77. *England in 1835*, iii. 133–4.
78. Thomas Hodgskin, *Travels in the North of Germany*, i. 59–60.
79. John Forster, *The Life of Charles Dickens*, 6th edn., 3 vols., London, 1872, i. 348–9.
80. John Taylor, *Records of my Life*, i. 184.
81. J. A. Mangan, *Athleticism in the Victorian and Edwardian Public School: The Emergence and Consolidation of an Educational Ideology*, Cambridge, 1981, chap. 2.
82. Lord William Pitt Lennox, *Percy Hamilton; or, the Adventures of a Westminster Boy*, 3 vols., London, 1851, i. 26–7.
83. *My Past and Thoughts: The Memoirs of Alexander Herzen*, trans. Constance Garnett, 4 vols., London, 1968, iii. 1119.
84. *Youthful Life, and Pictures of Travel: being the Autobiography of Madame Schopenhauer*, 2 vols., London, 1847, i. 81–2.
85. *Reise durch England und Schottland*, 2 vols., Leipzig, 1818, i. 236–7.
86. *Paupers and Pig Killers: The Diary of William Holland, A Somerset Parson, 1799–1818*, Gloucester, 1984, p. 37.
87. *Lettere sull'Inghilterra*, ed. Guido di Pino, Milan, 1944, chap. 7.
88. Richard Butterwick, 'The Visit to England in 1754 of Stanislaw August Poniatowski', *Oxford Slavonic Papers*, ed. C. M. Macrobert, G. S. Smith, and G. C. Stone, NS 25 (1992), 78.
89. F. C. Green, *A Comparative View of French and British Civilization*, London, 1965, chap. 4.
90. George Pinckard, *Notes on the West Indies*, 2nd edn., 2 vols., London, 1816, ii. 346–77.
91. *Briefe zur Characteristik von England gehörig; geschrieben auf einer Reise im Jahre 1784 von Heinrich von Watzdorf*, pp. 205–6.
92. Lord William Pitt Lennox, *My Recollections from 1806 to 1873*, 2 vols., London, 1874, i. 110.
93. Fanny Lewald, *The Italians at Home*, trans. Countess D'Avigdor, 2 vols., London, 1848, i. 239–40.
94. Prévost, *Adventures of a Man of Quality*, p. 132.
95. Peter Cunningham, *Two Years in New South Wales*, ed. David S. Macmillan, Sydney, 1966, p. 212.
96. Pierce Egan, *Boxiana*, 3 vols., London, 1930, i. 16.
97. *Paul's Letters to his Kinsfolk* in *Miscellaneous Works of Sir Walter Scott's*, vol. v, Edinburgh, 1870, p. 115.
98. *Great Britain in 1833*, ii. 114.
99. John Moore, *Mordaunt. Sketches of Life, Characters, and Manners, in Various Countries*, 3 vols., London, 1800, i. 233.
100. British Library, Add. MS 23646, fo. 59: Charles Rainsford's Journal.

101. Lord William Pitt Lennox, *Percy Hamilton; or, the Adventures of a Westminster Boy*, ii. 126.

102. E. W. Bovill, *English Country Life 1780–1830*, London, 1962, p. 169.

103. *The Diary of an Invalid being the Journal of a Tour in Pursuit of Health in Portugal Italy Switzerland and France in the Years 1817, 1818 and 1819*, 3rd edn., 2 vols., London, 1822, i. 198.

104. J. A. Mangan, *The Games Ethic and Imperialism: Aspects of the Diffusion of an Ideal*, London, 1986.

105. David Hackett Fischer, *Albion's Seed: Four British Folkways in America*, New York, 1989, p. 151. See also below, p. 151.

106. George Windsor Earl, *The Eastern Seas, or Voyages and Adventures in the Indian Archipelago, in 1832–33–34*, London, 1837, pp. 378–9.

107. C. F. Henningsen, *Analogies and Contrasts*, i. 72.

108. Pierre-Jean-Baptiste Nougaret, *Londres, la cour et les provinces d'Angleterre, Écosse et d'Irlande*, 2 vols., Paris, 1816, i. 435.

109. William Cobbett, *Advice to Young Men and (Incidentally) to Young Women in the Middle and Higher Ranks of Life*, London, 1926, pp. 258–60.

110. *Notes on England*, trans. W. F. Rae, London, 1872, p. 37.

111. *Sur les chemins de l'Europe*, pp. 27, 56, 142–3.

112. Revd John Davies Mereweather, *Diary of a Working Clergyman in Australia and Tasmania, kept during the years 1850–1853*, London, 1859, p. 135.

113. Carlo Denina, *Essai sur La Vie et Le Règne de Frédéric II, Roi de Prusse*, Berlin, 1788, pp. 400–2.

114. *Letters written during a Residence in England translated from the French of Henry Meister*, London, 1799, p. 167.

115. Wendeborn, *A View of England towards the Close of the Eighteenth Century*, i. 264.

116. *Observations sur Londres et ses Environs*, Paris, 1777, p. 79.

117. *The Travel-Diaries of William Beckford of Fonthill*, ed. Guy Chapman, 2 vols., Cambridge, 1928, i. 235.

118. *A Walk through Wales, in August 1797*, Bath, 1798, p. 182.

119. Louis-Antoine de Caraccioli, *Letters on the Manners of the French, and on the Follies and Extravagancies of the Times*, 2 vols., London, 1790, ii. 276.

120. *Letters written during a Residence in England translated from the French of Henry Meister*, pp. 234–5.

121. Leonore Loft, '*Le Journal du Licée de Londres*: A Study in the Pre-Revolutionary French Press', *European History Quarterly*, 23 (1993), 22.

122. Georgiana Chatterton, *Home Sketches and Foreign Recollections*, 3 vols., London, 1841, iii. 256–7.

123. *Memoirs of the Life of Sir James Mackintosh*, 2 vols., London, 1835, i. 174–5.

124. *The Works of George Eliot: Essays and Leaves from a Note-Book*, London, [1884], p. 73.

125. Roy and Dorothy Porter, *In Sickness and in Health: The British Experience*, London, 1988, p. 209.

126. Hester Lynch Piozzi, *Observations and Reflections made in the Course of a Journey through France, Italy, and Germany*, i. 141.

127. *Scarlet and Black*, Penguin edn., p. 290.

128. John Moore, *Mordaunt*, i. 86.

129. John Moore, *A View of Society and Manners in France, Switzerland, and Germany*, ii. 371.

130. S. E. Sprott, *The English Debate on Suicide from Donne to Hume*, La Salle, Ill., 1961, p. 159, prints the statistics employed by contemporaries, drawn from the London Bills of Mortality. The 19th-century evidence is analysed in Olive Anderson, *Suicide in Victorian and Edwardian England*, Oxford, 1987.

131. Charles Dédéyan, *L'Angleterre dans la pensée de Diderot*, p. 254.

132. T. Smollett, *The History of England, from the Revolution in 1688, to the Death of George the Second*, London, 1827, p. 237.

133. The argument is nicely summarized by Roy Porter, 'Civilisation and Disease: Medical Ideology in the Enlightenment', in Jeremy Black and Jeremy Gregory, eds., *Culture, Politics and Society in Britain, 1660–1800*, Manchester, 1991, pp. 154–83.

134. Roy Porter, *Health for Sale*, Manchester, 1989, p. 43.

135. Cornelius Webbe, *Glances at Life in City and Suburb*, pp. 233–4.

136. Francis Bamford, ed., *Dear Miss Heber: An Eighteenth Century Correspondence*, London, 1936, p. 66.

137. *Sydney Gazette and New South Wales Advertiser*, 24 Apr. 1803.

138. *Letters written during a Residence in England translated from the French of Henry Meister*, p. 166.

139. P. W. Clayden, *The Early Life of Samuel Rogers*, London, 1887, p. 446.

140. *The London Journal of Flora Tristan*, p. 18.

141. Amédée de Tissot, *Paris et Londres comparés*, Paris, 1830, p. 22.

142. *Observations sur Londres et ses Environs*, pp. 136, 83.

143. Henri Decremps, *Le Parisien à Londres, ou avis aux français qui vont en Angleterre*, 2 vols., Amsterdam, 1789, i. 207.

144. *Voyages de Montesquieu publiés par Le Baron Albert de Montesquieu*, 2 vols., Bordeaux, 1894, 1896, ii. 223.

145. Conte Giovanni Luigi Ferri di San Costante, *Londres et Les Anglais Par J. L. Ferri de St.-Constant*, 4 vols., Paris, An XII [1804], i. 208.

146. *Letters of a Russian Traveller 1789–1790*, p. 265.

147. *A View of England towards the Close of the Eighteenth Century*, i. 397.

148. Arthur Murphy, *The Englishman from Paris*, introd. Simon Trefman, Augustan Reprint Soc., 1969, p. 24.

149. *Le parisien à Londres, ou avis aux français qui vont en Angleterre*, i. 208–12.

150. J. C. Beltrami, *A Pilgrimage in Europe and America*, i. 213–14.

151. *Christmas at Bracebridge Hall*, London, 1924, pp. 183–4.

152. *A Memoir of the Life and Writings of the late William Taylor of Norwich*, i. 408.

153. C. H. Phipps, *The English in France*, i. 179–80.

154. M. Smith, *Balzac et l'Angleterre. Essai sur l'influence de l'Angleterre sur l'œuvre et la pensée de Balzac*, Londres, 1953, p. 165.
155. Lord John Manners, *A Plea for National Holy-Days*, London, 1843, p. 10.
156. Washington Irving, *Christmas at Bracebridge Hall*, pp. 183-4.
157. Friedrich Kielmansegge, *Diary of a Journey to England in the Years 1761–1762*, trans. Countess Kielmansegg [née Philippa Sidney], London, 1902, p. 214.
158. Carlo Denina, *An Essay on the Revolutions of Literature*, 2 vols., London, 1790, p. 255.
159. *Letters written during a Residence in England translated from the French of Henry Meister*, pp. 172-3.
160. J.-L. Borgerhoff, *Le Théâtre Anglais à Paris*, Paris, 1913, pp. 171 ff.
161. Amédée Pichot, *Historical and Literary Tour*, i. 212-13.
162. Henry Morley, *The Journal of a London Playgoer From 1851 to 1866*, London, 1866, pp. 224-5.
163. Alphonse Esquiros, *The English at Home*, 2nd ser., pp. 16-17.
164. V. A. C. Gattrell, *The Hanging Tree: Execution and the English People 1770–1868*, Oxford, 1994, p. 96.
165. Bombelles, *Journal de voyage en Grande Bretagne et en Irlande 1784*, p. 84.
166. *England und Schottland*, i. 84-5.
167. Victor Hennequin, *Voyage en Angleterre et en Écosse*, p. 311.
168. Pierre-Jean-Baptiste Nougaret, *Londres, la cour et les provinces d'Angleterre, Écosse et d'Irlande*, ii. 39-40.
169. Bombelles, *Journal de voyage en Grande Bretagne et en Irlande 1784*, p. 99.
170. Joseph-Alexis, vicomte Walsh, *Lettres sur l'Angleterre ou voyage Dans la Grande-Bretagne en 1829*, Paris, 1830, p. 315.
171. Adolphe Blanqui, *Voyage d'un jeune français en Angleterre et en Écosse pendant l'automne de 1823*, p. 18.
172. Catherine Sinclair, *Hill and Valley, or Hours in England and Wales*, Edinburgh, 1838, p. 44.
173. Cornwall Record Office, Journals of John Enys, EN 1800: 'A Sketch of a Northern Tour', 8 July 1783, p. 13.
174. [William Macritchie], *Diary of a Tour through Great Britain in 1795*, ed. David MacRitchie, London, 1897, p. 50.
175. John Gamble, *A View of Society and Manners, in the North of Ireland, in the Summer and Autumn of 1812*, p. 374; Nassau William Senior, *Journals, Conversations and Essays Relating to Ireland*, i. 284.
176. Chevalier de Lacoste, *Voyage Philosophique d'Angleterre, fait en 1783 et 1784*, 2 vols., London, 1786, ii. 177.
177. Haussez, *Great Britain in 1833*, i. 81.
178. P. G. Patmore, *Letters on England*, i. 24.
179. Haussez, *Great Britain in 1833*, i. 38.
180. Prince Pückler-Muskau, *Tour in England, Ireland, and France, in the Years 1828 and 1829*, 4 vols., London, 1832, iii. 325.

181. *De Londres et ses Environs*, pp. 19–20 (my translation).

182. *Journal de voyage en Grande Bretagne et en Irlande 1784*, p. 293.

183. Myron F. Brightfield, *Theodore Hook and his Novels*, Cambridge, 1928, p. 293.

184. Charles Johnston, *The Adventures of Anthony Varnish*, 3 vols., London, 1786, i. 97.

185. *Reise durch England und Schottland*, i. 409.

186. *Great Britain in 1833*, i. 98–9.

187. Charles Dédéyan, *L'Angleterre dans la pensée de Diderot*, p. 254.

188. *Letters of a Russian Traveller 1789–1790*, p. 270.

189. *The Memoirs of Charles-Lewis, Baron de Pöllnitz*, 2nd edn., 2 vols., London, 1739, ii. 463.

190. Lacoste, *Voyage Philosophique d'Angleterre, fait en 1783 et 1784*, i. 175–6.

191. *Observations sur Londres et ses Environs*, pp. 16–17; Henry Peckham, *The Tour of Holland, Dutch Brabant, the Austrian Netherlands, and Part of France*, London, 1772, p. 231.

192. Amédée de Tissot, *Paris et Londres comparés*, p. 113.

193. *Boswell's Life of Johnson*, ed. L. F. Powell, 6 vols., Oxford, 1934, ii. 72.

194. *Complete Works of William Hazlitt*, xvii. 156; George Gissing, *The Private Papers of Henry Ryecroft*, Oxford, 1987, p. 59.

195. John Carr, *The Stranger in Ireland*, p. 254.

196. John Milford, *Norway, and her Laplanders, in 1841*, London, 1842, p. 183.

197. *The Diary of Joseph Farington*, ed. K. Garlick, A. Macintyre, Kathryn Cave, 16 vols., New Haven, 1978–98, v. 1669.

198. John Wigley, *The Rise and Fall of the Victorian Sunday*, Manchester, 1980, p. 200.

199. R. H. Dalton Barham, *The Life and Remains of Theodore Edward Hook*, 2 vols., London, 1849, ii. 304.

200. e.g. *The History of Sir Charles Grandison*, 6 vols., Oxford, 1931, iv. 3.

201. Prosper Mérimée, *Études Anglo-Américaines*, ed. Georges Connes, Paris, 1930, p. 268.

202. Sir John Carr, *Descriptive Travels in the Southern and Eastern Parts of Spain and the Balearic Isles, in the Year 1809*, London, 1811, p. 106.

203. *The Works of George Eliot: Essays and Leaves from a Note-Book*, p. 191.

204. Gabriel-François Coyer, *Nouvelles observations sur l'Angleterre*, Paris, 1779, pp. 258–9.

205. Alphonse Esquiros, *The English at Home*, 2nd ser., pp. 202–3.

206. *Observations upon the United Provinces of the Netherlands*, 6th edn., London, 1693, p. 187.

207. *The Works of George Eliot: Essays and Leaves from a Note-Book*, p. 239.

208. Robin Reilly, *Josiah Wedgwood*, London, 1992, p. 134.

209. *London Quarterly Review*, 7 (1856–7), 386, reviewing Emerson's *English Traits*.

210. Coyer, *Nouvelles observations sur l'Angleterre*, pp. 138–40.

211. Doris Gunnell, *Sutton Sharpe et ses amis français*, p. 63.

212. *The London Journal of Flora Tristan*, p. 181.

213. *Briefe zur Characteristik von England gehörig; geschrieben auf einer Reise im Jahre 1784 von Heinrich von Watzdorf*, pp. 42–3.

214. *Sophie in London 1786 being the Diary of Sophie v. la Roche*, p. 213.

215. *Lichtenberg in England*, i. 14.

216. *Memoirs of Charles-Lewis, Baron de Pöllnitz*, i. 54.

217. *Letters from Italy, Describing the Customs and Manners of that Country, In the Years 1765, and 1766*, 2nd edn., London, 1767, p. 141.

218. Amédée Pichot, *Historical and Literary Tour*, i. 295.

219. *Paul's Letters to his Kinsfolk* in *Miscellaneous Works of Sir Walter Scott's*, v. 298 ff.

220. *The Case of the Unfortunate Bosavern Penlez*, London, 1749, p. 45.

221. J. G. Kohl, *Ireland, Scotland, and England*, p. 23.

222. *A Voyage to England*, p. 50.

223. *Great Britain in 1833*, i. 280–1.

224. Édouard de Montulé, *Voyage en Angleterre et en Russie, pendant les années 1821, 1822 et 1823*, i. 288.

225. *L'Angleterre au commencement du dix-neuvième siècle*, p. 365.

226. Richard Chenevix, *An Essay upon National Character*, ii. 229.

227. *J.-P. Brissot: Correspondance et Papiers*, ed. C. Perroud, Paris, 1912, p. 296.

228. *A Trip to Holland, being a Description of the Country, People and Manners*, 1699, p. 7.

229. Charles Dupin, *A Tour through the Naval and Military Establishments of Great Britain, in the Years 1816–17–18–19 and 1820*, London, 1822, p. 99.

230. Lord William Pitt Lennox, *Drafts on my Memory*, 2 vols., London, 1866, i. 142.

231. Edwin Hodder, *The Life and Work of the Seventh Earl of Shaftesbury*, 2 vols., London, 1887, i. 316.

232. *Complete Works of William Hazlitt*, xiv. 17.

233. John Richard, *A Tour from London to Petersburgh, from thence to Moscow, and return to London by way of Courland, Poland, Germany and Holland*, London, 1780, p. 65.

234. Édouard de Montulé, *Voyage en Angleterre et en Russie, pendant les années 1821, 1822 et 1823*, i. 276.

235. Alphonse Esquiros, *The English at Home*, ii. 264.

236. Charles Cottu, *De l'administration de la justice criminelle en Angleterre, et de l'esprit du gouvernement anglais*, Paris, 1820, p. 225.

237. Christopher Duffy, *The Wild Goose and the Eagle: A Life of Marshal von Browne 1705-1757*, London, 1964, p. 6.

238. Alexis de Tocqueville, *Journeys to England and Ireland*, trans. George Lawrence and K. P. Myer, London, 1958, p. 141.

239. *Calendar of State Papers and Manuscripts, Relating to English Affairs, existing in the Archives and Collections of Venice, and in other Libraries of Northern Italy*, viii. 110: Description of England in 1585.

240. Rosemary Ashton, *Little Germany*, p. 67.

241. *Essays Moral, Political and Literary*, p. 207.

242. 'The Jovial Cocker', John Horden, *John Freeth (1731–1808): Political Ballad-Writer and Innkeeper*, Oxford, 1993, pp. 141–2.

243. *Voyages en Anglois et en François d'A. de la Motraye, en diverses provinces et places de la Prusse Ducale et Royale, de la Russie, de la Pologne etc.*, London, 1732, p. 448.

244. Paul C. Weber, *America in Imaginative German Literature in the First Half of the Nineteenth Century*, New York, 1926, pp. 135–6.

245. *Londres et Les Anglais Par J. L. Ferri de St.-Constant*, i. 252.

246. *My Past and Thoughts: The Memoirs of Alexander Herzen*, iii. 1096. This is not to say that Englishmen did not learn the rules of Continental queuing. Balzac, travelling from Paris to Moscow, was dismayed by 'queues in which Englishmen were always first'. Graham Robb, *Balzac*, London, 1794, p. 379.

247. Alphonse Esquiros, *The English at Home*, 3rd ser., p. 95.

248. Steven Marcus, *Engels, Manchester, and the Working Class*, p. 90.

249. Carlo Goldoni, *Pamela Commedia di Carlo Goldoni Avvocato Veneziano translated into English With the Italian Original*, London, 1756, pp. 28–9.

250. Piozzi, *Observations and Reflections made in the Course of a Journey through France, Italy, and Germany*, ii. 181.

251. *An Inquiry into the Present State of Polite Learning*, London, 1759, in *Collected Works of Oliver Goldsmith*, 5 vols., Oxford, 1966, i. 299.

252. De La Vauguyon, *The Truth respecting England*, i. 55.

253. *Extracts from Mr. Burke's Table-Talk, at Crew Hall. Written down by Mrs. Crewe*, in *Miscellanies of the Philobiblon Society*, vol. vii, London, 1862–3, pp. 37–8.

254. Stefan Collini, *Public Moralists: Political Thought and Intellectual Life in Britain, 1850–1930*, pp. 189, 193.

255. *Letters of Matthew Arnold, 1848–1888*, ed. George W. E. Russell, 2 vols., London, 1895, i. 240.

256. Charles de Rémusat, *L'Angleterre au dix-huitième siècle*, i. 43–4.

257. Janet Ross, *Three Generations of English Women*, London, n. d. , pp. 69–70.

258. *Letters written during a Residence in England translated from the French of Henry Meister*, p. 147.

259. Price Collier, *England and the English from an American Point of View*, London, 1909, p. 24.

260. George Jacob Holyoake, *Sixty Years of an Agitator's Life*, i. 34.

261. C. F. Henningsen, *Analogies and Contrasts*, i. 321.

262. James Rutledge, *Essai sur le Caractère et les Moeurs des François comparées à celles des Anglois*, London, 1776, p. 119.

263. J. G. Lockhart, *Peter's Letters to His Kinsfolk*, 2nd edn., 3 vols., London, 1819, i. 42.

264. François Guizot, *An Embassy to the Court of St. James's in 1840*, London, 1862, p. 2.

265. *Crabb Robinson in Germany 1800–1805*, ed. Edith J. Morley, Oxford, 1929, p. 166.

266. *The Autobiography of Leigh Hunt*, ed. J. E. Morpurgo, London, 1949, p. 145.

267. J. Churton Collins, *Voltaire, Montesquieu and Rousseau in England*, London, 1908, p. 181.

268. *The Works of Mr de St. Evremont*, 2 vols., London, 1700, i. 518.

269. *The Englishman at Bourdeaux*, trans. Henry Beaumont, Dublin, 1763, p. 6.

270. *Letters from London: Observations of a Russian, during a Residence in England of Ten Months*, London, 1816, p. 45.

271. N. M. Karamzin, *Letters of a Russian Traveller 1789–1790*, p. 329.

272. *Complete Works of William Hazlitt*, x. 121.

273. Hélène Monod-Cassidy, *Un voyageur-philosophe au XVIIIe siècle: L'Abbé Jean-Bernard le Blanc*, Cambridge, Mass., 1941, p. 342.

274. J. G. Zimmermann, *Essay on National Pride*, trans. Samuel Hull Wilcocke, London, 1797, p. 38.

275. *The Life and Letters of Barthold George Niebuhr*, i. 118–19.

276. John Morley, *The Life of Richard Cobden*, 2 vols., London, 1896, i. 198.

277. Piozzi, *Observations and Reflections made in the Course of a Journey through France, Italy, and Germany*, ii. 140.

278. Ethel Jones, *Les Voyageurs français en Angleterre de 1815 à 1830*, p. 206.

279. *The Works of George Eliot: Essays and Leaves from a Note-Book*, p. 91.

280. Raumer, *England in 1835*, i. 61.

281. Oloff Napea, *Letters from London*, p. 28.

282. Thomas Fielding, *Proverbs of all Nations: Illustrated with Notes and Comments*, 2nd edn., London, 1826, p. xi.

283. *The Life Letters and Literary Remains of Edward Bulwer, Lord Lytton by his son*, 2 vols., London, 1883, i. 264.

284. *Briefe von und an Friedrich von Gentz*, ed. Friedrich Carl Wittichen, 3 vols., Munich, 1909–13, ii. 387.

285. H. Taine, *Notes on England*, p. 306.

286. Charles Dickens, *Sketches by Boz*, London, 1850, p. 115.

287. *Beauchamp's Career*, ed. Margaret Harris, Oxford, 1988, p. 160.

288. Claire Eliane Engel, *Figures et aventures du XVIIIe siècle: Voyages et découvertes de l'abbé Prévost*, Paris, 1939, pp. 228–9.

289. Quoted in W. H. Greenleaf, *The British Political Tradition*, vol. i: *The Rise of Collectivism*, London, 1983, p. 127.

290. *Bagehot's Historical Essays*, ed. Norman St John Stevas, New York, 1966, p. 88.

291. *Letters of Matthew Arnold, 1848–1888*, i. 9.

292. *Londres et Les Anglais Par J. L. Ferri de St.-Constant*, ii. 3.

293. Victor Hennequin, *Voyage en Angleterre et en Écosse*, pp. 118–20.

294. James Rutledge, *Essai sur le Caractère et les Moeurs des François comparées à celles des Anglois*, pp. 33–4.

295. *The Life Letters and Literary Remains of Edward Bulwer, Lord Lytton by his son*, i. 264.

296. Jean-Bernard Le Blanc, *Letters on the English and French Nations*, 2 vols., London, 1747, ii. 354.

297. N. M. Karamzin, *Letters of a Russian Traveller 1789–1790*, p. 207.
298. *Diary of Joseph Farington*, xiv. 5035.
299. *De L'Allemagne*, 2 vols., Paris, 1968, i. 167.
300. *Parliamentary Portraits*, London, 1815, p. 113.
301. James Peller Malcolm, *Anecdotes of the Manners and Customs of London during the Eighteenth Century*, 2nd edn., London, 1810, p. 393.
302. Felix Mac Donogh, *The Hermit Abroad*, 4 vols., London, 1823, i. 92–3.
303. *Mémoires et voyages*, p. 221.
304. Hester Lynch Piozzi, *British Synonymy*, ii. 172–3.
305. *Letters concerning the English Nation by Mr de Voltaire*, London, 1733, pp. 224–6.
306. R. Cru, *Diderot as a Disciple of English Thought*, New York, 1913, p. 30.
307. *A Picture of England*, 2 vols., London, 1789, ii. 171.
308. *Scarlet and Black*, Penguin edn., p. 290.
309. *Mémoires et voyages*, p. 238.
310. Louis Dutens, *Memoirs of a Traveller, Now in Retirement*, iv. 248.
311. Wendeborn, *A View of England towards the Close of the Eighteenth Century*, ii. 124, 181.
312. *Vanity Fair*, 24 Feb. 1877.
313. *Yesterday and To-Day*, 3 vols., London, 1863, iii. 229.
314. Edward George Earle Lytton Bulwer-Lytton, *Godolphin*, 3 vols., London, 1833, i. 226–7.
315. *Letters of Lady Louisa Stuart to Miss Louisa Clinton*, ed. Hon. James A. Home, Edinburgh, 1901, p. 240.
316. Hester Lynch Piozzi, *Observations and Reflections made in the Course of a Journey through France, Italy, and Germany*, i. 299.
317. *The Diary of Frances Lady Shelley*, ed. Richard Edgecumbe, 2 vols., London, 1912, ii. 2.
318. *Bagehot's Historical Essays*, p. 405.
319. Adolphe Blanqui, *Voyage d'un jeune français en Angleterre et en Écosse pendant l'automne de 1823*, pp. 335–6.
320. Frances Acomb, *Anglophobia in France, 1763–1789*, Durham, NC, 1950, p. 9.
321. *London and Westminster Review*, 27 (1837), 3.
322. Peter Marshall, '"Cornwallis Triumphant": War in India and the British Public in the Late Eighteenth Century', in Lawrence Freedman, Paul Hayes, and Robert O'Neill, eds., *War, Strategy, and International Politics: Essays in Honour of Sir Michael Howard*, Oxford, 1992, pp. 57–74.
323. *England und Schottland*, i. 286–9.
324. *The English in France*, iii. 268–70.
325. *De la misère des classes laborieuses en Angleterre et en France*, 2 vols., Paris, 1840, i. 147.
326. Robert Plumer Ward, *De Vere*, 3rd edn., 3 vols., London, 1827, i. 120.
327. Jill Pellew, 'Law and Order: Expertise and the Victorian Home Office', in Roy Macleod, ed., *Government and Expertise: Specialists, Administrators and Professionals, 1860–1919*, Cambridge, 1988, pp. 59–72.

328. Émile Boutmy, *The English People: A Study of their Political Psychology*, London, 1904, p. 108.
329. Alphonse Esquiros, *The English at Home*, 2nd ser., p. 305.
330. *The English at Home*, p. 363.
331. Allen McLaurin, 'Reworking "work" in some Victorian writing and visual art', in Eric Sigsworth, ed., *In Search of Victorian Values: Aspects of Nineteenth-Century Thought and Society*, Manchester, 1988, p. 29.
332. *Whigs and Whiggism: Political Writings by Benjamin Disraeli*, ed. William Hutcheon, Port Washington, 1971, p. 347.
333. Asa Briggs, 'Victorian Values', in *In Search of Victorian Values*, p. 25.

Chapter Two CANDOUR

1. Nicholas K. Robinson, *Edmund Burke: A Life in Caricature*, New Haven, 1996, p. 33.
2. John Forster, *The Life of Charles Dickens*, iii. 125.
3. Ludwig Wolff, *Briefe in die Heimath*, ed. Georg Lotz, 2 vols., Hamburg, 1833, i. 27.
4. *Extracts from Mr. Burke's Table-Talk, at Crew Hall*, p. 11.
5. *Nouvelles observations sur l'Angleterre*, p. 281.
6. Alphonse Esquiros, *The English at Home*, 3rd ser., p. 64.
7. Lord William Pitt Lennox, *Drafts on my Memory*, i. 75.
8. John Moore, *A View of Society and Manners in France, Switzerland, and Germany*, i. 138.
9. *The Memoirs of the Life, and Writings of Percival Stockdale*, 2 vols., London, 1805, i. 296.
10. *The Remains of the Late Mrs. Richard Trench*, ed. by her son the Dean of Westminster, London, 1862, pp. 204–5.
11. Simon McVeigh, *Concert Life in London from Mozart to Haydn*, Cambridge, 1993, p. 129.
12. *Music, Men and Manners in France and Italy 1770*, ed. H. Edmund Poole, London, 1974, p. 127.
13. *Memoirs of the Life of Sir James Mackintosh*, i. 93.
14. Béat Louis Muralt, *Lettres sur les Anglois et les François*, Cologne, 1725, p. 65.
15. John Griscom, *A Year in Europe*, 2 vols., New York, 1823, ii. 87.
16. August Hermann Niemeyer, *Beobachtungen auf Reise in und ausser Deutschland*, 4 vols., Halle, 1820–4, iii. 156: 'Reise durch einen Theil von Westphalen und Holland im Jahr 1806'.
17. M. de Blainville, *Travels through Holland, Germany, Switzerland, and Other Parts of Europe; but especially Italy*, trans. George Turnbull and William Guthrie, 4 vols., London, 1743, iii. 196.
18. *The Diary of Benjamin Robert Haydon*, ed. Willard Bissell Pope, 5 vols., Cambridge, Mass., 1960–3, i. 380.

19. *A Journey to Paris In the Year 1698*, ed. Raymond Phineas Stearns, Urbana, 1967, pp. 1–4.
20. John Moore, *A View of Society and Manners in France, Switzerland, and Germany*, i. 79.
21. P. G. Patmore, *Letters on England. By Victoire, Count de Soligny*, i. 249.
22. Lucette Desvignes-Parent, *Marivaux et l'Angleterre*, Paris, 1970, p. 97.
23. Arthur Murphy, *The Englishman from Paris*, p. 11.
24. Washington Irving, *Christmas at Bracebridge Hall*, p. 157.
25. *Memoirs of Charles-Lewis, Baron de Pöllnitz*, ii. 323; Francis Maximilian Misson, *A New Voyage to Italy*, 2 vols., London, ii. 239.
26. Christopher Hervey, *Letters from Portugal, Spain, Italy and Germany, in the Years 1759, 1760, and 1761*, 3 vols., London, 1785, i. 291.
27. W. L. Sachse, *The Colonial American in Britain*, Madison, 1956, p. 206.
28. *Londres et Les Anglais Par J. L. Ferri de St.-Constant*, i. 146.
29. Elizabeth Davis Bancroft, *Letters from England 1846–1849*, p. 31.
30. *De l'administration de la justice criminelle en Angleterre*, pp. 226–7.
31. Shirley Robert Letwin, *The Gentleman in Trollope: Individuality and Moral Conduct*, London, 1982, p. 18.
32. David Castronovo, *The English Gentleman: Images and Ideals in Literature and Society*, New York, 1987, pp. 44–5.
33. A. Smythe Palmer, *The Ideal of a Gentleman or a Mirror for Gentlefolks*, London, 1908, pp. 276–7.
34. *The Remains of the Late Mrs. Richard Trench*, p. 320.
35. J. Fenimore Cooper, *England*, i. 74–5.
36. *Moral and Historical Memoirs*, London, 1779, p. 7.
37. Ralph Waldo Emerson, *English Traits*, p. 121.
38. Lord William Pitt Lennox, *My Recollections from 1806 to 1873*, ii. 52–3.
39. Thomas Fielding, *Select Proverbs of all Nations*, p. xi.
40. James Moore Smythe, *The Rival Modes*, London, 1727, p. 26.
41. J. Fenimore Cooper, *England*, iii. 197.
42. Benedetta Craveri, *Madame du Deffand and her World*, London, 1994, p. 77.
43. *Complete Works of William Hazlitt*, x. 241.
44. Anthony Trollope, *Can You Forgive Her?*, ed. Andrew Swarbrick, Oxford, 1991, ii. 13.
45. Harriet Beecher Stowe, *Sunny Memories of Foreign Lands*, p. 127.
46. Philip Thicknesse, *Observations on the Customs and Manners of the French nation*, pp. 69–70.
47. Robert Plumer Ward, *De Vere*, ii. 114.
48. *The Remains of the Late Mrs. Richard Trench*, p. 128.
49. Nassau William Senior, *Journals kept in France and Italy from 1848 to 1852*, ed. M. C. M. Simpson, 2 vols., London 1871, ii. 225.
50. *Monthly Review*, 68 (1812), 382.
51. *State of the British and French Colonies in North America*, London, 1755, p. 78.

52. Revd John Davies Mereweather, *Diary of a Working Clergyman in Australia and Tasmania, kept during the years 1850–1853*, p. 268.

53. *Memoirs of the Public Life and Administration of the Right Honourable the Earl of Liverpool*, London, 1827, pp. 1–2.

54. *The King of Saxony's Journey through England and Scotland in the Year 1844*, pp. 36, 157.

55. *Lichtenberg in England*, i. 13–14.

56. *Observations and Reflections made in the Course of a Journey through France, Italy, and Germany*, ii. 246.

57. Pückler-Muskau, *Tour in England, Ireland, and France, in the Years 1828 and 1829*, iii. 124.

58. *The Yale Edition of Horace Walpole's Correspondence*, ed. W. S. Lewis, 48 vols., New Haven, 1937–83, xxxiii. 321.

59. *Sunny Memories of Foreign Lands*, London, 1855, pp. 195–6.

60. *Historical and Literary Tour*, i. 180.

61. *De L'Angleterre*, London, 1811, pp. 296–8.

62. William Howitt, *German experiences*, pp. 35–7.

63. *Notions of the Americans*, 2 vols., London, 1828, ii. 134–5.

64. Henry Goddard, *Memoirs of a Bow Street Runner*, introd. Patrick Pringle, London, 1956, p. 187.

65. *A Series of Letters of the First Earl of Malmesbury his Family and Friends from 1745 to 1820*, 2 vols., London, 1870, i. 193–4.

66. *The Parliamentary Diaries of Sir John Trelawny, 1868–73*, ed. T. A. Jenkins, Camden 5th ser. 3 (1994), p. 438.

67. *English Traits*, pp. 83, 129.

68. *London Chronicle*, 2 Oct. 1812.

69. Charles Robert Middleton, *The Administration of British Foreign Policy, 1782–1846*, Durham, NC, 1977, p. 16.

70. Harriet Beecher Stowe, *Sunny Memories of Foreign Lands*, p. 7.

71. *American Notes*, Oxford Illustrated Dickens, 1987, p. 25.

72. *A Journey from London to Genoa*, ii. 64–5.

73. *Sketches and Fragments*, London, 1822, pp. 39–41.

74. James Murphy, *Travels in Portugal*, London, 1795, p. 4.

75. *Briefe zur Characteristik von England gehörig; geschrieben auf einer Reise im Jahre 1784 von Heinrich von Watzdorf*, p. 25.

76. *On the Alien Bill by an Alien*, London, 1824; A. Defauconpret, *A Fortnight in London*, Paris, 1817, p. 10.

77. Benjamin Silliman, *A Journal of Travels in England, Holland and Scotland, and of Two Passages over the Atlantic, in the Years 1805 and 1806*, 2 vols., New York, 1810, i. 153, 155.

78. Calvin Colton, *Four Years in Great Britain*, New York, new edn., 1836, p. 94.

79. Rosemary Ashton, *Little Germany*, p. 41.

80. David Vincent, 'The Origins of Public Secrecy in Britain', *Trans. Royal Hist. Soc.* 6th ser. 1 (1991), 229.

81. Vere Foster, ed., *The Two Duchesses*, London, 1898, p. 365; *The Diary of Henry Hobhouse (1820–1827)*, ed. Arthur Aspinall, London, 1947, p. 12.

82. R. Therry, *Reminiscences of Thirty Years' Residence in New South Wales and Victoria*, introd. J. M. Bennett, Sydney, 1974, 1st pub. 1863, p. 456.

83. Anthony Trollope, *Phineas Finn*, ed. Jacques Berthoud, Oxford, 1982, p. 152.

84. Wendeborn, *A View of England towards the Close of the Eighteenth Century*, i. 25.

85. *Diary and Correspondence of Charles (Abbot) Lord Colchester*, 3 vols., London, 1861, i. 72.

86. Graham Robb, *Balzac*, p. 267.

87. *Lady Nugent's Journal*, ed. Frank Cundall, London, 1939, p. lxx.

88. Philipp Andreas Nemnich, *Neueste Reise durch England, Schottland, und Ireland*, Tübingen, 1807, p. 83.

89. Hugh Miller, *First impressions of England and its People*, London, 1847, p. 70.

90. *Letters and Papers of John Singleton Copley and Henry Pelham, 1739–1776*, Mass. Hist. Soc. Collections, 71 (1914), 239.

91. *The History of Sir Charles Grandison*, i. 216.

92. *London Chronicle*, 28 Aug. 1812.

93. *London Chronicle*, 22 July 1812.

94. William Byrd, *The London Diary (1717–1721) and Other Writings*, ed. Louis B. Wright and Marion Tinling, New York, 1958, pp. 83, 108.

95. M. E. Matcham, *A Forgotten John Russell*, London, 1905, p. 300.

96. *The History of Sir Charles Grandison*, ii. 214–15.

97. Adrien Fauchier-Magnan, *The Small German Courts in the Eighteenth Century*, London, 1958, pp. 77–8.

98. Samuel Richardson, *The History of Sir Charles Grandison*, ii. 216.

99. Letters at Sheffield City Archives, Wh. M, transcripts, to her daughter, 4 Mar. 1778.

100. Pat Rogers, *Literature and Popular Culture in Eighteenth Century England*, Brighton, 1985, pp. 54–5.

101. *Autobiography of Miss Cornelia Knight, Lady Companion to the Princess Charlotte of Wales*, 2 vols., London, 1860, i. 13.

102. Lydia Smith, 'Journal', *Mass. Hist. Soc. Proc.* 48 (1914–15), 531.

103. *Horace Walpole's Correspondence*, xxiv. 14.

104. *Thomas Platter's Travels in England 1599*, ed. Clare Williams, London, 1937, p. 189; Édouard de Montulé, *Voyage en Angleterre et en Russie, pendant les années 1821, 1822 et 1823*, i. 37.

105. Calvin Colton, *Four Years in Great Britain*, p. 92.

106. Alphonse Esquiros, *The English at Home*, i. 272.

107. *The London Journal of Flora Tristan*, p. 85.

108. T. Mozley, *Reminiscences chiefly of Towns, Villages and Schools*, 2 vols., London, 1885, i. 366.

109. Arthur Ponsonby, *The Decline of Aristocracy*, London, 1912, p. 79; Mary Ellen Chase, *In England Now*, London, 1937, p. 170.

110. Price Collier, *England and the English from an American Point of View*, London, 1909, p. 7.

111. *Voyage en Angleterre et en Écosse*, p. 174.

112. J. Michelet, *Sur les chemins de l'Europe*, p. 41.

113. Harriet Beecher Stowe, *Sunny Memories of Foreign Lands*, p. 21.

114. Edward Topham, *Letters from Edinburgh; Written in the Years 1774 and 1775*, London, 1776, p. 11.

115. C. G. Carus, *The King of Saxony's Journey through England and Scotland in the Year 1844*, pp. 32–3.

116. John Mitchell Kemble, *The Saxons in England*, i. 232.

117. Christopher Mulvey, *Anglo-American Landscapes: A Study of Nineteenth-Century Anglo-American Literature*, Cambridge, 1983, p. 69.

118. M. J. Daunton, *House and Home in the Victorian City: Working-Class Housing 1850–1914*, London, 1983, pp. 266 ff.

119. Archenholz, *A Picture of England*, ii. 45–6.

120. Alphonse Esquiros, *The English at Home*, i. 331.

121. *Londres et Les Anglais Par J. L. Ferri de St.-Constant*, i. 23.

122. Carola Oman, *The Gascoyne Heiress: The Life and Diaries of Frances May Gascoyne-Cecil*, London, 1968, p. 173.

123. P. G. Patmore, *Letters on England*, i. 68–9.

124. *Letters from London: Written during the years 1802 and 1803*, Boston, 1804, p. 30; *Our Old Home*, i. 151.

125. T. Mozley, *Reminiscences*, i. 96.

126. Alphonse Esquiros, *The English at Home*, 3rd ser., pp. 327–38.

127. Fanny Lewald, *England und Schottland*, i. 29.

128. *Crabb Robinson in Germany 1800–1805*, p. 18.

129. A. Alison, *Travels in France, during the Years 1814–15*, 2 vols., Edinburgh, 1815, ii. 256.

130. *Voyages de Montesquieu*, i. 143.

131. *Travels in the Two Sicilies, by Henry Swinburne, Esq. in The Years 1777, 1778, 1779, and 1780*, 2 vols., London, 1783, i. 68.

132. Henry Peckham, *The Tour of Holland, Dutch Brabant, the Austrian Netherlands, and Part of France*, p. 188.

133. *Tour in England, Ireland, and France, in the Years 1828 and 1829*, iv. 185.

134. Maria R. Audubon, *Audubon and his Journals*, 2 vols., London, 1898, i. 273.

135. *Journal by Frances Anne Butler*, 2 vols., London, 1835, ii. 67–8.

136. *The Diary of Philipp von Neumann*, ed. E. Beresford Chancellor, London, 1928, p. 48.

137. Thomas Macdonald, *Thoughts on the Public Duties of Private Life*, London, 1795, p. 47.

138. George W. E. Russell, *Fifteen Chapters of Autobiography*, London, [1915], p. 126.

139. Morris Tilley, *A Dictionary of the Proverbs in England in the Sixteenth and Seventeenth Centuries*, Ann Arbor, 1950, p. 315.

140. Matthew Consett, *A Tour through Sweden, Swedish-Lapland, Finland and Denmark*, London, 1789, p. 103.

141. Alphonse Esquiros, *The English at Home*, i. 138–9.

142. P. Gaskell, *Artisans and Machinery*, repr., London, 1968, pp. 63–4.

143. *The Memories of Dean Hole*, London, n.d., pp. 173–4.

144. Charles-Victor de Bonstetten, *The Man of the North, and the Man of the South; or the Influence of Climate*, New York, 1864, 1st pub. 1827, p. 23.

145. *Journeys to England and Ireland*, p. 96.

146. Ludwig Wolff, *Briefe in die Heimath*, i. 51–2.

147. Samuel Smiles, *Self-Help with Illustrations of Conduct and Perseverance*, p. 220.

148. *Youthful Life, and Pictures of Travel: being the Autobiography of Madame Schopenhauer*, ii. 24.

149. A. de Staël-Holstein, *Letters on England*, pp. 86–7.

150. *Letters written during a Residence in England translated from the French of Henry Meister*, p. 289.

151. François-Jean de Beauvoir, Marquis de Chastellux, *Travels in North-America, In the Years 1780, 1781, and 1782*, trans., 2 vols., London, 1787, ii. 204.

152. *Great Britain in 1833*, i. 44.

153. R. Bakewell, *Travels comprising Observations made during a Residence in the Tarentaise, and various Parts of the Grecian and Pennine Alps, and in Switzerland and Auvergne, in the Years 1820, 1821, and 1822*, 2 vols., London, 1823, i. 79–80.

154. Pückler-Muskau, *Tour in England, Ireland, and France, in the Years 1828 and 1829*, iv. 372.

155. Hester Lynch Piozzi, *Observations and Reflections made in the Course of a Journey through France, Italy, and Germany*, i. 50–1.

156. François Guizot, *An Embassy to the Court of St. James's in 1840*, pp. 175–6.

157. Sylvia Harcstark Myers, *The Bluestocking Circle: Women, Friendship, and the Life of the Mind in Eighteenth-Century England*, Oxford, 1990, p. 141.

158. C. H. Phipps, later Marquess of Normanby, *The English in Italy*, 3 vols., London, 1825, i. 100–1.

159. *The Remains of the Late Mrs. Richard Trench*, p. 169.

160. Lacoste, *Voyage Philosophique d'Angleterre, fait en 1783 et 1784*, i. 214.

161. *Memoirs of the Comtesse de Boigne*, ed. Charles Nicoullaud, 3 vols., London, 1907–8, ii. 144.

162. *The London Journal of Flora Tristan*, pp. 245, 251,

163. Charles Cottu, *De l'administration de la justice criminelle en Angleterre*, p. 226.

164. Henry Taylor, *The Statesman*, London, 1836, pp. 71–2.

165. Maria Edgeworth, *Letters from England 1813–1844*, ed. Christina Colvin, Oxford, 1971, p. 103.

166. Sir Ernest Barker, *Traditions of Civility: Eight Essays*, Cambridge, 1948, chap. 5.

167. Anne Eliza Bray [Mrs Charles Stothard], *Letters written during a Tour through Normandy, Britanny, and Other Parts of France, in 1818*, London, 1820, p. 66.

168. *Corinne ou l'Italie*, 2 vols., London, 1807, i. 277.

169. *The Diary of Frances Lady Shelley*, i. 79.

170. Marc-Auguste Pictet, *Voyage de Trois Mois en Angleterre, en Écosse, et en Irlande pendant l'Été de l'an IX (1801 v. st.)*, Geneva, 1802, p. 138.

171. *Mémoires historiques, littéraires et anecdotiques tirés de la correspondance philosophique et critique, addressée au duc de Saxe Gotha, depuis 1770 jusqu'en 1792, par le baron de Grimm et par Diderot*, 4 vols., London, 1813, iii. 405–6.

172. *Londres et Les Anglais Par J. L. Ferri de St.-Constant*, i. 201.

173. Alphonse Esquiros, *The English at Home*, 2nd ser., pp. 43, 51–9.

174. *Lady Morgan's Memoirs: Autobiography, Diaries and Correspondence*, 2nd edn., 2 vols., London, 1863, ii. 361–2.

175. *A Legend of the Rhine, Notes of a Journey From Cornhill to Grand Cairo and The Book of Snobs*, ed. George Saintsbury, London, [1908], p. 452.

176. John Timbs, *Club Life of London*, 2 vols., London, 1866, i. 248.

177. James Laver, 'Homes and Habits', in Ernest Barker, ed., *The Character of England*, Oxford, 1947, p. 463.

178. Hester Lynch Piozzi, *Observations and Reflections made in the Course of a Journey through France, Italy, and Germany*, i. 93.

179. *Briefe betreffende den allerneuesten Zustand der Religion und der Wissenschaften in Gross-Brittanien*, 4 vols., Hanover, 1752, i. 34; Wendeborn, *A View of England towards the Close of the Eighteenth Century*, i. 372.

180. *Travels*, i. 28.

181. *Memorials of the Life and Character of Lady Osborne and some of her Friends*, ed. by her daughter Mrs Osborne, 2 vols., Dublin, 1870, i. 195.

182. William Cobbett, *Advice to Young Men and (Incidentally) to Young Women in the Middle and Higher Ranks of Life*, p. 153.

183. Carl Philipp Moritz, *Journeys of a German in England in 1782*, trans. and ed. Reginald Nettel, London, 1965, p. 34.

184. Harriet Beecher Stowe, *Sunny Memories of Foreign Lands*, pp. 165–6.

185. Louis Simond, *Journal of a Tour*, ii. 219.

186. Susan Lasdun, *Victorians at Home*, New York, 1981, p. 31.

187. W. F. Mavor, *A Tour in Wales*, p. 19.

188. D. J. Greene, *The Politics of Samuel Johnson*, New Haven, 1960, p. 23.

189. *Correspondence of Emily, Duchess of Leinster (1731–1814)*, vol. i, ed. B. Fitzgerald, Dublin, 1949, p. 389.

190. Historical Manuscripts Commission, *Hastings MSS III*, p. 31; Geijer, *Impressions of England 1809–10*, p. 116.

191. John Griscom, *A Year in Europe*, i. 431.

192. Ludwig Wolff, *Briefe in die Heimath*, i. 17.

193. Leslie A. Marchand, *Byron: A Portrait*, London, 1971, p. 69.

194. Mark Bence-Jones, *Life in an Irish Country House*, London, 1996, p. 120.

195. J. Fenimore Cooper, *England*, i. 220.

196. *Great Britain in 1833*, i. 102–3.

197. *Œuvres complètes de Diderot*, 20 vols., Paris, 1875, ii. 382.

198. *My Contemporaries 1830–1870*, London, 1893, pp. 91–2.

199. *Tales of a Traveller. By Geoffrey Crayon, Gent.*, ii. 75.

200. Fanny Lewald, *England und Schottland*, i. 109.

201. *Complete Works of William Hazlitt*, xvii. 162.

202. Robert Southey, *Letters from England: by Don Manuel Alvarez Espriella*, 3 vols., London, 1807, i. 186.

203. Friedrich Ludwig Wilhelm Philipp, Freiherr von Vincke, *Darstellung der innern Verwaltung Grossbritanniens*, ed. B. G. Niebuhr, Berlin, 1815, p. 3.

204. Alphonse Esquiros, *The English at Home*, 2nd ser., p. 231.

205. P. Gaskell, *Artisans and Machinery*, repr., London, 1968, pp. 115–16.

206. *Bagehot's Historical Essays*, pp. 230–1.

207. *Modern Midnight Conversation, or Matrimonial Dialogues*, London, 1775, p. 188.

208. *Journal of Voyages and Travels*, compiled by James Montgomery, 2 vols., London, 1831, ii. 142.

209. *Lady Nugent's Journal*, p. 254; John Tosh, 'Domesticity and Manliness in the Victorian Middle Class: The Family of Edward White Benson', in Michael Roper and John Tosh, eds., *Manful Assertions: Masculinities in Britain since 1800*, London, 1991, pp. 67–8.

210. *Memories of Old Friends, being Extracts from the Journals and Letters of Caroline Fox of Penjerrick, Cornwall From 1835 to 1871*, ed. Horace N. Pym, 2 vols., London, 1882, ii. 238.

211. Michelle Perrot, ed., *A History of Private Life*, vol. iv: *From the Fires of Revolution to the Great War*, Cambridge, Mass., 1990, pp. 281, 343.

212. Marianne Baillie, *Lisbon in the Years 1821, 1822, and 1823*, 2 vols., London, 1824, ii. 201–2.

213. *English Traits*, pp. 112, 298.

214. Stefan Collini, *Public Moralists: Political Thought and Intellectual Life in Britain, 1850–1930*, p. 134.

215. J. Fenimore Cooper, *England*, iii. 6.

216. J. Foster Palmer, 'The Saxon Influence and its Influence on our Character as a Race', *Trans. Royal Hist. Soc.*, NS 2 (1885), 192.

217. *Parliamentary Portraits*, London, 1815, pp. 225–6.

218. *Bagehot's Historical Essays*, p. 226.

219. *Journeys of a German in England in 1782*, p. 157.

220. Luigi Angiolini, *Lettere sull'Inghilterra*, p. 27.

221. *The Correspondence of William Wilberforce*, 2 vols., London, 1840, i. 360.

222. Cyrus Redding, *Fifty Years' Recollections, Literary and Personal, with Observations on Men and Things*, 3 vols., London, 1858, iii. 94.

223. *Complete Works of William Hazlitt*, viii. 222.

224. *Charis. Ein Magazin für des Neuestes in Kunst, Geschmack und Mode, Lebensgenuss und Lebensglück*, 1804, pp. 181–2.

225. Felix Mac Donogh, *The Hermit Abroad*, i. 30.

226. Cyrus Redding, *Fifty Years' Recollections*, ii. 62.

227. Hon. Grantley F. Berkeley, *My Life and Recollections*, 4 vols., 1865–66, i. 65–6.

228. *The Journal of the Hon. Henry Edward Fox (afterwards fourth and last Lord Holland) 1818–1830*, ed. Earl of Ilchester, London, 1923, p. 203.

229. *Autobiography of Henry Taylor, 1800–1875*, 2 vols., London, 1885, ii. 313.

230. *Diary of Joseph Farington*, ix. 3465.

231. Ibid. v. 1915.

232. *Lettere e Scritti inediti di Pietro e di Alessandro Verri*, ed. Carlo Casati, 3 vols., Milan, 1879–80, ii. 98.

233. C. W. Brooks, 'Interpersonal Conflict and Social Tension: Civil Litigation in England, 1640–1830', in A. L. Beier, David Cannadine, and James M. Rosenheim, eds., *The First Modern Society: Essays in English History in Honour of Lawrence Stone*, Cambridge, 1989, p. 394.

234. Pierre-Jean-Baptiste Nougaret, *Londres, la cour et les provinces d'Angleterre, Écosse et d'Irlande*, ii. 12.

235. Jacques-Pierre Brissot, *New Travels in the United States of America. Performed in 1788*, London, 1792, p. 395.

236. Oloff Napea, *Letters from London*, p. 84.

237. S. H. Jeyes, *The Russells of Birmingham in the French Revolution and in America*, London, 1911, pp. 204–5.

238. John Forster, *The Life of Charles Dickens*, i. 389–90.

239. Prosper Mérimée, *Études Anglo-Américaines*, ed. Georges Connes, Paris, 1930, pp. 153–4.

240. Charles Pinot Duclos, *Voyage en Italie*, Paris, 1791, pp. 104–5.

241. William Archer Shee, *My Contemporaries 1830–1870*, London, 1893, p. 42.

242. Pückler-Muskau, *Tour in England, Ireland, and France, in the Years 1828 and 1829*, iv. 379.

243. *Diary of a Journey to England in the Years 1761–1762*, pp. 47–8.

244. *Reminiscences of Michael Kelly*, i. 71–2.

245. Walter L. Arnstein, 'A German View of English Society: 1851', *Victorian Studies*, 16 (1972–3), 202.

246. Frances Anne Kemble, *Further Records, 1848–1883*, 2 vols., London, 1890, i. 153.

247. Pierre-Jean-Baptiste Nougaret, *Londres, la cour et les provinces d'Angleterre, Écosse et d'Irlande*, i. 434.

248. *Oraisons Funèbres*, London, 1912, p. 19.

249. *Memoirs of the Life of Sir James Mackintosh*, ii. 205–6.

250. Ethel Jones, *Les Voyageurs français en Angleterre de 1815 à 1830*, p. 216.

251. De La Vauguyon, *The Truth respecting England*, i. 80.

252. *London Journal*, quoted David Nokes, *John Gay: A Profession of Friendship*, Oxford, 1995, p. 424.

253. *The Journal of the Hon. Henry Edward Fox (afterwards fourth and last Lord Holland) 1818–1830*, p. 49.

254. *The English Universities*, ed. Francis W. Newman, 3 vols., London, 1843, ii. 312–13.

255. Leslie A. Marchand, *Byron: A Portrait*, p. 316.

256. Washington Irving, *Tales of a Traveller. By Geoffrey Crayon, Gent.*, ii. 77; *English Traits*, Boston, 1856, p. 125.

257. Mabell, Countess of Airlie, *Lady Palmerston and her Times*, 2 vols., London, 1922, ii. 37.

258. John Forster, *The Life of Charles Dickens*, i. 55–6.

259. Henri Decremps, *Le Parisien à Londres*, i. 200.

260. C. H. Phipps, later Marquess of Normanby, *Matilda; a Tale of the Day*, 2 vols., London, 1826, i. 41.

261. W. B. Whittaker, *The Eighteenth-Century English Sunday*, London, 1840, p. 163.

262. Alphonse Esquiros, *The English at Home*, ii. 263.

263. F. Mac Donogh, *The Hermit in London: or, Sketches of English Manners*, 5 vols., London, 1819–20, ii. 118–19.

264. De La Vauguyon, *The Truth respecting England*, i. 74–5.

265. Amédée Pichot, *Historical and Literary Tour*, i. 230.

266. C. H. Phipps, *The English in France*, i. 183.

267. *Complete Works of William Hazlitt*, xvii. 354.

268. Hester Lynch Piozzi, *Observations and Reflections made in the Course of a Journey through France, Italy, and Germany*, ii. 214–15.

269. *English Traits*, pp. 125, 188.

270. Madame d'Avot, *Lettres sur l'Angleterre, ou deux années à Londres*, p. 63.

271. Carola Oman, *The Gascoyne Heiress: The Life and Diaries of Frances May Gascoyne-Cecil*, p. 260.

272. *Diary of Joseph Farington*, vi. 2410.

273. *Paupers and Pig Killers: The Diary of William Holland, A Somerset Parson, 1799–1818*, Gloucester, 1984, p. 252.

274. *Australia*, ed. P. D. Edwards and R. B. Joyce, St Lucia, Queensland, 1967, p. 53.

275. *Neueste Historische und Staats Bibliothek*, 1759, pp. 138–9, reviewing *L'Albionade ou l'Anglais démarqué*, Aix, 1759.

276. *The Greville Memoirs. A Journal of the Reigns of King George IV. and King William IV. By the late C. F. Greville., Esq.*, 3rd edn., 3 vols., London, 1875, i. 104.

277. *Memoirs of the Comtesse de Boigne*, ii. 231.

278. James Anthony Froude, *Thomas Carlyle: A History of His Life in London, 1834–1881*, 2 vols., London, 1884–5, i. 224, ii. 20, 87, 448.

279. Cyrus Redding, *Yesterday and To-Day*, 3 vols., London, 1863, i. 102–3.

280. S. Koss, *The Rise and Fall of the Political Press in Britain*, London, 1990, p. 1116; François Bédarida, *A Social History of England 1851–1975*, trans. A. S. Forster, London, 1979, p. 299.

281. Wilhelm Dibelius, *England*, London, 1930, orig. German 1922, p. 499.

Chapter Three DECENCY

1. *M. Misson's Memoirs and Observations in his Travels over England*, trans. John Ozell, London, 1719, p. 304.

2. *A Selection from the Diaries of Edward Henry Stanley, 15th Earl of Derby (1826–93) between September 1869 and March 1878*, ed. John Vincent, Camden 5th ser. 4 (1994), pp. 446–7.

3. Louis-Sébastien Mercier, *New Picture of Paris*, 2 vols., London, 1800, ii. 312.

4. *Diary of Frederick Mackenzie*, 2 vols., Cambridge, Mass., 1930, i. 111.

5. John Moore, *Mordaunt*, i. 341.

6. *Complete Works of William Hazlitt*, xv. 279.

7. Harriet Pigott, *Records of Real Life in the Palace and the Cottage*, ed. John Galt, 3 vols., London 1839, i. 169–70.

8. John Childs, *The Army of Charles II*, London, 1976, p. 216, and *The Army of James II*, Manchester, 1980, pp. 88, 95, 99.

9. W. A. Speck, *The Butcher: The Duke of Cumberland and the Suppression of the 45*, Oxford, 1981, pp. 145, 157, 199.

10. T. Pakenham, *The Year of Liberty: The Story of the Great Irish Rebellion of 1798*, London, 1969, p. 341.

11. *A Series of Letters of the First Earl of Malmesbury*, ii. 336–7.

12. R. E. Scouller, *The Armies of Queen Anne*, Oxford, 1966, p. 283.

13. Henry Matthews, *The Diary of an Invalid*, ii. 182.

14. *Fifty Years' Recollections*, i. 311.

15. Emma Sophia Cust, Countess Brownlow, *Slight Reminiscences of a Septuagenarian from 1802 to 1815*, London, 1867, pp. 169–71.

16. Adolphe Blanqui, *Voyage d'un jeune français en Angleterre et en Écosse pendant l'automne de 1823*, p. 330.

17. Raumer, *England in 1835*, ii. 120.

18. *Memoirs of Charles-Lewis, Baron de Pöllnitz*, ii. 456.

19. *Complete Works of William Hazlitt*, xvii. 154–5.

20. John Andrews, *An Account of the Character and Manners of the French; with occasional Observations on the English*, 2 vols., London, 1770, i. 58–9.

21. *Letters of Mrs. Adams, the Wife of John Adams*, 2 vols., Boston, 1890, p. 122.

22. Martin Lister, *A Journey to Paris in the Year 1698*, ed. Raymond Phineas Stearns, Urbana, 1967, p. 23.

23. *Observations upon the United Provinces of the Netherlands*, 6th edn., London, 1693, pp. 181–2.

24. *The Dutch Displayed*, London, 1766.

25. George Thompson, *Travels and Adventures in Southern Africa*, p. 29.

26. Charles Dédéyan, *L'Angleterre dans la pensée de Diderot*, p. 254. See below, p. 271.

27. Benjamin Waterhouse, *A Journal of a Young Man of Massachusetts*, Boston, 1816, repr. *The Magazine of History*, 1911, pp. 26–7.

28. *The Life and Adventures of John Nicol Mariner*, by Gordon Grant, London, 1937, 1st pub. 1822, p. 123.

29. Edward C. Mack, *Public Schools and British Opinion 1780 to 1860*, London, 1938, p. 165.

30. Heinrich Heine, *English Fragments*, trans. Sarah Norris, Edinburgh, 1880, p. 44.

31. Archenholz, *A Picture of England*, i. 40.

32. *Nouvelles observations sur l'Angleterre*, pp. 265–6.

33. Ferdinand Galiani, *Correspondance inédite de l'Abbé Ferdinand Galiani*, 2 vols., Paris, 1818, i. 200.

34. *L'Angleterre au commencement du dix-neuvième siècle*, p. 33.

35. *The History and Remarkable Life of the truly honourable Col. Jacque commonly call'd Col. Jack*, ed. Samuel Holt Monk, London, 1965, p. 185.

36. Georg Wilhelm Alberti, *Briefe*, i. 24.

37. John Andrews, *An Account of the Character and Manners of the French*, i. 58–9.

38. Archenholz, *A Picture of England*, ii. 123.

39. 21 May 1713.

40. W. B. Boulton, *The Amusements of Old London*, 2 vols., London, 1901, ii. 251–2.

41. Keith Thomas, *Man and the Natural World: Changing Attitudes in England 1500–1800*, London, 1983, pp. 173 ff.

42. Harriet Ritvo, *The Animal Estate*, London, 1990, p. 129.

43. Wendeborn, *A View of England towards the Close of the Eighteenth Century*, i. 383.

44. Madame d'Avot, *Lettres sur l'Angleterre, ou deux années à Londres*, p. 256.

45. *Voyage d'un jeune français en Angleterre et en Écosse pendant l'automne de 1823*, pp. 92, 94.

46. *L'Angleterre vue à Londres et dans ses provinces*, Paris, 1815.

47. *So Dearly Loved, So Much Admired: Letters to Hester Pitt, Lady Chatham from her relations and friends, 1744–1801*, ed. Vere Bindwood, London, 1994, p. 247.

48. *Un Prussien en France en 1792 Strasbourg—Lyon—Paris: Lettres Intimes de J. F. Reichardt*, trans. and annot. A. Laquiante, Paris, 1892, p. 409.

49. Emma Sophia Cust, Countess Brownlow, *Slight Reminiscences of a Septuagenarian from 1802 to 1815*, pp. 170–1.

50. C. F. Henningsen, *Analogies and Contrasts*, i. 162–3.

51. Robert W. Malcolmson, *Popular Recreations in English Society 1700–1850*, Cambridge, 1973, chap. 6.

52. Richard Holt, *Sport and the British*, Oxford, 1989, p. 116.

53. Michel Angelo, *Juvenile Sports and Pastimes*, 2nd edn., London, 1776, pp. 94–5.

54. *Londres et les Anglais Par J. L. Ferri de St.-Constant*, i. 283–5.

55. Béat Louis Muralt, *Letters describing the Character and Customs of the English and French Nations*, p. 38.

56. Samuel Sharp, *Letters from Italy, Describing the Customs and Manners of that Country, In the Years 1765, and 1766*, p. 175.

57. *Boxiana*, 3 vols., London, 1930, iii. 582.

58. V. G. Kiernan, *The Duel in European History: Honour and the Reign of Aristocracy*, Oxford, 1988, p. 102.
59. *The Memoirs of James Stephen Written by Himself for the Use of His Children*, ed. Merle M. Bevington, London, 1954, p. 113.
60. Bruce C. Daniels, *Puritans at Play: Leisure and Recreation in Colonial New England*, London, 1995, chap. 9.
61. See above, p. 47.
62. *Travels in North America, in the Years 1827 and 1828*, 3 vols., Edinburgh, 1829, iii. 147–8.
63. Charles Sealsfield, *The Americans as they are*, London, 1828, p. 26.
64. *The American Geographer*, new edn., London, 1794, p. 524.
65. Charles Sealsfield, *The Americans as they are*, p. 50.
66. Charles William Janson, *The Stranger in America*, London, 1807, p. 304.
67. Basil Hall, *Travels in North America, in the Years 1827 and 1828*, iii. 307.
68. *Port Philip Herald*, 13 Mar. 1845.
69. J. A. Mangan, *The Games Ethic and Imperialism: Aspects of the Diffusion of an Ideal*, London, 1986, p. 164.
70. *The Life and Adventures of John Nicol Mariner*, pp. 37–8.
71. *Letters written during a Residence in England translated from the French of Henry Meister*, p. 8.
72. Anthony Trollope, *Phineas Finn*, ed. Jacques Berthoud, Oxford, 1982, pp. 82–3.
73. *Complete Works of William Hazlitt*, xix. 267.
74. *A Collection of Letters, made by Sir Tobie Mathews Kt.*, London, 1660, 'To the Reader'.
75. *Diary of Joseph Farington*, xiii. 4676–7: 20 July 1815.
76. *Sydney Monitor*, 23 Mar. 1827.
77. Fanny Lewald, *The Italians at Home*, 2 vols., London, 1848, i. 75.
78. *Travels in North America, in the Years 1827 and 1828*, ii. 21–2.
79. Rousseau, *Émile*, Paris, 1992, p. 169.
80. J. C. Beltrami, *A Pilgrimage in Europe and America*, i. 363.
81. Haussez, *Great Britain in 1833*, ii. 11.
82. P. G. Patmore, *Letters on England*, i. 241.
83. René-Martin Pillet, *L'Angleterre vue à Londres et dans ses provinces*, pp. 131–5.
84. Fanny Lewald, *The Italians at Home*, i. 150–1.
85. Richard Chenevix, *An Essay upon National Character*, i. 176–8.
86. *England*, i. 182.
87. T. Wemyss Reid, *The Life, Letters, and Friendships of Richard Monckton Milnes, first Lord Houghton*, 2 vols., London, 1890, ii. 2.
88. Historical Manuscripts Commission, *Dropmore I*, p. 609.
89. *Letters written during a Residence in England translated from the French of Henry Meister*, p. 32.
90. S. H. Jeyes, *The Russells of Birmingham in the French Revolution and in America*, London, 1911, pp. 125–6.

91. 'Salvation' Murray, writing to Cyrus Redding's grandfather in England, Cyrus Redding, *Yesterday and To-Day*, i. 158.
92. *The Stranger in Ireland*, pp. 377, 469.
93. Thomas Hamilton, *Men and Manners in America*, Philadelphia, 1833, pp. 26–7.
94. *Diary of Joseph Farington*, v. 1850.
95. Washington Irving, *Christmas at Bracebridge Hall*, p. 181.
96. J. Fenimore Cooper, *England*, i. 200.
97. Helen Maria Williams, *Sketches of the State of Manners and Opinions in the French Republic, towards the Close of the Eighteenth Century*, 2 vols., London, 1801, i. 183–4.
98. *Crabb Robinson in Germany 1800–1805*, p. 147.
99. Alfred Iacuzzi, *The European Vogue of Favart: The Diffusion of the Opéra-Comique*, New York, 1932, pp. 334–5.
100. *Londres et Les Anglais Par J. L. Ferri de St.-Constant*, chap. 115.
101. Felix Mac Donogh, *The Hermit Abroad*, iii. 184.
102. *The Diary of Frances Lady Shelley*, i. 313–14.
103. *Notes on the West Indies*, ii. 407.
104. John Milford, *Observations, Moral, Literary, and Antiquarian, made during a Tour through the Pyrennees, South of France, Switzerland, the whole of Italy, and the Netherlands, in the years 1814 and 1815*, 2 vols., London, 1818, i. 25.
105. Anna Eliza Bray [Mrs Charles Stothard], *Letters written during a Tour through Normandy, Britanny, and Other Parts of France, in 1818*, pp. 77–8.
106. C. F. Henningsen, *Analogies and Contrasts*, i. 176–8.
107. C. H. Phipps, *The English in Italy*, i. 28.
108. John Forster, *The Life of Charles Dickens*, ii. 100.
109. C. H. Phipps, *The English in France*, iii. 113.
110. *Letters of Lady Louisa Stuart to Miss Louisa Clinton*, 2nd ser., ed. Hon. James A. Home, Edinburgh, 1903, p. 326.
111. *De l'administration de la justice criminelle en Angleterre*, p. 228.
112. R. Warwick Bond, ed., *The Marlay Letters 1778–1820*, London, 1937, pp. 86–7.
113. *Crabb Robinson in Germany 1800–1805*, p. 30.
114. Thomas Thornton, *A Sporting Tour through Various Parts of France, in the Year 1802*, 2 vols., London, 1806, i. 143.
115. Felix Mac Donogh, *The Hermit Abroad*, iv. 74.
116. *Table Talk*, ed. Carl Woodring, 2 vols., London, 1990, in *The Collected Works of Samuel Taylor Coleridge*, xiv. 60.
117. John Essex, *The Young Ladies Conduct*, London, 1722, p. 47.
118. Anna Eliza Bray [Mrs Charles Stothard], *Letters written during a Tour through Normandy, Britanny, and Other Parts of France, in 1818*, p. 19.
119. *Spectator*, 240.
120. William Brenchley Rye, *England as seen by Foreigners in the Days of Elizabeth and James the First*, p. 90.

121. *The Works of Adam Petrie, The Scottish Chesterfield*, Edinburgh, 1877, p. 26.
122. Louis-Sébastien Mercier, *Tableau de Paris*, 8 vols., Amsterdam, 1783, viii. 157–9.
123. Joseph Fiévée, *Lettres sur L'Angleterre, et Reflexions sur la Philosophie du XVIIIe Siècle*, Paris, 1802, p. 203.
124. *Letters from Edinburgh; Written in the Years 1774 and 1775*, p. 39.
125. Jérôme Lalande, *Journal d'un voyage en Angleterre 1763*, ed. Hélène Monod-Cassidy, Oxford, 1980, p. 91.
126. *Letters written during a Residence in England translated from the French of Henry Meister*, p. 282.
127. Pierre-Jean Grosley, *A Tour to London; or, New Observations on England, and its Inhabitants*, trans. Thomas Nugent, 2 vols., London, 1772, i. 255.
128. *Travels through Germany. With a Particular Account of the Courts of Mecklenburg*, 2 vols., London, 1768, i. 58.
129. *Travels in Italy, between the Years 1792 and 1798*, 2 vols., London, 1802, i. 312.
130. H. E. Busteed, *Echoes of Old Calcutta*, Calcultta, 1888, p. 123.
131. Alice Morse Early, *Two Centuries of Costume in America*, 2 vols., New York, 1903, ii. 721.
132. *South Carolina Historical and Genealogical Magazine*, 21 (1920), 43.
133. Harriet Beecher Stowe, *Sunny Memories of Foreign Lands*, p. 124.
134. William Pitt, *The Cabin Boy: being the Memoirs of an Officer in the Civil Department of H.M. Navy, well known by the Name of 'Billy Pitt', and who died at Malta in the Month of August, 1839*, London, 1840, p. 15.
135. Bombelles, *Journal de voyage en Grande Bretagne et en Irlande 1784*, pp. 88–9.
136. J. Churton Collins, *Voltaire, Montesquieu and Rousseau in England*, p. 20.
137. *L'Angleterre et les Anglais, ou petit portrait d'une grande famille; copié et retouché par deux témoins oculaires*, iii. 557.
138. *Observations on the Customs and Manners of the French nation*, p. 25.
139. British Library, Add. MS 32442, fo. 161.
140. Samuel Sharp, *Letters from Italy, Describing the Customs and Manners of that Country, In the Years 1765, and 1766*, p. 44.
141. *Horace Walpole's Correspondence*, xx. 339–40.
142. *Letters written during a Residence in England translated from the French of Henry Meister*, pp. 283–4.
143. Johanna Schopenhauer, *Reise durch England und Schottland*, i. 142.
144. Victor Hennequin, *Voyage en Angleterre et en Écosse*, p. 280.
145. *Letters written during a Residence in England translated from the French of Henry Meister*, pp. 284–5.
146. *Lettres sur L'Angleterre, et Reflexions sur la Philosophie du XVIIIe Siècle*, Paris, 1802, p. 203.
147. Archenholz, *A Picture of England*, ii. 136.

148. Marc-Auguste Pictet, *Voyage de Trois Mois en Angleterre, en Écosse, et en Irlande pendant l'Été de l'an IX*, p. 21.

149. Fanny Lewald, *The Italians at Home*, i. 137–8.

150. Fanny Lewald, *England und Schottland*, i. 346–7.

151. John Milford, *Peninsular Sketches, during a recent Tour*, London, 1816, p. 12.

152. William Pitt, *The Cabin Boy*, p. 153.

153. *Mémoires, Lettres et Pensées*, préface de Chantal Thomas, Paris, 1989, p. 220.

154. *Letters written during a Residence in England translated from the French of Henry Meister*, p. 170.

155. Philippe Berthier, 'Stendhal et les demoiselles de Westminster Road', in K. G. McWatters and C. W. Thompson, eds., *Stendhal et l'Angleterre*, pp. 295–304.

156. William Macritchie, *Diary of a Tour through Great Britain in 1795*, ed. David MacRitchie, London, 1897, p. 77.

157. *Impressions of England 1809–10*, p. 249.

158. *The Young Ladies Conduct*, p. 5.

159. Pollier, *Du Gouvernement des Moeurs*, Lausanne, 1784, p. 84.

160. A. Alison, *Travels in France, during the Years 1814–15*, i. 137.

161. *De L'Allemagne*, i. 66.

162. Charles William Janson, *The Stranger in America*, p. 87.

163. *Journal by Frances Anne Butler*, i. 259.

164. J. B. Moreton, *West India Customs and Manners*, London, 1793, p. 109.

165. *Sophie in London 1786 being the Diary of Sophie v. la Roche*, p. 249.

166. Adolphe Blanqui, *Voyage d'un jeune français en Angleterre et en Écosse pendant l'automne de 1823*, p. 76.

167. C. H. Phipps, *The English in Italy*, i. 103.

168. M. Smith, *Balzac et l'Angleterre. Essai sur l'influence de l'Angleterre sur l'œuvre et la pensée de Balzac*, London, 1953, pp. 141–2.

169. Béat-Louis Muralt, *Letters describing the Character and Customs of the English and French Nations*, i. 37.

170. *Journal of a Tour*, ii. 250.

171. Haussez, *Great Britain in 1833*, i. 89.

172. *Complete Works of William Hazlitt*, x. 250.

173. Madame de Staël, *Corinne ou l'Italie*, i. 273–4.

174. *L'Angleterre au commencement du dix-neuvième siècle*, p. 148.

175. *Historical and Literary Tour of a Foreigner in England and Scotland*, i. 350–1.

176. *Advice to Young Men and (Incidentally) to Young Women in the Middle and Higher Ranks of Life*, p. 226.

177. Amédée de Tissot, *Paris et Londres comparés*, p. 22.

178. *Journeys to England and Ireland*, pp. 191–2.

179. J. Fenimore Cooper, *England*, i. 187.

180. Hester Lynch Piozzi, *British Synonymy*, ii. 170.

181. C. F. Henningsen, *Analogies and Contrasts*, i. 320.

Chapter Four TACITURNITY

1. *ODEP* (1935), pp. 76, 392.
2. Frances Acomb, *Anglophobia in France, 1763–1789*, p. 11.
3. Charles-Victor de Bonstetten, *The Man of the North, and the Man of the South; or the Influence of Climate*, p. 102.
4. *Caspar Voght und sein Hamburger Freundeskreis*, ed. Kurt Detlev Möller and Annelise Tecke, 3 vols., Hamburg, 1959–67, ii. 19.
5. C. G. Carus, *The King of Saxony's Journey through England and Scotland in the Year 1844*, p. 36.
6. Lacoste, *Voyage Philosophique d'Angleterre, fait en 1783 et 1784*, i. 211.
7. Haussez, *Great Britain in 1833*, i. 27.
8. *Observations sur Londres et ses Environs*, p. 11.
9. J. Fenimore Cooper, *England*, i. 10.
10. *The London Journal of Flora Tristan*, p. 69.
11. J. G. Kohl, *Ireland*, London, 1843, p. 131.
12. R. Warwick Bond, ed., *The Marlay Letters 1778–1820*, pp. 86–7.
13. *Briefe in die Heimath*, i. 21–2.
14. Marianne Baillie, *First Impressions on a Tour upon the Continent, in the Summer of 1818*, p. 69.
15. *Notes on England*, trans. W. F. Rae, London, 1872, pp. 14 15.
16. Moritz, *Journeys of a German in England in 1782*, pp. 175–6.
17. Sir John Carr, *Descriptive Travels in the Southern and Eastern Parts of Spain and the Balearic Isles, in the Year 1809*, p. 73.
18. Wendeborn, *A View of England towards the Close of the Eighteenth Century*, i. 405.
19. Louis-Sébastien Mercier, *Memoirs of the Year Two Thousand Five Hundred*, Liverpool, 1802, p. 26.
20. *The Works of Walter Savage Landor*, ed. P. Earle Welby, 8 vols., London, 1876, iv. 281.
21. *Impressions of England 1809–10*, p. 146.
22. Heinrich Meidinger, *Briefe von einer Reise durch England, Schottland und Irland im Frühjahr und Sommer 1820*, pp. 4, 38–9.
23. Joseph Fiévée, *Lettres sur L'Angleterre, et Reflexions sur la Philosophie du XVIIIe Siècle*, p. 57.
24. *Letters of Matthew Arnold, 1848–1888*, ii. 229.
25. W. Cooke Taylor, *Notes of a Tour in the Manufacturing Districts of Lancashire*, pp. 8–9.
26. Anne-Marie du Boccage, *Letters concerning England, Holland and Italy*, 2 vols., London, 1770, i. 17.
27. J. C. Beltrami, *A Pilgrimage in Europe and America*, i. 329.
28. *Londres et Les Anglais Par J. L. Ferri de St.-Constant*, i. 206.
29. *Historical and Literary Tour*, i. 188.
30. *The London Journal of Flora Tristan*, pp. 263–4.

31. Ethel Jones, *Les Voyageurs français en Angleterre de 1815 à 1830*, p. 170.
32. *Londres et Les Anglais Par J. L. Ferri de St.-Constant*, i. 213–14.
33. S. H. Jeyes, *The Russells of Birmingham in the French Revolution and in America*, London, 1911, p. 105.
34. *Ireland, Scotland, and England*, London, 1844, pp. 113–14.
35. *De L'Allemagne*, i. 101.
36. R. Bakewell, *Travels comprising Observations*, i. 109–10.
37. *The Remains of the Late Mrs. Richard Trench*, p. 372.
38. Walter L. Arnstein, ed., 'A German View of English Society: 1851', *Victorian Studies*, 16 (1972–3), 186.
39. John Milford, *Observations, Moral, Literary, and Antiquarian*, i. 110–11; *The Diary of Philipp von Neumann*, p. 61.
40. *Letters from England 1813–1844*, p. 92.
41. Pierre-Jean Grosley, *A Tour to London*, i. 90.
42. Madame de Staël, *Corinna, or Italy*, 3 vols., London, 1807, i. 372–3.
43. Louis Simond, *Journal of a Tour*, ii. 143.
44. John Griscom, *A Year in Europe*, i. 262.
45. William White, *The Inner Life of the House of Commons*, ed. Justin McCarthy, 2 vols., London, 1897, i. 28, 41.
46. F. Mac Donogh, *The Hermit in London*, i. 81.
47. *A Pilgrimage in Europe and America*, i. 314.
48. J. Gamble, *A View of Society and Manners, in the North of Ireland, in the Summer and Autumn of 1812*, p. 304.
49. 'Tours of Lord Sheffield', British Library, Add. MS 34887, fos. 136–7: 19 Dec. 1763.
50. John Lough, *France Observed in the Seventeenth Century by British Travellers*, Boston, 1985, p. 215.
51. Alan Bell, *Sydney Smith: A Biography*, Oxford, 1980, pp. 51, 29.
52. *Monthly Review*, 69 (1812), 461, citing Cardinal Jean-Siffrein Maury (1746–1816).
53. Béat Louis Muralt, *Letters describing the Character and Customs of the English and French Nations*, p. 7.
54. Heinrich Heine, *Italian Travel Sketches*, trans. Elizabeth Sharp, London, 1927, pp. 231–2.
55. Alphonse Esquiros, *The English at Home*, 2nd ser., pp. 202–4.
56. G. A. Crapelet, *Souvenirs de Londres en 1814 et 1816*, p. 135.
57. *Briefe von und an Friedrich von Gentz*, ii. 395.
58. Jeremy Horder, *Provocation and Responsibility*, Oxford, 1992.
59. Alphonse Esquiros, *The English at Home*, 2nd ser., p. 143.
60. Alphonse Esquiros, *The English at Home*, 3rd ser., p. 95.
61. Count Édouard de Melfort, *Impressions of England*, i. 79 ff.
62. *Letters of Mrs Adams, the Wife of John Adams*, ii. 107.
63. Myron F. Brightfield, *Theodore Hook and his Novels*, Cambridge, 1928, p. 282.
64. Ralph Waldo Emerson, *English Traits*, p. 117.
65. *Our Old Home*, 2 vols., London, 1863, ii. 249.

66. *Life, Letters and Journals of Sir Charles Lyell, Bart.*, ed. Mrs Lyell, 2 vols., London, 1881, i. 122–3.

67. *The Diary of an Invalid*, i. 222.

68. John Andrews, *An Account of the Character and Manners of the French*, i. 158.

69. Raumer, *England in 1835*, iii. 30.

70. Alan Bell, *Sydney Smith: A Biography*, p. 190.

71. Felix Mac Donogh, *The Hermit Abroad*, ii. 67–8.

72. *The Court of London from 1819 to 1825*, ed. Benjamin Rush, London, 1873, p. 149.

73. Anna Eliza Bray [Mrs Charles Stothard], *Letters written during a Tour through Normandy, Britanny, and Other Parts of France, in 1818*, p. 7.

74. *Letters of Lady Louisa Stuart to Miss Louisa Clinton*, 2nd ser., p. 273.

75. Lady Newdigate-Newdigate, *The Cheverals of Cheveral Manor*, London, 1898, p. 24.

76. *Hill and Valley, or Hours in England and Wales*, pp. 362–3.

77. Anne-Marie du Boccage, *Letters concerning England, Holland and Italy*, i. 7.

78. Louis Simond, *Journal of a Tour*, i. 27; Raumer, *England in 1835*, ii. 55.

79. P. G. Patmore, *Letters on England*, i. 253, 255.

80. René-Martin Pillet, *L'Angleterre vue à Londres et dans ses provinces*, p. 324.

81. *Travels in France, during the Years 1814–15*, ii. 269.

82. Martin Murphy, *Blanco White: Self Banished Spaniard*, p. 63.

83. *Memoirs of a Family in Swisserland*, 4 vols., London, 1802, i. 166–7.

84. William Archer Shee, *My Contemporaries 1830–1870*, p. 73.

85. Christopher Hervey, *Letters from Portugal, Spain, Italy and Germany, in the Years 1759, 1760, and 1761*, ii. 508.

86. Wendeborn, *A View of England towards the Close of the Eighteenth Century*, i. 405–6.

87. Béat Louis Muralt, *Letters describing the Character and Customs of the English and French Nations*, p. 57.

88. *Letters written during a Tour through Normandy, Britanny, and Other Parts of France, in 1818*, p. 145.

89. *The Englishman from Paris*, p. 28.

90. *The Lounger*, 3 vols., Edinburgh, 1787, ii. 66.

91. John Moore, *Mordaunt*, i. 347–8.

92. *The Poetical Works of William Cowper*, ed. William Benham, London, 1908, pp. 136–7.

93. F. Holdsworth, *Joseph de Maistre et l'Angleterre*, Paris, 1935, p. 40.

94. Robert L. Patten, *George Cruickshank's Life, Times, and Art*, vol. i: *1792–1835*, London, 1992, p. 77.

95. Marcia Pointon, *Hanging the Head: Portraiture and Social Formation in Eighteenth-Century England*, New Haven, 1993, p. 159.

96. See Mary Vidal, *Watteau's Painted Conversations: Art, Literature, and Talk in Seventeenth- and Eighteenth-Century France*, New Haven, 1992.

97. Georgiana Chatterton, *Home Sketches and Foreign Recollections*, iii. 156–7.

98. J. Fenimore Cooper, *England*, ii. 129–30.

99. P. W. Clayden, *Rogers and his Contemporaries*, 2 vols., London, 1889, i. 422.

100. P. W. Clayden, *The Early Life of Samuel Rogers*, p. 423.

101. *Memoirs and Correspondence of Francis Horner, M.P.*, ed. Leonard Horner, 2 vols., London, 1843, i. 183.

102. Alan Bell, *Sydney Smith: A Biography*, p. 195.

103. Elizabeth Davis Bancroft, *Letters from England 1846–1849*, p. 75.

104. *Quarterly Review*, 59 (1837), 438–9.

105. *Edinburgh Review*, 32 (1819), 82–3.

106. *Correspondence of Emily, Duchess of Leinster (1731–1814)*, i. 231.

107. *Extracts from Mr Burke's Table-Talk, at Crew Hall*, pp. 14–15.

108. R. Nevill, ed., *The Reminiscences of Lady Dorothy Nevill*, London, 1906, p. 105.

109. Samuel Johnson, *Lives of the English Poets*, ed. G. B. Hill, 3 vols., Oxford, 1905, ii. 119.

110. Cyrus Redding, *Fifty Years' Recollections*, i. 289.

111. Chauncey Brewster Tinker, *The Salon and English Letters*, New York, 1915, chap. 12.

112. *Selections from the Letters and Correspondence of Sir James Bland Burges, Bart.*, ed. James Hutton, London, 1885, p. 60.

113. T. Wemyss Reid, *The Life, Letters, and Friendships of Richard Monckton Milnes, first Lord Houghton*, i. 190.

114. *The Remains of the Late Mrs Richard Trench*, p. 307.

115. Stephen Gill, *William Wordsworth: A Life*, Oxford, 1989, p. 422.

116. *Mémoires et Correspondance de Madame d'Épinay*, 3 vols., Paris, 1818, ii. 284–5.

117. *Horace Walpole's Correspondence*, xvi. 266.

118. Richard Foster Jones, *The Triumph of the English Language*, London, 1953, chap. 1.

119. *Spectator*, 135.

120. Louis-Antoine de Caraccioli, *Letters on the Manners of the French, and on the Follies and Extravagancies of the Times*, p. 273.

121. *A Voyage to England, Containing many things relating to the State of Learning, Religion, And other Curiosities of that Kingdom*, p. 70.

122. *The Manners and Customs Of the Principal Nations of Europe Gathered together by the particular Observation of James Salgado, a Spaniard, in his Travels through those Countries; and Translated into English by the Authors Care, Anno 1684*, sub. 'In Language' (not paginated).

123. Christopher Hervey, *Letters from Portugal, Spain, Italy and Germany, in the Years 1759, 1760, and 1761*, ii. 498–9.

124. N. M. Karamzin, *Letters of a Russian Traveller 1789–1790*, p. 318.

125. *Nouvelles observations sur l'Angleterre*, pp. 160–1.

126. *Souvenirs du Baron de Barante*, ed. Claude de Barante, 8 vols., Paris, 1890–1901, iv. 19.

127. *The Works of George Eliot: Essays and Leaves from a Note-Book*, p. 91.

128. Elizabeth Eastlake, *A Residence on the Shores of the Baltic*, 2 vols., London, 1841, ii. 3.

129. P. W. Clayden, *The Early Life of Samuel Rogers*, p. 304.

130. Historical Manuscripts Commission, *Charlemont MSS II*, pp. 165–6.

131. T. Wemyss Reid, *The Life, Letters, and Friendships of Richard Monckton Milnes, first Lord Houghton*, ii. 164.

132. J. Fenimore Cooper, *England*, ii. 52.

133. *The Saxon and English Languages reciprocally illustrative of each other*, London, 1798, p. 56.

134. Madame de Staël, *De L'Allemagne*, i. 111.

135. Henry Wansey, *An Excursion to the United States of North America, in the Summer of 1794*, 2nd edn., Salisbury, 1798, p. 20.

136. Devon Record Office, Sidmouth MSS, 38/7.

137. *Society in America*, 2nd edn., 3 vols., London, 1837, iii. 77, 72.

138. J. Fenimore Cooper, *England*, ii. 74–5.

139. *Diary, Reminiscences, and Correspondence of Henry Crabb Robinson*, selected and ed. Thomas Sadler, 3rd edn., 2 vols., London, 1872, i. 169; J. G. Lockhart, *Peter's Letters to His Kinsfolk*, ii. 148.

140. Edward Gibbon, *The History of the Decline and Fall of the Roman Empire*, ed. J. B. Bury, 7 vols., London, 1909, iv. 168.

141. F. Mac Donogh, *The Hermit in Edinburgh: or, Sketches of Manners and Real Characters and Scenes in the Drama of Life*, 3 vols., London, 1824, i. 118–19.

142. *The History of the Decline and Fall of the Roman Empire*, iv. 168.

143. Francis Jeffrey, *Contributions to the Edinburgh Review*, London, 1844.

144. *Lady Morgan's Memoirs: Autobiography, Diaries and Correspondence*, 2nd edn., 2 vols., London, 1863, i. 504.

145. Adam Potkay, 'Classical Eloquence and Polite Style in the Age of Hume', *Eighteenth-Century Studies*, 25 (1991), 49.

146. *The Works of Mr de St. Evremont*, i. 506–7. See Lawrence E. Klein, 'Gender, Conversation and the Public Sphere in Early Eighteenth-Century England', in Judith Still and Michael Worton, eds., *Textuality and Sexuality: Reading Theories and Practices*, Manchester, 1993, pp. 107–8.

147. *Memoirs of Charles-Lewis, Baron de Pöllnitz*, ii. 461.

148. *Corinne ou l'Italie*, ii. 369.

149. Ludwig Wolff, *Briefe in die Heimath*, i. 55.

150. John Carr, *The Stranger in Ireland*, p. 236.

151. David Collins, *An Account of the English Colony in New South Wales*, ed. Brian Fletcher, 2 vols., Sydney, 1975, i. lxxiii.

152. *The Life and Letters of Barthold George Niebuhr*, 2 vols., London, 1852, i. 132.

153. Pückler-Muskau, *Tour in England, Ireland, and France, in the Years 1828 and 1829*, iii. 159.

154. *Letters from Edinburgh; Written in the Years 1774 and 1775*, p. 66.

155. *Guardian*, 8 Apr. 1713.

156. Chauncey Brewster Tinker, *The Salon and English Letters*, p. 107.

157. *The History of Sir Charles Grandison*, i. 101.

158. *Sermons to Young Women*, 3rd edn., 2 vols., London, 1766, ii. 284.

159. *Diary Illustrative of the Times of George the Fourth*, 2 vols., London, 1838, i. 284.

160. Frances Anne Kemble, *Further Records, 1848–1883*, i. 33.

161. *The Greville Memoirs (Second Part). A Journal of the Reign of Queen Victoria from 1837 to 1852 by the late Charles C. F. Greville, Esq.*, 3 vols., London, 1885, i. 167–8.

162. Louis-Antoine de Caraccioli, *Voyage de la raison en Europe*, p. 85.

163. Hans Kohn, 'Arndt and the Character of German Nationalism', *American Hist. Rev.* 54 (1948–9), 795.

164. *The Memoirs of Madame Roland*, ed. and trans. Evelyn Shuckburgh, London, 1986, p. 81.

165. Friedrich Kielmansegge, *Diary of a Journey to England in the Years 1761–1762*, p. 255.

166. Archenholz, *A Picture of England*, i. 67.

167. *Reise durch England und Schottland*, 2 vols., Leipzig, 1818, i. 372.

168. *A Journal of Travels in England, Holland and Scotland, and of Two Passages over the Atlantic, in the Years 1805 and 1806*, i. 56, 59.

169. George Harris, *The Autobiography of George Harris*, London, 1888, p. 202.

170. G. A. Crapelet, *Souvenirs de Londres en 1814 et 1816*, p. 37.

171. Archenholz, *A Picture of England*, ii. 134; i. 192–3.

172. *De L'Angleterre*, London, 1811, p. 140.

173. *The Life and Letters of Barthold George Niebuhr*, i. 122.

174. London, n.d.

175. William Jacob, *A View of the Agriculture, Manufactures, Statistics, and State of Society, of Germany, and Parts of Holland and France*, London, 1820, p. 220.

176. A. de Staël-Holstein, *Letters on England*, p. 178.

177. *Can You Forgive Her?*, ed. Andrew Swarbrick, Oxford, 1991, i. 224.

178. *Journal of a Tour*, i. 55.

179. George Watson, *The English Ideology: Studies in the Language of Victorian Politics*, pp. 126–7.

180. Johan Caspar, Freiherr von Riesbeck, *Travels through Germany, in a Series of Letters; written in German by the Baron Riesbeck*, trans. Revd Mr Maty, 3 vols., London, 1787, ii. 252; the equally aristocratic Prince de Ligne, *Mémoires, Lettres et Pensées*, p. 339, made a similar remark.

181. *A Journey made in the Summer of 1794, through Holland and the Western Frontier of Germany, with a Return down the Rhine; to which are added Observations during a Tour to the Lakes of Lancashire, Westmoreland, and Cumberland*, London, 1795, p. 231.

182. *London Debating Societies, 1776–1799*, ed. Donna T. Andrew, London Record Society, 1994, p. xi.

183. Mary Thale, 'London Debating Societies in the 1790s', *Hist. Jnl.* 32 (1989), 84.

184. *Diary of Joseph Farington*, xv. 5362.

185. *'In My Hot Youth': Byron's Letters and Journals*, vol. i: *1798–1810*, ed. Leslie A. Marchand, London, 1973, p. 48.

186. T. Wemyss Reid, *The Life, Letters, and Friendships of Richard Monckton Milnes, first Lord Houghton*, i. 71.

187. Sir T. E. Colebrooke, *Life of the Honourable Mountstuart Elphinstone*, 2 vols., London, 1884, ii. 329.

188. F. Thistlethwayte, *Memoirs and Correspondence of Dr. Henry Bathurst, Lord Bishop of Norwich*, London, 1853, p. 153.

189. A. de Staël-Holstein, *Letters on England*, p. 178.

190. Louis Simond, *Journal of a Tour*, ii. 162.

191. J. Fenimore Cooper, *England*, ii. 75.

192. Calvin Colton, *Four Years in Great Britain*, pp. 137–8.

193. Martha Babcock Amory, *The Domestic and Artistic Life of John Singleton Copley*, Boston, 1882, p. 435.

194. Edward Michael Whitty, *St Stephen's in the Fifties: The Session 1852–3: A Parliamentary Retrospect*, introd. Justin M'Carthy, London, 1906, p. 39.

195. *Memoirs of the Life of Sir James Mackintosh*, 1835, i. 8.

196. *The Court of London from 1819 to 1825*, ed. Benjamin Rush, pp. 29, 279.

197. *Bagehot's Historical Essays*, pp. 209–11.

198. Grenville Fletcher, *Parliamentary Portraits of the present Period. Third Series*, London, 1862, pp. 6–7.

199. Amédée Pichot, *Historical and Literary Tour*, i. 382–3.

200. Henry Taylor, *The Statesman*, p. 11.

201. *Complete Works of William Hazlitt*, xvii. 8.

202. Friedrich Kielmansegge, *Diary of a Journey to England in the Years 1761–1762*, p. 163.

203. Michael Meehan, *Liberty and Poetics in Eighteenth Century England*, London, 1986, pp. 84–5.

204. *L'Angleterre au commencement du dix-neuvième siècle*, pp. 344 ff.

205. *A Selection of Thomas Twining's Letters 1734–1804*, ed. Ralph S. Walker, 2 vols., Lewiston, NY, 1991, i. 391, 406.

206. Ethel Jones, *Les Voyageurs français en Angleterre de 1815 à 1830*, p. 192.

207. R. B. Peake, *Memoirs of the Colman Family*, 2 vols., London, 1841, ii. 173.

208. Raumer, *England in 1835*, i. 232.

209. Oloff Napea, *Letters from London*, p. 215.

210. *Memoirs and Correspondence of Francis Horner, M.P.*, ii. 260.

211. *Diary of Joseph Farington*, ix. 3442.

212. *Complete Works of William Hazlitt*, xvii. 9–10.

213. *Bagehot's Historical Essays*, pp. 166–7.

214. *English Traits*, Boston, 1856, pp. 131–2.

215. Lévis, *L'Angleterre au commencement du dix-neuvième siècle*, p. 252.

216. *Lettere e Scritti inediti di Pietro e di Alessandro Verri*, ii. 92.

217. *The Autobiography of William Jerdan*, 2 vols., London, 1852–3, i. 85.

218. Grantley F. Berkeley, *My Life and Recollections*, i. 362.

219. Lacoste, *Voyage Philosophique d'Angleterre, fait en 1783 et 1784*, i. 249.

220. Grantley F. Berkeley, *My Life and Recollections*, i. 359.

221. *Great Britain in 1833*, i. 200.

222. Louis Simond, *Journal of a Tour*, i. 60.

223. Matthew Whiting Rosa, *The Silver-Fork School: Novels of Fashion Preceding Vanity Fair*, New York, 1936, p. 90.

224. *English Fragments*, pp. 82–3.

225. Raumer, *England in 1835*, ii. 275.

226. I. D'Israeli, *An Essay on the Manners and Genius of the Literary Character*, p. 166.

227. Alphonse Esquiros, *The English at Home*, 2nd ser., pp. 70–1.

228. Ralph Waldo Emerson, *English Traits*, p. 131.

Chapter Five RESERVE

1. *Another Traveller! or Cursory Remarks and Critical Observations made upon a Journey through Part of the Netherlands In the latter End of the Year 1766, By Coriat Junior*, 2 vols., London, 1767–9, i. 460.

2. James Peller Malcolm, *Anecdotes of the Manners and Customs of London during the Eighteenth Century*, p. 385. There were, however, two sides to the story of La Condamine's misfortunes. Sexual and financial scrapes brought him to the attention both of the law and newspaper readers; see *Gentleman's Magazine*, 1763, pp. 304–5.

3. Pierre-Jean Grosley, *A Tour to London*, i. 87.

4. *Histoire d'un voyage littéraire*, The Hague, 1735, p. 31.

5. Béat Louis Muralt, *Lettres sur les Anglois et les François*, p. 68.

6. Jacques Fontaine, *A Tale of the Huguenots, or Memoirs of a French Refugee Family*, introd. F. L. Hawks, New York, 1838, p. 146.

7. De La Vauguyon, *The Truth respecting England*, i. 169–70.

8. T. Wemyss Reid, *The Life, Letters, and Friendships of Richard Monckton Milnes, first Lord Houghton*, ii. 32.

9. Ralph Waldo Emerson, *English Traits*, p. 301.

10. *Observations on Mons. de Sorbiere's Voyage into England*, London, 1708, 1st pub. 1665, p. 109.

11. *Lettere e Scritti inediti di Pietro e di Alessandro Verri*, i. 402.

12. *A Trip through London*, London, 1728, p. 1.

13. *Lettere sull'Inghilterra*, pp. 217–18.

14. *Letters from London: Observations of a Russian*, pp. 28, 100.

15. *Observations sur Londres et ses Environs*, pp. 235, 183.

16. James Fenimore Cooper, *Notions of the Americans*, i. 230.

17. 'Journal', *Mass. Hist. Soc. Proc.* 48 (1914–15), 515.

18. Henri Decremps, *Le Parisien a Londres*, i. 91.

19. Wendeborn, *A View of England towards the Close of the Eighteenth Century*, i. 358.

20. Margaret Bain, *Les Voyageurs français en Écosse 1770-1830 et leurs curiosités intellectuelles*, Paris, 1931, p. 91.

21. 'Ansichten vom Niederrhein, von Brabant, Flandern, Holland, England und Frankreich', in *Georg Forster's sämmtliche Schriften*, 9 vols., Leipzig, 1843, iii. 381.

22. *L'Ami des Étrangers qui voyagent en Angleterre*, London, 1787, pp. 3-4.

23. *Briefe zur Characteristik von England gehörig; geschrieben auf einer Reise im Jahre 1784 von Heinrich von Watzdorf*, p. 154.

24. Lawrence Stone, in *Past and Present*, 108 (1985), 219, 222, defending his 'Interpersonal Violence in English Society, 1300-1980', *Past and Present*, 101 (1983), 22-33.

25. Benjamin Silliman, *A Journal of Travels in England, Holland and Scotland, and of Two Passages over the Atlantic, in the Years 1805 and 1806*, i. 163.

26. British Library, Add. MS 27827, fo. 144.

27. *Real Life in London*, 2 vols., London, 1821, i. 645-8.

28. Édouard de Montulé, *Voyage en Angleterre et en Russie, pendant les années 1821, 1822 et 1823*, i. 230-1.

29. *Travels*, iv. 81.

30. *Complete Works of William Hazlitt*, xix. 247-8.

31. *Burke's Works*, Bohn's edn., vii. 499.

32. *Diderot: Lettres à Sophie Volland*, ed. A. Babelon, 2 vols., Paris, 1938, ii. 72-3.

33. Ethel Jones, *Les Voyageurs français en Angleterre de 1815 à 1830*, p. 289.

34. François Guizot, *An Embassy to the Court of St. James's in 1840*, p. 175.

35. Maria R. Audubon, *Audubon and his Journals*, i. 124.

36. Lacoste, *Voyage Philosophique d'Angleterre, fait en 1783 et 1784*, i. 91 ff.

37. *Memoirs of the Comtesse de Boigne*, ii. 148.

38. Haussez, *Great Britain in 1833*, i. 28.

39. *The Remains of the Late Mrs. Richard Trench*, pp. 38-9.

40. Christopher Simon Sykes, *Private Palaces: Life in the Great London Houses*, London, 1985, p. 128.

41. J. C. Beltrami, *A Pilgrimage in Europe and America*, ii. 455.

42. George P. Fisher, *Life of Benjamin Silliman*, London, 1866, p. 191.

43. *Letters from England: by Don Manuel Alvarez Espriella*, ii. 307.

44. *Baroness von Riedesel and the American Revolution; Journal and Correspondence of a Tour of Duty 1776-1783*, revised trans. Marvin L. Brown, Jr., Chapel Hill, NC, 1965, p. 71.

45. *Correspondence of Emily, Duchess of Leinster (1731-1814)*, i. 395.

46. *A View of the Agriculture, Manufactures, Statistics, and State of Society, of Germany, and Parts of Holland and France*, London, 1820, p. 294.

47. C. H. Phipps, *Matilda; a Tale of the Day*, i. 194-5.

48. *A Great-Niece's Journals being Extracts from the Journals of Fanny Anne Burney (Mrs Wood) from 1830 to 1842*, ed. Margaret S. Rolt, London, 1926, p. 280.

49. Christian Augustus Fischer, *Letters during a Journey to Montpellier. Performed in the autumn of 1804*, London, 1806, p. 65.

50. i. 101.

51. *A View of Society and Manners in France, Switzerland, and Germany*, ii. 431, 433.

52. William Archer Shee, *My Contemporaries 1830–1870*, pp. 271–3.

53. *The Courts of Europe at the Close of the Last Century by the late Henry Swinburne, Esq.*, i. 237, 254.

54. Christopher Hervey, *Letters from Portugal, Spain, Italy and Germany, in the Years 1759, 1760, and 1761*, i. 425.

55. Devon Record Office, Sidmouth MSS, Mary Gaskell to Lady Sidmouth, 16 Jan. 1828.

56. *Lettere e Scritti inediti di Pietro e di Alessandro Verri*, i. 384–5.

57. *Memoirs of the Life and Peregrinations of the Florentine Philip Mazzei 1730–1816*, trans. Howard R. Marraro, New York, 1942, p. 117.

58. Countess of Ilchester and Lord Stavordale, *Life and Letters of Lady Sarah Lennox, 1745–1826*, London, 1904, p. 212.

59. *Crabb Robinson in Germany 1800–1805*, p. 21.

60. *Memoirs of a Traveller, Now in Retirement*, i. 224.

61. *Quarterly Review*, 59 (1837), 422.

62. Lady Mary Walker, *Letters from the Duchess de Crui and Others, on subjects Moral and Entertaining*, 2nd edn., 5 vols., London, 1777, iv. 124.

63. Francis Place, *Real Life in London*, i. 272.

64. *The Memoirs of Susan Sibbald (1783–1812)*, ed. Francis Paget Hett, London, 1926, p. 42.

65. *Reminiscences chiefly of Towns, Villages and Schools*, i. 85–6.

66. Édouard de Montulé, *Voyage en Angleterre et en Russie, pendant les années 1821, 1822 et 1823*, i. 154.

67. Hester Lynch Piozzi, *British Synonymy*, ii. 153.

68. *Georg Forster's sämmtliche Schriften*, iii. 377 ff.

69. Felicity Heal, *Hospitality in Early Modern England*, Oxford, 1990.

70. *Monthly Review*, 98 (1822), 159.

71. *An American Quaker in the British Isles: The Travel Journals of Jabez Maud Fisher, 1775–1779*, pp. 165, 220.

72. *A Journey made in the Summer of 1794*, pp. 158, 161.

73. Robert Gray, *Letters during the Course of a Tour through Germany, Switzerland and Italy*, London, 1794, p. 123.

74. *The Greville Memoirs (Second Part)*, i. 25.

75. *An American Quaker in the British Isles: The Travel Journals of Jabez Maud Fisher, 1775–1779*, pp. 42, 120.

76. Norman Scarfe, *Innocent Espionage: The La Rochefoucauld Brothers' Tour of England in 1785*, p. 143.

77. *Crabb Robinson in Germany 1800–1805*, p. 24.

78. Hester Lynch Piozzi, *Observations and Reflections made in the Course of a Journey through France, Italy, and Germany*, ii. 140.

79. Joseph-Alexis, vicomte Walsh, *Lettres sur l'Angleterre ou voyage Dans la Grande-Bretagne en 1829*, p. 247.

80. *Journal of a Lady of Quality*, ed. Evangeline Walker Andrews and Charles Maclean Andrews, New Haven, 1921, p. 78.

81. G. Heriot, *A Picturesque Tour made in the Years 1817 and 1820, through the Pyrenean Mountains, Auvergne, the Departments of the High and Low Alps, and in Part of Spain*, London, 1824, p. 21.

82. *Sketches of the Natural, Civil, and Political State of Swisserland*, 2nd edn., London, 1780, p. 63.

83. Luttrell Wynne, Travel notebooks, Cornwall Record Office, PD 455.

84. *Journeys of a German in England in 1782*, p. 113.

85. Edward Ward, *The London Spy*, 3rd edn., London, 1702, vii. 7; Robert Southey, *Letters from England: by Don Manuel Alvarez Espriella*, i. 119.

86. Joseph-Alexis, vicomte Walsh, *Lettres sur l'Angleterre ou voyage dans la Grande-Bretagne en 1829*, p. 323.

87. Sir Richard Phillips, *Modern London*, London, 1804, p. 137.

88. Oloff Napea, *Letters from London*, p. 249.

89. *Descriptive travels in the Southern and Eastern Parts of Spain and the Balearic Isles, in the Year 1809*, pp. 19–20.

90. *Impressions of England 1809–10*, pp. 123–4.

91. A. Alison, *Travels in France, during the Years 1814–15*, i. 9.

92. Devon Record Office, Sidmouth MSS, Henry Unwin Addington, 38/7.

93. Frances Trollope, *Domestic Manners of the Americans*, 4th edn., 2 vols., London, 1832, i. 136–7.

94. *Journal by Frances Anne Butler*, i. 135.

95. Isaac Weld, *Travels through the States of North America, and the Provinces of Upper and Lower Canada, during the Years 1795, 1796, and 1797*, 2nd edn., London, 1799, i. 123–4.

96. George Jacob Holyoake, *Sixty Years of an Agitator's Life*, i. 71.

97. *Music, Men and Manners in France and Italy 1770*, p. 103.

98. *Travels and Adventures in Southern Africa*, p. 40.

99. Geijer, *Impressions of England 1809–10*, p. 126.

100. *The Letter-Journal of George Canning, 1793–1795*, ed. Peter Jupp, Camden 4th ser. 41 (1991), p. 160.

101. Henry Peckham, *The Tour of Holland, Dutch Brabant, the Austrian Netherlands, and Part of France*, p. 107.

102. Louis-Philippe, *Journal de mon voyage d'Amérique*, ed. Suzanne d'Huart, Paris, 1976, p. 59.

103. A. Alison, *Travels in France, during the Years 1814–15*, ii. 82.

104. Charles Johnston, *Chrysal or the Adventures of a Guinea*, ed. E. Baker, London, 1908, p. 96.

105. *Recollections of the Public Career and Private Life of the late John Adolphus*, ed. Emily Henderson, London, 1871, p. 81.

106. *The Autobiography of Lieutenant-General Sir Harry Smith*, ed. G. C. Moore Smith, London, 1902, p. 341.

107. *The Diary of Colonel Peter Hawker*, ed. Sir Ralph Payne-Galloway, 2 vols., London, 1893, i. 130.
108. *Crabb Robinson in Germany 1800–1805*, p. 24.
109. Harriet Pigott, *Records of Real Life in the Palace and the Cottage*, ii. 8.
110. *First Impressions on a Tour upon the Continent*, p. 11.
111. *Lisbon in the Years 1821, 1822, and 1823*, i. 118.
112. J. G. Kohl, *Ireland*, p. 45.
113. Count Édouard de Melfort, *Impressions of England*, i. 9.
114. *Tales of a Traveller. By Geoffrey Crayon, Gent.*, ii. 71.
115. *Diderot: Lettres à Sophie Volland*, ii. 73.
116. Elizabeth, Lady Craven, *Letters from The Right Honorable Lady Craven, to his serene highness, The Margrave of Anspach, during her travels through France, Germany, and Russia in 1785 and 1786*, 2nd edn., London, 1814, i. 130.
117. W. Derry, *Dr Parr*, Oxford, 1966, p. 55.
118. *A. De La Motraye's Travels through Europe, Asia, and into Part of Africa*, 2 vols., London, 1723, ii. 147.
119. *A Kentish Parson: Selections from the Private Papers of the Revd Joseph Price Vicar of Brabourne, 1767–1786*, ed. G. M. Ditchfield and Bryan Keith-Lucas, Stroud, Glos., 1991, p. 160.
120. J. Michelet, *Sur les chemins de l'Europe*, p. 42.
121. John Marsh, MS Diary, Huntington Library, 1770.
122. *Sophie in London 1786 being the Diary of Sophie v. la Roche*, p. 140.
123. Marianne Spencer-Stanhope, *Almack's: A Novel*, 3 vols., London, 1826, ii. 231.
124. Pückler-Muskau, *Tour in England, Ireland, and France, in the Years 1828 and 1829*, iii. 312–13.
125. Maria Edgeworth, *Letters from England 1813–1844*, pp. 92–4.
126. John Cannon, *Samuel Johnson and the Politics of Hanoverian England*, Oxford, 1994, p. 21.
127. Sheffield City Archives, Wh. M, transcripts, 1, to Miss Mary Hervey, Zurich, 1766.
128. John Macdonald, *Memoirs of an Eighteenth-Century Footman*, ed. John Beresford, London, 1927, p. 85.
129. Henry Matthews, *The Diary of an Invalid*, ii. 46–7.
130. Louis-Sébastien Mercier, *Tableau de Paris*, i. 99.
131. Sarah C. Maza, *Servants and Masters in Eighteenth-Century France: The Uses of Loyalty*, Princeton, 1983, p. 252.
132. *The Memoirs of Madame Roland*, p. 160.
133. John Moore, *A View of Society and Manners in France, Switzerland, and Germany*, i. 365.
134. Ethel Mann, *An Englishman at Home and Abroad 1792–1828*, p. 147.
135. John Bramsen, *Remarks on the North of Spain*, London, 1823, p. 11.
136. George Pinckard, *Notes on the West Indies*, ii. 328–9.
137. *Sydney Monitor*, 3 Mar. 1828.

138. *Voyage Philosophique d'Angleterre, fait en 1783 et 1784*, i. 213.

139. *Diary of Joseph Farington*, x. 3752.

140. *A Kentish Parson*, p. 111.

141. *Diary of Joseph Farington*, xii. 4222.

142. Isaac D'Israeli, *Curiosities of Literature*, new edn., 3 vols., London, 1824, ii. 316.

143. Carl Philipp Moritz, *Journeys of a German in England in 1782*, p. 175.

144. Madame d'Avot, *Lettres sur l'Angleterre, ou deux années à Londres*, p. 238.

145. J. Gamble, *A View of Society and Manners, in the North of Ireland, in the Summer and Autumn of 1812*, pp. 359–60.

146. Walter L. Arnstein, ed., 'A German View of English Society: 1851', *Victorian Studies*, 16 (1972–3), 198.

147. Historical Manuscripts Commission, *Hastings MSS III*, p. 11.

148. *Gleanings from an Old Portfolio*, ed. Mrs Godfrey Clark, 3 vols., Edinburgh, 1895, ii. 12–13.

149. *The Remains of the Late Mrs. Richard Trench*, pp. 39–40.

150. *Miss Eden's Letters*, ed. Violet Dickinson, London, 1919, 25 Jan. 1837.

151. J. Fenimore Cooper, *England*, iii. 52–3; De La Vauguyon, *The Truth respecting England*, i. 53.

152. *So Dearly Loved, So Much Admired: Letters to Hester Pitt, Lady Chatham from her relations and friends, 1744–1801*, p. 136.

153. Archenholz, *A Picture of England*, i. 170.

154. Adolphe Blanqui, *Voyage d'un jeune français en Angleterre et en Écosse pendant l'automne de 1823*, p. 141.

155. *Memories of Old Friends, being Extracts from the Journals and Letters of Caroline Fox of Penjerrick, Cornwall From 1835 to 1871*, ii. 87.

156. *Letters of Dorothea, Princess Lieven, during her Residence in London, 1812–1834*, ed. Lionel G. Robinson, London, 1902, p. 3.

157. John Milford, *Observations, Moral, Literary, and Antiquarian*, i. 115.

158. J. B. Scott, writing in 1814, Ethel Mann, *An Englishman at Home and Abroad 1792–1828*, p. 116.

159. *Memories of Old Friends, being Extracts from the Journals and Letters of Caroline Fox of Penjerrick, Cornwall From 1835 to 1871*, i. 210–11.

160. *Letters of Lady Louisa Stuart to Miss Louisa Clinton*, 2nd ser., p. 99.

161. Doris Gunnell, *Sutton Sharpe et ses amis français*, p. 213.

162. *De Londres et ses Environs*, Amsterdam, 1789, p. 36.

163. *The Diary of an Invalid*, ii. 164.

164. *Italian Travel Sketches*, p. 203.

165. *Complete Works of William Hazlitt*, xvi. 194.

166. Martin Archer Shee, *The Life of Sir Martin Archer Shee*, 2 vols., London, 1860, ii. 152.

167. *Six Weeks in Paris, or a Cure for the Gallomania*, 3 vols., London, 1818, i. 97–8.

168. Edward Heneage Dering, *Georgiana Lady Chatterton*, London, 1901, p. 79.

169. Hon. Grantley F. Berkeley, *My Life and Recollections*, ii. 351.

170. Alphonse Esquiros, *The English at Home*, i. 135–5.
171. *England*, i. 104–5.
172. Richard Sennett, *The Fall of Public Man*, Cambridge, 1977, p. 81.
173. Edward Ward, *A Compleat and Humorous Account of all the Remarkable Clubs and Societies in the Cities of London and Westminster*, London, 1745.
174. *A History of Private Life: III. Passions of the Renaissance*, ed. Roger Chartier, Cambridge, Mass., 1989, p. 477.
175. Archenholz, *A Picture of England*, ii. 107–8; John Strang, *Germany in 1831*, i. 247–8.
176. Charles Marsh, *The Clubs of London; with Anecdotes of their Members, Sketches of Character, and Conversations*, 2 vols., London, 1828, i. 3.
177. George Gissing, *The Private Papers of Henry Ryecroft*, pp. 80–1.
178. J. G. Kohl, *Ireland, Scotland, and England*, p. 103.
179. *The London Journal of Flora Tristan*, p. 264.
180. Alphonse Esquiros, *The English at Home*, 2nd ser., p. 71.
181. Pückler-Muskau, *Tour in England, Ireland, and France, in the Years 1828 and 1829*, iii. 381.
182. Émile Boutmy, *The English People: A Study of their Political Psychology*, p. 114.
183. *Letters of a Russian Traveller 1789–1790*, p. 335.
184. Joseph Fiévée, *Lettres sur L'Angleterre, et Reflexions sur la Philosophie du XVIIIe Siècle*, p. 193.
185. Ellen Moers, *The Dandy: Brummell to Beerbohm*, London, 1960, p. 115.
186. *Memorials of the Life and Character of Lady Osborne and some of her Friends*, ed. by her daughter Mrs Osborne, 2 vols., Dublin, 1870, i. 191.
187. J. C. Beltrami, *A Pilgrimage in Europe and America*, i. 419.
188. *Letters from Edinburgh; Written in the Years 1774 and 1775*, pp. 66 ff.
189. *Lettere sull'Inghilterra*, p. 361.
190. *Memoir and Correspondence of Mrs. Grant of Laggan*, ed. J. P. Grant, 3 vols., London, 1844, i. 68.
191. *The Stranger in Ireland*, p. 251.
192. P. W. Clayden, *The Early Life of Samuel Rogers*, p. 184.
193. *General View of the Agriculture of the County of Cornwall*, London, 1811, pp. x–xi.
194. *A Journal of Travels in England, Holland and Scotland, and of Two Passages over the Atlantic, in the Years 1805 and 1806*, i. 56.
195. Friedrich Kielmansegge, *Diary of a Journey to England in the Years 1761–1762*, pp. 125–6.
196. Claire Tomalin, *Mrs. Jordan's Profession: The Story of a Great Actress and a Future King*, London, 1994, p. 33.
197. W. F. Mavor, *A Tour in Wales*, p. 46.
198. *Gleanings from an Old Portfolio*, ed. Mrs Godfrey Clark, i. 185.
199. *Memoirs and Correspondence of Francis Horner, M. P.*, i. 255.
200. *Letters of Lady Louisa Stuart to Miss Louisa Clinton*, p. 174.

201. Hester Lynch Piozzi, *Observations and Reflections made in the Course of a Journey through France, Italy, and Germany*, i. 106–7.

202. *Briefe zur Charakteristik von England gehörig; geschrieben auf einer Reise im Jahre 1784 von Heinrich von Watzdorf*, pp. 56–7.

203. A. B. Kurakin, *Souvenirs d'un voyage en Hollande et en Angleterre*, St Petersburg, 1815, p. 82.

204. John Moore, *A View of Society and Manners in France, Switzerland, and Germany*, i. 143–4.

205. Archenholz, *A Picture of England*, i. 110; Frances Ann Kemble, *Records of a Girlhood*, ii. 122; John Taylor, *Records of my Life*, 2 vols., i. 414.

206. Lionel Trilling, *The Liberal Imagination*, London, 1961, p. 209.

207. *Letters from London*, pp. 16–17.

208. The phrase was coined by Philip Gilbert Hamerton, *Human Intercourse*, London, 1884, p. 232, on reading *Democracy in America*, vol. ii, book 3, chap. 2.

209. *De Vere*, i. 329.

210. Calvin Colton, *Four Years in Great Britain*, p. 318.

211. Shirley Robert Letwin, *The Gentleman in Trollope*, p. 113.

212. Robert Baker, *Reflections on the English Language, In the Nature of Vaugelas's Reflections on the French*, London, [1770], p. 10; Philip Withers, *Aristarchus, or The Principles of Composition*, 2nd edn., London, [1789], p. 208.

213. *Life, Letters and Journals of Sir Charles Lyell, Bart.*, ii. 150.

214. *A Selection from the Correspondence of Abraham Hayward, Q. C. From 1834 to 1884*, ed. Henry E. Carlisle, 2 vols., London, 1886, i. 90.

215. *Diary of Joseph Farington*, v. 1810.

216. *Autobiography of Henry Taylor, 1800–1875*, i. 100.

217. *Recollections of the Public Career and Private Life of the late John Adolphus*, p. 80.

218. T. Wemyss Reid, *The Life, Letters, and Friendships of Richard Monckton Milnes, first Lord Houghton*, ii. 495.

219. Walter L. Arnstein, ed., 'A German View of English Society: 1851', *Victorian Studies*, 16 (1972–3), 200–1.

220. Devon Record Office, Sidmouth MSS, 38/7.

221. Lady Charlotte Bury, *Diary Illustrative of the Times of George the Fourth*, ii. 177.

222. Gertrude Lyster, *A Family Chronicle Derived from Notes and Letters Selected by Barbarina, the Hon. Lady Grey*, London, 1908, p. 209.

223. *Notions of the Americans*, i. 206–7.

224. *Edinburgh Review*, 37 (1822), 310–13.

225. C. H. Phipps, *The English in Italy*, ii. 296–7.

Chapter Six ECCENTRICITY

1. *L'Angleterre au commencement du dix-neuvième siècle*, p. 252.

2. *A Tour through Sicily and Malta*, 2 vols., Dublin, 1773, ii. 333.

3. *An Essay on the Revolutions of Literature*, trans. John Murdoch, p. 261.

4. Amédée de Tissot, *Paris et Londres comparés*, pp. 24–5.

5. C. F. Henningsen, *Analogies and Contrasts*, i. 87–8.

6. Lady Charlotte Bury, *Diary Illustrative of the Times of George the Fourth*, ii. 44.

7. Georgiana Chatterton, *Home Sketches and Foreign Recollections*, ii. 180–1.

8. *L'Angleterre et les Anglais, ou petit portrait d'une grande famille; copié et retouché par deux témoins oculaires*, iii. 350.

9. *Voyage en Angleterre et en Écosse*, pp. 50–1.

10. Susan Staves, *Married Women's Separate Property in England, 1660–1833*, Cambridge, Mass., 1990.

11. E. M. Butler, *The Tempestuous Prince: Hermann Pückler-Muskau*, London, 1929, p. 77.

12. J. C. Beltrami, *A Pilgrimage in Europe and America*, i. 470.

13. Janet Ross, *Three Generations of English Women*, London, pp. 71, 173.

14. Charles-Victor de Bonstetten, *The Man of the North, and the Man of the South; or the Influence of Climate*, p. 109.

15. *Nouvelles observations sur l'Angleterre*, pp. 231–2.

16. *English Fragments*, p. 5.

17. *Mémoires historiques, littéraires et anecdotiques tirés de la correspondance philosophique et critique, addressée au duc de Saxe Gotha, depuis 1770 jusqu'en 1792, par le baron de Grimm et par Diderot*, ii. 402.

18. pp. 12–13.

19. Alfred Franklin, *La Civilité, l'étiquette, la mode, le bon ton du XIIIe au XIXe siècle*, Paris, 1908, pp. 148–9.

20. Louis Simond, *Journal of a Tour*, i. 21.

21. John Alexander Kelly, *England and the Englishman in German Literature of the Eighteenth Century*, New York, 1921, p. 61.

22. J. G. Zimmermann, *Essay on National Pride*, pp. 78–9.

23. *Memoirs of Charles-Lewis, Baron de Pöllnitz*, ii. 436.

24. *Sophie in London 1786 being the Diary of Sophie v. la Roche*, p. 217.

25. *Lichtenberg in England*, i. 309.

26. Charles Dupin, *A Tour through the Naval and Military Establishments of Great Britain, in the Years 1816–17–18–19 and 1820*, p. 76.

27. A. B. Kurakin, *Souvenirs d'un voyage en Hollande et en Angleterre*, pp. 159–60.

28. *The Remains of the Late Mrs. Richard Trench*, p. 470.

29. *Diary of Joseph Farington*, xiv. 5102.

30. *Histoire Secrète de la Cour de Berlin*, 2 vols., Alençon, 1789, i. 251.

31. *A View of Society and Manners in France, Switzerland, and Germany*, ii. 91.

32. *Mémoires, Lettres et Pensées*, p. 632.

33. *Briefe zur Characteristik von England gehörig; geschrieben auf einer Reise im Jahre 1784 von Heinrich von Watzdorf*, p. 156.

34. *Memoirs of the Comtesse de Boigne*, ii. 149.

35. *Mémoires et Correspondance de Madame d'Épinay*, iii. 283–4.

36. Richard Sennett, *The Fall of Public Man*.
37. Robert Southey, *Letters from England: by Don Manuel Alvarez Espriella*, i. 137.
38. Lévis, *L'Angleterre au commencement du dix-neuvième siècle*, p. 6.
39. C. G. Carus, *The King of Saxony's Journey through England and Scotland in the Year 1844*, p. 26.
40. J. Michelet, *Sur les chemins de l'Europe*, p. 170.
41. *The London Journal of Flora Tristan*, p. 26.
42. *Letters from England: by Don Manuel Alvarez Espriella*, ii. 307.
43. Friedrich von Gentz, *Briefe von und an Friedrich von Gentz*, ii. 392.
44. G. A. Crapelet, *Souvenirs de Londres en 1814 et 1816*, p. 44.
45. Johanna Schopenhauer, *Reise durch England und Schottland*, ii. 16–17.
46. Luigi Angiolini, *Lettere sull'Inghilterra*, pp. 108 ff.
47. Bombelles, *Journal de voyage en Grande Bretagne et en Irlande 1784*, p. 293.
48. Phyllis Hembry, *The English Spa 1560–1815*, London, 1990, p. 108.
49. Pückler-Muskau, *Tour in England, Ireland, and France, in the Years 1828 and 1829*, i. 11.
50. John Macdonald, *Memoirs of an Eighteenth-Century Footman*, p. 86.
51. Norman Scarfe, *Innocent Espionage: The La Rochefoucauld Brothers' Tour of England in 1785*, p. 154.
52. *Almack's: A Novel*, ii. 209–10.
53. Prosper Mérimée, *Études Anglo-Américaines*, ed. Georges Connes, Paris, 1930, pp. 1–2.
54. *The Diary of Philipp von Neumann*, pp. 6–7.
55. J. C. Beltrami, *A Pilgrimage in Europe and America*, i. 354.
56. Elizabeth Davis Bancroft, *Letters from England 1846–1849*, p. 54.
57. *Notions of the Americans*, ii. 142–3.
58. Alexander Herzen, *My Past and Thoughts: The Memoirs of Alexander Herzen*, trans. Constance Garnett, 4 vols., London, 1968, iii. 1217.
59. *Letters written during a Residence in England translated from the French of Henry Meister*, pp. 4–5.
60. Madame d'Avot, *Lettres sur l'Angleterre, ou deux années à Londres*, p. 95.
61. Alexis de Tocqueville, *Journeys to England and Ireland*, p. 88.
62. François Bédarida, *A Social History of England 1851–1975*, trans. A. S. Forster, London, 1979, p. 294.
63. *Complete Works of William Hazlitt*, xx. 178.
64. Alphonse Esquiros, *The English at Home*, 2nd ser., p. 71; 3rd ser., p. 94.
65. Cyrus Redding, *Yesterday and To-Day*, iii. 230–1.
66. Ralph Waldo Emerson, *English Traits*, p. 146.
67. John Millar, *An Historical View of the English Government, from the Settlement of the Saxons in Britain to the Revolution in 1688*, iv. 370.
68. C. F. Henningsen, *Analogies and Contrasts*, i. 124.
69. *Mémoires et Correspondance de Madame d'Épinay*, iii. 193.
70. *Tour in England, Ireland, and France, in the Years 1828 and 1829*, iii. 115.

71. P. J. Rehfues, *Briefe aus Italien während der Jahre 1801, 1802, 1803, 1804, 1805, mit mancherlei Beilagen*, 4 vols., Zurich, 1809, ii. 69.
72. N. M. Karamzin, *Letters of a Russian Traveller 1789–1790*, p. 140.
73. *Guardian*, 26 Aug. 1713.
74. Ruth Kelso, *The Doctrine of the English Gentleman in the Sixteenth Century*, Urbana, Ill., 1929, p. 145; William Harrison, *The Description of England*, ed. Georges Edelen, Ithaca, NY, 1968, p. 145.
75. Hester Lynch Piozzi, *British Synonymy*, ii. 56–7.
76. *Complete Works of William Hazlitt*, ix. 214.
77. Frances Harris, *The Life of Sarah Duchess of Marlborough*, Oxford, 1991, p. 205.
78. J. A. Downie, *To Settle the Succession of the State: Literature and Politics, 1678–1750*, London, 1994, p. 95.
79. *So Dearly Loved, So Much Admired: Letters to Hester Pitt, Lady Chatham from her relations and friends, 1744–1801*, p. 169.
80. *The Twelve Letters of Canana*, London, 1770, p. 1.
81. *Voyage de la raison en Europe*, p. 85.
82. *A Trip to Holland, being a Description of the Country, People and Manners*, 1699, p. 9.
83. Patrick Joyce, *Visions of the People*, p. 329; W. Cooke Taylor, *Notes of a Tour in the Manufacturing Districts of Lancashire*, p. 292.
84. *Guardian*, 26 Aug. 1713.
85. Wendeborn, *A View of England towards the Close of the Eighteenth Century*, i. 52.
86. *Oxford in 1710 from the Travels of Zacharias Conrad von Uffenbach*, p. 68.
87. N. M. Karamzin, *Letters of a Russian Traveller 1789–1790*, pp. 334–5.
88. Robert Baker, *Reflections on the English Language, In the Nature of Vaugelas's Reflections on the French*, p. 18.
89. Kenneth Craven, *Jonathan Swift and the Millennium of Madness: The Information Age in Swift's A Tale of a Tub*, Leiden, 1992, p. 221.
90. *Journal des Dames et des Modes*, Frankfurt am Main, 11 Aug. 1800, p. 182.
91. Hélène Monod-Cassidy, *Un voyageur-philosophe au XVIIIe siècle: L'Abbé Jean-Bernard le Blanc*, p. 297; Béat-Louis Muralt, *Lettres sur les Anglois et les François*, p. 33.
92. Amédée Pichot, *Historical and Literary Tour*, i. 212–13.
93. F. Mac Donogh, *The Hermit in Edinburgh*, ii. 200–1.
94. *Lichtenberg in England*, i. 231.
95. John Richard, *A Tour from London to Petersburgh*, p. 4.
96. James Fenimore Cooper, *Notions of the Americans*, ii. 143; Charles Dickens, *American Notes*, p. 158.
97. Joseph Priestley, *Lectures on History and General Policy*, Birmingham, 1788, p. 523.
98. See above, p. 22.
99. *Anthropology from a Pragmatic Point of View*, trans. Mary J. Gregor, The Hague, 1974, p. 169.

100. Immanuel Kant, *Observations on the Feeling of the Beautiful and the Sublime*, trans. John T. Goldthwait, Berkeley, 1960, p. 104.
101. Archenholz, *A Picture of England*, i. 8–9.
102. Gerald Newman, *The Rise of English Nationalism, a Cultural History 1740–1830*, London, 1987.
103. Louis-Sébastien Mercier, *Tableau de Paris*, viii. 110–11.
104. *The Diary of Benjamin Robert Haydon*, i. 76.
105. Isaac D'Israeli, *Curiosities of Literature*, iii. 163–4.
106. Josephine Grieder, *Anglomania in France 1740–1789*, p. 116.
107. *Leipziger Mode-Magazin neuesten deutschen, französischen und englischen Geschmacks*, 1803, pp. 294–6.
108. *The Works of Mr de St. Evremont*, i. 516–17.
109. Louis Simond, *Journal of a Tour*, i. 187.
110. Revd George Davies, *The Completeness of the Late Duke of Wellington as a National Character*, London, 1854, p. 49.
111. Carola Oman, *The Gascoyne Heiress: The Life and Diaries of Frances May Gascoyne-Cecil*, p. 100.
112. C. A. G. Goede, *The Stranger in England; Travels in Great Britain*, i. 166–7; Haussez, *Great Britain in 1833*, i. 149–52.
113. *The Parliamentary Diaries of Sir John Trelawny, 1858–1865*, Camden 4th ser. 40 (1990), p. 186.
114. Martin Sherlock, *Lettres d'un voyageur anglois*, 2 vols., London, 1780, ii. 160.
115. *A Memoir of the Life and Writings of the late William Taylor of Norwich*, i. 521.
116. *A Dissertation on the Origin and Progress of the Scythians or Goths*, London, 1787.
117. *Lettere sull'Inghilterra*, pp. 152, 186.
118. C. P. Courtney, *Isabelle de Charrière (Belle de Zuylen)*, Oxford, 1993, p. 227.
119. *Spectator*, 562.
120. Serge Serodes, 'Les Anglicismes chez Stendhal', in K. G. McWatters and C. W. Thompson, eds., *Stendhal et l'Angleterre*, pp. 367–77.
121. W. H. Bruford, *Culture and Society in Classical Weimar, 1775–1806*, Cambridge, 1962, p. 32.
122. See Conclusion, n. 4.
123. F. McEachran, *The Life and Philosophy of Johann Gottfried Herder*, Oxford, 1939, p. 30.
124. *Observations and Reflections made in the Course of a Journey through France, Italy, and Germany*, i. 206.
125. Patrick Coleman, 'The Idea of Character in the *Encyclopédie*', *Eighteenth-Century Studies*, 13 (1979–80), 21–48.
126. Richard Wendorf, *The Elements of Life: Biography and Portrait-Painting in Stuart and Georgian England*, Oxford, 1990, pp. 295–6.
127. *Memoirs of the Life of Sir James Mackintosh*, i. 174–5.
128. John Barrell and Harriet Guest, 'On the Use of Contradiction: Economics and

Morality in the Eighteenth-Century Long Poem', in Felicity Nussbaum and Laura Brown, eds., *The New Eighteenth Century: Theory, Politics, English Literature*, New York, 1987, pp. 132–3.

129. *Memoirs of Baron Stockmar. By his Son Baron E. Von Stockmar*, ed. F. Max Müller, 2 vols., London, 1872, i. 295.

130. *Leipziger Mode-Magazin*, 1804, pp. 205–6.

131. *Le Parisien à Londres*, i. 85.

132. Thomas Andrew Green, *Verdict According to Conscience: Perspectives on the English Criminal Trial Jury 1200–1800*, Chicago, 1985, pp. 281 ff.

133. *Boswell's London Journal 1762–1763*, ed. Frederick A. Pottle, London, 1950, p. 47.

134. *Self-Help with Illustrations of Conduct and Perseverance*, pp. 3–4.

135. World's Classics edn., Oxford, 1991, p. 488.

136. *Historical and Literary Tour of a Foreigner in England and Scotland*, i. 187.

137. *Records of a Girlhood*, i. 151.

138. *Diary of Joseph Farington*, xii. 4221, 4231.

139. John Timbs, *English Eccentrics and Eccentricities*, 2 vols., London, 1866, i. 142–6.

140. Ibid. i. 49–56, 87–93.

141. Émile Boutmy, *The English People: A Study of their Political Psychology*, p. 120.

142. *Macready's reminiscences, and Selections from his Diaries and Letters*, ed. Sir Frederick Pollock, 2 vols., London, 1875, i. 221.

143. Peter D. G. Thomas, *John Wilkes: A Friend to Liberty*, Oxford, 1996, p. 209.

144. *Eccentric Biography*, 2nd edn., 2 vols., London, 1803, i. 132–3.

145. Edith Sitwell, *The English Eccentrics*, London, 1933, p. 185.

146. Julia Blackburn, *Charles Waterton, 1782–1865: Traveller and Conservationist*, London, 1989, p. 4; the remark is attributed to the novelist Graham Greene.

147. Henry Matthews, *The Diary of an Invalid*, ii. 228.

148. John Timbs, *English Eccentrics and Eccentricities*, i. 95–8, 132–3.

149. Stefan Collini, *Public Moralists: Political Thought and Intellectual Life in Britain, 1850–1930*, p. 111.

150. *On Liberty*, London, 1859, p. 120.

151. *The Autobiography of The Hon. Roger North*, ed. Augustus Jessop, London, 1887, p. 85.

152. John Forster, *The Life of Charles Dickens*, iii. 124.

153. *De L'Allemagne*, i. 106.

154. *Mémoires et voyages*, pp. 244–5.

155. Daniel Levier, 'Anatomie de l'Excentricité en Angleterre au XVIIIe siècle', in Michèle Plaisant, *L'Excentricité en Grande-Bretagne au 18e Siècle*, pp. 9–24.

156. *Journal des Dames et des Modes*, Frankfurt am Main, 11 Aug. 1800.

157. C. G. Carus, *The King of Saxony's Journey through England and Scotland in the Year 1844*, p. 40.

158. *Voyage en Angleterre et en Écosse*, pp. 89–90.

159. *English Hours*, London, 1905, pp. 117–18.

Conclusion MANNERS AND CHARACTER

1. Herbert Spencer, *An Autobiography*, 2 vols., London, 1904, i. 32–3.
2. Ethel Jones, *Les Voyageurs français en Angleterre de 1815 à 1830*, pp. 287–8.
3. P. W. Clayden, *Rogers and his Contemporaries*, i. 205.
4. *Observations on the Feeling of the Beautiful and the Sublime*, p. 104.
5. Lothar Bucher, *Der Parlamentarismus wie er ist*, 3rd edn., Stuttgart, 1894, p. 7.
6. Alphonse Esquiros, *The English at Home*, i. 134.
7. P. G. Patmore, *Letters on England*, i. 244.
8. Jonas Hanway, *Earnest Advice, Particularly to Persons who live in an habitual Neglect of Our Lord's Supper*, London, 1778, p. 33.
9. Stefan Collini, *Public Moralists: Political Thought and Intellectual Life in Britain, 1850–1930*, p. 341.
10. Robert Colls and Philip Dodd, *Englishness: Politics and Culture 1880–1920*, London, 1986; Peter Mandler, 'Against "Englishness": English Culture and the Limits to Rural Nostalgia, 1850–1940', *Trans. Royal Hist. Soc.* 6th ser. 7 (1997), 155–76, and 'The Consciousness of Modernity? Liberalism and the English "National Character", 1850–1940' in M. Daunton and B. Rieger, eds., *British Modernities, 1850–1940*, Berg, forthcoming.
11. Jeffrey Richards, *Films and British National Identity From Dickens to Dad's Army*, Manchester, 1997, chaps. 11 and 12, where, as so often, it is assumed that the British and the English character are synonymous.
12. Geoffrey Gorer, *Exploring English Character*, London, 1955.
13. *England and the English*, 2 vols., New York, 1833, i. 29.
14. Robert Mattlé, *Lamartine Voyageur*, Paris, 1936, pp. 278–9.
15. *English Traits*, p. 294.

Index

undifferentiated proscription 16
local/state gov't control to 80-1
separation 105-7
leisure 163
london advertising to proprietors 230
professionality Tab 233
middle class character 7 grammar 316